D1206931

Date Due

ECONOMICS AND MAN

THE IRWIN SERIES IN ECONOMICS

Consulting Editor
LLOYD G. REYNOLDS
YALE UNIVERSITY

AMES *Soviet Economic Processes*

ANDERSON, GITLOW, & DIAMOND (Editors) *General Economics: A Book of Readings* rev. ed.

BALASSA *The Theory of Economic Integration*

BEAL & WICKERSHAM *The Practice of Collective Bargaining* 3d ed.

BLAUG *Economic Theory in Retrospect* rev. ed.

BORNSTEIN (Editor) *Comparative Economic Systems: Models and Cases*

BORNSTEIN & FUSFELD (Editors) *The Soviet Economy: A Book of Readings* rev. ed.

BRANDIS *Economics: Principles and Policy* rev. ed.

BUCHANAN *The Public Finances* rev. ed.

CARTTER *Theory of Wages and Employment*

CARTTER & MARSHALL *Labor Economics: Wages, Employment, and Trade Unionism*

DAVIDSON, SMITH, & WILEY *Economics: An Analytical Approach* rev. ed.

DAVIS, HUGHES, & McDOUGALL *American Economic History: The Development of a National Economy* rev. ed.

DOLL, RHODES, & WEST *Economics of Agricultural Production, Markets, and Policy*

DRUMMOND *The Canadian Economy: Organization and Development*

DUE *Government Finance: An Economic Analysis* 3d ed.

DUE & CLOWER *Intermediate Economic Analysis* 5th ed.

DUNLOP & HEALY *Collective Bargaining: Principles and Cases* rev. ed.

FELLNER *Probability and Profit: A Study of Economic Behavior along Bayesian Lines*

ECONOMICS AND MAN

JOHN S. GAMBS, Ph.D.

Professor Emeritus

Hamilton College

JEROME B. KOMISAR, M.A.

Lecturer in Business Enterprise and Accounting

State University of New York at Binghamton

Third Edition • 1968

RICHARD D. IRWIN, INC., Homewood, Illinois

IRWIN–DORSEY LIMITED, Nobleton, Ontario

THIRD EDITION

First Printing, March, 1968

Library of Congress Catalog Card No. 68–17048

PRINTED IN THE UNITED STATES OF AMERICA

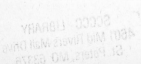

To our children
Louise Martha and John Frederick Gambs
Harriet, Wade, Frances, and Aurenna Komisar

PREFACE

Economics and Man is inspired by the liberal arts tradition. By this we mean, among other things, that it seeks values beyond those of professional training. The large, encyclopedic textbooks are admirable in many ways, but chiefly admirable for students who major in economics and who intend to make economics their life work. Their rigor, their thoroughness on small points, their copious diagrams, make them indispensable to the economics major, but less useful to the student in the liberal arts. Indeed, many competent sophomores, after being dragged through 800 large pages, sometimes double-columned, come out at the other end in a fog instead of in the light, having derived few educational values of any kind from a year of bewildering study. We find that the muse who presides over the art of leaving things out is more difficult to serve than the one who governs the art of including everything but the kitchen stove.

Strictly defined, the liberal arts embrace only the trivium and quadrivium of the medieval curriculum. More loosely we may say that the liberal arts are the branches of study that free the mind—free it from superstition, fear, prejudice, special pleading, bias, and from the narrowness of the local and parochial. They lead toward self-knowledge and self-realization and give the mind sea room. All of the social studies are admirably fitted to achieve such aims. This book, by suggesting that Anglo-American economics do not answer all questions, by indicating the value of other social sciences to economics, by a somewhat more searching inquiry into method, conforms perhaps more closely to the liberal arts tradition than other textbooks. The mood sought for in these pages is, we believe, the mood of the liberal arts: not, "Here is the truth about economics," but rather, "Let us explore economic ideas together to see what truths they do contain."

To a greater degree than other elementary volumes, this one attempts to be "terminal." By this we mean that students, with the aid of an instructor, need not go much beyond these pages to get a mature and sophisticated view of economics. We believe that many textbooks achieve easy pedagogical victories by being dogmatic, by excluding conflicts of viewpoint, and by avoiding the difficult task of fostering the attitude of suspended judgment. Justification for this procedure is usually found in the argument that students will, in later courses, develop the healthy and tolerant skepticism that informs the thought of our more competent economists. But for most students there is no second or third course—particularly not in general theory. If they are ever to learn that the most mature economists have the most misgivings about economics as a science, they have only one chance to learn—in the elementary and final course. This is obviously a challenge to pedagogical skill. It is hoped that this book will be helpful to those who have decided to accept that challenge.

This volume makes several clean breaks with current styles in textbooks. One is to rely on what might be named the "comparative method." This means that *Economics and Man* somewhat resembles textbooks in philosophy, which teach by contrasting the views of Stoics, Hegelians, positivists, and others. We have often wondered why economists have made so little use of the comparative method as a pedagogical device on the elementary level. Work in the history of doctrines is, of course, part of the graduate school program; but we believe it is helpful at the very start, and that belief has done much to shape this book. The reader should not, however, infer from this that *Economics and Man* is a primer in the history of economic thought. The arrangement is topical, not chronological. It will become clear to the reader that this method of stimulating thought flows from a conviction of the authors that much economic theory is still—despite impressive scientific gains in the past quarter of a century—as close to philosophy as it is to science.

Though brief as textbooks go, the present volume is of wide scope and reveals more about the whole, wide land of economic thought than most introductory texts reveal. This is done at the expense of an exhaustive treatment of price theory—though basic training is included—and of various other matters contained in other books. But we believe it gains in breadth what it loses in depth. To some, this book may lack that quality which is widely known as "rigor"; but it does contain difficult ideas—though not always in the areas in which difficulty is to be found in our most widely used textbooks. It is a book *about* economics rather than *on* economics. It takes students on a visit to economists' workshops and shows them how different men have approached their tasks; it does not impose methods of working or thinking.

This book has a moderately long history. It was begun by John S. Gambs in 1946 and published by the Columbia University Press in 1952—under the title of *Man, Money and Goods*. The next thing was that Richard D. Irwin, Inc., decided it could be made into a textbook. Dr. Sidney Wertimer of Hamilton College was persuaded to help convert it into a textbook, and the Gambs-Wertimer version appeared in 1959. Dr. Wertimer became Dean Wertimer and the pressure of his new duties prevented him from taking part in the revised edition of 1964. Jerome Komisar helped in the preparation of that edition. Now John Gambs and Jerome Komisar have revised it again for a third edition. The major single change this time is the addition of a new chapter on poverty, a subject that has rather suddenly engrossed public attention. Facts and figures have, of course, been brought up to date. The chapters on taxation, agriculture, and foreign trade have been extensively revised. Hardly a page of the old has been left untouched; countless changes, though sometimes small, have been made to increase clarity and readability. A few new diagrams have been added.

In previous editions we have thanked those who have helped us and to them we renew our thanks. We owe a debt to Joseph Haden, of the International Labor Office, who allowed us to use material he had brought together on poverty. We are grateful to the Columbia University Press for allowing us to incorporate, without restriction, a good deal of the material originally contained in *Man, Money and Goods*.

JOHN S. GAMBS
JEROME B. KOMISAR

February, 1968

TABLE OF CONTENTS

xiii

Chapter 1 | ECONOMICS AND ECONOMISTS

Definitions

What is economics all about? It is often defined as the science of wealth or as the study of how mankind gets its living. Statements like this are certainly useful, but they are also too general. When we try to take the next step, we get into trouble. We meet difficulties in pinning economics down because its practitioners are in disagreement about the scope and nature of their science, and attempts to particularize lead to protests from opposing schools of thought. The only definitions on which agreement is possible are broad ones like those given above, or humorous ones like "Economics is whatever an economist wants to talk about."

The reader may have misgivings about studying a science in which disagreements arise at the very start. His doubts are indeed well founded, but should not too quickly turn him away. After all, there are still differences of opinion even in astronomy and phyics, chemistry and biology. Psychology remains a free-for-all. No considerable field of knowledge is so completely understood that all of its scholars speak with the same voice. The process of reaching a balanced conclusion often requires a sifting of the testimony of contradictory witnesses. In any event, stress on differences should not obscure the fact that all sciences, including even economics, agree on many things. There is, besides, an enormous store of historical and descriptive matter—economic facts—that is well worth knowing and concerning which there is little dispute. We shall hope that the burden placed on the reader of suspending judgment and viewing the same things in different lights will not be too heavy.

One of the dominant schools of the day looks upon economics as a study of what happens when we try to reconcile the scarcity of things with the insatiable wants of human beings. Most things worth having, except the air we breathe, are scarce—scarce enough, at least, to

3

command a price and not to be available to all in generous quantity. Among the less dominant and dissenting schools is one that considers the study of the disposal of scarce goods too restrictive. Some members of this class focus their interest on the moral codes, business practices, social institutions, legal framework, and the like under which we get our food, clothing, and shelter. They study an economic system—capitalism, for example—in much the same way that an anthropologist studies the Klamath Indians or some primitive tribe of a South Sea island. They ask, and try to answer, questions that have little to do with the disposal of scarce goods.

The student may find it helpful to examine the definitions given below. They represent the thought of several periods and schools. In these definitions the older phrase "political economy" is more or less equal to the modern word "economics."

Oeconomy, in general, is the art of providing for all the wants of a family, with prudence and frugality. . . . What oeconomy is in a family, political oeconomy is in a state (Sir James Steuart, 1712–1780).

. . . .

Writers on Political Economy profess to teach, or to investigate, the nature of Wealth, and the laws of its production and distribution: including directly or remotely, the operation of all the causes by which the condition of mankind, or of any society of human beings, in respect to this universal object of human desire, is made prosperous or the reverse (John Stuart Mill, 1806–73).

. . . .

Political Economy treats chiefly of the material interests of nations. It inquires how the various wants of the people of a country, especially those of food, clothing, fuel, shelter, of the sexual instinct etc., may be satisfied; how the satisfaction of these wants influences the aggregate national life, and how in turn, they are influenced by the national life (Wilhelm Roscher, 1817–94).

. . . .

Political Economy or Economics is a study of mankind in the ordinary business of life; it examines that part of individual and social action which is most closely connected with the attainment and with the use of the material requisites of well being. Thus it is on the one side a study of wealth; and on the other, and more important side, a part of the study of man (Alfred Marshall, 1842–1924).

. . . .

Economics is a study of the "community's methods of turning material things to account" (Thorstein Veblen, 1857–1929).

.   .   .   .

Economics . . . is concerned with that aspect of behavior which arises from the scarcity of means to achieve given ends (Lionel Robbins, 1898–   ).

.   .   .   .

. . . Economics is . . . a social science; that is, it deals with the behavior of men in organized communities. Its special province is the behavior of social groups in providing the means for attaining their various ends (Wesley Mitchell, 1874–1948).

.   .   .   .

The theory of economics . . . is a method rather than a doctrine, an apparatus of the mind, a technique of thinking, which helps its possessor to draw correct conclusions (John Maynard Keynes, 1883–1946).

A few comments on the above may help. The first definition, by Steuart, was conceived before much formal and sustained thought by a succession of scholars had been given to what we now name "economics." Steuart was a mercantilist, primarily interesed in the wealth of the British crown and its capacity to support a navy, pay soldiers, and build and maintain the King's highways. His concern was not with the nation as a whole—the artisans, farmers, and other men of low degree. In contrast, the next definition, by Mill—a very acceptable definition even today—does consider the society as a whole. It also calls attention to the "laws of . . . production and distribution," which are still at the forefront of economic interest. With the exception of the definition given by Lionel Robbins, all of the others reach down—like Mill—into the entire community. Veblen and Mitchell are dissenting economists, as we shall see later in the book. Yet both echo the phrase of Marshall, a major orthodox economist, about "the attainment . . . of the material requisites of well being." Marshall, Robbins, and Mitchell place emphasis on human behavior. This is a desirable emphasis, lest we forget because of our shorthand way of speaking that human beings are the cause of economic phenomena. For example, economists are much concerned about the rise and fall of prices; but prices do not rise and fall. Human beings mark them up or down. The majority of American standard or orthodox economists would endorse the definition given by Marshall, not only because it is a good one, but also because of his great authority. Yet Robbins'—so completely different—would also meet with great favor. What economists like about this pithy definition is that it goes to the heart of an issue which engrosses many of them: how to reconcile scarcity or the niggardliness of nature with the unlimited desires of man. Economists like to say they will not be needed in heaven. The reason is that in paradise, wants are few and resources boundless. Its inhabitants will never have to decide how much to spend and how much to save, how heavily to tax, how much butter to give up in order to have guns.

The definition given by Keynes, the most widely acclaimed economist of the 20th century, is a rather puzzling one. Economics is here defined partly as a "technique of thinking." What does this mean? Obviously, any organized body of knowledge directs the mind in ways that are foreign to other organized bodies of knowledge. The chemist thinks about how atoms combine, whether they combine explosively or quietly, what happens when you restructure the atoms of a molecule. In this sense, we get a unique "technique of thinking" in almost any specialized activity, including economics; indeed, even baseball, football, and other sports impose a special technique of thinking. But is this all that Keynes has in mind? Certain well-known techniques of thinking include induction and deduction. Behaviorist psychologists—at least in the early days—reduced thinking to inaudible speech; the philosopher John Dewey described thinking as problem solving. Without clarifying, Keynes seems to claim for economics a unique method of ascertaining truth—one which is either a substitute for or an addition to the more widely known methods suggested above; something you would not find in a book of logic, only in a book of economics. If this is his meaning, we must reject the definition, for the method of scientific investigation and techniques of thought are the same for all kinds of data; and in any case, there is a difference between the concerns and data of economics and the method of studying it—a difference which is not recognized in the Keynesian definition.

The question whether economics is really a science cannot be answered easily. Astronomy, chemistry, and physics have spoiled us with their split-second accuracy and such infallibility of prediction that we are inclined to look with disdain at the social sciences. Biology has not scored the successes credited to the physical sciences, but it still outpaces economics by a good deal. If, however, science is thought of as an attitude, a willingness to put aside prejudice, self-interest, and the unverified wisdom of authority, then economics will fare moderately well.

The earliest writers on economic subjects failed most of the tests of scientific objectivity. Slavery was a good thing ethically, or a bad thing, depending on the writer; buying and selling were good under some conditions, bad under others. Like some of the early biologists— Georges de Buffon, for example, to whom the lion was proud and disdainful, the ideal combination of strength and agility—the ancient Greek writings evaluated economic pursuits as either lowly or lofty. Trade and moneylending were unnatural and mostly for rogues. This sort of praise, dispraise, or admiration lies in the realm of ethics or honorific taxonomy rather than in the field of matter-of-fact science. Neither biology nor economics, if scientific, may use value-laden words to describe their objects of study.

The Middle Ages were no improvement, though toward the end of the period one or two writers did come up with matter-of-fact generalizations of wide application. The period of mercantilism, beginning about 1500, saw a considerable contraction of the area of applied ethics, unverifiable belief, and transcendental sanctions. The mercantilists did, to be sure, accept the imponderable value of a strong nation-state; but once this had been accepted, they went on to study economic activity scientifically enough. Many of the ancient prescriptions were abandoned. Trade and business enterprise were studied rather than judged. The payment of interest and moneylending became acceptable. Agriculture (meaning, among the Greeks, farm management, not the toil of the slave) stopped being the only productive occupation worthy of noble minds. As the centuries and decades passed, unpleasant or controversial subjects were studied objectively and often quantitatively: Business cycles, trade-union activity, the unequal distribution of income—all came under scrutiny. The "ought" or "should" of the older economists slowly became the "what" and "how" of contemporary scholars.

It must not be thought, however, that economics has become a completely value-free science. It has in this respect the same ambiguous quality that medicine has. A study of medicine teaches the physician to sharpen pain or reduce it; to break or mend bones; to cure the sick or cause exacerbation; to kill or give life. But he is so deeply indoctrinated in our ethical code that he rarely makes a choice; he palliates suffering, heals and sustains life without debating the issues. In somewhat the same way, an economist is able to formulate policies that increase or decrease wealth, that bring prosperity or depression. But, following the ethical code of the society around him, his policy recommendations seek to increase wealth, curb gross inflationary movements, and smooth out the troughs and peaks of the business cycle. In addition to these values, he accepts other kinds of values: that private property is good, that prices determined in a competitive market are just, that the consumer's freedom to choose is akin to a natural right. All of these are debatable, but they are not much debated by the standard economists of the Western world. It is doubtful whether an economist can be effective unless he does carry on his study within the confines of the value system just suggested. It is part of the common sense of our culture. Still, we must note that Nikolaus Copernicus, Charles Lyell, and Charles Darwin could never have made their great contributions if they had not strayed beyond the boundaries of the received doctrines of their day: the earth was flat and stationary; man and his world had been created 6,000 years ago. They broke from the theology of their day. Most economists do not.

But after all is said and done, and proper exceptions are made, it must be affirmed that economists do study many problems objectively, without bias and with the inquiring attitude of other scientists. If perfection has not yet been achieved, progress over the decades must be recorded. Most social scientists have worked reasonably hard to strip away class interest and bias, to crush down their private prejudice or aspirations, to squash their own fantasies of what constitutes a good society, and to study what is there, not what might be or should be. Serious efforts are made to look at the world as it really is, advance hypothetical explanations, and then verify them. All of this is part of the scientific attitude.

To sum up, then: If science is to be defined as a point of view toward the unprejudiced collection and organization of knowledge, then it must be said that economics tries hard to conform to this point of view, that it is making progress but still has some distance to go. As for exactitude and ability to predict, economics cannot, in the calculable future, compete with astronomy, physics, and chemistry. Many of its forecasts do come true. But there are too many variables in economics. The assassination of a President causes the stock market to go down; an untimely frost in Florida sends up the price of oranges; an unexpected invention may promptly cause unforeseen unemployment; in 1967, American Catholic bishops permitted meat eating on Friday, and it is doubtful whether any economist was then able to predict the effects of this decision on the fishing industry.

What Economics Is Not

We shall better be able to understand what economics is all about if we consider some of the things that it is not. Economics has been defined as "the science of wealth," but this does not mean that it teaches individuals how to pile up personal riches. The word "wealth" as it is used by economists does not mean a great store of valuable possessions. It means, rather, anything having value, as when we say "the wealth of a laborer lies in the strength of his muscles."

The knack of acquiring riches for personal use is not within the province of economics but forms part of the arts of business; and economists are not necessarily successful businessmen, though a few have been very good ones. Not many have met a payroll, but their job is not to run stores or factories or even to say much about how they should be run. Their concern is more often regional, national, or international in scope. Is a high interest rate good or bad for a nation? Should a country like ours increase or reduce tariffs? It may be asked how a man can be expected to understand the whole economic system if he has had no experience running even a corner drugstore. But the question is really silly. A good captain of the *Princess Italia* is not necessarily a competent gondolier. And a man who runs a successful diner is not necessarily an expert on foreign trade though he serves Brazilian coffee and Japanese tuna. Business and economics have much in common, of course, but they are also vastly different. A businessman is identified with the success of an individual firm. An economist—unless he has become an adviser to business—has small interest in any individual firm; his interest lies in the wealth and prosperity of the whole nation—indeed, of all nations. We are of course speaking here of his public or professional function as compared with his private life. With his savings, he may buy TV common and prayerfully hope, like any other American citizen, that it will go up 50 points in 50 days. As an economist he may deplore a rapid rise in the stock market and may even write letters to *The New York Times* urging that the interest rate be increased to prevent a runaway stock market. The first great book in economics, written by Adam Smith and published in 1776, is entitled *An Inquiry into the Nature and Causes of the Wealth of Nations*, and perhaps this title is as good a short definition of economics as can be found. Such an inquiry has little to do with how to manage a supermarket or make a killing on the stock exchange. In his capacity as a scholar, the economist has the further task of enlarging human understanding.

Economics should not be mistaken for technology. Teachers in the grades sometimes visit dairies or canneries with their classes, hoping that the children are learning economics. Such excursions provide an excellent technical background for economic study, of course; but unless some truth about economics is cleverly disengaged, the excursion contributes little to economic wisdom. Going through a penicillin factory may give your family physician a useful insight into the technology of drug making, but many excellent doctors have never seen medicine being made. Economics is not often concerned with the detailed processes of manufacture, though this varies somewhat with the problem studied. As we shall see in a later chapter, the word "production," when used in economic discourse, means something quite different from technical process.

Problems of a Simple Economy

Perhaps the best way to understand what economics is about is to make one of those experiments in imagination that are so much a part of the economist's method of study.

Suppose a group of 100 college students on their way to spend their junior year abroad are shipwrecked and safely cast ashore on a fruitful tropical island. They will most likely improvise an economic system almost immediately. Committees will be formed to search for springs of fresh water. Some of the men will gather food—bananas, shellfish, and so on. Another committee will be chosen to build signal fires and otherwise attempt to communicate with the outside world.

The girls will perhaps cook and arrange songfests in the evening as a form of recreation. Already we see emerging basic characteristics of an economic system: division of labor and allocating of people to suitable tasks.

Suppose, now, that weeks and months pass, that the castaways have given up hope of early rescue, that they behave better than the young people in *Lord of the Flies,* and that they decide that they must plan for a long stay on the island. They have to begin to make permanent rules and to organize their economic activities on a long-run basis. One of the first economic rules may be that those who do not work may not eat, unless, of course, they are ill or severely handicapped physically. The committee on production may decide to propagate 100 new banana trees and to build a long dormitory for the men and another for the women. Now they are deep in truly economic decision. Why propagate banana trees? Why 100 rather than 200? Why not date palms or coconuts? (We assume all are available.) Why communal dormitories? Why not let each individual thatch himself a grass hut of his own? What mechanism was used to arrive at these decisions? Did they vote? Did they delegate economic planning to a powerful executive committee? Regardless of whether one of these or other mechanisms is used, their aim will be to combine their abilities and the resources of the island in such a way as to secure a high degree of community satisfaction. This is the essence of an economic arrangement. Anything else would be haphazard.

No doubt many of these questions can be worked out easily enough, for the community is small and homogeneous, and the products of this lush island are abundant enough to prevent quarrels about the basic necessities of life. Though there may be a coconut-and-date clique opposed to a banana faction, the issue of what to produce is a small one, for nature offers few choices and promises little beyond the basic necessities. Since convertibles, electricity, television, and mink coats are impossible to get, the question of how to share them does not call for decision, and the economic system will be simple. But even so, there exists a well-defined economic system. Rules and decisions are made as to what can be produced most advantageously while satisfying group wants, how much to produce, who is to perform what tasks, and how the joint product of the group is to be divided.

If, now, this community of castaways becomes a permanent

settlement, if its members marry and have children, if population expands and wealth accumulates, the economic system becomes more complex, and formal government arises as the economy develops. New resources—perhaps ores or oil—are found; surpluses are developed which permit the creation of public works and capital, that is, irrigation canals, a water and sewer system, roads, barges, a harnessed waterfall to grind foods. New rules—now called laws—have to be made about who gets what, for now there is more to get. The question of property ownership arises in more acute forms than it did when there were only 100 people, all of whom knew one another, and when almost everything, except very personal things like toothbrushes, belonged to everybody and to nobody. Men who work on roads may be given unique shells as evidence that they have put in so many hours on community or public projects and are entitled to a share of the community's food, shoes, and beer. Pretty soon a traffic in shells begins to arise. Some workers on the roads have more shells than they need. Other men are willing to acquire these shells and may be willing to exchange their surplus food or clothing for shells. A custom has grown up that men may be excused from community work if they surrender some of their shells to the government. Now we have money and price—and how are prices determined? Will the government post lists that state the value of bananas, fish, and clothing in terms of shells, or will it allow people to bargain as they please?

At length, perhaps only after several generations, the economy will become even more complex. Now there are taxes and foreign trade and public debt. Economists will appear. Some will reexamine the rules and traditions that have grown up—often grown up haphazardly—as to who gets what or why so many bananas are being produced. They will become experts in the rules and laws governing the dividing-up of the things produced and may suggest that certain changes in the rules would benefit the community and remove inequities. Some would study the balance between present and a possibly increased future consumption. That is, does the government absorb too much of the community labor, brains, and material in long-run road building, thereby depriving the community of things it might enjoy here and now? Others would study this shell business. What happens when new beds of shells are discovered? They might find that shells could be used generally as tokens or counters in any kind of exchange of goods and services, and would urge the government to find ways of issuing more shells and of encouraging their use in all transactions. Still others, addicted to statistics, would try to find out how much the island was producing each year. And if it produced less in one year than in another, they would try to find reasons: physical reasons, such as hurricanes or drought, and "economic" reasons, such as high taxes or low wages that discouraged production or the exhaustion of the land by a too intensive cultivation—though this is partly physical as many economic phenomena undeniably are.

The economic problems that we have noted in our imaginary community are almost the same as those of the most advanced economies of the modern world. Theirs are perhaps easier to study because the mechanism used to make decisions is still fairly simple and thus still easily open to view, and is less obscured by millennia of custom. Study of any modern society is harder, but we study the same things, basically—why we produce what we do; who gets what we produce; whether we can produce more efficiently or distribute the product better to promote the general welfare; what man-made barriers inhibit steady production; how we allocate people to their tasks.

How Some Decisions Are Made in a Contemporary Economy

The process of making such decisions in contemporary American society is partly concealed because we are so accustomed to making decisions that we are not really aware that we are making them, just as we are usually unaware of our breathing or of our heartbeats. Our decisions arise from three principal sources: our cultural heritage, our government, and our price system. Let us follow this train of thought for a moment.

Perhaps our basic decisions are the product of our culture. There is no mass production in the United States of snails, togas, or dandelion greens, because our culture has rejected all three; we do not find them good or useful, even though they are as good, functionally and esthetically, as raw oysters, dinner jackets, and iceberg lettuce. Bridal white—rather than red or yellow—is used for wedding gowns, and this is a mere cultural decision. We buy more Bibles than Korans, because we are born in a Christian society. Thus our traditions, beliefs, religion, eating habits, and clothing habits determine in part what we produce and buy and sell.

Secondly, we make many decisions through our governments,

which we elect, on the federal and local planes. We have decided against opium, unless prescribed by a physician. We decide, through taxes, to increase our decrease our personal purchasing power and, within limits, to equalize our incomes. Washington decides through tariffs and similar devices (such as import quotas) to make us pay dearly for certain foreign goods and thereby to encourage certain American industries to expand. Through government, we plan our roads, schools, armaments, police protection, pensions, unemployment benefits, telephone and electric rates, travel fares, and a multitude of other things.

The remaining economic decisions are made, as we sometimes say, by the private sector of our economy through the mechanism of price. As consumers, we are rationed by our pocketbooks; that is, we buy popular cars or air-conditioned luxury automobiles, depending on our incomes. This automatically determines that many Fords, Plymouths, and Chevrolets are produced, while relatively few Cadillacs, Imperials, and Continentals are manufactured, for only a few people can afford the big cars. The forces of supply and demand operating in a relatively free market are active determinants of prices, wages, and salaries in this free sector; hence, we say, the market determines what is to be produced. The dollars we spend as consumers are to some degree ballots to guide production. Thus, enthusiastic spending for some new product, such as color television sets, is equivalent to voting that more sets be produced.

The economist's job in our society—as it would be in simpler societies—is to study all of our decision-making forces, practices, and traditions, and to decide whether they are promoting the general welfare. Economists scrutinize the economic decisions of government with the same end in view. Are tariffs too high? Are social security pensions too low? Are the forces of supply and demand being obstructed in their beneficent operation by private coercion?

When we speak of the general welfare or appraise any form of economic performance, the question of human values comes up. What is welfare? How much do economists think we should eat? How good should our houses be? How many nonessentials should we have? Should pretty and modish clothes be produced for women, or should only utilitarian, long-lasting garments be produced for all?

Economists have no true answer to this question of what welfare is, for it is not really an economic question, but lies in the realm of value, that is, of ethics or philosophy. On the whole, economists respond to the question of values by accepting those of the society in which they find themselves. Thus, increases in production are usually among the goals of economists, provided the increases do not encourage the expansion of vice or crime as would an increase in the production of heroin. The reason economists approve of increased production is clear: Our culture approves of more, more, and more. Again, they support, as most people in the Free World do, the institution of private property. In societies as highly developed as ours, economists accept the prevailing view that nobody should be allowed to starve to death; hence, they have in depression recommended WPA's, public assistance, and at all times public homes for the infirm, incurable, and mentally defective. The economist believes, as most Americans and Western Europeans believe, that moderate inequalities of income serve many useful purposes; on the other hand—again like most Westerners—they also believe not only that vast, unjustified, and fortuitous inequalities are intrinsically "bad," but also that they militate against a "good" thing, namely, increases in production. Since the depression of the 1930's, one ethical value has bulked large in economic thought, namely, that great depressions should not be allowed to happen again; indeed, the search for economic stability has become one of the major preoccupations of the science of wealth.

The economist works within a given ethical framework and tries to find ways in which the society can achieve its values insofar as they are tied up with economic activity. The ends, or aims, or goals of economic activity are set by the culture of a nation; the economist is concerned with the means of achieving some of these goals—not all, for some of the ends and means may not touch the economic world in any significant way, as in the fields of theology or art.

The Profession of Economist

In our quest for a definition of economics—or rather, in our survey of what economics is all about—it may help us to take a look at the profession: how large it is, what economists do, and in what areas they concentrate their activities.

Attempts to count the number of economists in the United States run into difficulties because of certain problems of classification. Above, we made a rather sharp division between businessmen and economists; the former, we said, worked for the welfare of a firm, the latter for the welfare of the nation or even of the world. But now, what happens when an economist, trained in the theory and practice of improving the human condition, becomes an adviser to a business firm? Is he a businessman now and no longer an economist? And where do we put teachers of advertising, marketing, and management? Knowledge of such subjects is primarily of aid to business enterprise and only secondarily to the society as a whole. That is one problem. Another problem relates to extent of training. Can we say of a young B.A. who has majored in economics in a liberal arts college that he is an economist? Probably not. The question of counting would be simple if we licensed economists as we do physicians and lawyers, and established precise standards for licensing: a holder of a Ph.D. (or equivalent) from a department of economics of a standard university, employed either as a teacher, civil servant, or official of the United Nations and affiliated organizations. This would simplify our task but might be too restrictive.

A rather limited census of American economists—though less restrictive than the one suggested just above—published by the National Science Foundation, counted 12,143 economists in 1964. A different count, made by an agency of the federal government in 1960, found about 20,000 economists. If we split the difference, we can arrive at 17,000 for the mid-1960's—an arbitrary figure that we shall nevertheless use as the basis for further discussion. This makes economics one of the sciences with relatively few practitioners. More economists profess their vocations than meteorologists or sociologists; they are, however, vastly outnumbered by chemists, physicists, mathematicians, and biologists—chemists in particular. Compared with the standard professions, economists are exiguous. The nation supports 17 times as many physicians, 12 times as many lawyers and judges, and almost 12 times as many clergymen.

Economics is a masculine occupation. The ratio is one woman out of 25 men. In 1964, 364 men received Ph.D.'s in the subject, but only 17 women. The largest geographic concentration of economists is to be found in the state of New York; next comes the District of Columbia; and third, California. This gives us the heavy concentration of 17 economists per square mile in the national capital—equal to the density of the whole population of the United States in about 1881.

Any single figure on the annual salaries of economists is likely to be misleading, as so many measures of central tendency are. In 1964 the arithmetic average of 12,000 economists studied by the National Science Foundation came to $13,670. The median, however, was lower—$12,000. The range was from $100,000 to less than $5,000. But these things vary with age and experience, and omit some 5,000 economists who were not caught in the Foundation's net. It goes without saying that a typical economist of about 25 might get only one third as much as a typical economist of 50. These figures relate only to salaries. Writers of economic textbooks and popular books, con-sultants, and lecturers may be able to build up their total incomes appreciably—rumor has it that a few have become millionaires, mainly through royalties. On the whole, academic salaries prevail in the profession, since so many of its members are teachers; but among teachers, they do pretty well.

The broad field of economics may be divided into numerous subfields of specialization such as foreign trade, money and banking, taxation, general theory, economic growth, and various other areas, many of which are listed as course descriptions in college catalogs. Excluding agricultural economics and business subjects such as ac-counting, administration, and marketing, the largest number of spe-cialists is found in the category of general economic theory. The money and banking specialists come next. Economists who specialize in welfare, population, economic history, and the history of economic thought are at the bottom of the list. Somewhere in the middle, we find labor economics and foreign trade.

The profession does not lend itself to TV and movie-script glamour as do the professions of the physician, detective, and lawyer. But economists do find tasks well above the humdrum level; they take part, often as delegation advisers, in high-level international confer-ences where they may meet heads of states and some of their chief ministers; in recent years, many economists have been invited to give counsel to the governments of underdeveloped nations, and their professional travels to the corners of the earth have placed them against colorful scenes and events.

The field of economics is diverse. One practitioner may spend most of his time settling grievances in labor disputes; another may be studying uncertainty in the obscure market of put and call options. Some are moral philosophers who operate rather high in the stratosphere; others advise hardheaded businessmen as to whether or not they should expand their operations or where to build new plants. In their work for the federal government, they compile statistics relating to changes in the cost of living, study effects of support prices on agricultural production, follow international trade and fluctuations in the value of foreign currencies. There are a dozen Federal Reserve banks in our larger cities; they employ economists to help determine whether interest rates should rise or fall, to study the demand for loans, to consider the advisability of buying or selling government bonds. The Treasury has its taxation experts. Economists are scattered throughout such special agencies of the United Nations as the Food and Agricultural Organization, the World Bank, the Monetary Fund, and the International Labor Organization, doing on a world scale what the economists of national governments do on a national scale. A large fraction of them are concerned with a problem which has come to the fore only in recent years, namely, the economic development of backward areas. Economists with this interest suggest programs for increasing the levels of living—that is, increasing production—in such places as Libya, Bolivia, and Iran.

In Europe, many economists have risen to exalted positions in government. It is not hard to tick off the names of half a dozen recent prime ministers or ministers of state who at some stage were economists. In the United States a characteristic mistrust of learning in a field where common sense is widely assumed to be the best guide has prevented us from giving high place to economists. Yet even here, this seems to be changing. Recent chairmen of the President's Council of Economic Advisers have played large political roles and have become public figures; one of them, Gardner Ackley, made the *Newsweek* cover in 1966; as this is being written, President Lyndon B. Johnson is just recovering from surgery, and among the first to visit him after the operation was Ackley. One former senator and one former ambassador, Paul Douglas and John Kenneth Galbraith, are among our most distinguished economists.

Few economists are rewarded by a popular and lasting fame. Adam Smith and John Maynard Keynes are indeed known a few rods beyond the circle of cultivated men and women, but not by many others. In 1954, Columbia University Press sent a questionnaire to a selected group asking this question: What eminent persons in various fields, living in 1954, would be remembered in 2154? T. S. Eliot won in poetry, Pablo Picasso in painting, and so on. Keynes won in economics but had to be disqualified, since he died in 1946. But scores of those queried followed the rules of the game and put down the name of some living economist. However, so few votes went to each of the eligible economists that the Press scratched the category and recognized no winner. It is doubtful whether the situation would be much different today. A great economist does not become visible as easily as an Ernest Hemingway, an Igor Stravinsky, or a Frank Lloyd Wright. Actually, to become great, an economist must be more than an economist. He must do more than make mere discoveries, as the great physical scientists do. Adam Smith and Keynes were persuasive enough to change or at least direct Western thought into new pathways. Karl Marx, too, was a great economist; but his real greatness consisted in his ability to remold a whole culture.

Howard R. Bowen, a well-known American economist, has written so well about some of these matters that he deserves to be quoted at length:

The economists of the United States are a small heterogeneous group without strong professional consciousness or powerful professional organization. They face public attitudes that are often indifferent and sometimes hostile. Their status as viewed by the public is lower than that of other learned professions. Nevertheless, economists exert an important—and probably growing—influence in American life—an influence that is entirely disproportionate to their numbers or to the offices they hold. This influence is due primarily to the increasing public interest in economic affairs, an interest which has grown out of this generation's experience with depression, war, inflation, high taxes, enlarged scope of government, labor conflict, and the world-wide threat to the capitalistic system itself. The advice of technically trained economists is sought by government, private business firms, trade associations, labor unions and other groups. Economists frequently appear as expert witnesses before Congressional Committees and public boards. Because economics has become a leading study in schools and colleges, and because citizens of all classes have become intensely interested in economic affairs, economists are able to exert significant influence through their teaching, writing and lecturing. Frequently the research studies and theoretical investigations of economists lead the way to new public policies in fields such as taxation, banking, anti-trust, labor legislation, foreign trade or national defense.

It is not to be inferred, however, that most economists are sitting at the right hand of policy-makers guiding the destiny of the country day by day and in detail. The great majority of economists work in relatively obscure and even humble jobs as teachers, as research workers, and in various minor posts as administrators or research assistants. Few of them ever see, much less advise, Senators or Cabinet Members or leading businessmen. Only a few economists ever occupy positions of direct power and influence or are consulted directly by men of decision. Yet the influence of all is felt and their combined impact is very great. Collectively they are custodians of our accumulated economic knowledge from the past, they are scholars continuously extending this knowledge and advancing new ideas, they are teachers patiently disseminating this knowledge, and they are consultants applying it to particular policy problems. The role of those few economists who are in direct contact with policy-workers should not be overemphasized. They serve as one link by which the knowledge of the entire profession is transmitted to those who can make use of it. The other—and perhaps most important link—is education in all its ramifications. It is primarily through education at all levels that the knowledge of professional economists is brought to bear on social problems. I know few economists who are not also educators in some sense.[1]

Summary and Conclusions

In this chapter, we have only reached toward a definition of economics, and reaching without grasping is perhaps as much as we need to do, since no short definition is likely to satisfy anybody or to clarify anything. Perhaps the most widely acceptable definition would in some way relate to the problem of reconciling illimitable wants to scarce resources. We have sought to discover essential economic problems and to describe some of the tasks of those who have chosen to profess economics as a vocation. Whether they study banking, foreign trade, or any of the other specialties, they study it for the purpose of benefiting the nation—or mankind—rather than the individual. Now, before we take up economic theory proper, let us look at some of the principal features of the American economy.

[1] Howard R. Bowen, "Graduate Education in Economics," *American Economic Review*, Vol. XLIII, No. 4, Part 4 (September, 1953), pp. 33, 34.

QUESTIONS FOR REVIEW AND DISCUSSION

1. Define, in your own words, each of the following terms:
   a) Economics
   b) Economist
   c) Social science
   d) Division of labor
   e) Technology
   f) Scarce resources

2. Do all economic systems need each of the following institutions to run smoothly: banks, stockbrokerage houses, and advertising firms?

3. An economics major attending Sweetriver College is surprised to learn that his six-hour course, Advertising and Marketing 101–2, does not count toward his major. What argument is the head of the economics department likely to make when he denies the student credit for this course?

4. In the early 1960's, most economists urged policies that would have sought to reduce unemployment. Is such action dictated by science or a system of values, or by both?

5. What is meant by the "economic problem"? Under what conditions would this problem not exist?

6. In your text, Lionel Robbins is quoted as stating that economics concerns itself with "behavior which arises from the scarcity of means to achieve given ends." Who gives the "given ends," or how are they given?

7. "The successful businessman is not an economist, and a good economist is not a businessman. These two specialties cannot exist in one man at one time." Do you think the statement is true? Explain.

8. Most undergraduates feel that the physical sciences have been more "successful" than the social sciences. Why do you think they have this attitude?

Chapter 2

THE AMERICAN
ECONOMY

Institutional Characteristics of Capitalism

As part of our introductory work and before going on to a study of economic theory, we should spend a little time on a descriptive survey of the American economy. The United States is a moderately self-sufficient, industrial, advanced, capitalist economy of about 200 million souls. Let us break up this statement into smaller pieces. To say that we are "moderately self-sufficient" means that unlike England and Holland, we do not—considering our size and wealth—rely heavily on imports, for we grow and mine such a diversity of things in our variegated regions that a vast cutting-down of imports would not prevent us from getting along tolerably well. It is true that we would miss our morning coffee, that there would be less sugar for our cereal, and that we would in other ways have to change our habits of consumption; but we could get along with very little from the outside world.

When we speak of our economy as being "industrial," we refer to the fact that it is technologically well equipped, unlike that of such underdeveloped nations as Peru or Egypt—or, for that matter, of our own nation before the Civil War. An industrial economy embraces more than machines or the ability to apply recent discoveries in physics and chemistry to production; it requires an industrially literate population, bred to mechanization—to turning valves, opening switches, operating telephones, driving cars, obeying red and green signals, keeping machinery oiled, and the like. The ordinary person must be able to read complex directions, to recognize dangers—such as uninsulated electrical wires lying about—to travel without fear under exact rules in cars, airplanes, elevators, and subways. In short, an industrial society is one that has, uses, understands, and perhaps even loves machines and accepts their stern discipline.

By "advanced," we mean well endowed in worldly goods. How

well endowed? It is generally known that the United States leads the
world in this respect. W. W. Rostow, noted economist and civil servant, has made some interesting observations on this point. Until
recently, he says, we were economically in the most advanced stage
still subject to classification, "the age of high mass-consumption." By
this, he means the stage at which electric-powered household gadgets
and the automobile became available to the average family. We
entered this stage in about 1920, earlier than any other nation and just
a little before Canada and Britain. Japan and the great nations of
western Europe did not get there until the 1950's. But, Rostow
observes, the United States seems to be emerging from this stage and
going on to something new. He is not yet prepared to define this new
stage, but he does point out that our ever-growing prosperity is being
put into larger families. We now have our cars, he seems to say, our
dishwashers and blenders, our TV sets and social security. What next
for America? Babies? The rapid growth of population between 1945
and 1964 seems to confirm this thesis; but in recent years, population
growth has decelerated.

    We now come to our fourth and last adjective to describe the
American economic system—capitalist. By "capitalist," we do not, of
course, refer to the caricatures of fat, greedy businessmen in the
Communist press. Our word is derived from "capital"; and by this,
we mean—and so do the economists of all nations, including the
Russian—machines, factories, steamships, tractors, trucks, and all
man-made or man-developed things used to produce other goods or to
transport other goods for processing and to market. Thus, in one
sense, all cultures except those of the most primitive food-gatherers
have used capital and have been capitalistic. The canoe that transports to the hunting ground, the snare that entangles birds, the net,
the pointed stick that stirs the ground for planting—all these are
capital.

    About the middle of the 19th century, the adjective "capitalist"
began to be applied to nations that had large accumulations of capital
and in which further accumulation was proceeding rapidly—that is,
to countries like England, Holland, the United States, France, and so
on. However, it also began to be perceived, particularly by economic
historians, that along with the accumulation of capital, there had
developed a changed viewpoint about economic life in general. In

other words, a capitalist nation was not merely a feudal country that had somehow managed to acquire a lot of steam engines, spinning jennies, and railroads; or a mercantilist nation that had got hold of automatic looms, a telegraph system, or powered machinery to pump water out of mines. What competent observers saw was that along with the growth of capital had come a changed point of view about life; there was a new belief system with new values; a new philosophy had come to underlie the production and acquisition of goods. Thus, as time passed, it came to be realized that the relationship between the word "capital" and such words as "capitalism" or "capitalistic" was very tenuous. For example, the Communist nations want nothing more than to equal or excel the free nations in their accumulation of capital. But they profess to despise capitalism and capitalists. Thus, "capital" is, everywhere, something used to make something else, from a spade to a gargantuan earthmoving machine; from an apple reserved to make canned applesauce to a vast steel plant that makes the steel that is used for the cans in which the applesauce is preserved and sold. But capitalism is a point of view, a way of life, a belief system, one of the many cultural complexes of the world's history.

What is this point of view that characterizes capitalism, that makes it different from feudalism, mercantilism, communism, social-ism, fascism, or any of the other isms that have dominated economic life since man first appeared? One wishes the question could be answered simply and definitively. An ism is at least as hard to de-scribe as a human personality—indeed, it is a personality of a sort—with all its complexities, inconsistencies, and mysteries. It is like an old friend whose behavior you can predict today but whose behavior baffles you completely tomorrow.

We can safely say that one basic tenet of a capitalist country is the right to hold and protect private property. This right is highly developed and covers not only tangible things such as land, buildings, and cars, but also all sorts of nonmaterial things such as a patent or copyright, an unspecified part of a corporation (share of stock), and brand names and trademarks. The chief difference between commu-nism and capitalism is that communism does not recognize the right to own the means of production, whereas capitalism does. Thus, our factories, railroads, land, trucks, and apartment buildings are pri-vately owned; in Russia, they are owned by the government. By comparison with feudalism, our property is alienable. Neither duke nor serf could sell "his" land, for it was not really "his"; and the noble could not sell his title, such as earl or baron, as a modern man can sell a valuable name he owns, such as Buick.

Although the right to hold private property under capitalism is highly developed, it is not indefeasible. If the government or a public utility needs a piece of land, the owner may be forced to sell regardless of his wishes. We do of course compensate the owner in accordance with the principles of law; confiscation is not tolerated. The assumption is made that in such a case the public interest is paramount. The "public interest" is an elastic phrase, subject to reinterpretation as time goes on and human needs change.

Perhaps the second most striking ideological aspect of a capitalist economy is the fact that the free and unplanned making and spending of money incomes are the norm of economic behavior. And the corollary to this is that almost everything has a price and is salable or purchasable. This last is not meant cynically, and there are many obvious exceptions, such as the soldier's patriotism, the professional man's integrity, and countless other forms of unpurchasable virtue. But in most of the ordinary affairs of life, there are few things worth having that money cannot legally procure at a price that is known or pretty clearly established. To most of us, this seems such an obvious thing that readers may wonder why the point is emphasized. But we have to go back only a few years to find cases in which money could not legally get us everything we wanted. During World War II, we needed money *and* ration coupons to get gasoline, steak, or shoes. Socialist and communist economies tend to supplement or even supplant the money and price system with rationing or arbitrary assignment even in peacetime. A few hundred years ago, artisans were often not permitted to wear the same kinds of clothes as the upper classes, even if they had enough money to buy them. But today, any successful gangster may have the same tailor as the Cabots and the Lodges.

Similar observations may be made about the acquisition of money—the opposite of spending. Few occupations or ways of profit making (crime excepted) are closed in a capitalist society; hence, few ways of making money are disbarred. Indeed, moneymaking is so generally reputable that at times it even confers a kind of spuriously sympathetic reputability on dubious transactions. Dealers in black markets in wartime are tolerated though they interfere with military planning—and perhaps they are endured because moneymaking seems to us to be so much the right thing to do.

Like free money spending, free moneymaking is not and has not been tolerated in all societies. In the Middle Ages, many ways of making money were forbidden or at least frowned on. The medieval concept of the just and unchanging price meant that one should not take advantage of scarcities to raise prices and make a speculative profit, and it also meant that one should not attract the customers of others by undercutting prices. Receiving interest on loans was wrong. Buying and selling of land was restricted. The peasant had his land; it did not occur to him, as it does to a modern farmer, that he might buy up his neighbor's fields or sell his own. Nobody was supposed to acquire more possessions than befitted his station in life. Capitalism is quite different and makes rather a virtue of rising above a lowly station.

One striking way of demonstrating the significance of a belief system is to assume that by some magic, Americans would wake up one morning with the ethical values and mental habits of Hindus. It is doubtful whether American capitalism—optimistic, welcoming change, energetic, and anxious to get ahead—could long survive such a radical alteration in beliefs. Hindus are indifferent or actively opposed to many things we cherish, from juicy steaks to "bettering one's self." Their doctrine of *karma* imposes a fatalistic acceptance of their status. Under the Hindu belief system, our prosperity would soon decline, because so many of our goods would appear unnecessary or frivolous to the Hindu mind. A lot of stuff would simply not be bought. Stocks in stores would back up, factories would lay off their men, and a depression would set in.

A very basic tenet of the capitalist point of view is that every person benefits not only himself but also the entire society by seeking his greatest good or gain in an occupation freely chosen. To be sure, this must be done under certain restraints and conditions. The restraints are the well-known ones of law and moral code; we do not seek gain by robbing our neighbor. The conditions are set by competition in a society that encourages economic freedom. But as in all ideologies, deviations and derogations are tolerated.

For example, we cannot tolerate the waste of four airlines flying the short distance from Natchez to Mobile, and our government would not permit it. We do a little inconsistently tolerate the lesser waste of four gas stations at almost any intersection. Our ideology opposes planning and assumes that competition plans better than human beings could—hence the four gas stations. But public transport involves such large outlays of money for rails, stations, airports, radar, and weather-reporting systems that we do tolerate—partly for these reasons and partly for others—government planning in this area. The ideology stands there as the basic principle from which as few derogations as possible are permitted. Sometimes the derogations do not make much sense; oftener, they do.

Although we are indeed a capitalist country with a vast amount of economic freedom by comparison with the remainder of the world, governmental intervention in business affairs is considerable. The amount of restraint, licensing, price-fixing, and subsidization is enough to make us wonder whether we have not returned to the age of mercantilism. Licenses of one sort or another are required to start almost any new transport company or television or radio station. Firms selling electricity, gas, water, or telephone service must charge prices fixed by a governmental agency. A vast number of persons and firms are subsidized in one way or another: farmers, producers of oil, war veterans, certain needy or physically handicapped groups, airlines, advertisers, homeowners, shipbuilders, owners and employees in tariff-protected goods, owners of heavy trucks, and small businessmen. The federal government conducts a vast pension business (social security), not to mention a host of other activities from running the Panama Canal to running military PX's; state governments administer a vast educational "business"; and our list is by no means exhausted. In all this, we are like most of the other capitalist nations of the world. We do differ from some of the major ones, however, in that American airlines, telephone and telegraph companies, and railroads are not governmentally owned.

Before leaving the difficult task of trying to describe our belief system and the actual deviations from it, mention should be made of our attitude of tolerance toward economic instability. The economic instability of capitalist economy is not related to such external events as droughts, floods, great plagues, or the chronic and debilitating warfare of the medieval period or the Reformation. The trouble is internal or endogenous. As will be seen later, the admirable freedom of choice we have in getting and spending our money incomes may also lay waste our powers. Though coordinating forces do exist and will be discussed in the next chapter, they are not always strong enough to prevent the instability that reveals itself through inflation, depression, recession, unused manufacturing capacity, or unused labor power (unemployment).

It is true that the fully planned societies, Russia being the most obvious example, also endure unemployment, unused plant capacity, and inflation. There is a difference, however. Unemployment in the Soviet system seems to arise from a breakdown of planning, from the blundering of a ministry, the miscalculation of a commissar, and, in general, the fallibility of men. Some person, board, or agency botched things or did not foresee a bottleneck; and the penalty may be agricultural underproduction, inflation, or idleness of men. And presumably, the blunderers are held responsible. Under capitalism, no person or board or bureau is to blame. Stability is everybody's business and hence nobody's business.[1] As a result, we are vulnerable to an uneven growth, sudden and sharp stock market declines as in the spring of 1962, and massive unemployment as in the 1930's. The capitalist viewpoint, historically, has accepted this instability in much the same spirit that we accept the weather. A depression has been defended as a salutary "shake-out," or as a necessary exhalation after a deep breath, or as a desirable rest after a period of growth. Inflation, which robs us attritively and diverts the brains of business from production to the conservation of pecuniary capital, is a feature of capitalism. In the last 30 years, this viewpoint has changed somewhat, for both capitalism and its capitalist belief system are evolutionary. Most economists believe that human action can forestall depression and block inflation without doing violence to the basic principles of capitalism, but many businessmen and members of government do not share this belief. That is, they feel that the remedies proposed will do substantial damage to that set of institutions and beliefs which we call capitalism. The issue is still a matter of public debate.

[1] It is true that the Employment Act of 1946 places responsibility of a sort on the federal government to maintain high levels of employment, and it is true that public opinion is more tolerant today of governmental intervention to maintain prosperity than it was before 1930; yet the facts are substantially as set forth in the text above.

Facts and Figures about the U.S. Economy

We have a population of more than 200 million persons to draw on for our economic activity. Out of this total, about 40 percent are money-makers—that is, they are receivers and therefore in most cases producers of income. The remaining 60 percent are children, older people, housewives, and special groups such as the institutionalized criminal and insane. Thus the average income receiver carries a burden of 1½ consumers who do not work or, at least, whose work is not rewarded by a cash income. One fairly large group of producers does not receive paychecks. This group includes all housewives who stay at home and all others who perform family chores.

Excluding these domestic tasks, the American people produce enough to give them a national income close to $800 billion. If we divide this figure by total population, we find that equal sharing would award everybody about $4,000. This suggests that the typical family of four would get $16,000 annually. But in the United States, as seems to be true in all countries of the world, income is rather un-evenly distributed—so much so that the arithmetic averages used above are not very good measures of American prosperity. Averages sometimes measure something less than nothing at all. Two grand-parents of 65 and their three grandchildren, all about two years old, have an "average" age of 27 years; but this figure is meaningless, since it does not come close to describing any age in the group—the figures do not cluster around a central tendency. The same kind of fault inheres in income data as well as in many other basic figures of the economy. To get a figure with greater meaning, we shall first have to dispense with the typical family of four and then with the arith-metic average. We shall use as the group of persons involved the "spending unit," defined by the Survey Research Center of the Uni-versity of Michigan as all persons living in the same dwelling and belonging to the same family who pool their incomes to meet their major expenses, though this may also apply to any single person living alone. Next, for the measure of central tendency, we shall use the median—that is, the income of the middle spending unit. This is analogous to the figure found by the teacher who arranges her papers in order from 98 percent to the lowest, 40 percent, let us say. If she has 31 students, the 16th paper will be exactly in the middle, and the grade on it would be the median. Now, the middle spending unit in the United States in 1964 had a median income of $6,556, less than half the income of our typical family above ($16,000). One reason for this discrepancy, as we have said, is the large inequality of incomes here and elsewhere. A second is that median figures for 1968 are not yet available. They will probably be higher. In our own country, in 1964, the lowest 10th of all spending units got one one hundredth of the total money income; the highest 10th, beginning at $13,700, got thirty hundredths of the total.[2] The $4,000 average per capita income discussed above is a national figure. Great variation in personal income exists among the states. In 1966 the citizens of Mississippi reported an average income of only $1,751, and those of South Dakota only $2,355, while the residents of Connecticut enjoyed an average per capital income of $3,678, and those of California $3,449. If anything, these figures do not fully reflect the differences that exist among the states, for an "average" tends to hide from view both poverty and affluence, as we have just seen.

How we spend this money is interesting. If we use urban families of wage earners and clerical workers as our standard, 25 percent of all income spent (after income taxes) goes for food, beverages, and tobacco. Studies by the Twentieth Century Fund indicate that the average American consumes 1,500 pounds of food yearly. Not quite one third of our income goes for housing. Nearly 9 percent goes for apparel, with women and girls spending a little more than men and boys. Transport runs to about 13 percent, and medical care about half as much. What's left over goes for personal care, reading, recreation, and miscellaneous.

That is, of course, one useful way of looking at our expenditures. Another approach yields other results. Our military expenditures (excluding the war in Vietnam) probably run to $80 billion a year; it is impossible to be exact, since we find difficulties in classification. For example, we are spending money to send a man to the moon. Is this military? If we are prepared to accept the figure of $80 billion, then we can establish that this is about 13 percent of our national income. Our expenditure for education is about 5½ percent of national in-

[2] *Statistical Abstract of the United States*, 1966, p. 335.

come. Highway expenditures run to over $12 billion a year. In ordinary years, we sell about nine million passenger cars to the American public. Assuming that they sell for an average of $3,000 each, including the usual extras, we spend about $27 billion a year on new cars, or close to 5 percent of our national income; but of course, we also spend for gas, insurance, replacement parts, and repairs. Automobiles are a most expensive item in our culture. They are said to account for one fourth of all retail sales. This embraces gasoline and the gas tax but does not include insurance.

Let us return for a moment to the $80 billion that we spend for the military or defense. This is obviously a vast figure. We do of course spend more for food and for shelter, but the defense figure constitutes one of the largest fractions of the national income, and military needs provide direct or indirect employment to hundreds of thousands. To be sure, not all of what is being produced for defense could be foregone, even if war were renounced by all nations and disarmament were a reality. For example, over three million men and women now in the armed forces would have to consume food, clothing, and shelter, whether in uniform or out. Still, there is cause for anxiety in the thought that any suggested step toward international peace arouses the fear of unemployment in the minds of tens of thousands. Economic statesmanship of a high order could prevent catastrophe, of course; but at best, there would be many dislocations, and it is never safe to count on the emergence of great economic statesmanship just because it is needed. A Damoclean sword does overhang our economy. If we beat our spears into pruning hooks, the sword may not fall; but it is there.

The Firms That Produce Our Goods and Services

In the continental United States, there are about 11.4 million business establishments, including about 3.5 million farms. It would be hard to pick out the most striking characteristic of this huge phalanx that ministers to our material needs. Perhaps the salient feature would be the relative absence of the middle-sized firm. In many sectors of the economy a few giant firms dominate production, as in automobiles, steel, utilities, oil, electric equipment, and others. Many of the remaining firms are pygmies by comparison; they are gleaners after the mammoth harvesters have passed by. A typical small store takes in around $200 daily; the A & P takes in about $15 million daily; Sears Roebuck takes in about 25 percent more. Disparities are not so great in agriculture; but even here, the top 9 percent produces as much as the bottom 91 percent.[3] There are, of course, some areas in which big business is not represented at all, such as barbershops and beauty shops; repair shops for automobiles, shoes, television sets, and washing machines are small.

When American business is big, it is really big. The assets, for example, of a small automobile company (American Motors) are about 3½ percent of the assets of General Motors, a $13-billion company. The assets of General Motors are about 37 percent of the assets of American Telephone and Telegraph. A $50-million company is really nothing—certainly not big business, for it is only one seventieth the size of such multibillion-dollar companies as General Electric or Standard Oil of Indiana. And yet we are not a land of big business only; to get our work done, we need several million small firms, ranging in size from small diners to independent department stores nine stories high—and *they* are small potatoes!

The legal arrangements adopted to carry on production are of interest. Most farms and 73 percent of all nonfarm firms are individually owned. About 10 percent of the nonfarm firms are partnerships. In law, there are important differences between individual proprietorships and partnerships, but they have so little economic effect that these differences need not detain us. Only about 16 percent are corporations; the remaining 1 percent are of mixed types. The corporation thus appears on the surface to have minor importance. But as we have already intimated, the corporation is the standard form for big business to take, and its weight is therefore much greater than its small numbers suggest.

Corporations are curious legal entities owned by thousands and even hundreds of thousands of people scattered all over the world, usually interested in what their corporation is doing so long as dividend checks come in regularly. Rarely do more than a very few—relative to the total number—of the part owners meet together to discuss affairs relating to their property. Indeed, the majority cannot,

3 Edward Higbee, "Now the Non-Farmer Asks for Parity," *New York Times Magazine*, June 2, 1963, p. 15.

for physical reasons. Our largest corporation, American Telephone and Telegraph, has about two million stockholders. They would occupy the 20 largest stadiums in the United States, with enough left over to fill some of the vastest stadiums abroad, plus the imposing bullfight arena in Mexico City. And few other big-name companies could squeeze a majority of their stockholders into the seats of Houston's Astrodome.

If one thinks of structure alone, the stockholders are the ultimate and omnipotent managing force of a corporation. They elect the directors, a governing board of perhaps 20 or 30 men. The directors choose the president, who is the operating head and who manages the corporation under the policies and scrutiny of the directors. If the directors and president pursue a course of action that displeases the stockholders, the latter may vote the directors out of office and get new ones who will fire the president. No doubt this description holds good for many small corporations with perhaps a couple of hundred stockholders, none of whom owns a disproportionately large share of the total stock outstanding. (Stockholders' votes are weighted in accordance with the number of shares they hold, usually one vote for each share of stock.)

For large corporations with hundreds of thousands of stockholders, the above description is meaningless. To be sure, the structure is still the same: On paper, stockholders elect directors; directors choose the president; stockholders can throw directors and president out of office. But in actual practice in a going concern, initiative comes from what we shall name "insiders"—the directors, the president, and perhaps a few of his closest advisers and officers, and in some instances a few very large stockholders. The vast majority of stockholders simply ratify the decisions of insiders. The insiders form a self-perpetuating club, relatively free from general stockholder control or supervision; so long as reasonable dividends are paid with reasonable frequency, stockholders take little interest in what is going on and vote their absentee ballots as the insiders propose. Usually, voting is confined to the selection of directors—the reelection of those whose terms expire or the replacement of those who resign or die. Questions about pricing the product, raising or lowering dividends and wages of production workers, or expanding or contracting operations are not often submitted to stockholder voting.

Occasionally, a few stockholders, usually rather large ones (but not necessarily insiders), and also men of considerable experience in business, seek to gain control of a corporation, oust the directors and officers, and capture the machinery of management. They can do this by setting in motion a campaign not unlike a political campaign. They send letters to stockholders attacking the present management; they urge them to turn the rascals out, just as is done in campaigns for senators, governors, or mayors. They promise a better administration, larger dividends, and the like. Sometimes, this is done in good faith, and the incumbents really are rascals or at best timid and incompetent; sometimes, it is done simply to get control and occasionally to lay hands on an overful treasury. If the insurgent group is able to persuade enough stockholders to vote for its candidates and its program, control of the corporation passes into its hands. What has been wrested from the old group by the new is, of course, power and control, not property. The old insiders did not own the corporation any more than the President and Congress of the United States own the nation; the new insiders do not own anything either, except that both groups probably hold a few thousand shares of stock of the many thousands outstanding. Even where a new group lays hands on a well-filled treasury, the money over which power has been secured must be handled with circumspection. If increased dividends are to be paid, all stockholders must get increased dividends. If the new officers are to get higher salaries and allowances than the old, increases must be made legally and in accordance with corporate rules—or the rules must be changed according to proper procedures.

Most of the large corporations lead relatively uneventful lives. There are no insurgents; the corporation is run by a trained bureaucracy. The first aim of the officers is of course to make reasonable profits; the second is to reconcile the conflicting interests that swirl around a large company. Labor must be kept appeased; stockholders must be kept satisfied; antitrust prosecutions must be avoided; consumers must feel they are getting their money's worth; the claims of the various departments must be adjudicated; specified goals must be achieved; and of course, as in politics, those holding office strive to keep themselves in control. Although profits obviously come first if the corporation is to survive, the pursuit of maximum possible profits is not always the dominant goal. Interviews with corporation officials suggest that they seek to attain certain targets, such as 30 percent of

the market or 20 percent profit, rather than undefined yet maximum
profit goals. After all, the top men in a corporation have no strong
incentive to push profits beyond a certain point. Their salaries are
fixed, and though they may get bonuses for extra profits, they have
usually reached the point where extra dollars can mean little to them.
Salaries are high, often much higher than the salary of the President
of the United States. Much of their travel and entertainment is at
company expense. Their prestige is enormous. The economic empires
they rule may be larger than any one of the 30 smallest nations of the
world. In the councils of the world's mightiest, their opinions may
weigh more heavily than those of many heads of state, and their terms
of office may last longer. Men of this kind need not push for maximum
possible profits. They are more likely to have goals of prestige: a
larger and more powerful company, an improved public image, and a
reputation for producing the best product, whether justified or not.

In conclusion, it must be clear that the large corporation is
something more than a king-size model of the corner bakery. The
motivation of the managers, the absenteeism of its owners, and the
divorce of management and ownership all point to qualitative rather
than quantitative differences. Some corporations are in the business of
owning enough shares of other corporations to control them; they are
known as "holding companies," and their purpose is to secure unified
action over several corporations. There are even holding companies of
holding companies of holding companies. On paper, any such company would have to acquire 51 percent of the stock of another
company before the controlling company could feel sure of its capacity to dominate the policies of the second corporation. In actual
practice, 5 to 10 percent is enough. Thus the first holding company
may control a $100-million operating company by buying only $5
million worth of stock; the second holding company could control the
first holding company by making an investment of only $250,000;
and a third could control the second by investing a paltry $12,500.
There are cases on record in which holding companies have controlled
a million dollars for every thousand invested at the top. The device is
not normally used, as might be inferred from the example just given,
to superimpose several layers of control on a single company, but
rather to bring together several operating and producing companies
under unified management.

There is obviously nothing inherently wrong about holding companies, but one wonders whether it is in the public interest to go so very far in separating ownership from management. Holding companies, though financial rather than industrial in purpose, may nonetheless supply useful guidance and integration to the underlying companies that produce actual goods and services. Many of them— particularly the older public utility holding companies—have, however, been exploitative in purpose and caused loss to small investors.

We cannot dwell too long on holding companies. There are several more things worth noting about an ordinary corporation. Like a college, it has life everlasting; it continues to function as an entity even after the death of a whole generation of presidents, directors, and stockholders. Legally, it is a person, and we even think popularly of it as having personality. The United States Steel Corporation, formed in 1901, has probably by now lost virtually all the officers, stockholders, and directors it had nearly seven decades ago. Yet United States Steel has acquired as distinct a character as any well-known college or university. A corporation may of course decide to perish— that is, liquidate its affairs and go out of business—but it is not compelled to do this, as a partnership or individual business must, when an owner dies. A corporation stockholder has limited liability. This means that no investor need legally lose more than he puts into the business. If you buy 10 shares of General Motors, thus investing $700 in the company, you can never lose more than $700, no matter what fantastic debts an ineffective management may contract. This privilege of limited liability applies also to directors, presidents, and vice presidents of corporations. They manage without assuming any financial risk, except, of course, the amount they have invested, which may be very little or, in rare cases, nothing at all. In short, they can wreck the company at little or no pecuniary loss. This privilege is not shared by the individual proprietor or partnership.

It is generally argued that one great advantage of the corporation is that by pooling the savings of thousands of people and limiting the risks they take, immense sums of money can be placed under one management to direct vast and beneficent projects. This is a fact, of course, but it is not very clear to whom this is an advantage and who is benefited. Taking present technology into account, it is doubtful whether any industrial plant, to achieve maximum efficiency, requires a larger investment than three quarters of a billion dollars—and a sum of this magnitude in only a few industries. The large American fortunes are such that several hundreds of millions could be found in numerous families and many partnerships. From the viewpoint of the public interest, a strong case can be made for the argument that we are overendowed with oversized firms. The corporation and the holding company are mixed blessings.

The corporation, particularly the very large corporation, has aroused much speculation and some foreboding in the minds of many economists and social philosophers. Many would hold that the insiders of a few hundred of the largest companies form the most powerful group in our nation; that they influence important legislation; that they shape consumers' demand rather than supply consumers' wants; that by their influence on the press and broadcasting, they debase our language, beliefs, and ethics. One observer reminds us that the "giant corporation is not the individual economic unit writ large," so often assumed in the theory of competitive price.[4] Adolf A. Berle, Jr., though expressing hope for a benevolent evoluton of corporate power, also cautions us against certain dangers. It is generally assumed that old-fashioned competition among many small firms performed a regulatory function in the public interest; but, says Berle, the kind of competition that now exists among a few corporations is of a different sort and has different effects. Who supplies the regulatory function that was formerly supplied by competition among many small firms? The reply—stated here too briefly to do justice to Berle—is that the force of public opinion, the threat of governmental control, and the statesmanship of the officers will keep these vast aggregations of economic (and hence political) power in line. John Kenneth Galbraith, economist and many other things besides, sees the vast power of the corporation held in reasonable check by the countervailing power of "big" labor, by farmers organized politically to get their subsidies, and by the probable rise of other countervailing forces when and if needed to curb abuses of power. In other quarters the modern large corporation has been described as a bureaucracy in which officials, following an unimaginative routine, have displaced the great innovating businessmen of previous centuries. The scope of this chapter and indeed of this book is not large enough to permit our

[4] Center for the Study of Democratic Institutions, *The Corporation and the Economy* (Santa Barbara, 1959), p. 7.

going much further into this matter. Chapter 16, on the preservation of competition, will have something more to say about the large corporation. In the meantime, we can only conclude that a relatively new kind of organization for the production of goods and services dominates much of American life.

Summary and Conclusions

In this chapter, we have taken some of the dimensions of the American economy—population, working force, average and median incomes of its inhabitants, and what people buy with their incomes.

We have also sought to describe some of its chief institutions and the nature of its belief system. In the field of production of goods and services, we find an interesting bimodality—many stores, farms, and other enterprises often producing rather little of the total for all of their numbers: and on the other hand, a few large enterprises often producing the major part of a product.

The larger productive units usually take the form of the corporation or holding company. The structure of both is rather interesting legally. It is quite different from that of the small, individually owned firms. It makes possible a wide separation of control from ownership. A rather large industrial empire can be controlled by a relatively small investment. The simple profit motive is, in a large corporation, diluted—or possibly enriched—by other motives.

QUESTIONS FOR REVIEW AND DISCUSSION

1. Define, in your own words, each of the following terms:
   a) Capitalist economy
   b) Communist economy
   c) Median
   d) Distribution of income
   e) Corporation
2. The types of goods and services we produce and consume are dictated by our "biological needs and cultural demands." Discuss. Is a woman's hat the response to a cultural or biological need? What about shoes, cornflakes, or newspapers?
3. The American economy is often called a "mixed economy." What does this mean?

4. Why would a nation be accounted poor if 60 percent of its national income were spent on food?

5. The service industries now employ the largest fraction of the U.S. labor force. Would this have been true 100 years ago? Would it be true of India today? Explain your replies.

6. Define capital. Which, if any, of the following could never in any circumstances be classed as capital: a puppy, a quart of strawberries, or a dozen roses?

7. Using the materials in your text and any further information you can get from other textbooks or encyclopedias, draw organization charts for a corporation; for a holding company.

8. Where does a belief system come from? How does an individual acquire a belief system?

9. Much more easily than can individuals, great corporations are able to raise sums as huge as $25 billion, thus enabling them to build up great manufacturing and service establishments. Are these establishments wholly in the public interest? Give reasons for your reply.

10. Sometimes the phrase "Protestant ethic" is used to describe the underlying spirit of a capitalist society. What is this? Use an encyclopedia or book on European history to find the reply.

PART II

Standard Economic Theory

Chapter 3

INTRODUCTION TO STANDARD ECONOMIC THEORY

Theory and Common Sense

We are now passing through the entrance gates to standard economic theory. This chapter may be looked upon as a briefing session for what lies ahead. In the next hundred pages or so we shall be exploring an unfamiliar land, namely, the field of economic theory; and in this chapter, we shall form some preliminary notions about the terrain. We need first to be clear about the nature and role of theory in any science and about the value of simplifying assumptions generally in human thought. From this, we shall go on to see what simplifications and abstractions have to be made by economists in particular before they can do their work. The topics in this chapter may not always, at first sight, appear to be related to one another; but this should not cause confusion if the reader will remember that all topics are related to the functions of a briefing session—to the problem of making easier the comprehension of the remainder of this book.

There are several types of economic theory; and we shall first discuss, in Part II, what your authors will designate as "standard economic theory" or, more simply, "standard theory." Economics has not, like physics and geometry, reached a state of theoretical development that wins global assent to its elementary propositions. There are many disagreements, and at least three types or systems of theory are visible in the world today. The first is standard economic theory. This is the kind that dominates economic thinking in the free Western world in schools and among government officials. It represents majority opinion in the Free World. A second is the Marxian school that, emasculated, has been at least partly incorporated into the belief system of the Communist world. The third is the so-called "institutional school" that claims a minority group in this country and a few like-minded adherents elsewhere in the Free

World. All three types will be discussed in their proper places. This chapter introduces only standard theory.

College students who have taken geometry and physics are already inured to the demands of theoretical thought, even if they are not quite aware of the fact that they have learned scientific method-ology. But it is desirable in the teaching and the learning of economics to dwell for awhile, as we shall now do, on the meaning of a theoreti-cal approach in any field, and we shall move from widely understood concepts in physics and geometry to less widely known concepts in economics.

Theory is often in conflict with the testimony of common sense or of down-to-earth observation. It is, for example, easy enough to describe in a general way how a feather and a stone will behave if dropped from the Washington Monument; but what requires imagina-tion and a willingness to deny the evidence of common sense is to realize that feather and stone would strike the earth at the same instant but for resistance of the air. In a vacuum, thistledown and a steel ball plunge to earth at the same speed.

Now, the remarkable thing is that theoretical physicists are more concerned about how things drop in the vacuum than they are about how things drop in the real world; and this is true despite the fact that in the real world, only one fall in several trillions takes place in even a partial vacuum. This one exceptional or experimental case is, however, the important one to the physicist. Indeed, this exceptional occurrence is the basis of the law of falling bodies. The law conflicts with the daily observations of the ordinary man, but it is the first important step in comprehending reality. It is used in problems relating to the trajectory of projectiles, ballistic missiles, and artificial satellites, and in various other practical ways. The law that bodies undisturbed by resistance fall at equal speeds from the same height is the fundamental fact. This being known, it is easy to make allowances for certain interferences such as air resistance.

This is only one example of how the events of an unreal world help us to understand the real world. In the field of geometry, we encounter the same paradox. Billy E. Goetz of Massachusetts Institute of Technology, in speaking of geometry, has gone so far as to say that some of the most useful things to mankind are figments of the imagination:

A straight line has no width, no depth, no wiggles, and no ends.

There are no straight lines. We have ideas about these non-existent impossibilities: we even draw pictures of them. But they do not exist. . . .

A straight line hasn't even a definition. . . .

A point has no dimensions, no existence and no definition. . . .

Euclid lists twenty-three definitions which define more than twenty-three figments of the imagination. Next he postulates an ability to draw straight lines from point to point, to project these straight lines indefinitely in either direction, and to draw circles; all manifest impossibilities. . . .[1]

And yet, Goetz goes on to say, out of these manifest impossibilities and figments of the imagination come the countless useful practical applications of geometry.

The Abstractions of Economics

Economic theory, like physics and geometry, has its heroic abstractions and exceptional cases as handmaidens to theory. They sometimes demand a denial of the testimony of common sense. Perhaps the best way of introducing the student to theoretical ways of thinking in economics is to describe the abstract world within which the economist reasons. There are three fundamental "figments of the imagination," to use Goetz's words, that we shall have to accept if we are to make progress in standard theory—first, a perfectly competitive market; second, buyers, sellers, producers, and consumers who are devoid of all motives except economic motives; and third, an economic world beneficently organized by price. We now elaborate these concepts in turn.

A perfectly competitive market—like a line or a point, or a perfect vacuum—does not exist on this earth. But it facilitates economic reasoning if we assume the existence of such a market. What is a perfectly competitive market like?

In a general and hazy way, we all know what is meant by competition. A brochure put out by the United States Steel Corporation some years ago defined the commonsense notion of competition as follows: "The action of two or more sellers in attempting to secure the same piece of available business." And most of us feel that a

---

[1] "The Usefulness of the Impossible," *AAUP Bulletin*, Vol. XLII, No. 2 (Summer, 1956), pp. 275–76.

competitive economy is one permeated by such actions. This is a tolerably good statement of the popular notion.

For the economist, this is not good enough. To begin with, the United States Steel definition leaves out the buyers' side, as at a country auction, where two or more buyers try to outbid each other for an available antique. That is, there is competition among buyers as well as sellers. But there is much more to it than that. For the concept of perfect competition to be useful to the economist, the competition must really be perfect—like the impossible perfection of Euclid's lines. First, each individual buyer and seller must do so insignificant a business that if any one of them should drop out of the market, his contribution would hardly be missed, and price would not alter perceptibly—as a lighted candle contributes virtually nothing to the heating of a large room. This condition is, for sellers, almost met in many kinds of farming; it is doubtful whether any cabbage grower produces enough cabbage to affect price if he should drop out of the market. It is not met in the case of tobacco buying, for among our cigarette companies there are a few huge buyers who, if they did not buy, would wreck the market. It is not met in the case of many industries, as in automobiles or aluminum, in which half a dozen companies or less sell about 70 percent of the product, or more.

A second condition of perfect competition is an absence in the market of various restrictions. Restrictions may be set by the government which would forbid the operation of new radio and TV stations, airlines, railroads, and certain kinds of trucking companies without a license. Some restrictions fall into the domain of racketeering, as when unions, businessmen, and politicians combine to threaten the destruction of new entrants into certain businesses—laundries, bakeries, cleaning and pressing establishments, and the like. Certain states restrict people from entering certain occupations by a detailed licensing system. In some states, you have to have a license if you want to become a threshing-machine operator, a scrap tobacco dealer, or an egg grader. Immigrration laws prevent a smooth flow of human services across borders.

A third condition is equal knowledge of buyers and sellers of relevant market facts. If this condition really obtained, it would mean the end of advertising as big business—a rather paradoxical outcome in the minds of those who believe that advertising is the soul of competition. There would be nothing true, false, or borderline that a seller could tell a buyer about his product, for the buyer would already know everything. But knowledge goes beyond familiarity with the product. It includes knowledge of other, better markets. It would make impossible the picking-up of a rare coin, stamp, or book at as absurd bargain or the trading of a few Woolworth trinkets to savages for much ivory and gold.

A fourth condition is that products be homogeneous. Relative to the total, there are few such commodities, and most of them are to be found in the basic products—number 2 yellow corn, black pepper, pig aluminum, granulated cane sugar, and the like. You may buy exactly the same bacon for 69 cents at a supermarket as you buy in a truly fancy grocery at 80 cents. But the products are not homogeneous; they are differentiated. At the swank grocer's, you do not serve yourself or stand in line; you can have your bacon delivered; you can have it charged; you get attentive service from a well-mannered salesman. From the economist's viewpoint, the two commodities, though the same in the home economics laboratory, are different. In one case, you buy only bacon. In the other, you buy bacon plus extreme courtesy, delivery, charge privilege, convenience, and an environment of good breeding. Many things in our society are differentiated primarily through trademark, surface design, scent, or other unimportant quality. Thus, many tires, soaps, and toothbrushes are equally good in accomplishing their function but are distinguished in the minds of people only by design and maker's name. So long as consumer loyalty can be won by externals, so long do we have a differentiated rather than homogeneous commodity.

We need scarcely put down as our last point the obvious fact that there must be no collusion among buyers on the one hand or sellers on the other. And of course, there must be no monopoly elements in the market. Formal, overt collusion may be relatively infrequent. But what shall we say of the ladies who, at the Tuesday Literary Club of a small town, discuss the servant problem, wages, and afternoons off? Will they not, as a result of their chitchat, pursue similar policies with respect to their domestic workers? If a large steel company raises prices and all others follow, what then? This kind of lockstep presents real difficulties when antimonopoly prosecutions arise in our courts.

Now, all of this does not mean that economists never speak of imperfect markets or of monopoly. They make many descriptive studies of the actual forms that imperfect competition and monopoly take. They also treat these matters theoretically. The handling of problems in the realm of imperfect competition has been highly developed in the past 30 years. But it is still true that an assumed system of perfect competition is the first approximation, and that many of the guiding principles of current economics arise out of the assumptions of perfect competition.

The Economic Man

We come to our second observation underlying economic theory: What kind of people operate in these markets? This perfectly competitive world is peopled by perfectly economic men. Their psychology, as viewed by the economist, is fairly simple. They do not love or hate or do stupid or heroic things or dreamily recite poetry in a glen. They just buy and sell and work and rent their land and organize their enterprises, always with a view to making the most profit or the least loss, or getting the most satisfaction or productivity from their purchases. They are lightning calculators, always able to tell whether the pleasure of getting $3.75 is just about equal to putting in an hour of overtime; always pretty decisive about whether they will get more pleasure from a $6.00 theater ticket than from a $6.00 necktie.

The intelligent economist does not really believe that people are like that. What he believes is that one aspect of human nature is sufficiently like that to warrant his making these assumptions when he engages in purely economic reasoning. When he searches for a wife or a friend, he looks for a more versatile mind; but when he ponders the wider effects of an increase in taxes, he goes back to his simply motivated economic man, to his profit maximizer, his animate slide rule.

The Automatic Organization of the Economy

The third basic abstraction of standard economic theory involves the concept of organization, or cohesiveness, of the economic world.

What is the cement, spit, or gravitational force that keeps it from flying apart? If one thinks hard about economic life—the hard kind of thinking Isaac Newton did when he wondered why the apple went down instead of up—one begins to wonder why there is any order at all in economic life. How amazing our economic organization is can be appreciated if one stops to ponder the logistics of a Sunday school picnic. That requires a general chairman with almost dictatorial power; careful planning; various subchairmen in charge of food, recreation, and transportation, also vested with authority; plus endless telephone conversations about watercress sandwiches with mayonnaise. All this central direction for just a few hours' picnicking! And yet there is no central direction for our vast American economic system which feeds 200 million people more or less adequately three times a day, transports them billions of miles from sun to sun, and finds a bed for nearly all nearly every night. To be sure, economic life is not unplanned in detail. Each businessman plans for the welfare of his firm. Government is an organizing force—perhaps a greater one than most people realize. But even so, there is no overall planning.

There are other evidences of unenforced order in our economic life. There is proportion, and there is economy. It is rare that two men are sent to do the job of 10. Bulldozers are not used to shovel away a few pecks of dirt, and power shovels are not used to dig postholes. There are—except for one or two tiny ones that occasionally pop up in human interest stories—no farms on Manhattan Island. Materials like wood or gold, brick or sapphires are always dedicated to their special and "proper" uses. Prices are roughly the same for the same things over wide areas; it is clear that there is a system of interrelated prices. Yet, except for price-fixing by some manufacturers and other bodies, it is equally clear that there is no central price-fixing commission. All of these evidences of order are impressive—as impressive in their way as the order of the solar system, which prevents planets from colliding and keeps the stars in their courses.

Adam Smith is to be credited with explaining how the economic system organizes itself automatically, and his theories have not been much improved on by later standard theorists. First, according to Smith, we must consider that man seeks his own interest and is naturally adapted to "trucking and barter." Besides having a propensity to specialize in production, he creates surpluses: The shoemaker produces more shoes than he can wear, the farmer more food than he can eat, the weaver more cloth than he can use. What is more natural, then, than for each to seek to exchange his surplus for another man's surplus? Thus the first and basic organizing force is that men naturally take to the kind of economic life we now have, making different things and exchanging what they do not need.

The second organizing force is the action of price on a free market. On this, Smith is less clear; what follows includes the ideas of others. If too many shoes are being made, considering demand, their price will fall in the presence of a free market and the absence of government controls. It may fall below the cost of production of the less efficient shoemakers; and if so, some men, at least, will stop making shoes. The supply will then go down, and prices will therefore go up. If too many have dropped out of shoemaking, the prices will rise again; they may go so high that some of the shoemakers will reenter their trade. This process of trial and error will continue back and forth until a balance or equilibrium is reached. And so for all other commodities.

Price has the further function of ordering scarce goods to their "highest" uses. Here is a huge tract of land. It can be used for anything from a farm or golf course to an oil refinery or base for skyscrapers. What decides how it shall be used? Price. The owner will of course sell to the highest bidder; the highest bidder is the one who can make the best (most productive and hence most profitable) use of the land. Thus, all of us are insured against frivolous or trifling uses not only of land but also of labor and capital and natural resources, for they are similarly used to best account. Those who would use any kind of good to perform trivial functions are outbid by those who are able to use it most productively. To be sure, a very wealthy man may buy rich farmland precisely because he wishes to keep it unproductive and wishes to insure privacy, elegance, and quiet for himself. But exceptions are not important in the aggregate.

Several considerations help to make the process of price adjustment smoother than it might seem at first glance. One is the almost unlimited possibility of substitution—the protein in cheese for the protein in eggs, or flying machines for orchard-spraying machines. Another is the eternal exchange of market information. Men and women love to talk about prices. Unintentional eavesdropping in subways, hotel lobbies, and restaurants almost anywhere in the world is rewarded by such sounds as "$5,'" "only $1," "75 francs," "30 bob." Through all means of communication from the telephone to the grapevine, news quickly gets around about shortages, oversupply, or faltering or unshrinking demand. Men act in response to this knowledge because proper and timely action yields a profit. But proper and timely action also rectifies a shortage or an oversupply or appeases vigorous demand. Nature abhors an economic vacuum, that is, an unexploited opportunity for profit. Somebody always steps in to fill the vacuum and make the profit—and hence meets a human need.

Many standard economists pondering the explanations given above have tended to see something deeper, something more than mere economic organization. They would say that the desire of each purchaser to buy cheap, of each seller to sell dear, of each man to work at the most highly paid occupation or invest in the most profitable business—that all these forms of individual selfishness result in the greatest good to the greatest number. Bernard Mandeville, as early as 1714, saw at least dimly this paradox, which he wrote about under the title *The Fable of the Bees; or, Private Vices, Publick Benefits.* Going perhaps a little further than the economists later went, he wrote:

> All Trades and Places knew some Cheat;
> No Calling was without Deceit.
>
> Thus every Part was full of Vice,
> Yet the whole Mass a Paradise.

Scandalized complaints were lodged against the book; it was condemned and publicly burned; but Adam Smith and other economists, not to mention the average citizen of today, accept the idea that the vice of self-interest is transformed into a public benefit by the magic of economic process. Alexander Pope came closer than Mandeville to striking the right note with his couplet:

> Thus God and Nature formed the general frame
> And bade self-love and social be the same.

Whether or not one agrees with the theories of economic organization here put forward—and they are open to question, as we shall see later—they are admirable in that they seek to do certain very important things. They are an ingeniously devised bridge between the individual and society, between freedom and order, between anarchy and organization, between atomism and pattern, between egoism and altruism. They are, if equally valid, as important in the realm of economics as the law of gravity is in astronomy. Both account for the forces that hold things together in worlds that have no central direction by deliberate human act.

Needless to say, such a world is static. There are no wars, revolutions, depressions, or inflation. The stock market does not suddenly take fright because a President of the United States becomes ill, and there is no frenzied speculation in land and stocks as there was in the 1920's. Growth of industries and of population and of demand for goods is orderly, sustained, and never explosive.

The last few pages may be thought of as describing an economic model. We all know that a working model of a 707 jet is a small representation of the real thing—not only small but even if done carefully to scale very much simplified. For example, it would not contain real food in the refrigerators—indeed, not even real refrigerators. World globes used to teach geography are also models, never with trees and grass or actual water in the seas, usually not even with model mountains and valleys; but the globes serve very well for purposes of study or instruction and as aids in surface or aerial travel.

Now, we cannot always represent large, complicated ideas—like the operation of our economy—by actual, tangible, working models, though a few of our economic processes have been so represented. For example, a system of tubes containing colored water can be arranged to show the flow of money from various groups in the community to other groups. But the concept of the competitive, self-organizing, and self-regulating economy cannot be made into a model; at any rate, the loss in effort expended would not be worth the gain. But it is not really very important to have actual, material working models. We can construct models in our heads; and as a matter of fact, models of the imagination are one of the commoner devices of science. Economists today often speak of their models; and when they do, they speak of models in the mind rather than of tangible miniatures. The most comprehensive economic model of all is the one we have described in recent pages—a competitive economic world, peopled by economic men, self-regulating and self-equilibrating. The student will understand economic theory, particularly standard economic theory, if he learns to solve problems with this model in his mind.

With this kind of model, it is possible to predict what will happen in the real world; and if the real world were quite close to the model, economists could predict much better than they do. Unfortunately, what goes on in the real world is sometimes quite different from what happens within the limits of the model. But after all, this kind of difficulty arises even in physics. Thus the physicist can predict exactly what will happen to a steel ball and a feather dropped into the top of an airless pipe 550 feet tall. But if he simply drops ball and feather from the Washington Monument, he cannot predict. The feather may float into an open truck carrying crates to Baltimore, from where they will—with the feather sticking to one of them—be shipped to Djibouti.

How far off in abstraction an economist goes can be best appreciated by taking an actual case. Paul Wells, an economist, was studying the benefits and burdens of excise taxes, that is, taxes on goods such as liquor, tobacco, luggage, perfume, and the like. At the beginning of his article, he suggests the kind of model with which he proposes to work, partly as follows:

> This paper will present a theory of the incidence of both the burdens and benefits an excise tax exerts in a two-person, two-factor, two-commodity, perfectly competitive world. . . . We shall demonstrate [certain] conclusions for our two-dimensional world, and then consider how far it is possible to go in generalizing from it.[2]

We can be sure that the man on the street would not go about discussing the benefits or burdens of the cigarette or liquor tax in this way—by describing what goes on in a two-person, two-commodity world. Although this is perhaps an extreme case of abstraction, it does suggest how some economists go about solving some of their problems.

Miscellaneous Simplifications

For many purposes, economists make a lot of other simplifications. They often speak of "the interest rate" or "the rate of wages" as

[2] Paul Wells, "A General Equilibrium Analysis of Excise Taxes," *American Economic Review*, Vol. XLV, No. 3 (June, 1955), p. 345.

if there were only one rate of interest or one wage rate. There are, of course, many interest rates, ranging in recent years from as low as 1½ percent on some kinds of loans to perhaps 30 percent for loans on unpaid balances if you buy clothes on time. And any large factory may have as many as 100 wage rates, ranging from $1.40 to $6.50 an hour. Still, it is often convenient to speak of *the* wage rate. We cannot be sure that economists can always define what they mean by these phrases. The figure is not the average figure—at least not always— and anyhow, there are many kinds of averages: weighted, unweighted, arithmetic, geometric, mode, median, harmonic. Neither is it the lowest figure nor the highest. Yet, when properly used, the phrases should not create confusion. If we say, "The interest rate went up in 1956," or "The wage rate increased enormously between 1946 and 1953," everybody knows what we are talking about.

Another simplification is that often economists speak as if there were no intermediaries between manufacturers or farmers and the final consumer. We say, "A manufacturer's costs rise 10 percent, which he is immediately able to pass on through higher prices to the consumer"—we say this as if nobody stood between, no jobbers, wholesalers, or retailers. For many purposes, this is all right. In similar fashion, economists sometimes omit brokers' and salesmen's commissions, interest on loans, and the like. These items are not always omitted, of course. They are sometimes made the direct object of extensive study. But they can often be brushed aside on certain levels of analysis.

Economists frequently slur over the difference between expectation and fact. Thus, they will say, "A farmer plants 100 acres of cabbage at a price of 4 cents a pound, but only 15 acres at a price of 3 cents." Now, obviously this means anticipated price. It takes about four months to produce cabbage. In this period, anything can happen to supply (through drought and other growing conditions) or to demand (through war or medical discovery); therefore, anything may happen to previously anticipated cabbage prices. Yet much fruitful economic reasoning assumes that expectations tally with fulfillment. Indeed, the gap is often completely ignored.

Economists sometimes use a kind of shorthand in their thinking that positively frightens the man on the street. For example, most

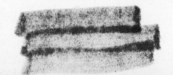

economists believe and proclaim resoundingly that tariffs and similar restrictions on foreign trade diminish the wealth of nations. To any man who works or invests in a tariff-protected industry, such as pottery and china, the doctrine of free trade seems to be a doctrine of impoverishment conceived in malevolence and insanity, for it is clear that competition from Europe and the Far East would soon reduce the American industry to rubble. Economists know this, of course; and few would—if seriously working on the problem—leave the industry to perish overnight. They would probably suggest a lowering of tariffs by stages, gradually, over a five-year period. They might suggest government loans to help the industry convert to some new type of operation—the manufacture of porcelain insulators perhaps.

Another and somewhat similar issue arises over certain reforms that seem to be nonchalantly proposed by economists, but that to others seem to attack the very heart of American institutions. For example, and to oversimplify, most economists believe we could stave off both inflation and depression if a quick way were found to raise or lower income taxes temporarily when inflation or depression threatens. Under our system of government, one way, and perhaps the best way, to get timely cuts in taxes would be to give the President authority to change rates for a period not to exceed six months by a percentage not to exceed 5 percent. However sound this may be economically, it is objectionable politically. Congress is proud of its prerogative as tax legislator. Everyone fears that a first-term President, either himself unscrupulous or surrounded by unscrupulous advisers, would see a depression coming when the season for reelection rolls around and would cut taxes whether we needed a reduction or not. Politically, few things succeed like tax reduction.

All kinds of economic proposals, from tax cuts to tariff cuts, from unemployment compensation to agricultural price supports, open up opportunities for bribery, graft, chiseling, and all of the frauds developed since governments first began, or they demand institutional changes. The economist cannot do much about this, just as the physician cannot do much about cures that are expensive or that place almost impossible demands on a sick man's patience. The economist feels that certain goals demand a high price in the form of integrity or institutional change, that it is the job of the police to go

after the people of low integrity, and that not all institutions are so sacred as to warrant retention forever.

Summary

This chapter has touched on a number of things that are intended to facilitate the study of economic theory. Foremost among them has been a consideration of some of the curious unrealities imposed on thought by theory of any kind. We then picked up three important unrealities of standard economic theory—the nature of a competitive market, the nature of the economic man, and the forces that are assumed to hold the economy together. These three unrealities may be combined in the mind to form an economic model, that is, a sort of imaginary machine whose processes resemble those of the actual world sufficiently to be useful for many purposes.

QUESTIONS FOR REVIEW AND DISCUSSION

1. Define, in your own words, each of the following terms:
   a) "Figment of the imagination"
   b) Theory
   c) Substitution
   d) Models
   e) Price
2. What are the chief organizing forces in the economy of the United States?
3. What is "standard" economic theory? What other types of economic theory are mentioned in your textbook?
4. Why would competition fail if buyers and sellers did not have equal knowledge?
5. What role would advertising have in a perfectly competitive economy? Why?
6. What reply would a standard theorist give to the following statement: "Only the perverted, insane, or hypocritical would state that an economy based on self-interest can yield social good."
7. How do "theoretical ways of thinking" differ from other methods used to form intellectual conceptions?
8. The word "competition" means one thing when used at a meeting of the American Economic Association and quite another thing when it is used by the ordinary citizen in a discussion of competition in the automobile industry. What is the difference?

THE THEORY OF
PRODUCTION

What Is a Product?

Not so very long ago the whole of theoretical economics was divided into four principal parts—production, exchange, distribution, and consumption. This seemed to be very logical, for it took commodities up the steps from original production through sale to final consumption. Many books were organized in such a way as to take major account of these four great topics. Economics has become vastly more complicated since those days, and so much emphasis has been placed on the avoidance of depressions and inflation, and the attainment of economic growth and development, that contemporary textbook writers do not use this fourfold classification. It has certain virtues, however, and we shall follow it vestigially here in Part II. This chapter will be devoted to production; the next two chapters will discuss exchange and distribution. Not much will be done about consumption, but that topic has never been very well developed in economics anyhow.

Since production in economics does not mean quite the same thing as it does in common speech, we must try to comprehend the economists' special use of the word. First, we should note that production may refer to both tangible and intangible things. Produce in general falls into two categories—services and commodities. By services, we mean the services of actors, professional ballplayers, physicians, clergymen, salesmen, and the like. In the early days of economic theory, there was some question as to whether services were products or not since, it was argued, they perished at the moment of production (movies and recordings were of course unknown). They had quaint arguments on this matter. One, maintaining the modern position, said that if a ballerina's dance was not a product, then fireworks could not be counted as produce, either, since they, too, ceased to exist after their first use. To meet the argument that a bootblack was not productive, the counterargument was made that the bootblack was not really different from the bootmaker, who was admittedly productive. The bootmaker took needle, thread, and leather and converted them into boots. The bootblack took brush, polish, and dirty boots and converted them into clean boots.

Today, economists unanimously agree that services as well as tangible goods belong in the class of produce. And they use the words "goods" or "commodities" to cover both. The question still remains, however, as to what goods and services are economic. If Colin yanks Colette back onto the sidewalk to prevent her getting hit by a speeding truck, he has performed a great service—but not an economic service. If an apple grower gathers together a bushel of apples matched in size, each of which has exactly two worms, neither more nor less, he has done a tedious job and produced a rare thing, but it is doubtful whether that bushel of apples will count as an economic product.

In our society the simplest test as to whether a thing is, in an economic sense, a product—and hence part of society's production—is whether it appears in a market and has market value. If its value can be stated in terms of dollars and cents and it enters the market, then the thing was "produced." So true is this that the word "productivity" may often be made equivalent to the phrase "income-producing capacity." Thus, if a baker divides his operations into two parts, breadmaking and cakemaking, and his net income from cakes is greater than from bread, we would say that cakemaking is the more productive part of his business. And this would be true despite the fact that he may actually bake and sell twice as much bread as cakes.

Any good or service that meets the test of possessing market value has utility, and many economists would say that the act of production is the creation of utilities. A few things that have utility do not go on the market, however. Air is the most obvious example. Economists refer to it as a "free good," along with fish in the ocean or drinking water in a mountain brook. Such goods stop being free when they are processed and brought to market—the fish as frozen fillets, perhaps, and the water in five-gallon demijohns from mineral springs. As we shall see more clearly later, some goods of high utility have low market value. Thus, bread and milk are cheaper than caviar and vodka, but bread and milk are the more important pair from the viewpoint of biological survival.

Production and the Division of Labor

From the early days of modern economic thought, men have realized that productivity increases as specialization increases. Productive specialization is often referred to as "the division of labor." If several people are working together to produce and sell something—rustic outdoor tables, for example—they will probably produce more if they divide their labors. One or two may go to woodland to cut down all the saplings used. Another may attend to the power sawing, another to assembling, and still another to selling. This would ordinarily be a more productive way of making lawn furniture than if each one gathered wood, cut, assembled, and sold. The same is true of regional specialization. We have more and cheaper bananas and coffee because certain regions specialize in these products than we would have if each nation tried to grow its own tropical produce, for this would mean a vast and expensive system of hothouses in the temperate climates.

There are many reasons why divided labor is more efficient than undivided labor. One is that it permits workers to develop special skills. A similar one is that it permits society to use more advantageously the special gifts with which some people are born, such as a quickness of physical response, grace, strength, and the like. Workers need not learn to use too many tools. In a series of processes a place can be found for people of low endowments to work effectively, thus releasing the more gifted for the more difficult tasks.

Manufacturing processes in advanced societies are marked by a highly developed division of labor, though we find it in primitive societies and even among birds, bees, and ants. In our society, one man may do nothing but tighten a bolt or two as a half-finished refrigerator goes by on a moving belt. Because division of labor has, in conjunction with the machine, helped to destroy skilled crafts like tailoring, bootmaking, and cabinetmaking, the belief prevails that the subdivided tasks are deadening, that tightening a bolt hour after hour, day after day, turns a man into a robot. The evidence under this heading is not clear; some men and women seem to enjoy their repetitive jobs; and trade unions are more interested in high wages, low hours, good grievance procedure, and the like than in diversified jobs. No doubt the human spirit can soar higher in the ministry, the sciences, or statesmanship, but it does not follow that a cooper in a handicraft society is greater-souled than the punch-press operator.

How far one can go in subdividing labor efficiently is an issue of some interest. Chaos would result if in driving an automobile, one person specialized in steering, another in braking, and a third in manipulating the accelerator—yet something like that is done to control ocean liners. A few great monarchs are said to have had one cook who specialized in baking, another in boiling, a third in cooking game, a fourth in preparing fish, and so on. This seems excessive and even ridiculously wasteful for an establishment that normally serves only a few people; but it might be a very good idea for a luxury hotel that serves 5,000 meals a day.

The Four Factors of Production

Early in the modern history of economic thought, students of the subject gave attention to the element or elements underlying production. Some thought that the underlying element was labor. Every commodity, they said, was made up of labor and labor alone. This, of course, does not deny that things are composed of such chemical elements as hydrogen, oxygen, carbon, nitrogen, and the like. From the economic viewpoint, the chemical composition of goods has no relevance. Now, it is true that labor is a large component of all goods and services—around 75 to 80 percent of their total value—but other things go into goods as well. A turnip contains some of the land it grows in; it may also in a sense contain part of the tractor which prepared the turnip field. Out of such speculation, standard economic theory has come to the conclusion that four elements are basic to the productive activities of any society—labor, land, capital, and a special form of labor which may be named entrepreneurship (from the French word *entrepreneur,* one who undertakes, contracts, adventures, tries). Each of these terms has a special meaning, at least a shade different from that of ordinary life. They are given their economic definitions below:

1. *Labor,* meaning almost any kind of labor—head, hand, or back. Labor may be pleasant, as it presumably is for various types of artists and professionals, but it is frequently distinguished from

physical or mental play (like tennis or chess) by its disagreeableness. "Labor is the use of the body for other than pleasure," as a bright sophomore put it. The reward of labor is named *wages*.

2. *Land,* meaning almost any gift of nature, like a waterfall or an Adirondack lake as well as land itself. Again the sophomore speaks: "Land is God's gift to man—it does not imply only dirt." The reward of land goes to its owner, of course; its name is *rent*.

3. *Capital,* meaning a variety of things—connected, however, by one concept, namely, that of previous saving. Tractors, power shovels, steel mills, and automatic looms—all are capital partly because some people, not necessarily the present users, had to save out of their incomes in order that such large equipment could be bought and employed in the process of production. Capital may loosely be thought of as the opposite of consumption goods, such as peaches, turkeys, and wine. But this can be misleading. To a restaurateur, peaches, turkey, and wine are things he uses in the process of production (serving meals to diners); hence, they form part of his capital along with his stoves, skillets, china, napkins, and the rest. The apple you eat is a consumer's good, but an apple owned by a cider mill is capital. It is something diverted from the production stream to make something else—cider, in this case. The owner of capital, like the owner of land, receives a property income; its name is *interest*. Sometimes the receiver of interest is not quite aware of the fact that he is receiving payment for the productivity of capital. He thinks he is getting 4 percent on his money. But his money is probably now in the form of a bond or similar piece of paper; and if it is a bond like a Pennsylvania Railroad bond, the money he paid for it was used to buy a length of steel rail or part of a coach or locomotive.

4. *Entrepreneurship,* which refers to the special productive service of the policy-making person or board of any business establishment—to the special contribution of the big boss: his judgment; ability to combine land, labor, and capital in the most fruitful proportions; labor-management skill; inside knowledge; market information; lucky hunches; sixth sense about business affairs; good contacts with persons informed on business and political matters; discretion; poker face; ability to pick good lieutenants; aplomb when testifying before legislative committees; and the like. The entrepreneurial reward is named *profit*.

The classification of the four factors of production is not thoroughly satisfactory. Who, for example, is the entrepreneur in a modern corporation—the chairman of the board, the president, or the stockholders who must vote on certain basic politices? Why is such a sharp difference made between land and capital? Is not one of the most productive assets of any civilization its accumulation of knowledge, its discipline, its ability to absorb inventions into its culture? And where is all this listed among the productive factors? It is doubtful whether any economist is thoroughly happy about this four-leaf clover of productive agents, but it is the best we have, and we shall use it.

We often speak of these four elements as the factors or agents of production. The idea behind this is very simple: If you have land to work on, some machines or tools or raw materials to work with, and a few employees and an owner-boss, you can go ahead and start producing, whether you produce physical things like clothing, or services as in a retail establishment. An advantage in this classification—indeed, the idea behind it all—is that incomes go only to the people representing these four groups. In other words, any money that anybody earns can be put under four categories—wages, rent, interest, and profits, or variants thereof, such as salaries (wages) or dividends (profits). Thus the standard economic theorist divides producers, or productive agents, into categories that are also useful to him when he gets around to his theory of distribution. A theory of distribution, as will appear in Chapter 7, is a theory that explains why people get the incomes they do.

One who ponders this explanation may object that many incomes do not fit into the categories—for example, gains from speculation, as in the case of professional stock market operations, or from the royalties of a book or invention. Gains from speculation are indeed a little difficult to classify. One could meet the difficulty by saying that speculation cannot exist in those perfect markets in which everybody has equal and perfect knowledge; hence, it does not occur in a model of pure competition, with which we are now concerned, and can occur only in "imperfect" economies, with which we are not concerned at the moment. Other economists would say that speculation, not unlike retailing or wholesaling, has its productive aspects and that its reward is similar to profits. As for royalties from books and inventions, they are merely rewards to labor; they are thus a form of wages

or salary. To be a wage or salary, payments need not come in pay
envelopes on Friday night.

The Law of Diminishing Returns

As has already been intimated, the process of production is
simply to bring these four factors together and to put them to work.
But the important question is: In what proportions? How much land
to how many farm laborers? How many delivery trucks for a department store? How many cows in a pasture? The arranging of factors in
varying proportions causes a phenomenon to arise, under static conditions, that is referred to as "the law of diminishing returns." The
word "law" is perhaps too lofty a word to use in this connection; but
something really does happen, and that something has been measured
in various ways, perhaps mostly in the growing of plants. Agricultural
experiment stations have ascertained how much an extra dose of water
will increase yields, and have done the same with fertilizer. In
general, the results are the same: At first, equal doses of water (or
fertilizer) increase yield enormously. Later the increase attributable
to each dose declines, though total yield continues to rise, at least for a
while. This is the law of diminishing returns. It has been extended to
cover doses of anything at all—for example, doses of labor in an
automobile plant or doses of land in the building of a large apartment house.

The first evidence we have of consciousness among economists
that equal increases of only one factor of production would bring a
diminished product is to be found in Thomas Robert Malthus' famous
principle of population. Since this principle—though but a mere
application of the law of diminishing returns—has become a rather
important economic doctrine in its own right, we shall digress briefly
to explain and evaluate it.

Malthus, a clergyman later turned economist, got into an argument about 170 years ago with his father concerning the perfectibility
of man. That is, they debated whether man had within himself the
power to overcome his greed and various other lower passions and to
live a utopian life.

The son disagreed with his visionary father and, brooding later
on their discussion, wrote a paper which he felt would prove once and
for all the impossibility of man's perfecting himself to the point where

vice, hunger, pestilence, and war would disappear from human life. His argument was that man tends to propagate more rapidly than the food supply can be increased to meet his needs. If in a perfect society a larger percentage of people lived out their full span of life in health and prosperity, the pressure of population on food would soon become intolerable, and everybody would have to go on short rations. Ultimately, there would again be starvation; and starvation, he felt, was the source of many human evils such as infanticide, war, and cannibalism. On the other hand, such positive checks to population as war and pestilence had at least the function of making life tolerable for those who survived.

Translated into the language of diminishing returns, what Malthus said was: If you hold constant three factors of production—namely, land, capital, and entrepreneurship—and if, then, you keep increasing the fourth factor—namely, labor—the product attributable to each equal accession of population will inevitably decline. Population meant labor to him, principally farm labor, because in 1800 agriculture was the chief occupation. The three other factors, he felt, would remain constant because the earth embraces a finite and limited amount of land which cannot be increased or decreased, at least not in significant quantity. As for entrepreneurship and capital, they too would remain constant, in his opinion, partly because the technology of those days, though progressing rapidly, had not yet suggested the fabulous changes that would come.

The Malthusian doctrines created a great stir when they were published. Critics pointed out that a sort of reverse Malthusianism also holds true. People may be poor in a country which does not have a sufficient population, as they were in America in 1650. Others argued that plants and animals reproduce at least as freely as human beings do, and since plants and animals are human foods, Malthus started off from a false assumption. Similar to this is the argument that each person, though admittedly born with a mouth to feed, is also born with two arms and hands for work. This last criticism has no validity because it ignores the law of diminishing returns, which says that as the number of hands increases, their efficiency declines if all else is held constant.

The whole Malthusian question is a hard one. It has been shown that as countries become rich, the birthrate declines; we in the rich United States have fewer children per family than the poor of Asia.

And some people argue that when the people of the East themselves produce more (become richer), they will also limit the number of their children. We cannot say that mankind will outstrip its food supply because we do not know whether man's ingenuity will enable him to produce increasingly. By constantly changing the methods of production, our improving technology may perpetually nullify the law of diminishing returns. Indeed, it is a static law, operating only when the four factors of production remain unchanged in quality. We do not know whether the great populations of the East will accept birth control as easily as did those of the West. Whatever may be the defects of Malthus' theory, one must at least concede that a finite world cannot support infinite additions to its population; whatever its merits, one must at least concede that the Western world has not had to face the issues that Malthus presented in the way in which he presented them. We shall have more to say on this subject in the last chapter on economic growth.

We must now return from our digression to the use of the law of diminishing returns in current economic thinking. The figures in Table 4–1 summarize the result of an experiment performed by the University of California in 1917 and serve to quantify the notion of diminishing returns.[1]

The phrase "law of diminishing returns" is so often used loosely in popular language that the student should be on guard against its

TABLE 4–1

FUNCTIONAL RELATIONSHIP BETWEEN DOSES OF WATER AND ALFALFA YIELD

(Yield Numbers Rounded and Approximate)

(Column 1) Depth of Water Applied (in Inches)	(Column 2) Alfalfa Yield (Tons per Acre)	(Column 3*) Increase per Acre Attributable to Each Dose (Marginal Product)
0	3.5	...
12	6.0	2.5
24	8.0	2.0
36	9.0	1.0
48	9.3	0.3
60	8.7	—0.6

* Note on column 3: The amounts in this column are named "marginal product." They are arrived at by subtracting each number in column 2 from the next succeeding number in column 2. Thus, to get the first marginal product, 2.5, we subtract 3.5 from 6.0.

[1] University of California Agricultural Station, *Bulletin No. 280*, May, 1917. This bulletin was first brought to the attention of economists by F. C. Mills.

improper use in economic discussion. Popularly, the phrase may be uttered by an amateur gardener who, after weeding in the hot sun for an hour, exclaims wearily, "I've come to the point of diminishing returns." What he means is that he is sick and tired of his job and is ready to sit in the shade with a cool drink. This is not economics. On a less popular level, but still erroneously, the point of diminishing returns is sometimes thought of as the point at which total product either declines or stops increasing. In Table 4–1, that situation is shown at 60 inches, where yield per acre has actually declined from 9.3 to 8.7 tons (column 2). This, too, is wrong. Actually, diminishing returns begin almost immediately and should be looked for in column 3, the point at which the product attributable to a new dose has reached its height and begins to decline, that is, at 12 inches. Thus the point of diminishing returns is the turning point where marginal product (for definition of this phrase, see note under Table 4–1) is greatest but begins to decline. It is like the moment of midnight, which ends one day and begins another.

Cost of Marginal Product and Revenue

Beginning students often get the idea that a smart businessman stops producing when marginal product begins to go down. This would mean, using Table 4–1 and assuming that all water used must be paid for, that the alfalfa grower would buy 12 inches of water but no more. This is not true. Businessmen do not stop producing or adding new doses at the point of diminishing returns. Businessmen are more likely to stop producing at the point where the cost of the extra dose is no longer justified by the revenue derived from the marginal product. Thus, if alfalfa in the field sells for $13 a ton and if 12 additional inches of irrigation water can be bought at $10 per acre, it will pay a farmer operating under the conditions of Table 4–1 to use 36 inches of water instead of only 24, even though he is well past the point of diminishing returns (see Table 4–2). He makes a profit of $3 on this last dose. If he were to buy another dose of 12 inches of water, he would lose money. The water would still cost $10, but he would grow only an extra (or marginal) three tenths of a ton. This would be worth three tenths of $13, or $3.90. No use spending another $10 to get an additional return of only $3.90; there would obviously be a loss of $6.10.

TABLE 4–2

PROFITABILITY OF PRODUCING BEYOND POINT OF DIMINISHING RETURN

(Column 1) Depth of Water (in Inches)	(Column 2) Marginal Product per Acre	(Column 3) Price Received at $13 per Ton for Marginal Product (Column 2 × $13)	(Column 4) Cost of Each Additional Dose of Water	(Column 5) Gain or Loss (Column 3 − Column 4)
0	...	......	...	......
12	2.5	$32.50	$10	$22.50
24	2.0	26.00	10	16.00
36	1.0	13.00	10	3.00
48	0.3	3.90	10	− 6.10
60	−0.6	− 7.80	10	− 17.80

This is a rather important point in standard economic theory and will come up again in a later chapter in a more sophisticated form, where we shall use not only the concept of the cost of the marginal unit but also a concept known as "marginal revenue." But this is anticipation. For the moment, we can forget about marginal revenue.

It may be objected that few alfalfa farmers have access to tables like the one printed above and that there must be millions of business-men who have no similar tables applicable to the other factors of production, such as labor or machines or land, for the law of dimin-ishing returns holds good for any input that any businessman uses in production. No doubt this sort of adjustment is made by trial and error, without tables. But unless a businessman is pretty shrewd about whether he ought to spend extra money on an extra waitress or another refrigerating unit, he may be headed for disaster. He may be un-educated and may never have seen the outside of an economics text-book, but if he can rightly say, "It don't help me none to hire no extra delivery boy 'cause he don't hardly pay for hisself"—if he knows this much, he is on the way to business success.

Substitution and Lowest Cost

If farmers had nothing to think about except an extra dose of water and grocers nothing to think about except an extra delivery boy, life would be much easier for them and for most businessmen. The problem is harder, however, because the factors of production are substitutable for one another within certain limits. If, for example, wages go up rather high, a factory owner will try to substitute labor-saving machinery for manpower. If a farmer wishes to increase his wheat yield at a time when extra land near him is too dear to buy or rent, he will use more fertilizer on the land he has or in other ways cultivate his land more intensively. The builder of skyscrapers substitutes additional stories of a building (capital) for land; by building higher, he houses more people on the same amount of land. Substitution in general, whether of the factors of production or in consumers' goods, is much more widely practiced than is generally realized. Clothing can be substituted for petroleum; you do this by wearing warmer clothes around the house and turning down the thermostat. Various forms of capital may be substituted for one another. In swimming pools, you can either run in new water frequently; or by using a pump, filter, and chemicals, you can recirculate the same water again and again.

The above discussion leads us to the heart of the problem of production in a capitalist society. The essential thing is, of course, to produce as cheaply as possible. Now, cheap production is an economic problem, not a technological problem. From the purely technological point of view, there is no unique combination of land, labor, raw materials, and other capital that will permit an entrepreneur to produce, say, 1,000 pairs of shoes a day. He can use many men or many machines instead; his factory can sprawl over several acres or be contained within a relatively few square yards. Regardless of the combination he chooses, unless it be totally devoid of sense, he can produce 1,000 pairs of shoes daily. But merely to produce shoes is not enough. He must produce at lowest unit cost, or he will be undersold by competitors. In other words, he must produce economically. And economically, there is a unique combination. Unless he searches out the best combination and finds it, substituting now one factor, now another, until the lowest unit cost is achieved, he will lose out, for we may be sure that his competitors will find the point of least cost.

Summary

In this chapter on production as seen by the economist, we have tried, first of all, to define produce or, to put it differently, to define the act of economic production as contrasted with an engineering view of production. The first difference lies in the nature of a product: To an engineer, it is a thing; to an economist, it is a utility. And sometimes, in one or two easy steps, it becomes an income, or profit. The next difference lies, of course, in the realm of costs. To the engineer, scientist, and amateur gardener, costs are, within broad limits, irrelevant. But the businessman cannot produce oxygen as does the professor of chemistry. It would be too expensive. And if all expenses were taken into account, each perfect rose probably costs the amateur gardener much more than it costs the commercial grower. Mere production is fairly easy, but production at lowest cost is difficult. We have also identified the four agents of production. Production, we further found, is enhanced by the division of labor. The law of diminishing returns, a fundamental concept of a static economic system, is true enough in some ways, as our alfalfa table indicated; but in its applicability to a dynamic society, it leaves something to be desired. The important point was made that production does not stop when marginal product declines; it stops, at least in the perfectly competitive market we have assumed, when the cost of the last dose equals the price offered in the market. Allied to the law of diminishing returns is the Malthusian principle, which, like the former, envisages a dreary future for mankind. Though the principle was propounded more than a century and a half ago, our technology has not stayed still long enough to allow it to exert its force on our society.

QUESTIONS FOR REVIEW AND DISCUSSION

1. Define, in your own words, each of the following:
   a) Goods and services
   b) "Free good"
   c) Productivity
   d) Factors of production
   e) Wages
   f) Rent
   g) Interest
2. List and discuss the four factors of production. Would you include "knowledge" under any of these four? Explain.
3. Construct an arithmetic example that will illustrate the law of diminishing returns. Of what importance is this law to the theory of production?

4. Why is production continued after the point of diminishing returns is reached? Construct an arithmetic example to prove your answer.

5. Of what importance is the Malthusian doctrine to the modern world?

6. Is a tuna fish swimming freely in the Pacific Ocean a free good or a product? Could you convert a free-swimming tuna into a scarce good? How?

Chapter 5

THE THEORY OF
VALUE

A Brief History of the Theory of Value

This chapter and the next inquire into what standard theory has to say about the value of things we use up directly as consumers. The word "value" in economics is very close in meaning to the word "price." There are some differences: "Price" must always be stated in terms of a national currency, but "value" is a general concept; money itself is subjected to the forces of valuation and therefore cannot be used as the ultimate yardstick. For many purposes, however, economists tend to use the words interchangeably. The price of things we do not directly consume, such as land or factory labor or the leather a shoemaker buys for further processing, is governed by the same principles as govern the prices of consumers' goods. Still, there are some small differences, and it will be convenient to discuss nonconsumers' prices separately in Chapter 7.

Why does a fountain pen cost 50 times more than a plain penholder? Why do radios and chairs cost about the same? The first modern answer given to such questions was that the value of things depended on the average amount of labor congealed in them. On this theory, chairs and radios must require about the same number of days or hours to manufacture. Adam Smith, David Ricardo, and Karl Marx are among the great names associated with this doctrine.

The labor theory of value, even in its most naïve form, has a certain usefulness, for many things that require very little labor are normally cheap. But it is only a rough guide. In a farmer's market the same bunch of carrots may sell at 15 cents in the morning and at 10 cents in the evening of the same day; obviously, the 10-cent carrots contain as much congealed labor as the 15-cent carrots.

Later economists expanded the labor theory to include all the costs of production. "Costs of production," incidentally, does not mean exactly the same thing to the economist as to the businessman.

71

The economist includes a reasonable gain to the businessman as a cost of production; the businessman, however, thinks of this same benefit as his profit—the difference between cost and selling price. The economist, viewing the entire process from the outside, recognizes the fact that businessmen would not produce or resell at retail if they did not receive a return; and this return is a cost, like any of the other costs of production.

The total-cost-of-production theory does indeed provide a fuller explanation of value than labor costs alone, but even this has flaws— the same flaws as the labor theory of value, for things often sell at more or less than their average cost. On the other hand, costs of production are a useful and often reliable guide to price or value.

But the basic flaw in the cost-of-production theory is that it does not take account of the usefulness of a commodity. It would cost quite a lot to get a hogshead of snow from Greenland to New Orleans unmelted, and snow is not without its usefulness; but who really needs Greenland's snow? By contrast, it costs plenty to fly a kilo of wild strawberries from France to New York, fresh and edible. But people are prepared to pay several dollars for this delicacy. In other words, demand and desirability have an influence on price. And this brings us to the next stage in the development of thought on economic values.

The next major step in value thinking was to go to the other extreme. In the last quarter of the 19th century, economists rose to say that nothing had any inherent value—no permanent value congealed in it. Human beings were the evaluators; nothing is cheap or dear but thinking makes it so. Stanley Jevons (1835–82) and the Austrian Karl Menger (1840–1921) are usually credited with having made this dialectical contribution to economic thought, though the same idea had come to the minds of others before them. But Jevons and Menger added a little twist to this idea which made the difference between a merely interesting statement and an analytical tool that economists could manipulate to get certain useful results.

Here is the little twist. Seeking the value of things as a class is the wrong approach to value theory. What is important is to think of the usefulness of separate units in a class. Thus, as a consumer of butter, I want very little of it, just an occasional pat. Indeed, several hundred pounds of butter delivered at the same moment—remember, I cannot resell under the ground rules of this chapter, for we are talking about value to consumers only—would be quite a nuisance to me. On the other hand, there are times when I am willing to pay $1 a pound; and for a small square served in a restaurant, I pay at the rate of $2 or $3 a pound. A young man will be willing to pay $1,000 for his fiancée's engagement ring, but he cannot be induced to buy her a second or third diamond ring unless the price is appreciably lowered. He prefers to use the money to furnish the prospective home. Thus, value depends on units already available. That was the Jevons-Menger twist: As consumers, we evaluate one unit dearly; successive units are evaluated at less, and additional units may have no value at all.

This type of economic thinking, which goes forward by steps or units or dosages is known as marginal analysis, for the last unit under consideration is the marginal unit. It is the unit which, though still desirable, has the least utility to the individual concerned. It is not necessarily the last unit in a chronological sense, just as it is not really the seventh hot dog that causes an internal disturbance. The seventh is exactly like the first or any other in the series. It has no special virtue; it apparently produces a special effect only because it was preceded by six others like itself. Seven hot dogs cause disturbances; the seventh sausage, in itself, does nothing; it is inherently like the others.

Jevons, Menger, and later the American John Bates Clark (1847–1938), and their disciples, worked on the marginal utility concept of value, exploring every path suggested, including a few blind alleys. Many economists felt that these marginal savants had discovered something important and realized that the old labor and cost-of-production theories were deficient. Others felt that the new unit valuation procedure alone could not explain much. It was subjective; it involved, they said, circular reasoning and the creation of an indefensible standard of social value. In this situation, Alfred Marshall (1842–1924), an English economist, appeared. He fused the marginal theories and the older theories in a way that composed outstanding differences between most of the pro- and antimarginalists.

To understand what Marshall did, we must go back a little. Men had long observed that supply and demand were related to price: Reduce supply, up goes price; reduce demand, down goes price. This being true, why did Adam Smith, Ricardo, Jevons, Menger, and the others go out of their way to explain price by inventing the labor and other theories of value? Our answer must be a guess, but we have the right to assume that supply and demand seemed too obviously simple to them. Everybody knows that supply and demand exert a strong influence on price. But was there not something beyond this truism— something deeper, more permanent, more profoundly woven into the very fiber of each commodity or perhaps in human beings themselves? In posing this question, they were partly right. To explain value or price by glibly saying "supply and demand" is to explain very little. Something more profound is needed. But the something more profound is to be found neither in the commodity to be valued nor in the soul-searching of a buyer, but in the words "supply" and "demand" themselves. This is what Marshall discovered. His method, therefore, was to scrutinize the full meaning of the phrase "supply and demand." In doing this, he found that both the objective and the subjective theories of value had important contributions to make, as we shall see.

What Marshall and his followers said, in effect, was something like this:

1. Adam Smith, Ricardo, John Stuart Mill, and others, by embracing the labor or cost-of-production theories of value, placed emphasis on supply, on the niggardliness of nature, on the obstacles to supply. Jevons and Menger emphasized human valuation, that is, demand. By studying supply and demand and their interaction, a synthesis of the two viewpoints is made.
2. Problems of value would be clarified if we introduced the dimension of time. What happens in the short run is quite different from what happens in the long run. By making proper allowance for time, we shall be able to break up a hard question into several easier ones.

Here, we have the guideposts of the standard economic theory of value during much of the past half century. Its task has largely been to study supply, demand, their action and interaction over short and long periods, and the effect of price itself on the quantities bought or produced.

The Demand Schedule

We now proceed to the main headings under the above outline and begin by scrutinizing in turn the words "demand" and "supply."

Demand for consumers' goods is governed by Jevons' principle

of diminishing utility—the principle that the more we have of anything, the less we want any more of it, and, therefore, the less willing
we are to pay for increased quantities of it. This principle is embodied
in tables known as "demand schedules"—much used by the practitioners of standard theory. Table 5–1 is an example of such a
schedule.

TABLE 5–1
Mrs. Smith's Weekly Demand Schedule for Butter

At $2 or more a pound, Mrs. Smith will not buy butter regularly; she
will buy only for holidays, normally using margarine, goose fat, and
other substitutes.

At $1.50, Mrs. Smith will buy one pound of butter weekly. This is only
enough to use sparingly at the table. Her other butter needs are met
by substitutes. She makes no cookies, cakes, or the like.

At $1.10, Mrs. Smith will buy two pounds of butter. She still uses substi-
tutes for many of her needs, but the real thing can be used more
freely at table and on a few cooked vegetables.

At 85 cents, Mrs. Smith will buy three pounds of butter. No close
substitutes are required, but butter is still too expensive for cookies
and cakes.

At 65 cents, Mrs. Smith will buy four pounds of butter. Cookies and
cakes are beginning to appear.

At 55 cents, Mrs. Smith will buy five pounds of butter. Cookies, cakes,
candies, and hard sauce appear.

At 45 cents or less, Mrs. Smith will buy six pounds of butter. Now there
will be hollandaise sauce on broccoli. She will more freely bestow
cookies on the neighbors' children.

At 45 cents, the end of Mrs. Smith's demand schedule is reached,
for even at 30 cents or 20 cents a pound, she has no use for more
butter, fears overdosing her family with cholesterol, and will not buy
more than six pounds weekly.

One thing to keep straight about such a schedule is that it
expresses the whole range of demand at some given period of time
only. It tells us nothing about how much butter Mrs. Smith will buy if
she unexpectedly inherits a large fortune or if her husband's salary is
doubled or reduced, or how she might readjust the amounts spent on a
whole list of foods, including butter, if the prices of meat and coffee
were to rise sharply. Each price-quantity combination in the schedule

equally well expresses her judgment on how best to balance a sacrifice of money with a benefit in the form of butter, but only under unchanged circumstances. It follows, then, that her demand is not greater when she buys six pounds at 45 cents than when she buys two pounds at $1.10. Both combinations express with equal accuracy her demand for butter and her reluctance to part with money. But if Mrs. Smith should suddenly become very wealthy, her demand might become greater; in that case, her entire schedule would have to be revised upward before it could express her willingness to buy more butter at every price now given in the schedule. Indeed, our revision might have to carry the price up to $50 or even $100 per pound, for if Mrs. Smith were really in the chips, there would be no ordinary limit to the price she might be willing to pay.

Since geometric diagrams of demand will later be used to study price, let us at once convert Mrs. Smith's demand schedule into a geometric figure (Figure 5–1). The reader may also wish to see how increased demand is represented on a diagram. The dotted line in Figure 5–2 represents the hypothetically increased demand of Mrs. Smith after a modest inheritance. This is contrasted with the line representing the demand schedule already diagrammed (Figure 5–1).

FIGURE 5–1

MRS. SMITH'S DEMAND CURVE

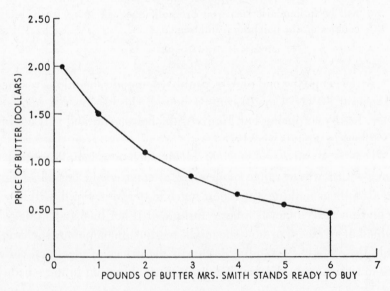

FIGURE 5–2

MRS. SMITH'S INCREASED DEMAND CURVE

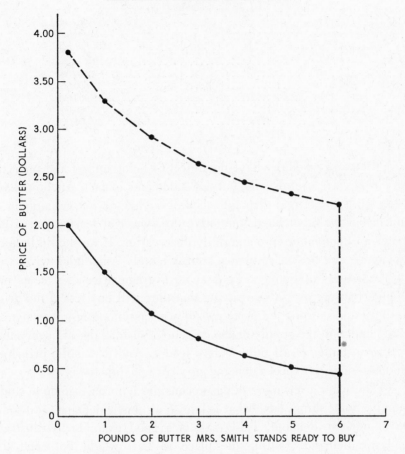

In the United States, there are perhaps 50 million Mrs. Smiths. Each has a weekly butter schedule more or less like *the* Mrs. Smith's. Some are much better off and are willing to buy seven or eight pounds at $10 a pound. Low-income households will not buy freely even at 30 cents a pound. Some poor people are passionately fond of butter and will give up other things for it; some rich people do not like it and will buy very little of it, even if cheap. But for all that, the majority of the schedules will follow the general pattern: More is bought at low prices than at high prices.

We can add up all the demand schedules of all the housewives and get a collective demand schedule, like in Table 5–2.

TABLE 5–2
AMERICAN HOUSEWIVES' COLLECTIVE DEMAND SCHEDULE
FOR BUTTER FOR ONE WEEK

Price per Pound	Approximate Purchase (in Pounds)
$10.00	1,000,000
5.00	4,000,000
2.00	11,000,000
1.50	15,000,000
1.00	23,000,000
0.50	39,000,000

Demand schedules have the defect of being unreal and unverifiable. They are useful tools, but not statements of fact. Attempts have been made to get real demand schedules. They do not yet amount to much. On the other hand, the curve does meet at least some of the criteria of common sense and daily observation. If we should happen to know—and this we can know approximately—that housewives will buy x pounds of butter a week at an average price of y cents per pound, then we are safe in saying that they will buy less if the price goes up and more if the price goes down (assuming no other significant change in the supply-demand picture, such as the discovery that eating no butter at all relieves hay fever). And that is the principal thing economists expect a demand curve or schedule to say.

There are a few more things to consider before we go on to study supply. Some things have what is known as elastic demand, and some have inelastic demand. Table salt is a good example to illustrate inelastic demand. Cutting the price in half would not send the housewife rushing downtown to buy and feed her children more of this delicacy—that is, a substantial drop in price would have little effect on her purchases. On the other hand, a substantial rise in price would not vastly curtail the amount used. Many common objects of small value and infrequent use are characterized by inelastic demand— carpet tacks, Mother's Day cards, medicines, and the like. Elastic demand is the exact opposite: Small increases or decreases in price have powerful effect on the quantity bought. The best cuts of meat, good wines, fur coats, and the like are normally objects of elastic demand. On the whole, there are few acceptable substitutes for goods of inelastic demand and many for goods of elastic demand.

To be a little more precise, if a relative decline in price, let us say 10 percent, brings forth an increase in the quantity demanded of greater relative magnitude than the change in price, in this case more than 10 percent, demand is said to be elastic. If, however, the 10 percent decline in price calls forth less than a 10 percent increase in the quantity demanded, demand is considered inelastic. The elasticity of demand can also be determined by observing what happens to the amount consumers spend on a product after a price change. A larger total is spent by the consuming public on commodities of elastic demand when price goes down; but when demand is inelastic, the total spent goes down as the price goes down. The figures in Table 5–3 will clarify the issues just discussed.

TABLE 5–3

Price	Percent Change in Price	Demand	Percent Change in Demand	Total Amounts Spent by Population of Centerville
STEAK: ELASTIC DEMAND				
$1.50 per pound		100		$1,500
$1 per pound	−33⅓%	175	75%	1,750
CARPET TACKS: INELASTIC DEMAND				
20 cents per box		800		160
12½ cents per box	−37½%	880	10%	110

It should also be noticed that theory makes no provision for the urgency of human needs or the breadth of human desires. The poor family that cannot afford enough food is considered to have a low demand for food—not because they do not want it, but because their wants are ineffective in the market. They cannot bid up prices. Demand is not demand unless there is money behind it. In this sense of the word, we must rule that most American women have no demand for mink coats, star sapphires, or Florida vacations. The proof is that the majority of women do not buy these things.

The Supply Schedule

Supply is the converse of demand. The higher the price, the greater the amount that will be offered for sale. Some of the reasons for this are obvious: Many owners of things locked up in storage or of animals on the hoof will, if prices suddenly rise, quickly and glee-fully unstore or slaughter their possessions for the favorable market. In the longer run, manufacturers are stirred to greater productive efforts if prices, and therefore profits, promise to remain high. Supply, like demand, is not some fixed quantity, but is a way of speaking of the resistances or costs of bringing goods into being. Lying behind the supply of a good are its human costs—often great sacrifices, as when workmen are killed in coal-mine explosions or when corporation officials sacrifice their health to worry and frustrations.

A basic generalization about supply is that a price increase calls forth a larger volume of production, which in turn may go so far as to increase the cost of production. This fundamental concept can, like demand, be shown on a schedule, and such a document is named a "supply schedule"—quite as significant in standard theory as is the demand schedule. Table 5–4 is an example of a supply schedule; its appropriate diagram will be found in Figure 5–3. At 1,500 bushels of corn, we reach, for all practical purposes, the end of Farmer Brown's supply schedule. Even at an anticipated $3 per bushel, he could scarcely try to produce more than 1,500 bushels. Costs have risen too much; wages have gone up; fertilizer has gone up, and not only that, it is doubtful whether the plants can use extra food advantageously. There is some doubt as to whether he could make appreciably greater gains by producing more. See Figure 5–3 for the supply curve.

FIGURE 5–3

FARMER BROWN'S SUPPLY CURVE

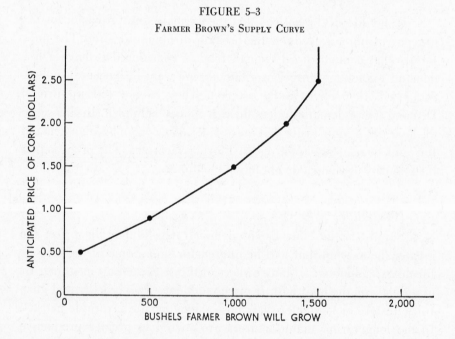

BUSHELS FARMER BROWN WILL GROW

TABLE 5–4

At the Anticipated Price per Bushel:	Farmer Brown Is Willing to Cultivate Enough Land and Plant Enough Seed to Produce:	Remarks
$0.50	100 bushels of corn	At this price, there is so little money in corn that Farmer Brown would rather go fishing than devote himself seriously to corn growing; he will not use fertilizer and will do little cultivating; it will be almost a volunteer crop. But he does produce 100 bushels because he needs the cash proceeds for tax money.
0.90	500 bushels of corn	At 90 cents, corn is a fairly good crop; it warrants some fertilizing and cultivation. On the other hand, the price is not good enough to warrant renting additional land or taking on another hired man or neglecting cows and chickens, painting of barn, or spraying of apple trees.
1.50	1,000 bushels of corn	At $1.50, corn is really worth a considerable effort and an appreciable outlay. Premium seed is worth buying; fertilizer may be used freely even though its price may have gone up, since all farmers are expanding their production of corn. The barn and the apple trees may be neglected, and a hired man is worth taking on.
2.00	1,300 bushels of corn	Two dollars a bushel is almost an unprecedented figure. At this price a 6 percent loan may be made to permit renting additional land. Not only the barn and the apple trees may be neglected, but also the cows and the chickens. An additional horse or hired man could be used; or instead, perhaps the old tractor could be traded in for a new and more reliable one.
2.50	1,500 bushels of corn	The price of $2.50 is a fine one, but it has its drawbacks, because now everybody is corn-crazy. Fertilizer costs have risen. New tractors cannot be delivered until autumn. All nearby land has been taken up. Hired men are not available. But every effort should be exerted to grow and harvest a large crop.

Like demand curves, supply curves are creatures of the imagination. They are merely a way of saying two things:

1. As prices (**price expectations**) rise, producers are willing to put more goods on the market.

2. Omitting special cases, costs of production under static conditions rise if the amount produced is appreciably increased (assuming that the economy is not in a deep depression or otherwise producing far below capacity).

Supply curves, too, may be elastic or inelastic: Elastic ones refer to commodities whose production responds vastly to small price increases or decreases; inelastic ones, to commodities that respond less to price changes. In January, after Thanksgiving and Christmas feasting is over, most available turkeys have been consumed. A large price increase for turkeys in the dead of winter would not do much to bring forth appreciable quantities of the birds. On the other hand, the willingness of the public to pay only a little more for knitting needles would probably bring forth enormous quantities. It is not difficult to install knitting-needle machinery in metalworking plants. Our farm problem has been exacerbated by inelasticity of supply. Farmers are not quite so rational as the imaginary Farmer Brown of a page or two back. They usually plant a bumper crop regardless of price expectations; they refuse to drop out of farming even after years of losing money; they keep on rolling up surpluses regardless of price. This is one form that inelasticity of supply can take—continued production as if price were irrelevant. Inelastic supply is characteristic of tree and bush crops such as coffee, tea, and cocoa; the bushes and trees, in total ignorance of world prices, yield crops at their own pace. If demand rises suddenly, prices shoot up fast because supply cannot be increased. Unfortunately for growers in the warm and underdeveloped nations, it is often likely that demand remains stable or declines—we now use synthetics instead of rubber—while trees and bushes keep producing tons of unwanted tropical goods.

Formation of Price

So now we have demand schedules and curves and supply schedules and curves. What do we do with them? We bring together the schedule makers. In the theater of our imagination, we make demanders and suppliers confront each other in a market and watch to see what happens. The demanders are potential buyers, with their schedules; the suppliers are potential sellers, with their schedules. The combined schedules in Table 5–5 (and diagramed in Figure 5–4) are a sort of box score of the economic game as it stands in a free and competitive wheat market just before sales are made.

TABLE 5–5

COMBINED SUPPLY AND DEMAND SCHEDULES FOR A SMALL WHEAT MARKET

If the Price per Bushel Is:	Buyers Are Willing to Buy:	And Sellers Are Willing to Sell:
$1.40	5,000 bu.	2,000 bu.
1.50	4,500	2,500
1.60	4,000	3,000
1.70	3,500	3,500
1.80	3,000	4,000
1.90	2,500	4,500
2.00	2,000	5,000

In a market to which buyers and sellers have come with inten-
tions summarized in Table 5–5, the price will have to be $1.70, and
the amount bought and sold will be 3,500 bushels. The price is spoken
of as the equilibrium price. This is the point at which there is a meeting of minds, and since a characteristic of a true market is that there is
only one equilibrium price, those who do not buy or sell at $1.70
withdraw. Some potential buyers and some potential sellers are disappointed. The disappointed buyers will presumably find substitutes,

FIGURE 5–4

PRICE DETERMINATION ON A SMALL WHEAT MARKET

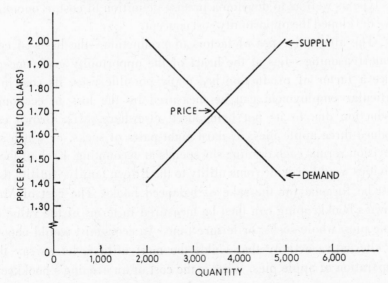

do without, or wait for the price to go down. The disappointed sellers will presumably hold their grain in storage, hoping for a better day; some may decide to use the grain directly to feed their chickens or other livestock. Figure 5–4 represents what is contained in Table 5–5 and the explanations above. The diagram shows the point at which the two sloping lines meet and cross. Price and quantity are found on the vertical and horizontal lines, respectively. It is almost unnecessary to add that the equilibrium price symbolizes, in the real and complex world, a value toward which actual prices tend. Some buyers will pay more and some less than $1.70, but $1.70 is the point to which deviating prices seek to return. The concept is like that of an ocean liner under way. The boat is rarely level, but after each roll or pitch, it seeks to right itself again.

Opportunity Cost

Farmer Brown's supply schedule is based on the costs he assumes in the production of corn. Most of them are easily measured— the price he must pay for seed times the quantity he uses; the 6 percent interest rate he pays at the local bank times the amount he borrows; the going price of fertilizer multiplied by the amount he uses. But what is the cost of his own labor? What value can be placed on the evenings his wife devotes to bookkeeping or on his sons' efforts at keeping the farm machinery operational? To handle problems of this type as well as to develop a precise definition of cost, economists have developed the opportunity cost concept.

The alternative use of factors of production—the basis of economic reasoning—lies at the heart of the opportunity cost concept. Since a factor of production has many possible uses, its cost in a particular employment can be measured by the loss in economic production due to its not being used elsewhere. Mrs. Brown can produce three apple pies, or darn eight pairs of socks, or watch six television reruns each evening she spends at accounting. Each of these activities would provide some utility to the Brown family—utility that must be forgone for the sake of balanced books. The cost of Mrs. Brown's bookkeeping can then be measured in terms of the value of apple pies, whole socks, or leisure time. An economist would choose the alternative activity that yields the most utility—let us say the preparation of apple pies. What is the cost of an evening's bookkeeping? Three pies or the amount of money the family must spend at the local bakery to replace them.

Opportunity costs, though of major importance to a theoretical economist attempting to analyze problems in terms of what will benefit the total society, may have little relevance to individual behavior within an economy. The following example should help to clarify this point.

Hobart H. Hopgood, having taken a four-year Bachelor of Arts degree at State University and a five-year nonstudent graduate program at Berkeley, assumes a position as the mid-western representative of Household Appliance, Inc. The job necessitates frequent and extensive travel. Two modes of transportation are available—plane and automobile. He calculates the cost of travel by car would be $1,200 a year, $800 of this being depreciation; by air, $1,100 a year.

To reduce this hypothetical problem to its simplest form, we shall not consider savings of time and matters of personal convenience. We shall state that Hobart will fly because of the $100 saving. An economist, looking at the problem from society's rather than Hobart's point of view, would make a different decision. "The depreciation on the automobile is overstated," he would reason, "for new-car prices contain a monopoly profit that does not reflect factor costs, and a large part of the price of gasoline consists of tax revenues which do not measure destroyed resources. On the other hand," the economist would continue, "the cost of air transportation is understated. Since all levels of government seem to subsidize local airlines, the cost of flying Hobart around is actually greater than what he pays for his tickets. From society's vantage point, driving destroys resources valued at $900; flying costs society $1,500. Hopgood should drive." If Hobart H. Hopgood is an economic man, he will not take the economist's advice.

One of the reasons for the love affair between economists and the competitive model described in Chapter 3 is that under conditions of perfect competition, there need be no difference between an individual's and an economist's estimate of cost. Competitive firms, at least when in their long-run equilibrium position, sell their produce at a price equal to the costs of the factors of production used. If an economy consists entirely of competitive markets, then prices are a measure of opportunity costs. Under conditions of imperfect competition, however, the prices at which output is sold are higher than the costs incurred in production and are therefore greater than the opportunity costs. Such a situation does not allow for the perfection in the allocation of resources envisioned in the competitive model, for the individuals in the economy respond to market price—a measure of their personal opportunity costs—not to the abstract opportunity costs relevant to society.

One final word before we leave opportunity costs. This concept is useful in the examination of far larger problems than are evidenced by a single supply schedule or Hopgood's transportation dilemma. What is the cost of a jet bomber? It can be stated in dollars, but it may be better viewed as the commodities that could have been produced by the resources used to build the plane—a large suburban grade school, a college student center, a battle in the war on poverty; or the cost of a foreign military venture—state universities, rejuvenated urban centers, safety on the nation's highways. In short, the cost of things may be measured by the cost of things forgone to get them.

Economic Time

The above is a sort of rough-and-ready account of how economists use supply and demand schedules; but it has not suggested how the element of time is used in analysis of the pricing process. *Time* in economics is not really time at all, but rather an attempt to distinguish between forms of behavior in the shorter and longer runs of events. We must make the assumption that the relations of supply and demand for a commodity call forth very different kinds of calculation on the part of a manufacturer or other supplier, depending on whether the kind of action he takes is rare, occasional, or customary. In many ways the idea is not unlike our own behavior as consumers. On rare occasions, like honeymoons, we spend money at a rate that would be ruinous if persisted in for long. This would be our short-run rate of spending. Our long-run rate of spending is such that income and outgo must balance. In similar fashion, in the short run, suppliers may sell below costs; but obviously, no supplier can do this in the long run.

Actually, there are three "runs" that economists talk about. The first run is not named a "run," but instead is named the "market period." The second is the "short run," and the third is the "long run." Let us see how each of these situations affects action.

In the market period, costs play a minor role in price determination. If too many farmers bring too many raspberries to market on Saturday morning, they will have to sell them for what they can get, regardless of cost. But now we must account for opportunity cost. If the farmers are offered too little for their raspberries, many will withdraw them from the market because they would rather take the berries back home and use them within the family—deep-freeze them, make jam, or give them away to appreciative neighbors. They might, besides, be able to salvage the quart boxes and crates in which the berries are packed and use them some other time. Thus, we find that even when producers are in a ruinous and temporary squeeze between heavy supply and light demand, they still must be offered a price high enough to cover the cost of an alternative use for the berries (and the crates). If, on the other hand, few farmers bring berries to market, and if the demand is strong, then berries will, on that market, sell very high—quite possibly at a price two or three times higher than the cost of production of the least efficient grower. This observation further confirms the general principle of market-period price, namely, that cost of production plays only a small role in determining price. The principle works both ways—toward excessively low and excessively high prices.

The second case is the short run. Here, total costs play a larger but not yet decisive role. Let us assume that a small clothing manufacturer, Jones, finds himself in a slack period. X, a buyer, offers him a rather bad contract for 20,000 pairs of blue jeans—bad in the sense that the $40,000 offered is lower than total costs. Should Jones accept or reject the contract? At first glance, it would seem that no manufacturer would be insane enough deliberately to produce at a loss. Better to lock up the factory until business picks up again and take a trip to Florida. But no—it *does* make sense to produce at a loss under certain conditions.

To understand this kind of seeming insanity, we must first view costs as being of two types, fixed and variable. Fixed costs are costs that go on at the same rate whether Jones's factory is temporarily closed while he is in Florida or whether it is working full blast. These include rent, salary to a watchman, insurance, certain taxes, interest on borrowed funds, and the like. Let us assume that over the three-month period required to produce 20,000 pairs of blue jeans, fixed costs run to $3,000. This is not unlike certain situations we meet as consumers. If an elderly couple buys a car that they use only for Sunday church and midweek shopping, certain costs will be as great as those incurred by an active young salesman who drives 30,000 miles a year. Insurance will be about the same as will the decline in value on account of obsolescence and the sacrifice of income from the $3,000 that the automobile cost—a sum that might have been invested at 5 percent to bring the couple dividends, now forgone, of $150 a year.

The second kind of costs is named variable costs. These are the immediate costs of production—what Jones would have to pay to get clothing workers, for thread, cloth, electricity, and so forth, if he accepted the contract. These are comparable, in the automobile analogy just above, to the costs of gasoline and oil, which are not fixed but vary enormously, depending on whether the car is driven 1,000 miles annually or 30,000.

If, now, the variable costs for producing the 20,000 pairs of blue jeans amount to $38,000 and the fixed costs are $3,000, then total costs are $41,000. But X offered Jones only $40,000. Should Jones accept? If this is the best offer that Jones can expect to get during the slack season, he should accept, for this reason: By accepting the contract, he will lose only $1,000; by rejecting it, he will lose the whole of the $3,000 of fixed costs. How so? We must look at the matter a little more closely. If he does go to Florida and shuts his plant, his total income and costs are as follows:

Income		Costs	
	$0	Fixed	$3,000
		Variable	0
Totals	$0		$3,000
	Loss $3,000		

If he stays and produces, his income and costs are as follows:

Income		Costs	
	$40,000	Fixed	$ 3,000
		Variable	38,000
Totals	$40,000		$41,000
	Loss $1,000		

Thus, it actually pays a manufacturer to produce at a loss and to sell below costs during the short run. It is, of course, also possible to make abnormally high profits in the short run. If the demand for blue jeans were great, Jones might have refused to accept less than $60,000 for the 20,000 pairs. This might continue for a rather long time, possibly for years, but Jones could not enjoy this enviable position indefinitely in a competitive market with free entry. If manufacturers of blue jeans were making inordinate profits, other entrepreneurs would soon enter the blue-jeans business, add to the supply, and cause the price to fall.

In the two cases noted above, the raspberries and the blue jeans, we have seen that, of the two forces that determine price, demand plays a greater role than costs.

The last case to consider is the long run. In the long run, no producer will continue indefinitely in business unless prices received meet all costs of production incurred (including a reasonable profit). Briefly, in the long run, prices must cover costs. Or to put it differently, in the long run, prices and costs tend toward equality in a competitive society.

The process involved in bringing about this equality in a completely competitive industry is fairly obvious. Let us assume the industry is that of color TV sets. When they are first produced, the demand for these new sets is great, and the price is high. High prices invite a swarm of manufacturers to enter this business and swell production. The volume of TV sets now becomes so great that prices decline. Low prices will weed out the least efficient producers, that is, producers whose costs are above the prices offered. But weeding out these inefficient producers reduces the number of sets produced and tends to raise prices again, though not to so high a point as before. After seesawing a while, the price-demand-supply relations of the industry will reach an equilibrium, and cost of production will approximately equal price.

The easy statement, "Cost of production will approximately equal price," conceals a very real difficulty. Whose cost? If the price of the TV sets (paid to all manufacturers) is $500, we may rightfully assume that the most efficient among them can turn the sets out for an average cost of $400 to $495. Only the least efficient manufacturers among those remaining in the business (after the weeding-out process described just above) run average costs up to $500. Thus, we must change our simple "price equals cost" formula to "price equals the cost of the marginal producers." Or we can move in the direction of great abstraction and assume that in the very long run, in a truly competitive economic system and with other things remaining unchanged, all manufacturers will become equally efficient and will incur approximately equal costs in making the same television sets.

In any event, the thing really worth noting is that a rough equality prevails between prices and costs of production in the long run. Some readers, disappointed in this seemingly obvious conclusion, may remember that Adam Smith nearly 200 years ago said substantially the same thing, and so did Ricardo and Mill and others. Well, the answer to that is that Smith, Ricardo, and Mill were really pretty fuzzy about cost of production and did not see the point at which cost of production is affected by demand. Later economists found subtleties that others had not seen, saw the interplay of supply and demand through costs of production, and gave us a more perceptive theory. They developed the concept of supply and demand schedules and the useful graphs we have presented. And of course, they emphasized the differences among market period, short run, and long run. Only in the long run is there a tendency to equality between price and cost. In the shorter run the story is different: The forces of demand take precedence and are of greater import than total costs in price determination.

Applications of Value Theory

We have in the preceding pages of this chapter made an elementary survey of price theory, one of the basic areas of economic study. It may be a little surprising to many students to be brought up short and told that they have completed a most significant unit of standard economic theory. "So what?" they may say, and "What use is it?" Certainly, it does not help anybody to fix a price. If an antique table is to be sold, no amount of monkeying around with supply and demand curves will help either buyer or seller to work out a proper price. Much better to get an appraisal by an expert on antiques than to consult the most distinguished economist in the world. Price theory is no good at fixing price tags.

Some economists describe price theory as the basic logic of

economics, as the tool which can be used to attack many problems. It
is the algebra of the science of wealth. Let us see how this algebra may
be used to throw light on two economic problems: (1) Who pays an
excise tax? (2) Do wage increases in an industry cause much unemployment? The first problem sticks very close to the issue of prices of
things used up by consumers, as defined in the first paragraph of this
chapter. The second problem explores other uses to which the same
techniques may be put.

For the first case, we shall assume a completely competitive
industry in which the products are interchangeable or virtually so. A
good example might be the men's plain black umbrella industry. The
selling price is $5. Let us further assume, to simplify things, that the
producer sells directly to the consumer. The government now levies an
excise tax of 50 cents on each umbrella sold. This tax is in the first
instance levied on the producer; he must buy government stamps for
his umbrellas as cigarette makers do, and must paste a stamp on each
of his products. Who ultimately pays the 50 cents? The producer?
The consumer? Is the cost of the stamp shared by both? A supply-and
demand diagram will give us an answer of sorts.

In Figure 5–5 the two solid black lines in the form of a large X

FIGURE 5–5

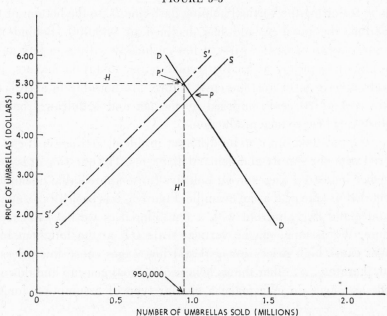

describe the industry before the tax. They are labeled *DD* and *SS* for demand and supply. Umbrella makers are selling one million umbrellas yearly at $5 each. Now the 50-cent tax is imposed. This action does not change the demand line *DD*, because the tax has no effect on demand; it does not cause more or less rain or make umbrellas more or less attractive. It does, however, change the supply line *SS*. The supply line may be viewed, a little inaccurately, as a cost line; and if the government forces umbrella makers to paste a 50-cent stamp on each umbrella, then costs are raised, and the old supply line *(SS)* is affected. A new dot-and-dash supply line *(S'S')* is therefore drawn. In the diagram, this new line is exactly 50 cents above the old line *SS*. That is, the vertical distance between *SS* and *S'S'* is a distance which, if measured along the price scale at the extreme left of the diagram, equals 50 cents.

The fact that *S'S'* lies 50 cents higher than *SS* does not mean that the price is 50 cents higher. The new price is to be found at the intersection of *DD* and *S'S'*, which point is labeled *P'*. If we now measure the height of *P'* with the aid of the horizontal helping dash line labeled *H*, we find that it cuts the price scale at $5.30. This means that the manufacturer must absorb 20 cents of the cost of each stamp.

Not only has the price gone up, but also the quantity sold has declined. At $5, one million umbrellas were sold. At $5.30, as we can see by following the vertical helping dash line *H'* to the bottom of the diagram, the number sold has declined to 950,000. Behind this decline lie two causes: First, a few customers willing to buy at $5 are unwilling to buy at $5.30; second, a few umbrella makers, just barely able to meet average costs before, are not able to absorb the extra cost of 20 cents imposed by the tax and withdraw from the industry. Others reduce production.

We now take up a quite different problem, and again it can be solved with our supply-and-demand diagrams. The question at issue is whether increased wages in an industry cause appreciable unemployment. Let us take coal as an example. Figure 5–6 is basically a supply-and-demand diagram, but with a few inferences we have not made before. We assume, on the vertical scale *OY* at the left, that high wages cause high prices for coal and low wages cause low prices— that, therefore, all other things being equal, coal goes up and down in price as wages do. We make a similar type of assumption for the

FIGURE 5–6

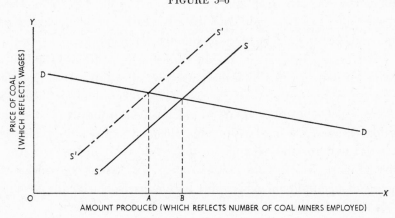

horizontal line *OX*, which in previous diagrams has measured quantity produced and sold. The assumption is that a definite relationship exists between number of men employed and amount produced and sold; i.e., few men produce little coal, many men produce much coal.

Next, we draw in a big, solid-line *X*, which represents demand and supply (*DD* and *SS*). But we have drawn our *DD* line as a very gentle slope from left to right. This we did because we are assuming that the demand for coal is quite elastic. Such a line, by traveling far from left to right with but a slight loss of elevation, indicates that slight changes in price cause large changes in the quantity purchased. The reader must not, however, carry away the impression that all flattish demand or supply curves are elastic throughout their length. Something depends on the scales used, but other reasons prevail which we cannot now pursue. To return, we have the right to say that the demand for coal is elastic because it has so many substitutes—oil, gas, hydroelectric power, insulation, open wood fires, even wool sweaters and socks.

We start, then, with all the assumptions made above, and the two solid lines in Figure 5–6. A change occurs, however: The union has negotiated a large wage increase. This increases the cost of coal (other things remaining equal; we do not take into account various ways in which a wage increase might lead to greater efficiency). The wage increase does not make coal more attractive; therefore, we do nothing about the *DD* line. But we do draw a new supply line *S'S'*. We now drop perpendiculars from the intersections to the *OX* line. These measure off quantities sold and thereby mark off the numbers unemployed. The line *AB* suggests the number of unemployed.[1]

Now, let us draw a similar diagram for the antibiotics industry. Here is an industry in which there are few substitutes. It is true that we formerly recovered from diseases without antibiotics—although many did not—but most of us would not be willing to try the old-fashioned cures. We shall assume that demand in this industry is very inelastic; and for this reason, we draw *DD* as a line of very steep slope (Figure 5–7). Our new distance *AB*, which measures the amount of unemployment, is short by comparison with the distance *AB* of the coal industry.

FIGURE 5–7

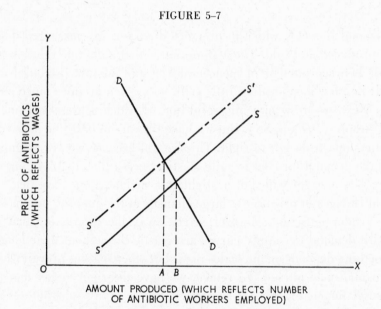

AMOUNT PRODUCED (WHICH REFLECTS NUMBER
OF ANTIBIOTIC WORKERS EMPLOYED)

Thus, by the use of our price-theory diagrams, we conclude that high wages may cause large unemployment in industries that make products having elastic demand and relatively little in industries of

[1] The student should be warned that in the two examples here given (coal and antibiotics), your authors have vastly oversimplified the problems. The discussion is, they believe, most useful pedagogically, even though it falls somewhat short of elegant economic analysis. The examples have the virtue of tying together several concepts developed in this chapter and the preceding one, and of handling a complex problem simply. They have the defect of skipping over the demand and supply curves for labor.

inelastic demand. And earlier, we learned about how an excise tax is split. To be sure, we have greatly oversimplified and have neglected such things as the possibility of substituting machines for labor. But our examples do clearly suggest that supply and demand curves are not intended to be used in estimating prices, but in the solution of a wide range of economic problems.

Summary and Conclusions

In this chapter, we have gone to the very heart of standard economic theory—a study of value, or of price formation in a competitive market. As has been well known in Western culture during the period of recorded history, the forces of supply and demand have a strong effect on price. But this is not quite enough. To use our general knowledge as an economist must, we need such auxiliary concepts as marginality, elasticity, demand and supply schedules, fixed and variable costs, and short- and long-run periods. Additional aids to reasoning may be found in graphic representations of supply schedules and demand schedules. Our final conclusion is that in competitive markets, price in the long run equals cost of production, but this is not necessarily true in the market period or in the short run.

QUESTIONS FOR REVIEW AND DISCUSSION

1. Define, in your own words, each of the following terms:
    a) Value
    b) Utility
    c) Demand
    d) Supply
    e) Elasticity of demand
    f) Elasticity of supply
2. What limits the usefulness of the labor theory of value?
3. Demand and supply schedules of red shoes:

Quantity Supplied (Thousands)	Price per Pair	Quantity Demanded (Thousands)
120	$12	80
110	11	90
100	10	100
90	9	110
80	8	120

What will the market price of red shoes be? What quantity of red shoes will be produced? What will be the change in the quantity produced and the price charged if demand increases by 10 percent? Diagram your solutions.

4. Analyze why a disequilibrium price—a price which is above or below the intersection of the supply and demand curves—must change. Use diagrams.

5. Discuss the concept of diminishing marginal utility. Construct a demand schedule for white shirts for each of five individuals, assuming that each individual has different tastes and preferences. How can these data be used to construct a composite demand curve for white shirts?

6. Give several examples of opportunity costs. Did Robinson Crusoe ever have to pay any opportunity costs?

7. A family budgets $4 for butter and margarine. It buys five pounds of margarine at 50 cents a pound and two pounds of butter at 75 cents a pound. A new process cuts the cost of margarine first to 43 cents, later to 33 cents, and finally to 13 cents a pound. With each decrease in price, the family buys one additional pound of butter and one pound less of margarine; at the same time the family stays within a few pennies of the total it has budgeted for a spread. Draw the family's demand curve for margarine. How does it differ from ordinary demand curves? Can any generalization be made about the law of diminishing utility when superior substitutes are available?

Chapter 6

VALUE UNDER

IMPERFECT

COMPETITION

Monopoly Price

The last chapter dealt with competitive price. Before we can safely leave the theory of price, we have another job—to suggest some of the problems of pricing under conditions of monopoly and quasi monopoly.

Monopoly price works like this: Assume that a man really invents a better mousetrap, after all, and patents it—one that does not snap at your fingers, is permanently baited, and automatically reduces the carcass to a little heap of sterile ashes. He makes his traps in small quantity at first and finds they cost him $3 apiece. Since his product is unique, he has no guide in the form of a going price for a similar gadget already on the market. Initially, his marketing policy is a complete blank except for one fact: Price must cover his costs and yield a profit. In these circumstances, it would not be completely absurd to charge as much as $25, for surely several hundred Americans every year would wish to buy so efficient a trap at that price. Neither would it be absurd to charge $4 or $5, for then tens of thousands of customers annually would want to buy. The inventor would, if wise, balance the advantage of small sales at a high profit against mass sales at a low profit.

After puzzling out the price-quantity enigma, he may reach the conclusion that the best chance for greatest total profit is to pursue a medium course: medium price—perhaps $7.50—and medium sales.

But one more thing must be taken into account. Our inventor had figured that his costs would be $3 per *Mousoleum*—the name he has given his product. This figure is meaningless except as a sort of anchor to his preliminary calculations. Costs of producing vary with quantity. Perhaps the cost will go down to $2.50 if 1,000 are produced monthly. And if 10 times that many are built, costs may go down even lower. Costs go up eventually as they did for Farmer Brown in the preceding chapter; but for a while, they tend to go down. Thus, our mouse-catching man has to juggle a third variable, cost. Selling price, quantity sold, and cost: These three sliding figures have to be adjusted in such a way as to yield a maximum gain. He may discover that he should cut his selling price far below $7.50, thereby picking up several new layers of customers; and because of the reduced cost per unit as well as great volume, he may realize an even greater overall profit than his earlier calculation had indicated.

One of the ways in which this adjustment or computation may be made discloses a basic proposition of price theory: To maximize gains, any firm produces up to the point at which marginal cost equals marginal revenue. Since we have not yet defined the two terms "marginal cost" and "marginal revenue," we shall do so at once.

Total, Marginal, and Average Cost

We shall begin with total cost, since the concepts of marginal cost and average cost depend upon it. Total cost is the sum of all costs incurred by the entrepreneur in the production of a specific quantity of output. This cost includes payments to labor, land, and capital, as well as a return to entrepreneurship. Reading from column 3 in Table 6–1, the total cost of producing five units of Mousoleums per week is $1,250; the total cost of producing six units per week is $1,614. Note that "unit" is defined as a batch of 100.

Marginal cost is the extra cost of producing an additional unit of something. If our monopolist increases his production from five to six units per week, his total cost of production rises from $1,250 to $1,614 per week. The increase in total cost due to the production of the sixth unit is $364. In other words, the marginal cost of the sixth unit is $364.

Average cost is the total cost of production divided by the number of units produced. Thus, if the total cost of producing five units of Mousoleums is $1,250, the average cost of each unit is $250, or $1,250 divided by 5. If the total cost of producing six units is $1,614, the average cost of each of the six units is $269.

When plotted on graph paper, the average cost curve and the marginal cost curve have characteristic shapes and relationships. Average costs usually look like a rocker. Marginal costs usually resemble the business end of a hockey stick, and the curve always intersects the average cost curve at its lowest point. Figure 6–1 shows this characteristic relationship. The plotting of the actual figures given in Table 6–1 will be found in Figure 6–3.

TABLE 6–1

AVERAGE AND MARGINAL COSTS OF PRODUCING MOUSOLEUMS

(Column 1) Number of Units of Mousoleums Produced Weekly (at 100 per Unit)	(Column 2) Average Cost of Each Unit	(Column 3) Total Cost (Column 1 × Column 2)	(Column 4) Marginal Cost per Unit (Subtract Each Item in Column 3 from the One Following)
0	....	......	....
1	$330	$ 330	$330
2	275	550	220
3	258	774	224
4	251	1,004	230
5	250	1,250	246
6	269	1,614	364
7	312	2,184	570
8	380	3,040	856

FIGURE 6–1

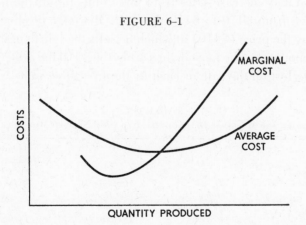

MARGINAL COST

AVERAGE COST

COSTS

QUANTITY PRODUCED

From costs, we now move over to receipts. For this, Table 6–2 becomes home base. Total revenue tells us how much, gross, the seller of a product receives. If our Mousoleum monopolist sells three units at $470 per unit, he receives $1,410 in total revenue.

Marginal revenue is the change in total revenue caused by a

change in the number of units sold. If our monopolist increases his sales from three units at $470 each to four units at $410 each, his total revenue increases from $1,410 to $1,640. The increase in total revenue, in this case $230, is the marginal revenue attached to the sale of the fourth unit. Marginal revenue tells us how much more the seller will gross as he moves from one position to the next, that is, how much more he will get if he sells five units instead of four, or 10 instead of nine.

Average revenue is total revenue divided by the number of units sold, much as average cost is total cost divided by the number of units produced. If total revenue is $1,640 when four units are sold, average revenue is $410. This figure, $410, is equal to the price the buyer will pay for each of the four units; price and average revenue are always equal. The concept of average revenue is therefore not different from the concept of price as developed in the last chapter, and the average revenue schedule is a demand curve.

Under monopoly conditions, marginal revenue is always lower than average revenue. This is because the monopolist must lower price in order to increase sales. Reading from Table 6–2, in order that our monopolist may increase sales from three units to four units, he must lower price from $470 to $410 per unit. His total revenue does not increase by the price ($410) at which he sells the fourth unit, but by a smaller amount. For he must deduct from the $410 the $60 of possible revenue he lost on the sale of each of the first three units because he

TABLE 6–2

AVERAGE AND MARGINAL REVENUE RECEIVED FROM SELLING MOUSOLEUMS

(Column 1) Number of Units of Mousoleums Sold Weekly (at 100 per Unit)	(Column 2) Average Revenue (Price)	(Column 3) Total Revenue (Column 1 × Column 2)	(Column 4) Marginal Revenue (Subtract Each Item in Column 3 from the One Following)
0	....	......	....
1	$590	$ 590	$590
2	530	1,060	470
3	470	1,410	350
4	410	1,640	230
5	350	1,750	110
6	290	1,740	− 10
7	230	1,610	− 130
8	150	1,200	− 410

lowered price. In other words, his marginal revenue is $410 minus $180, or $230.

The average and marginal revenue curves of a monopolist usually appear in elementary textbooks as two straight lines sloping downward, the marginal revenue line being below the average revenue line. Their characteristic relationships are shown in Figure 6–2. Note that the marginal revenue line has a steeper slope.

FIGURE 6–2

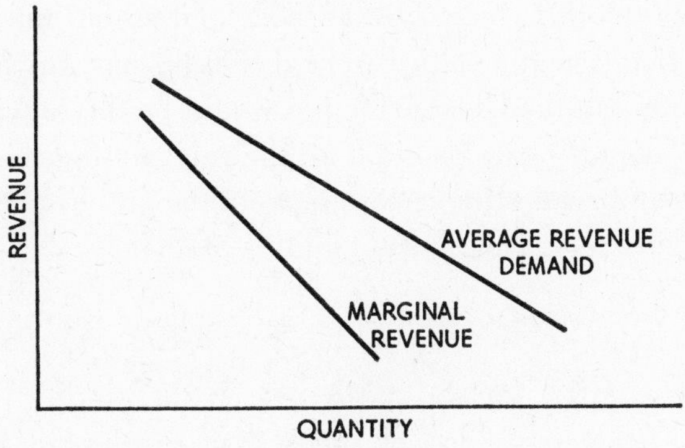

The Determination of Monopoly Price

Now we have the data required to solve our problem. The reader will remember it to be as follows: How can the Mousoleum monopolist determine his best-profit point? Well, he can do two things. He can subtract total costs in Table 6–1 from total revenue in Table 6–2 and find out at what rate of production his profit is highest. Table 6–3 shows how this works out.

TABLE 6–3

Number of Units Produced and Sold	Total Revenue (from Table 6–2)	Total Cost (from Table 6–1)	Profit
0	......	......	......
1	$ 590	$ 330	$ 260
2	1,060	550	510
3	1,410	774	636
4	1,640	1,004	636
5	1,750	1,250	500
6	1,740	1,614	126
7	1,610	2,184	— 574
8	1,200	3,040	— 1,840

Table 6–3 tells us that his greatest profit will be $636, achieved if he produces three or four units. This, of course, means 300 to 400 Mousoleums weekly, since we made each unit equal to a weekly batch of 100. This solution (300 to 400) is not as accurate as one could wish. Our trouble lies in the fact that we are using integers, or whole numbers, with which readers are familiar. In the calculus, with which some readers may not be familiar, the numeral 2 does not follow 1, and 4 does not follow 3. Instead, there is an infinite gradation of numbers between two integers. Thus, after 2 would come some such figure as 2.00000001, then 2.00000002, and so on, until we finally reached 3. If our mathematics were different, our answer would be more accurate, but the basic principle would be the same.

Our monopolist can also plot all the relevant figures given in the above tables and read off his answers from the graph. Such a graph is drawn in Figure 6–3. The relevant figures plotted are:

> Average cost, or *AC* in the graph
> Average revenue, or *AR* in the graph
> Marginal cost, or *MC* in the graph
> Marginal revenue, or *MR* in the graph

The critical place to look for the solution of the problem is the point at which *MR* and *MC* intersect. If, now, you drop a line (1) from the point of intersection to the horizontal quantity line at the bottom (*X*-axis), it will fall at four units, one of the points indicated in Table 6–3. Thus the monopolist can learn from the graph, as he does from the table, that he should produce four units. The price at which he ought to sell, and the profit he will get, can also be read off the graph. Follow the line (1) upward until it meets the *AR* line. The point of intersection, measured along the *Y*-axis, tells him what price he should charge per unit. The price is $410 per hundred, or $4.10 per Mousoleum. His total profit is the shaded rectangle. Its area is the difference between average revenue and average cost (a difference of $159) multiplied by the number of units sold, and, as in our table, is $636.

It is perhaps the basic tenet of price theory that the point at which *MR* and *MC* intersect marks the point at which profit is greatest —or if not profit, at least the most satisfactory output for the firm. The price arrived at by the procedure described above is the equilibrium price. This means it is the point to which price returns if there

FIGURE 6–3

MONOPOLY PROFIT

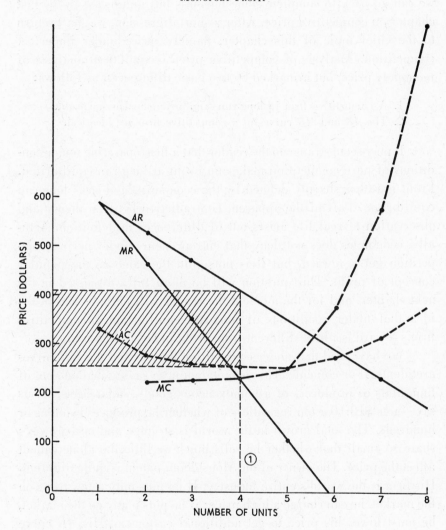

NUMBER OF UNITS

are temporary disturbances in the market and the price at which the firm is most satisfied to sell and produce.

A Digression on MC and MR under Perfect Competition

The preceding paragraph applies primarily to a monopolist. But it also applies in almost every particular to a firm under conditions of pure competition. Now that we understand the *MC* and *MR* curves, we can go back to complete some business left unfinished in the last chapter on competitive price. After a short digression, we shall return to the chief topic of this chapter, namely, price under imperfect competition. Analysis of competitive price is similar to analysis of monopoly price, but is marked by two basic differences, as follows:

1. A competitive firm in long-run equilibrium makes no profit.
2. The *AR* and *MR* curves of a competitive firm are identical.

It may seem strange to the reader that a firm operating under conditions of pure competition makes no profit at long-run equilibrium. Profit is rather sharply defined by the economist, and so is long-run equilibrium. Part of the apparent contradiction between theory and observation of real life arises out of differences in definition. Actually, economics does not deny that entrepreneurs under perfect competition get a reward, but it is not quite the same as the popular concept of profit. This question will be more fully discussed in the next chapter, and for the moment the reader will perhaps accept the idea that under conditions of long-run equilibrium a competitive firm's reward is a little different from profit in the usual sense.

We have said that under competition the *AR* and the *MR* curves are identical or coincide. This is tantamount to saying that one out of thousands of producers of a homogeneous good—sugar beets, let us say—gets $12.10 a ton regardless of whether he produces two tons or hundreds. The total grown in the world is so huge and one grower's share so small that whether he sells much or little, he alone cannot affect the price. The owner of the Mousoleum patent is quite different. His firm is the world's entire industry. If he puts only a few traps on the market, he can charge a high price; if he puts many on the market, he must lower his price to get additional customers. His *AR* curve goes down as he produces more, and the *MR* curve goes down with it, even more steeply. But under competition the *AR* curve is a steady, horizontal line. For the sugar beet grower, it stays level at $12.10 a ton, as in Figure 6–4. The *MR* line also stays steady at $12.10 per ton; that is, each successive ton sells at $12.10, too. Thus, *MR* and *AR* coincide.

We now turn to the cost curves. Unlike the revenue problem, the cost problem of the monopolist and of the competitive producer is the

FIGURE 6–4

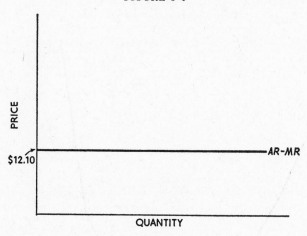

same. Whether you are a monopolist or a cometitor, you have to face exactly the same facts of life as a producer: Fixed costs per unit at low production are quite high; and at excessive production, variable costs per unit rise; but between the extremes lies an area of most efficient—and hence cheapest—production. In short, the sugar beet man, like the mousetrap man, will have two cost curves; again, one will look like a rocker, the other like a hockey stick. These two lines and the *MR* line will all intersect at the same point. That point indicates the spot at which the sugar beet man (or any person operating under perfect competition) is operating most efficiently. Table 6–4 and Figure 6–5 show what happens. By referring to the graph, it

TABLE 6–4

Number of Tons of Sugar Beets Grown	Cost per Ton	Total Cost	Marginal Cost
0	......	....	
1	$15.40	$ 15.40	$15.40
2	14.30	28.60	13.20
3	13.50	40.50	11.90
4	12.80	51.20	10.70
5	12.30	61.50	10.30
6	12.10	72.60	11.10
7	12.10	84.70	12.10
8	12.20	97.60	12.90
9	12.40	111.60	14.00
10	12.90	129.00	17.40
11	13.50	148.50	19.50

FIGURE 6-5

BEET GROWER'S EQUILIBRIUM RATE

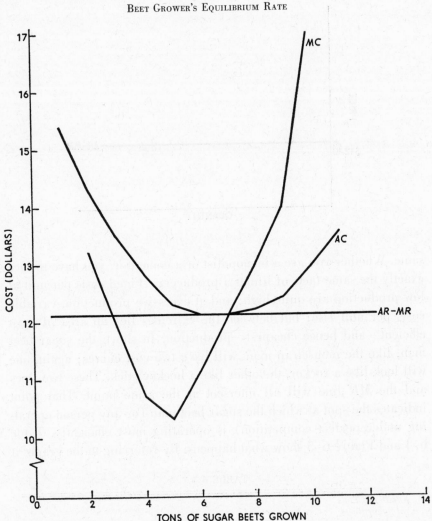

TONS OF SUGAR BEETS GROWN

will be seen that the three lines intersect above the quantity of seven tons—the point up to which our sugar beet grower should produce, and beyond which he should not go.

Much has been made of the fact that under perfect competition, *AR*, *MR*, and *MC* all touch at the lowest point on the *AC* curve. It is considered by some economists to be almost an act of Providence that the most satisfactory position for the entrepreneur is also the most

satisfactory position for the consumer, since the point coincides with
the lowest cost of production.

This suggests a genuine harmony between buyer and seller under
conditions of perfect competition. What's best for producers is also
best for consumers. This works out so well that the reader may even
suspect that the figures have been rigged to achieve this outcome. It is
true, of course, that the figures are hypothetical and that in this sense
they have been rigged, but let us see what would have happened if
they had not been rigged at all. If our figures had indicated that the
AC curve lay wholly above the *AR–MR* line, never touching it (as in
Figure 6–6), then we would have been talking about a sugar beet
grower who cannot long exist, for his costs are always above the
$12.10 price.

FIGURE 6–6

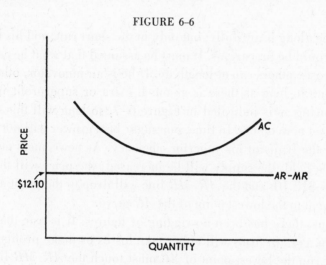

A sugar beet grower who can never get his costs down to the price
of $12.10 must find some other vocation. He will go bankrupt even-
tually. But what about the very efficient grower whose cost line dives
under the *AR–MR* line, as in Figure 6–7? He would be making a
rather handsome profit, and the consumer would not be getting the
benefit of his lower cost. The reason for this is that if the price *is*
$12.10, and if he can sell all he produces at $12.10, he would be silly
to offer his beets at less than the market price.

Certainly, for a while the sugar beet grower of Figure 6–7 would

FIGURE 6–7

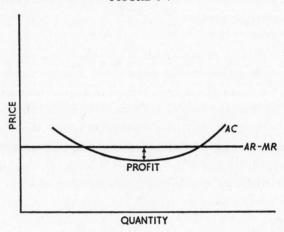

be getting along beautifully, but only in the short run, and his hold on profits would be precarious. It must be assumed that what he can do to reduce costs, others can at length do. If he is an innovator, others will copy him. So long as there is as much extra or superprofit in sugar beet growing as is indicated in Figure 6–7, so long will this occupation attract newcomers. In time, our sugar beet grower will not be able to enjoy the fruits of his superior efficiency. As newcomers enter this profitable field, the supply will be increased; the price will therefore go below $12.10, and the *AR–MR* line will drop to the point at which it is tangent to the lowest point of the *AC* curve.

Thus, there has been no rigging of figures. It is true that in the short run, certain firms will either take losses or make profits; but in the long run the lowest point of *AC* must touch the *AR–MR* line, and *MC* will intersect at this point of tangency.

Monopolistic Competition

We now return from our digression on perfect competition to continue our work on price in imperfectly competitive markets. Standard theory has long been able to discuss convincingly certain relationships among supply, demand, price, and costs in either a purely competitive market or a monopolistic market. But the trouble is that few things are sold on either type of market. Just as there is little pure competition, so there are few pure monopolies. Thus the standard theory of prices rarely touched the real world directly. Only in recent decades have economists concerned themselves with the great middle ground of imperfect competition, quasi monopoly, and the like. Three major names are involved here—Piero Sraffa, Edward Chamberlin, and Joan Robinson. Joan Robinson is, incidentally, the first and only woman economist to be associated with any significant original work in theoretical economics. There are, to be sure, many quite competent women economists. Beatrice Webb, with her husband, has done brilliant work in economic history; but in original price theory, which is the core of standard theory, Joan Robinson stands alone.

One of the leading ideas in this relatively new department of theory is that most producers, if they can, try to create a partial monopoly for their products by differentiating them from similar products. But this monopoly is a rather frail one because substitutes are so easily available. Nearly all monopolies are threatened by substitutes; even our Mousoleum man of a few pages back had to take into account the fact that poison and spring traps could also launch mice into eternity. But we made the assumption that the new mousetrap was unique and excelled all others; it was a genuine innovation. You can, however, create feebler monopolies without innovation or improvement. For example, basic differences among toilet soaps are inconsequential, except for those few that have definite medicinal qualities or contain a bactericide. Despite great similarity among soaps, you can, by wrapping, advertising, and perfuming, create a soap with monopolistic properties—let us name it *Langorous Lady*. You can, by the laws of trademarking, forbid others to use your name and package design. You are the whole of the *Langorous Lady* industry, as any monopoly is the whole industry. If you succeed in presenting your product successfully, you will develop many loyal customers who would never think of using another soap, not even if you raise prices a little—to four for 98 cents from three for 69 cents. (It is often wise, when raising rices, to throw the housewife off balance by changing the size of the package and presenting her with problems of arithmetic that cannot easily be solved as she pushes her cart through the supermarket and tries to control her two runaway toddlers.) Your advertising has been so successful that you have created inelastic demand in many faithful buyers. Yet your position is not so strong as is the position of the manufacturer of the Mousoleum. Despite the success of your advertising and of the attractiveness of *Langorous Lady*'s wrapping and scent, many customers know that you are simply selling toilet soap, no better and no worse than dozens of other brands. Though you have differentiated your product, you have not created a strong monopoly.

Thus, under these new conceptions, one sees a quite different world from the world of perfectly competitive theory. It is a world of flimsy monopolies rather than of competing firms; for this reason, it lies in the sphere of monopolistic competition. And this applies not only to tangible trademarked goods but also to service establishments: chains of pagoda-shaped ice-cream palaces with cerise roofs along the highways; motels that display a coat of arms, with shield gules and vert. Most of the small amenities of retail shopping, such as air conditioning, soft carpets, and pretty salesgirls, are gestures in the direction of monopolistic competition.

Few things are undifferentiated. To find examples of products that are completely homogeneous and undifferentiated, one has almost to abandon the field of retail trade and go into the commodity markets outside the final consumer's ken—flour, hard winter, New York; corn, number 2 yellow, Chicago; zinc; lead; or silver. Only a few years ago, most vegetables were undifferentiated products. But now, with frozen peas and spinach and mashed potatoes in powdered form— branded and widely advertised—this last refuge of homogeneous commodities in retail trade is disappearing.

The demand curve as seen by the individual firm in a monopolistically competitive industry is not the horizontal line of the competitive industry as we portrayed it in Figure 6–4. It is instead like a monopolist's curve as seen in Figure 6–2, the average revenue, or demand, curve. This, in turn, is like the demand curve for a whole industry. The reason, to return to our example, is that your firm is the whole *Langorous Lady* soap industry. Whether you sell 1,000 or 3,000 cases a day may make quite a difference in the price you get. The price you set is your price, not the price set by others. If by a successful advertising campaign you have been able to identify your soap with sophistication, high fashion, and great wealth, if your soap is one of only two or three brands available in the shops of the Waldorf-Astoria or the first-class sections of luxury ocean liners, then you can charge a high price. It will be in your interest to produce and sell relatively little; for if you flood the market with it, the price will have to go down to the level that can be afforded by consumers of low income and less exclusiveness.

Outcomes under Imperfect Competition

It would be rather tedious to go into the geometry and further implications of this difference between the two demand curves, and probably unnecessary except for those who wish to go on to specialize in economic theory. There are, however, a few generalizations arising out of the theories of monopoly, monopolistic competition, and other forms of imperfect competition that are worth reporting. Perhaps the first and most interesting is that firms under imperfect competition produce less goods and sell them at higher prices than they would under perfect competition. But this statement requires qualification. Under the nomenclature of imperfectly competitive theory, an industry that is comprised of or is dominated by only a few large producers is named an "oligopoly"—that is, monopoly shared by a few. Now, in some industries the costs of erecting an optimum firm are so large, and the share of the market an optimum firm can supply so great, that maximum efficiency requires oligopoly. Studies made by engineers and economists have clearly demonstrated that the automobile industry would be pretty inefficient and costs high if each of 200 firms should supply one two-hundredth of the market. The firms would be too small, and their low volumes would not permit them to use the most efficient means of production. Steel and aluminum provide similar examples. In some industries, therefore, a few large sellers—that is, oligopolies—can produce more cheaply than would the hundreds of firms demanded by the model of perfect competition. Whether the cheaper costs of oligopolies are always passed on to the consumer is, however, an open question. Even when an oligopoly is necessary for maximum efficiency, it cannot be expected that its firms will produce at the lowest cost possible. Under imperfect competition the firm must curtail output before attaining lowest average cost in order to maximize profits. Therefore, while an oligopoly may be the most efficient producer, it will not in fact produce as efficiently as would be possible. Economics has not yet devised any solution to this unhappy situation, though attempts are being made to deal with this type of problem through public utility regulation.

A second generalization about imperfect competition follows directly from the first. Under conditions of imperfect competition, there will be less demand for factors of production than under conditions of perfect competition, simply because less production uses up less labor, material, and land. Less demand for factors of production will lead to lower prices paid for these factors. Thus, imperfect competition does not permit as efficient use of factors of production as does perfect competition. The inefficient use of land, labor, and capital is clearly seen in cases of monopsony (one buyer) and oligopsony (several buyers). When the market for a factor of production has only one or at most a few buyers in it, each buyer can have great control over the price paid and the quantity used of the factor. If the monopsonist or oligopsonist wishes to maximize profits, he must use his market power to pay this factor of production a lower price than would be paid under perfect competition. This lower price will normally result in less of the factor's being supplied; thus, less of it will be used. We can now see that when the imperfect competitor, whether producer or purchaser, acts to maximize his profits, he prevents the most efficient allocation of the factors of production.

A third generalization is that imperfect competition increases instability in our economy, causing business cycles to be more violent than they would be in a perfectly competitive economy. Under perfect competition, price fluctuation may be expected to influence economic actions in such a way as to maintain high levels of economic activity. If consumer spending would decline, the prices of consumer goods would also decline. These declines would tend to increase consumer purchases and so move the economy back to a high level of performance. Under imperfect competition, however, prices do not fluctuate freely. In fact, price rigidity seems to be a common characteristic of imperfect competition. This price rigidity weakens the power of the price mechanism to stabilize the economy; it thus contributes to economic fluctuations.

A fourth generalization is that the partially monopolistic position of many firms does not necessarily enhance their profits. There is a tendency for them to share limited amounts of business. Examples are small neighborhood barbershops or the four gasoline stations at an intersection.

Another interesting contribution of the theory of imperfect competition is that it has provided a place for explaining phenomena that were not explicable under perfect competition. Advertising is one. In the model of a perfectly competitive society, with equal knowledge of the market and of goods on both sides, it does not pay a seller to tell a buyer anything about the product. He already knows all there is to know. If a shampoo makes handsome suitors flock around a girl, she will know it, and it is a waste of money to tell her. But the theory of imperfect competition assumes that she is abysmally ignorant about the virues of the shampoo and concludes that, through advertising, the horizontal demand line of a firm can be changed to a downward-sloping line. Theory has at last found a place for the well-known fact that advertising creates or manipulates demand, that it is a cost based on rational calculation. The theory of imperfect competition clarifies at least two other phenomena that were not easy to explain under the earlier theory.

One of them is price wars, and the other is the sale of the same commodity at different prices. One hears of railroad wars in the past, of gasoline wars today, and of other kinds of price wars, but never of cauliflower or rhubarb wars. The reason is that many forms of agriculture are carried on under conditions that approximate pure competition reasonably well. But railroads and gasoline do not sell on perfect markets; hence the possibility of price wars. Cauliflower and rhubarb growers get no benefit, long run or otherwise, from underselling their neighbors; the price is fixed by the forces of competition, and they will sell their whole product to the commission merchant at that price, neither more nor less. On imperfect markets a price war may do somebody some good—or at least, somebody thinks good may come of it.

The selling of the same product for two prices is not uncommon in American business. Thus a great tire maker will stamp some of his tires with his own well-known name and will stamp others with a name selected by a mail-order house. The first tire will sell for a few dollars more than the other, although the two are exactly the same. To the consumer, of course, there will seem to be a difference, for he is not told that the two tires are identical. This, again, does not happen under perfect competition. No cabbage grower has ever been seen labeling half his cabbage *Jones's Cole Slaw King* and the other half *Smith's Corned Beef Companion.* For slightly different reasons, railroads have also charged two prices. They had only partial monopolies on long hauls and therefore sometimes engaged in price wars for runs like the one from New York to Chicago. But locally, they had complete monopolies; here, they charged more per mile—and of course, there were no price wars, for war requires two or more.

Game Theory

Dissident economic theory, which will be treated in a later chapter, has long called attention to the existence of conflict and disharmony in economic life. Standard theory has never paid much attention to this until fairly recently, when John von Neumann and Oskar Morgenstern in 1944 published a now famous work on the theory of games and economic behavior. This new theory of games, which has been taken up by others, goes far beyond the probability theory with which bridge players and poker players have at least a passing acquaintance—as, for example, that the odds are 11 to 1 against filling an inside straight. This new theory discriminates between such games as chess and poker. In the former, all moves are in the open; in the latter, secrecy and bluff are of the essence. Military men have found game theory to be useful in helping them to reason about who will attack whom first, the nature of "credible deterrents," and new concepts of strategy in the nuclear age. Like standard theory, which talks of maximizing income or profits or utility and minimizing losses or costs or disutility, this new theory also speaks of maximization, but of maximizing one or more things in a world in which others are trying to do the same, often at each other's expense. It is said that the theory was developed by close observation of the poker tables at Princeton, and that economists all over the country now justify their nights out at gambling by arguing that they are trying to make breakthroughs in game theory.

All of this is most interesting, and some of it is applicable to the problems of imperfect competition. One can think of a duopoly (only two sellers in a market) as being a game similar to two-handed poker.

Thus, game theory might shed more light on what the (virtual) duopoly of American Can and Continental Can is doing than would analysis of its curves of marginal revenue and marginal cost. Buyers of tobacco for cigarette companies are said to constitute an oligopsony. Here, several buyers have an interest in common—to buy cheaply. But they also have an opposing interest: Each would like to buy more cheaply than the other. And of course, on the other side, you have many sellers, not to mention the people who fix support prices in the Department of Agriculture, some of whom want the public welfare and others of whom want votes. This is the kind of problem to which game theory might address itself, though it is doubtful whether it is mature enough to provide a better analysis at this time than that provided by the experience, empirical knowledge, and intuition of people who know the tobacco business well.

In the study of imperfect competition, we detect an element of strategic or tactical thinking more nearly resembling war or warlike games. Oligopolists and duopolists are likely to ask themselves such questions as: What is my rival going to do next? If I cut (or raise) prices, will he follow me? How will his advertising counter my claim that my pills will give the fastest relief? If I put my product in a new and attractice container, can he find an even more attractive one? Thus, economic activity, instead of being the sort of naïve, aboveboard price-quality competition envisaged in standard 19th-century theory, becomes a kind of battle in which feints, bluffing, secrecy, scouting, and espionage play large roles. And this, of course, opens up rather wide vistas heretofore unexplored by standard theory.

Summary and Conclusions

In this chapter, we have further discussed the theory of value with special applications to imperfect competition. Under monopoly, we learned about the all-important marginal revenue and marginal cost curves, the intersection of which is supposed to guide all producers in determining their best output or size. We found that the theory of imperfect competition helps to describe our economy more realistically than the theory of perfect competition and helps to explain the ubiquitous phenomenon of advertising and the less common one of price wars. Economists, like social scientists and military men, see much hope in the newly developed theory of games. The problems of imperfect competition are among the problems that seem to get most illumination under the light shed by this new theory.

For several reasons, economists deplore the pervasiveness of imperfect competition. First of all, they believe that prices are higher than they would be under more nearly perfect competition. Secondly, they wonder whether the large advertising industry—mainstay of product differentiation—can lay claim to a desirable allocation of resources. The gross income of the industry, above $15 billion annually, is equal to that of each of several major industries, such as furniture and household appliances. Here, then, is a sizable amount of human effort that responds only feebly to the consumers' dollar votes. We have to take what we get or get nothing at all, as when we turn off the TV in despair. We get cardboard spaceships with our boxes of cereal; with dog food, we get miniature whisk brooms. Many of us do not want to be forced into buying such trash, for it is not free despite the fact that it is made to appear so. We must of course note the fact that some advertising, particularly some local advertising, is in the consumers' interest. We do want to know where and when the hockey game will be played tonight; what movies are in town; whether the supermarket has a weekend special on chuck roast. Worse even than the waste of advertising is the waste of the business cycle; and we can be pretty sure that imperfect competition contributes to economic instability.

In monopoly, it is quite clear that resources are not allocated as the consumer desires them to be. If, for example, our Mousoleum sells a million at the price of $15 but would sell five million under competition at $2, then less steel, labor, copper, land, and the like are devoted to Mousoleums than consumers would like, if offered a choice. When one contemplates the extent of imperfect competition and oligopoly in the monetary economies of the Western world, one wonders how truly the consumers' dollars really do register consumer preferences and guide resources into the employments that best reflect consumer desires. One almost has the feeling sometimes that consumers never really get a chance to choose what they want, but rather are asked to select only among things offered. Thus, their selection is negative—sometimes even a choice of the lesser evil than of the greater good. In any event, most economists believe that markets more nearly perfect than those we have would more closely register the true desires of consumers and would better allocate our scarce resources.

We have now gone through basic training in one aspect of price theory—the prices of consumers' goods. But price theory also extends to the incomes of human beings, that is, their wages and the interest, dividends, and rents they receive. The next chapter will discuss prices of this sort, for incomes are, as the reader will see, a kind of price, too.

QUESTIONS FOR REVIEW AND DISCUSSION

1. Define, in your own words, each of the following terms:
   a) Average total cost
   b) Average revenue
   c) Marginal cost
   d) Marginal revenue
   e) Monopoly
   f) Monopolistic competition
2. In what ways do monopolies impede the proper allocation of resources?
3. Examine advertisements in a daily newspaper and in a national magazine. Would you say that more information is contained in newspaper ads than in magazine ads? What new information of significance and credibility is contained in ads of liquor, beer, soft drinks, cigarettes, telephone companies, foods, autos, shampoos, spark plugs, storage batteries, cat and dog foods, perfume, watches, and radio and TV sets?
4. How much freedom does a competitive firm have in deciding how much will produce, what method of production it will use, and what price it can charge? What effect do the constraints on a competitive firm have upon the efficient operation of an economy?
5. Answer question 4 with respect to a monopoly.
6. Point out differences among oligopoly, monopoly, and monopolistic competition. Could all, under certain conditions, lead to a socially desirable allocation of resources?
7. What are oligopsony and monopsony? Have you encountered any real-life examples of either?
8. Given the following information about the demand for a monopolist's product and his costs of production, determine:

a) The quantity he should produce to maximize profits
b) The price he should charge for his product
c) The monopoly profit he should attain

Use diagrams as well as tables to obtain your results.

Price	Quantity Demanded	Total Costs of Production
$6	100	$ 650
5	200	800
4	300	1000
3	400	1250
2	500	1600
1	600	2100

Chapter 7

DISTRIBUTION:
FACTS AND THEORY

Introduction

The second great topic of economic analysis under its theory of value is the distribution of income. This is a major subject, for, as we saw in Chapter 1, a fundamental concern of economics is the answer to this question: Who gets what? After the yachts and baked beans and swimming pools and nutcrackers have been produced, we must find out how they are apportioned. Obviously, the people with the largest number of dollars at their command normally get the largest and best share of the product. Thus, our problem is, in a sense, a study of why Leonard Billingham de Noyer gets a six-figure income, while Tony gets $973 a year. But it is not quite that, for, as revealed in Chapter 5, economic science does not put definite price tags on goods or on the worth of a service. It can only shed light on what considerations enter into the making of prices.

Distribution is one of the thorniest subjects in the world. For thousands of years the human race has been asking why some people wear silks and feed on filet mignon while others have only coarse smocks and crusts of bread. It is the subject of some of our better known and more sardonic phrases:

> To him that hath shall be given.
>
> The rich get richer, and the poor get poorer.
>
> When Adam delved and Eve span,
> Who was then the gentleman?

Differences in income are used to fan the flames of class hatred. Office rivalry, jealousy, and envy often turn on differences of earnings. One of our first speculations about a new acquaintance is whether his income is high, low, or average. We think a very great deal about the distribution of income, though we rarely use those words.

What Statistics Reveal

Distribution can be studied in two ways, statistically and theoretically. The first method tells us what the facts are; the second seeks to explain the facts. Statistical study can tell us at least two important and quite different things: (1) what income receivers actually get and (2) what certain selected categories of income receivers get by comparison with others. Let us look into each of the two sets of facts before we go on to theoretical explanations.

If we consider families in households as the income-receiving units, we can summarize the distribution of income in the United States in Table 7–1.

TABLE 7–1*
MONEY INCOME, PERCENT DISTRIBUTION OF FAMILIES IN
HOUSEHOLDS BY INCOME LEVEL, 1964

Family Income	Percentage of Families in Each Class
$ 0–$ 2,999	18
3,000– 4,999	17
5,000– 9,999	43
10,000– 14,999	16
15,000 and over	6
	100

* Adapted from *Statistical Abstract of the United States*, 1966, p. 316.

The first class, from $0 to $2,999, was chosen because this is the class of undeniable poverty, an issue that will be discussed in a later chapter. We shall be more precise in that chapter, but we can foresee at this point that nearly one fifth of all American families lies close to the poverty zone. Looking at the other end of the scale, we find that only six families out of 100 live in the bracket of $15,000 and above. Although a family of four earning the minimum figure in the bracket may be considered affluent enough, even these families must live within relatively narrow bounds. They may be able to do some of the things listed below, but they cannot do all of them after paying income taxes and meeting the ordinary expenses of life such as food, clothing, routine medical care, modest recreation, and insurance:

Live in a $30,000 house.

Send two children to college at the same time.

Own and run two cars.

Pay for orthodontia for one teen-ager and acne treatment for the other.

Take a trip to Europe (or similar extended travel) every three years, tourist class.

Own and operate a swimming pool.

Drink four martinis before dinner (two for each adult).

Belong to the country club.

Engage seriously but modestly in a sport (golf, fishing, boating, mountain climbing, etc.).

An interesting and much-used way of representing the distribution of income graphically is through the Lorenz curve. If the distribution of income were absolutely equal, all the spending units (families and unattached individuals) would get the same amount of money; in that event, 10 percent of the spending units would get 10 percent of the total income, 20 percent of the units would get 20 percent, 30 percent would get 30 percent, and so on. This could be plotted as in Figure 7–1, and the line labeled "equal" would represent this situation. When, however, incomes are unequal, the two per-

FIGURE 7–1

LORENZ CURVE SHOWING DISTRIBUTION OF U.S. INCOME, 1964

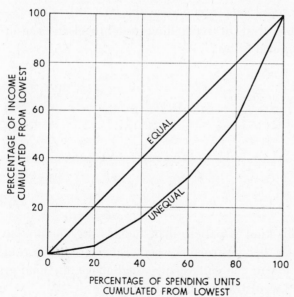

PERCENTAGE OF SPENDING UNITS
CUMULATED FROM LOWEST

centages vary: The lowest 10 percent of the spending units may get less than 1 percent of the income, and the highest 10th may get 26 percent of the whole. Plotting the actual figures cumulatively gives us a bent line, like the line marked "unequal" in Figure 7-1. The two lines together form a bow; and the wider the bow, the greater the inequality.

The Lorenz curve suggests no standards to help us evaluate the facts that it reveals. Very few sane people in the world, whether conservative, liberal, communist, or socialist, advocate absolute equality of income. What many people do advocate is a more nearly equal distribution of income—one still based on differences in ability or productivity, or some other standard that would commend itself to persons holding the usual human values. We do believe that some people are more equal than others—to use George Orwell's phrase— but we have no standard for judging exactly how much they should be more equal. This is, of course, a question of values and ethics and is, in some senses, outside the realm of economics. However, statistics applied to economics does yield relevant facts which may be used to inform an ethical judgment.

A variety of biological traits arrange themselves according to a common pattern. The height of full-grown men within the same culture, the weight of summer squash selected at random from the same species and geographic area, the IQ's of teen-agers—these and countless other traits of living things order themselves according to the scheme suggested below:

Categories	Percent of Cases Measured
Small	5
Below average	20
Average	50
Above average	20
Large	5
	100

It is this kind of pattern that students presumably have in mind when they ask their instructors whether they are being graded "on the curve." Following the pattern suggested above, the final grades in an economics class of 100 might be as follows:

Grades	Number of Students
A	5
B	20
C	50
D	20
E (failures)	5
	100

The "curve" in question would be a smoothed curve similar to the one based on the figures given above. If thousands of cases and a larger number of classes (A, A—, B+, B, B—, C+, etc.) were used, the curve would resemble the normal curve of error shown in Figure 7–2. The curve is bell-shaped and possesses bilateral symmetry. So many natural phenomena were observed to conform to this curve that in the latter part of the 19th century, conformity was all but elevated to a natural law. We do not now believe that this is the only way in which things order themselves in nature, but it still serves as a norm for a wide variety of phenomena.

FIGURE 7–2

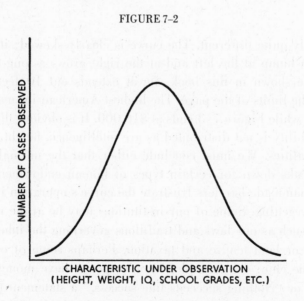

CHARACTERISTIC UNDER OBSERVATION
(HEIGHT, WEIGHT, IQ, SCHOOL GRADES, ETC.)

If, now, we plot actual family income in the United States against number of families receiving a certain income (Figure 7–3), we get a curve similar to the normal curve of error—at first blush. But

FIGURE 7–3*

DISTRIBUTION OF FAMILY PERSONAL INCOME, 1950

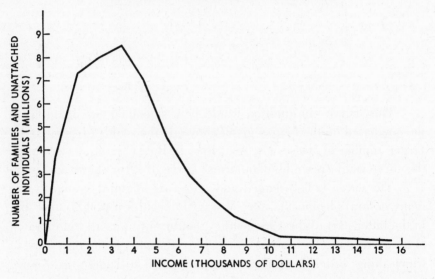

* Adapted from material contained in F. C. Mills, *Introduction to Statistics* (New York: Henry Holt & Co., Inc., 1956), p. 60.

it is really quite different. The curve is clearly skewed; it suddenly rises to a hump at the left and at the right grows a long tail which cannot be shown in this book, for it extends out 10 feet or more beyond the limits of the page. The highest American income is in the millions, while Figure 7–3 ends at $16,000. It is obvious that income-getting ability is not distributed as are intelligence, height, and most other qualities. We must conclude either that the normal curve of error breaks down for certain types of human endowments or that certain man-made barriers frustrate the curve's operation in the field of money getting. Some of our institutions may be at the root of the trouble, such as our laws and traditions governing the inheritance of property or land tenure and taxation. Perhaps some of our adages supply the clue; for example, "You've got to have money to make money," or "Nothing succeeds like success," a statement that draws attention to a happy upward spiral in individual affairs but also suggests an unhappy downward spiral if one gets started off on the wrong foot.

But the real point to stress about the actual curve (Figure 7–3) and the normal curve (Figure 7–2) is that when economists talk about the virtue of unequal incomes at the same time that they talk of the benefits of greater equality, they probably mean that they would like to see American incomes conform more closely to the normal curve than they do—no 10-foot tails and a less sudden rise to a hump at the left.

Distribution of Income by Productive Shares

As readers already know from the discussion in Chapter 4 on the theory of production, standard economists recognize four factors of production—land, labor, capital, and entrepreneurship. Since distribution is, in standard theory, the converse of production, it follows that there are four—and only four—income streams, namely, rent, wages, interest, and profits. Any income may be classified under one of these four headings. Many incomes are mixed, of course, and for both accounting and economic purposes should be broken down into their elements. Jones may, for example, have to report on his income tax form a total income of $18,000 annually. Of this, $15,000 may be wages (salary) as a G.E. executive, $1,000 rent on a farm inherited from his grandfather, $1,000 profit in the form of dividends on $25,000 worth of stock, and another $1,000 interest on savings and loan accounts. If, in addition, he should receive royalties on books or patents, these would be wages.

The question we seek to answer in this section is: How much does each productive agent get? Or to put it differently, what share of the national income goes to land and what share to labor, to capital, to entrepreneurship? Well, the largest share quite obviously goes to labor, since so many income receivers labor in some way or other. The remaining three incomes are often classed together, perhaps a bit illogically, as "property incomes"—illogical because the entrepreneurial function is really a special kind of labor. However, the so-called "property incomes" taken together add up to something considerably less than the wage total.

To give exact figures on these magnitudes is impossible. Statistics are indeed published by the government that approximate the sizes of our four categories, but they do not quite follow the economists' categories. Ingenious individuals have derived the desired figures from several sources and have come up with various estimates. We can perhaps settle for the following estimate to cover recent years: Wages and salaries account for three fourths of the national income; much of what remains is profit; rent and interest together account for less than 5 percent.

One rather remarkable thing about the above figures is that the ratios of three quarters for labor income and one quarter for property income have seemingly remained fairly constant for many years. There have, however, been intragroup shifts. Apparently, rents and interest have lost to profits; and within the labor category the blue-collar worker has gained, per employee, at the expense of the white-collar worker.

What Theory Reveals: Supply and Demand

Leaving the facts behind, we now proceed to the theory of distribution. The theory underlying distribution is twofold. First, the factor's reward is equivalent to his price, that is, to the resultant of the forces of supply and demand. To put this a little differently, each income or reward is looked upon as a price; and the price of each factor, like the prices of consumers' goods studied in the last two chapters, is, under competition, fixed by supply and demand. Land in Manhattan is in greater demand and in relatively shorter supply than in Death Valley; hence the price is higher and the landowner's income greater. The second part of the theory holds that there is a relationship between what each factor receives and his product at the margin. This needs explanation and will be discussed more fully in the next section. These two parts are not in conflict. On the contrary, they are complementary; each supports the other. One can join them into a single statement by saying that under perfect competition the forces of supply and demand will operate to make any producer's income equal to his marginal product (expressed in money).

The supply-and-demand theory is the easier one to explain and understand. Let us start with that one. As we have already learned, to speak of "the interaction of the forces of supply and demand" is not enough when we study price. We must examine both demand and supply and understand more clearly how they interact. We now proceed to examine demand, and then supply, in relation to the factors of production.

The demand for land, labor, and capital is a special kind of demand; or rather, the demand exists only in a special group of the population, namely, the managers or the entrepreneurial group. In preceding chapters, we studied everybody's demand for an infinity of things that could be used up directly (food) or worn out (shoes), or that agreeably stimulated the senses (perfume or fireworks). Here, we study the demand of a few people for a very few categories—land, labor, and capital. The demanders are the managers or entrepreneurs. It is true that many of us who are not entrepreneurs are in the market for the labor of servants or for land to build our own houses on; but it will make things easier if we forget about that, because our demand as consumers for factors of production is small compared with the demand of entrepreneurs. We shall think only of the demand of factory owners, store owners, bankers, and the like for the land, labor, and capital used strictly for business purposes. We should, however, realize that many of us who are not ordinarily entrepreneurs may have our entrepreneurial moments. Many demure spinster schoolmarms think about their stocks and bonds as shrewdly as the most hardened businessman. A large, frequently overlooked class of entrepreneurs is the farming class. When all is said and done, however, the group of demanders on whom we focus our interest in this chapter is a much smaller group of demanders than that of preceding chapters.

The demand for land, labor, and capital is a derived rather than a direct demand. We want bananas because they are nutritious and taste good. The average businessman or entrepreneur wants workers or machines not for such reasons, but because workers and machines are needed to produce things that they can sell to us. Many of us stop eating bananas only when some sort of inner voice tells us that to eat more might have undesirable consequences. Entrepreneurs never stop hiring workers for this simple biological reason or because workers no longer please them or because it would be more fun to use their money on some other factor of production. The factory owner stops hiring workers and renting land and buying capital largely because he thinks that the demand for his product does not warrant an expanded output. Although the individual producer stops hiring land, labor, and capital at the point at which *MC* equals *MR*, as we saw in the preceding chapter, all the producers together in a given industry stop hiring the factors of production when the demand for their product, at a given price, has been met. The amounts bought are always related to the amount of the finished product that the consuming public will and can absorb, or at least that entrepreneurs think will be absorbed.

The amounts bought are also related to the relative prices of the factor of production. Within limits, each agent of production may be used in place of the others. The ground for an airport may be leveled as in China during World War II with shovels, baskets to carry earth in, and swarms of unskilled laborers; or as in this country, with bulldozers, steam shovels, trucks, and relatively few workers, most of them highly skilled. Either way may be cheap or dear, depending on many things, mainly prices. But what should be especially noted is that labor and capital are often interchangeable. The same thing applies to land. If land is cheap, a thousand-bushel wheat crop may be grown on 100 acres without much use of fertilizer or entrepreneurial skill or labor. If land is dear, fertilizer, tender care, and scientific knowledge will be used to grow the same crop on one third the acreage; that is to say, managerial skill, labor, and capital are substitutes for land. In short, demand for one factor of production may often be converted, if its price is too high, into demand for another.

Entrepreneurs will ever be watchful to keep down costs; and in doing this, they will constantly be comparing the usefulness to them of less labor, more capital; more land, less capital. This is partly a technological question, of course, for technology often dictates the only reasonable combination of the factors of production. A bus or truck, for example, has one driver's seat, one steering wheel, and one set of pedals; three drivers operating at the same time would wreck the vehicle. But technological considerations are not always the determining ones. More often, the determining factor is purely economic: Is it cheaper to use more men than additional machines, or more fertilizer than additional acres?

There are even greater differences between consumers' goods and the factors of production on the supply side than on the demand side. If peole want more consumer goods and are willing to pay more for them, the forces underlying supply will quickly respond by increasing their amount. Increased price does not, however, as certainly call forth all the factors of production.

The quantity of land, for instance, is not appreciably increased by high prices; it is fixed. Some land can be "made" or redeemed by irrigation, filling-in, pushing back the sea with dikes, and so forth.

Improved transportation may bring some land nearer a given center and may relieve population pressure on that center. Still other things can be done; but speaking broadly and strictly, an increased demand (or price) does not call forth *new* land in appreciable quantity. It may of course call forth new sellers of old land, but that is something else. Other important gifts of nature, like waterfalls, caverns, and magnificent scenery, are similarly fixed in quantity. Thus the rents paid for the use of land are more vigorously affected by the state of demand than by variations in supply. This explains why, when demand improves, fortunes can be made out of relatively small parcels. There is no way of increasing the land area of Manhattan Island, and that is why land values there have not merely gone up—they have become fantastic. On the other hand, inability to shrink the amount of land available locally when demand falls helps to explain why families that once were rich can now be land-poor.

Theory of Distribution: Marginal Productivity

We have intimated that productivity is at the basis of demand for the factors of production. But of course, the demand is not for free-floating productivity or productivity run wild. No bakery would long employ a baker who, having a passion for wedding cakes, insisted on working half the night every night, baking six-story nuptial confections in quantitites far beyond the number that customers might reasonably be expected to buy. This would be a waste of flour, sugar, fuel, and labor. The productivity desired is not physical productivity, but value productivity: How much can he add to the income of the firm? In other words, not how many tons or dozen or reams, but how many dollars does the factor add to the income? Obviously, no entrepreneur will pay $1,000 for units of land, labor, or capital unless he expects to get back at least $1,000.

This fact takes us to the marginal value productivity theory of distribution. (Actually, the phrase "marginal revenue productivity" is more commonly used than "marginal value productivity"; we shall hereafter use the former, more generally accepted phrase.) The theory was first put forward by John Bates Clark, an American, at the turn of the century. It can be applied to any factor of production but is usually demonstrated through its applicability to labor's share of the national income. It is quite abstract in the sense that a distressingly large number of unreal assumptions have to be made, but it has dominated the scene for some 60 years.

To comprehend the theory, it will help us to imagine that all the productive equipment of a nation can somehow be concentrated in one vast factory and farm—a single, giant workplace which has the magic ability to expand and contract in conformity with the number of workmen on the job. We must also imagine that we are concerned with a general wage rate—some sort of average, let us say—and that we are not concerned with the large differences between the wages of the aristocratic toolmakers and the lowly sweepers. Let us, in this particular case, assume a newly created nation of five million souls which has not yet worked out exactly what it wants from its economic system and which, by a method of trial and error, is trying to determine its wants —how many goods it wants, how much leisure, how many employed, and so forth.

During the first week of trial, two million men and women are sent to work in the factory-farm, and they produce a certain product at a certain value. But the nation finds that the quantity is not quite great enough; and the next week, they add a batch of 200,000 workmen. This new batch—taken in isolation—may produce less per capita than did the first swarm of two million, because of the operation of the law of diminishing returns. Indeed, this diminution in production may have begun even before. Had we divided the original two million into batches of 200,000, each might very well have produced less than the preceding batch. Figure 7–4 represents this situation. Each slender rectangle symbolizes the yearly revenue product of 200,000 workers. Each value rectangle is shorter than the preceding one, for we assume here that diminishing returns began immediately (actually, the second 10,000 may have produced more than the first 10,000, but we can disregard this). At 2.2 million workers the society is satisfied and stops adding them.

The question now is: What does the working class get as its average wage? According to Clark's theory, in a competitive society with institutions like ours the worker gets his "product," that is, the share of the total product attributable to his efforts. In Figure 7–4 the last worker is paid an amount equal to the height of his production rectangle—the last one, which stands at a height of $3,000—meaning

FIGURE 7–4

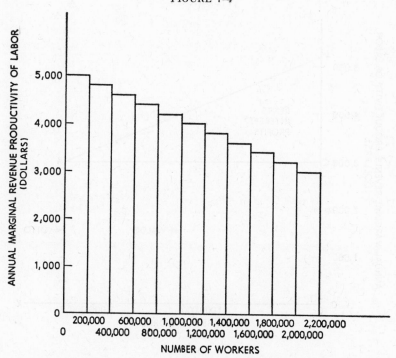

NUMBER OF WORKERS

a wage of $3,000 a year. But what about other workers, those who stand at the left of the last batch of workers and whose production rectangles go up as high as $5,000? Is each batch of 200,000 workers paid a different wage? The answer from experience is no; and to understand why this is so, we must look into Clark's theory a little more closely. Actually, Clark did not quite say that each worker gets his product. What he really said was that each worker got a wage equal to labor's marginal revenue product.

To understand better what this means, we must draw a slightly different figure, Figure 7–5. This figure is derived directly from Figure 7–4. The tops of the rectangles are connected by a line, and then the rectangles themselves are knocked out. Any line perpendicular to OX and stopping at AY may be thought of as representing a worker and his product. Thus the vertical line near the middle of the diagram symbolizes Waldo, whose product is $4,000. If a million more employees are hired after Waldo—that is, if the society goes on hiring successive batches until we get to Otto—the product of addi-

FIGURE 7-5

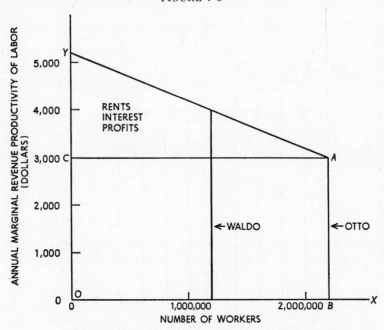

tional workers declines. Thus, if 2.2 million workers are employed, Otto produces relatively little and therefore can be paid relatively little—only $3,000. But if Otto is paid only $3,000, then Waldo will also be paid only $3,000, for they are interchangeable. And what is true of Waldo is true of all employees; all are substitutable for Otto, and are paid, as he is, only labor's marginal product—that is, Otto's product. The rectangle *OBAC* represents the total wage bill of the society. This leaves to landlords, capital, and entrepreneurship the triangle *CYA*. And to repeat, the wages of each workman are equal to the marginal (last) wage of $3,000.

It may seem unfair that Waldo should get only as much as Otto. The diagram suggests that Waldo produces much more than Otto and that he should get more. But Waldo and Otto—and anybody else in the working force—are assumed to be equivalent to one another in native ability, industriousness, and so forth. The only circumstance in which Waldo would get a wage equal to the height of his line is if the whole society had decided to stop producing when Waldo was added to the working force. At that point the working force would have been a very small one; and since the supply would have been small, wages would have been high. But because more than two million people went to work, the supply was enlarged, and wages for all went down.

As has been intimated just above and earlier in the chapter, this marginal revenue productivity theory is really a dressed-up supply-and-demand theory, sketching out how supply and demand operate. It can be made to say that if the number of workers is large relative to demand, the wage will be low—as measured by Otto. If the number offering to work is small, wages will be higher—as measured by Waldo.

The marginal revenue productivity theory of wages explains what happens under competition. There are, obviously, imperfectly competitive conditions in markets for the factors of production just as there are in markets for consumers' goods; and the theory can be adapted to meet such situations. Everybody knows that some unions, at least, exert power akin to monopoly power. On the buyer's side, employers sometimes constitute monopsonies, duopsonies, or oligopsonies. Sometimes, there is only one employer in an area; sometimes, two who exchange wage rate information; and sometimes, many come together in associations the main concern of which is the industrywide or areawide wage bargain. It is assumed that under such conditions, wages may be above or below the competitive wage.

Further Considerations: Land, Capital

It was awkward enough to explain the marginal productivity theory when applied to the rewards of labor; it would be even more awkward to explain how it applies to the rewards of land and capital —rent and interest—but the basic idea is the same and is applicable to these two factors of production as well. Both land and capital are, like labor, productive. Standard economic theory holds that land and capital are rewarded in accordance with their marginal revenue productivity. And this is equivalent to the statement that their value or reward depends on the forces of supply and demand. There are, however, a few special twists in the analysis of incomes from land and capital that justify additional observations.

Rent is the income arising out of a gift of nature, and the income goes to its owner. Thus a strict use of economic terms would forbid us to say, "I rented a rowboat" or "We rented a cabin in Maine last summer." Boats and houses are not gifts of nature. Sometimes, economists use the words "economic rent" or "pure rent" to emphasize that they are not talking about the fee paid for the temporary use of a man-made good.

One can clarify one's concept of rent if one thinks of two farms, equal in size, in proximity to market, and in every other way except productivity. Even the amount of labor and capital used and the entrepreneurial skill applied are the same. But because of the inherently different qualities of the soil, one produces 500 bushels of wheat more than the other. In that event the difference in rent between the two farms would reflect the money equivalent of 500 bushels of wheat. Of course, the landlord, not the farmer, gets this money in a society that sanctions the private ownership of land.

The pure theory of rent may also be clarified if one thinks of land as being characterized by a perfectly inelastic supply curve, that is, by a vertical straight line. This means that the amount of land can be neither increased nor decreased whether rents be high or low. This obviously is quite different from anything we have learned about commodities for the consumer. If the demand for paper napkins should suddenly rise, prices would rise, and this would call forth an increased quantity. But the supply of land cannot be increased or diminished[1] by change of demand or price. This suggests the reason for skyscrapers in the downtown areas in big cities and also why skyscrapers in a sparsely settled community would be uneconomic.

A basic concept in rent theory is that high rents do not cause high prices; low rents do not cause low prices. Causality runs the other way. Low prices cause low rents; high prices cause high rents. If wheat sells at $1 a bushel, rents will be lower than if wheat sells at $2. These observations lead to the interesting paradox that rent is not a cost to the society as a whole, though it is a cost to the individual firm or entrepreneur. If a farmer grows wheat and pays $1,000 annual rent—the economically proper rent for his land—he looks on the $1,000 as a cost. But from the viewpoint of the entire society, rent is

---

[1] Pure theory rules out of consideration those small additions or subtractions of land that, in fact, can be made. Through irrigation and drainage, we have increased the supply of habitable and arable land, and through erosion lost some of it. But the assumption is made that such changes in supply are minimal.

not a cost. To demonstrate the point, let us take another farmer who cultivates such poor land that his rent is zero—or virtually zero, a token payment of $10 annually. The society's demand and the economy's capacity to supply it have already set the price of wheat at $2 a bushel, and this price is sufficient to encourage our rent-free farmer to grow wheat. His yield is only 5 bushels an acre. This no-rent wheat sells for $2, as does all other wheat. Another farmer elsewhere, using the same amount of capital and labor and satisfied with the same profit, can grow 30 bushels an acre. The price for his wheat is also $2. This farmer on more fertile ground will gross a higher income than the rent-free farmer, but he must pay rent. No landlord would allow such fertile land to stay in a tenant's hands rent-free. The landlord is the one who is able to collect, in the form of rent, the difference between the two farmers' net incomes. Buyers still pay $2 a bushel, for there has been no change in the supply-demand relations. The payment of rent is a private transaction between farmer and landowner; the buyer of wheat was not affected.

This should warn us to look with a skeptical eye on those merchants who invite us to come to their out-of-the-way stores for bargains because they operate in low-rent areas. There may be occasional truth in this, but the great supermarkets and cut-rate drugstores and Macy's and Gimbel's operate mostly in high-rent areas. Most things can be bought as cheaply or even more cheaply on Fifth Avenue in New York as on Main Street in a dreary hamlet of 200 souls. Rent in the village is low, but from a mercantile viewpoint the land is unproductive; few people pass by to make purchases.

Now, this theorem about rent is of interest primarily in a society that recognizes the private ownership of land. If the government owned all the land, it could and probably would charge rent; but this rent, instead of going to the private incomes of landlords, would presumably go into the general funds of the government, as taxes do. We may assume that other taxes in such a society would then be lower, since land rents (pure rent, economic rent) would run into a pretty sum. This idea underlies the once-popular doctrines of the American reformer, Henry George (1839–97). He proposed that all rental income be taxed away from the landlord; the proceeds from this tax alone would, he thought wrongly, be sufficient to run the government. Under the "single-tax" slogan, he appealed to a wide audience.

One final item: Rent may, by extension, he thought of as any gift of nature, even a personal gift, such as Joan Baez's ability to charm audiences. Let us assume that she would sing and record for us if her income were only $7,000 a year; she'd rather sing at this wage than sell insurance or run a deluxe motel. But we shower her with many thousands a year. The difference between what is required to call forth her song and what she actually gets is rent, an unnecessary payment for the gift with which she has been graced.

The reward to capital, because of its special nature, also requires a few observations. Economists are always insisting, quite properly, that capital consists of things like trucks, factories, and materials such as raw cotton waiting to be made into cloth, or strawberries into jam. (Such items are productive and therefore yield income.) And yet the income from capital is named interest, which we all think of as a percentage paid for the use of loanable funds. Perhaps one reason for the apparent lack of correspondence between capital and the name of its reward is that capital, being more heterogeneous than land or labor, seeks a common denominator. It is more convenient to speak of a 5 percent reward to the owner of $1 million than to speak of the marginal revenue product of lathes, hydraulic presses, looms, bottle-capping machines, and strawberries—all worth $1 million. Another reason is that physical, tangible capital is built up through loans of money. An expanding airline does not borrow two new airplanes; it borrows $20 million with which to buy two new airplanes. To confuse things still further, the personal experience that most of us have with interest payment revolves around a consumer's good rather than a capital good. Pop borrows money from the bank to buy the family car, which is not capital. We ran into the same problem when we studied the wages of labor. Our butlers, household cooks, and maids are not productive in the same sense that Otto and Waldo were. Obviously, there is a sympathetic relationship between the wages of labor, whether employed by an entrepreneur or by a family for personal service; obviously, too, there is a similarly sympathetic relationship between interest rates, whether the loan was made to an entrepreneur for a power shovel or to a merry couple that wants to throw a $1,000 party on its 10th anniversary. But in the case of both interest and wages, it will help us to understand the argument of standard eco-

nomic theory if we think primarily of the entrepreneur's demand and
neglect the consumer's demand.

The origin of capital is savings. If we ate up the whole crop of
strawberries in the spring, there would be no strawberry jam for our
breakfast biscuits in December. If nobody were prepared to suspend
his consumption of steel in the form of motorboats, autos, refrigerators, stoves, and the like, we would be short of steel for ocean liners,
railroad equipment, lathes, and all other goods belonging in that vast
category of durable productive equipment which forms part of our
capital endowment. Somebody has to save at some point, and one may
look on this saving either as not eating four boxes of strawberries in
season or as not spending $2, the price of the strawberries. Again, by
deciding that we can get along as a one-car rather than a two-car
family, we not only save money but also liberate a certain quantity of
steel that somebody else can put into a punch press or diesel locomotive. Until about 50 years ago, economists were so much impressed
by this fact that interest was frequently looked upon as a sort of
reward for abstinence.

For many people, saving is rather automatic and would be
engaged in even if there were smaller rewards than are now available,
or even no reward at all, simply because most of us who can afford it
want to build up funds for our old age, for a rainy day, or for the
education of our children. As we shall see more clearly in the next
chapter, the amount saved in any society seems to be more closely
related to the income of the society than to the interest rate, and the
equality between the amount saved and the amount invested is established by changes in income.

Most of us who save are not true investors; we do not directly
convert our savings into tangible capital. Instead, we put our money
into banks, insurance companies, and building and loan associations.
These institutions try to complete the total act of investment by
lending the money to actual entrepreneurs. In young or underdeveloped countries, such as India, Mexico, or the United States in frontier
days, the rate of interest is high; in older, rich nations which already
have a vast amount of capital, interest rates are low.

The ordinary man may find it hard to accept the idea that
interest depends on marginal revenue productivity and is likely to say

that interest is some sort of reward for risk; and for proof, he may offer as evidence the fact that risky loans, such as those made to obscure citizens by small loan companies, bear necessarily high interest rates, whereas loans made to General Motors have lower rates. This is true, but economists believe that even the safest loans—for example, those made to the United States government—must bear a "pure" rate of interest, say 2½ percent. As for the small loan company that lends at 30 percent, the economist would say that 2½ percent is still pure interest; the remaining 27½ percent is insurance for safety. In short, in many rates of interest as quoted, only part is pure interest; the rest is not interest at all, but some sort of insurance against default or a charge for the expenses of bookkeeping and collecting.

Profits

The last share, and in some ways the most difficult to analyze, is profit—the entrepreneur's reward. First of all, we must, as in the case of rent and interest, distinguish between pure profit (if any) and apparent profit. Let us say that Jenkins runs a prosperous little hardware store and averages $12,000 a year as net income from his business. Is this all profit? Probably not. Let us assume that he owns the building and land and that they are worth $100,000. Now, Jenkins could give up his hardware store, its headaches and responsibilities and risks, and take a cushy government job at $7,000 a year. Then he could rent out his $100,000 piece of property and get a net income of $5,000 from it. With these two incomes, totaling $12,000, he would be as well off in money as if he were running the store. He would not be his own boss; but in most other ways, things would be easier for him than when he ran his shop. Jenkins, as a storekeeper, never made any profit. To make a profit, he would have had to make more than $12,000 a year when he was an entrepreneur. Had he made $14,000 in the store and were he able to get only $12,000 by hiring his person and renting his property, then and only then would he have made a profit—in this case, $2,000. Thus, we must define profit as a return which an entrepreneur receives over and above the incomes he might get from alternative employments of his land, labor, and capital. And this is a fancy way of saying that profit is something beyond wages, rent, and interest. Viewed in this light, it is quite believable that a majority of our entrepreneurs make no profits at all. The small farmers, the little storekeepers, the owners of hot-dog stands—any one of them could probably do as well or better if he took a job and invested his money in bonds and blue-chip stocks.

But there are profits, of course. There is income above and beyond the income attributable to the wages of a manager, the rent on his land, and the interest on his capital. What is this payment for, and how does it depend on supply and demand? Economists do not, as a matter of fact, have a very good theory of profits, and supply-and-demand analysis does not help very much. Have you ever heard of anybody's demanding entrepreneurs or of somebody's increasing or decreasing the supply of them? Even schools of business do not turn out entrepreneurs as medical schools turn out physicians or law schools lawyers. Business school graduates usually take jobs as business employees; few become entrepreneurs.

Profits in a dynamic and competitive society are often thought of as the rewards for handling uncertainty with success, for making innovations that end prosperously, and for assuming uninsurable risks (an uninsurable risk is unlike the risk of fire, personal loss from which may be avoided by fire insurance). This is not a very convincing argument to all economists, since every group in the community—worker, landlord, capitalist, and consumer—assumes uninsurable risks and gains or loses by life's uncertainties. Technological change threw harness makers out of work when autos took over. It can of course be argued that they were partly entrepreneurs, at least insofar as they made some original choice of vocation, and that, like many others, they were unsuccessful entrepreneurs and paid a penalty. But this seems to be stretching definitions. We might as well say that a bride was a successful entrepreneur because her silver anniversary finds her still with her doting husband, two lovely cars, and two lovely grandchildren; she might have turned out to be a lonely, impoverished widow.

But to return: Profits may also arise from successful monopolizing. This immediately takes us out of the basic competitive model of standard economic theory. Monopoly is contrary to our sense of economic ethics, and monopoly profit must be considered an unjustifiable or exploitative income. And then there are windfall profits. The

English often use as an example the draper who happens to have on hand a large consignment of black cloth when the sudden death of the sovereign unexpectedly plunges the nation into a period of mourning. The price of black cloth goes up, of course, at such a time, and the draper is all set to make his windfall profits. Such profits are obviously transient and infrequent.

In a static competitive society, theory deduces that profits in the long run do not exist. In such a society, there is no risk, uncertainty, or innovation, since it is in equilibrium—which in this context means that you cannot find a better job or investment than you already have. Thus, profit in a competitive economy seems to make its appearance only under dynamic conditions; and yet something must be paid under all circumstances to induce a person to take on the responsibilities of entrepreneurship, something beyond the wage he would get doing almost exactly the same job for somebody else. Whatever that sum is might be named normal profit, and transient or windfall profit above this sum might be named abnormal profit. Economists are not, in their writings, very consistent about separating these two concepts, perhaps partly because profit theory is a bit hazy anyhow. One professor we know always ends his lectures on profit as follows: "Ladies and gentlemen, if I have been able to confuse you, then I have succeeded in clearly explaining the modern theory of profit."

Businessmen often complain that too many people, including academic economists, think of "profit" as a dirty word. As far as academic economists are concerned, this is not a just accusation. In a society like ours, normal profits are absolutely necessary to supply us with the talent needed to direct an enterprise. Abnormal profits are also needed, at least temporarily, to attract resources from areas in which they are not needed or wanted to areas in which they are. If jai alai should suddenly excite the widespread and almost passionate interest that basketball and bowling have aroused in recent years, a few fortunes might quickly be made by those on the ground floor. The continued though temporary opportunities to make big money would facilitate the transfer of resources from products and services that consumers want less to those they want more—in this case, jai alai. When the transfer has been made and a jai alai equilibrium established, the function of abnormal profit making is terminated, and entrepreneurs in this field should be making only normal profits.

Economists are, to be sure, dubious about the economic usefulness of other kinds of profits. Though some forms of speculation have
economic value, some do not; and speculation which is close to mere
gambling or which is based on rigging the market or spreading false
information is of no aid to increased production, price stability, or
full employment, three values supported by most economists. The
superprofits of monopoly or quasi monopoly are also frowned upon
by economists as inhibiting the best use of resources. It is really
monopoly, quasi monopoly, and gambling that are the dirty words in
the economists' lexicon; profit is not one of them.

Summary

In our society, we settle the thorny question of who gets what by
paying monetary incomes to the factors of production. These incomes
are the prices paid to the owners of land and capital, and to labor and
entrepreneurs for their services. As in all societies known to history,
there is in our society considerable inequality of incomes.

The prices paid to labor and to the owners of land and capital
are determined, under conditions of more or less perfect competition,
by the forces of supply and demand. The demand for these three
factors is a derived demand—that is, we care very little about what
utilities are directly supplied by them. We care about their capacity to
produce utilities. In other words, what we look for among the factors
of production is their productivity. Their capacity to produce arouses
demand for them. On the supply side, we are struck by the fact that
land is of inelastic supply and that it cost mankind nothing to
produce. Otherwise, issues relating to the supply of factors of production are not radically different from what they are for other things.

Profit is a special case. Here, supply-and-demand theory seems
to break down. Normal profit is a sort of minimum payment required
to get the services of an entrepreneur. Abnormal profits in a competitive society are desirable and economically useful if they are the spur
needed to attract resources away from the production of goods that
consumers desire less to the supplying of goods consumers desire
more. Thus, abnormal profits should be transitory. When profits are
abnormally high for a long time, something is wrong; it may be

monopoly or some form of permanently exploitative advantage institutionally protected.

QUESTIONS FOR REVIEW AND DISCUSSION

1. Define, in your own words, each of the following terms:
   a) Income distribution
   b) Marginal revenue product
   c) Profits
   d) Property incomes

2. "Under the theory of distribution, the average worker does not receive his marginal revenue product, but rather the marginal revenue product of the last worker hired." Discuss.

3. How does the condition stated in the question above tend to guarantee the efficient allocation of labor?

4. "The most effective way unions can raise wages is to limit the supply of labor." Discuss.

5. "The existence of abnormal profits in a competitive industry eventually leads to a more efficient use of factors of production, but the existence of monopoly profits is only a sign of inefficient resource allocation." Discuss.

6. Discuss the relationship between the law of diminishing returns and the theory of distribution.

7. "Standard theory's theory of distribution is not a theory of distribution at all, but merely a theory about the pricing of those factors of production that are bought and sold in the marketplace." Discuss.

8. How are salaries in a nonprofit institution determined, since the productivity of teachers, government employees, and the like cannot be measured?

THE NATIONAL

INCOME

Macroeconomics: Its Importance

This chapter and the next enter a field of study named "macroeconomics." As everyone knows, the word element "macro" is derived from the Greek word *makros,* which means "long in extent or duration" and hence "large" or "great." The brand of economics studied in the past few chapters is named "microeconomics" and is, on the whole, concerned with price and value. Speaking broadly, macroeconomics studies the overall performance of the economy, particularly the total national income, its fluctuations, and the reasons for changes in its volume. Macroeconomics is a pretty important branch of economics. Its subjects are good times and hard times, inflation and deflation. It is also of great political importance, for men and governments are often elected or defeated according to the amount of confidence they inspire in their capacity to keep the nation prosperous. Although economists suggest or help to formulate policies in countless fields—taxation, foreign trade, and agriculture—the grand lines of policy are those related to the steady increase of a nation's income.

What Is a Nation's Income?

It is often easier to understand a concept if we simplify almost to the point of absurdity, and this we shall now do. Basically, a nation's income is like Robinson Crusoe's income. If Robinson Crusoe produces a spear, then he receives a spear as income. Until Friday arrives, Crusoe is the whole nation; and what he produces as landlord, worker, entrepreneur, and capitalist is his to enjoy as consumer. That spear of his is a product if we think of him as combining in his person the four factors of production; it is his income if we think of him as a consumer.

143

What is true of Crusoe is also true of a vast nation like ours. Every year, we produce millions of automobiles and billions of pounds of food and myriad services from appendectomies to lectures on economics, not to mention such minor items as dog tags, harpsichords, and zithers. All this is our product. All this is our income. We can, as consumers, get the product away from the producers by giving them money; and we are prone to think of the money we get as our income. And this is true. But our real income is the goods and services we can get away from the producers; what we really want is the goods and services, not the money. People do not want money income; indeed, soon after payday, most people have little of their money left; they have exchanged their money income for real income—for meat, potatoes, shoes, gasoline, medical service, payments on the car and washing machine, and so on, all of them goods and services.

To recapitulate and reiterate: A nation's product is its income. What we make as producers is what we get as consumers. There are, of course, some exceptions to this. A few nations receive aid from other nations or, like Israel, from private citizens. Thus, they can consume more than they produce. These exceptions are not very important. A seeming exception is imports. We Americans do not produce bananas, coffee, or Scotch whisky, yet we consume all three. But to get these goods, we must give up some of our product in the form of exports. Thus, although we can consume some things we do not produce, we must produce an excess above our needs to be able to get such things as coffee and cameras away from Brazil and Japan. We do not produce exactly the same things we consume, but we do have to produce a quantity equal in value to what we consume.

Now, one of the problems of this chapter is to inquire into ways in which we measure this product or income. It would be cumbersome to the point of impossibility to make an exhaustive list of all the goods and services we produce. There would be hundreds of thousands of items, expressed in such different measures as dozens, tons, pounds, barrels, gallons, and bushels. If it were possible to make a true inventory of what we produce, it would fill volumes, and its unwieldiness would make it all but useless except for a very few purposes.

In our kind of pecuniary society, we have an easy answer to the problem of adding a bushel of apples to a gallon of milk and a ton of

steel and an appendectomy and a zither. We find the price of each unit
and then add the prices. Although the statistical work is formidable,
we do have enough facts and figures to add up the prices of most of the
things that get to market. For reasons which we shall go into later, this
is not a precise measure of our net national product, but it is a very
good measure and a useful one. And this figure is also our income—
or rather, it is fairly close to our income. Both figures are somewhat
contaminated by extraneous items, and both are imperfect for other
reasons.

The figures we can most easily get hold of and most quickly
publish for the guidance of government officials and businessmen are
not true figures of our net product or income, but they are close to the
truth. If their deficiencies are understood, they can be used with considerable safety for many practical purposes. The figures that come
close to measuring the income of our nation are known by the following names:

> Gross national product
> Net national product
> National income
> Personal income
> Disposable personal income

Let us look at each in turn to see what they do measure and what
they leave out, and to form some opinion of how close they come to
"true" national income.

The Gross National Product and the Net National Product

When we talk about a nation's income, we run into several
concepts. In this, the income of a nation is not unlike the income of an
individual. A businessman thinks of gross income (everything he
takes in) and of net income (gross income minus expenses). A blue-
collar or salaried worker may have a weekly income of $100, but a
"take-home" pay or disposable income of only $80—which means that
$20 went for taxes, union dues, pension, and perhaps other items, and
that he has only $80 of clear or disposable income.

The first quantity we shall discuss is a nation's "gross national
product." This figure is perhaps the most widely used of the national
income statistics—so widely known that almost all people interested

in public questions know its significance and refer to it by the initials GNP. It is loosely analogous to the concept of "gross income" in a business establishment, although there are important differences. The crudest concrete and elementary notion of the GNP, though incomplete, would be a vast pile in which everything produced by a nation in a given period would be dumped—apples, automobiles, beds, camping equipment, and so on through the alphabet to zippers, zwieback, and zymometers. But this would not include all, for you must also include intangibles that you cannot dump onto the pile, such items as the services of the actor, barber, chauffeur, doorman, equerry, and postilion, down to the zoology professor—services ranging from manicures to brain surgery. Thus the real GNP includes all the final products and services of a society brought into existence over a given period, usually a year.

The easiest and most accurate way of adding all these disparate things to form a single, manageable total is, as we have said, to use the common denominator of price. Thus, if the value of all the items totaled $0.5 trillion in 1960, we could say that the GNP for 1960 was $500 billion—which is, incidentally, very close to the real figure.

Now, in performing this addition, we must be sure to avoid double-counting—that is, to count only the final product. Thus, if we count an automobile and value it at $3,000, we cannot give additional values to the separate parts of the automobile, such as its tires, batteries, spark plugs, and light bulbs. But this does not mean that we can never count tires, batteries, spark plugs, and light bulbs; we do count such things as part of the GNP if they stand alone and are sold as separate and final products—as replacements, for example. It is not always easy for economists and statisticians to decide what is a final product and what is not; their decisions are sometimes arbitrary. But they do a pretty good job and are constantly on their guard against counting the same things twice.

There is one troublesome item in the GNP, a sort of impurity that appears when we convert the pile of goods and services into their monetary value. That item is the sales tax and similar consumer taxes. When we add the prices of goods and services as sold to final consumers, we are forced to include the increase in price demanded by government sales tax, excises, and property taxes. These taxes are neither services nor goods, but they do increase prices and artificially swell the total; thus, on the one hand, we get a false total. On the other hand, as long as these taxes remain relatively unchanged from year to year, they do not detract too much from the usefulness of the figure. Our interest is not so much in the accuracy of the total as in the accuracy of annual changes. What we usually care about is whether a nation's income is going up or down or standing still. And this the GNP gives us with tolerable accuracy. In any event, as we shall see a little later, we do have another measure of the nation's income—one that does subtract these taxes.

We must take note of another exaggeration in the GNP. The vast pile of goods that composes our annual product includes within it goods destroyed in the process of production. As we make and transport goods and offer services, the things used in these processes wear out. Farmer Brown's tractor is used up a little each year and finally goes to the junkyard. One can almost say that some of the tractor has been absorbed by each bushel of corn he harvests. Thus, while he has been producing wheat, he has also been destroying a tractor. The nation may be 7,000 bushels of corn richer as the result of Farmer Brown's activity, but it is also poorer by one sixth of a tractor, assuming he has to buy a new one every sixth year. When, therefore, we say that 7,000 bushels have been contributed to the GNP by Farmer Brown, we ought somewhere to make a deduction for the loss of part of a tractor. But the GNP does not deduct this loss. And what is true of wheat and tractors is true of almost anything else produced. The barber produces a haircut, but slowly destroys scissors, clippers, and razors and diminishes his store of witch hazel; the taxi driver produces rides, but he destroys his taxi month by month; and so it goes for almost any product that could be named.

We can and do subtract for this; but when we do, we no longer have the GNP but a less widely known measure of the nation's income, the net national product, or NNP. This quantity is equal to the GNP minus the things that had to be destroyed in order to produce it. To put things in more technical language, NNP equals GNP minus capital consumption allowances. During the 1960's the NNP has averaged about 91 percent of the gross product. Thus, to get 100 units of GNP, we have to destroy nine units of national wealth. In other words, the overall rate of loss was 9 percent of GNP.

So far, we have, by implication, looked at the GNP only in terms of producers—a huge pile of goods and services brought together by Farmer Brown, barbers, brain surgeons, zwieback makers, zoology professors, and millions of others. Let us look for a moment at the kinds of people who go to this pile to satisfy their needs. In one sense, everybody goes to this source of all goods—babies for bottles and rattles, teen-agers for dance records, rich men for race horses and yachts, and poor men for baked beans and codfish balls. We should like to divide this motley crowd into four categories which may at the moment seem arbitrary but which will be useful in our later work. The first category will include the final, private consumers of goods; the second, domestic investors, that is, buyers of capital rather than of goods for personal use; the third, exporters; and the fourth, government. The first two groups present no problem; obviously, consumers and entrepreneurs withdraw consumers' goods and capital goods, respectively. But government and exporters are a little differ- ent. The government's withdrawals range widely, from paper clips to atom bombs; they are neither consumers' goods in the ordinary sense nor capital in the entrepreneur's sense. Withdrawals by exporters are made on behalf of other nations. Our interest is not really in exports but rather in the excess of exports over imports. Let's look at the problem this way: Importers bring into the United States all kinds of things—Italian olive oil, Scotch whisky, Brazilian coffee, Guatemalan bananas, and so forth. Obviously, this is not part of the GNP of the United States. To make them our own, we have to pay for them with part of our GNP—with wheat, machinery, jet airliners, and so forth, which are shipped out of the country in exchange. These goods, though produced here, we do not count as part of our GNP, since we have substituted for them the coffee, bananas, and other products intro- duced by importers. Now, if we export more goods than we imported (measured by value), as we normally did in the 1950's and early 1960's, then that excess may be counted as part of our GNP. With this clarification, we can now take a look at the percentages of the GNP absorbed by each of the four claimants during a recent typical year (1966) (see Table 8–1). The percentages are relatively stable and from year to year vary by only two or three points, except the small export figure, which varies by only a half point or less.

We can make an equation concerning the GNP by taking the four categories of Table 8–1—an equation which will be useful to us later.

TABLE 8–1
THE DISTRIBUTION OF GROSS NATIONAL PRODUCT, 1966

Recipient	Percentage of GNP Received
Personal consumption expenditures	62.8
Gross private domestic investment	15.8
Net exports of goods and services	0.6
Government purchases of goods and services	20.8
	100.0

It is as follows: $Y = C + I + E + G$. Here, Y is the GNP; C is personal consumption expenditure; I is investment; E is excess of exports over imports; and G is government expenditures. Although we must postpone discussion of why GNP fluctuates, it is quite obvious at this point that if any item on the right-hand side of the equation is increased, then Y also increases. Thus, we may say, to take an example, that if the government increases its spending, the GNP of the nation will rise.

The National Income

We now come to our third measure of a nation's income. The first was the GNP, widely known and used. The second, which we dismissed rather hastily, was the NNP, or net national product. The one to be described in this section is the "national income."

The quantity named national income, though less widely known than the GNP, is a cleaner and leaner figure. It is not only closer to the true income of a nation, but the concepts underlying it have perhaps greater economic significance. This measure of a nation's income lays emphasis on the receiving (or income) side of the equation, rather than on the product side. But of course, as we have already said several times, the two are really the same; Robinson Crusoe gets what Crusoe makes. To be sure, even in the simplest society, you might in November harvest crops or shoot deer (produce food) that you would consume (use as income) only in January of the following year. Thus, in any given arbitrary period, there might be some discrepancy between product and income. But this discrepancy is small and does not really detract from the basic proposition that product equals income. Statisticians recognize this problem in gathering income statistics and make allowances for it.

Since income equals product, we ought to be able to get at the value of the product of a nation by adding up the incomes of its inhabitants. As a matter of fact, we can and do, and we find that the difference between the process of (1) valuing total product and (2) adding all incomes is very small—so small that it can be attributed to faulty reporting rather than any logical unsoundness in our proposition.

Now the economist recognizes only four basic sources of income —land, labor, capital, and entrepreneurship. Thus, if we add up all the incomes from these sources, we should get the true national income; and this figure should also add up to the true national product—the GNP with proper deductions for sales (and similar) taxes and capital allowances. And this is true in fact. If we add up the four incomes, we get a figure which does equal the GNP minus those two contaminating quantities (indirect business taxes and capital allowances).

Let us check this against the actual figures as given for a recent year (1966). We shall first approach national income from the income side by adding the incomes of all recipients of profit, wages (including salaries), rent, and interest. A little unfortunately for us, the government does not collect figures in such a way as to conform precisely with the four rigorously defined categories of economic theory. The Department of Commerce uses five categories, but these five cover approximately the same ground as do the economist's four. The categories, with the income assignable to each of the five, are reported for 1966 as shown in Table 8–2.

TABLE 8–2

	In Billions
Compensation of employees	$433.3
Proprietors' income (business, professional, farm)	57.7
Corporation profits	80.2
Rental income of persons	18.9
Net interest	20.0
National Income	$610.1

Now, let us approach the problem from the other end and derive national income by using the product approach (see Table 8–3).

You will see that the national income figures derived in two

TABLE 8–3

In Billions

Gross national product	$739.6
Subtract: Capital consumption allowance	63.1
Net national product	$676.5
Subtract: Indirect taxes	65.5
National Income	$611.0

different ways are quite close. They can be made to tally exactly by taking into account a few small items that we have neglected. We neglected an item of $2.3 billion named "business transfer payments." This relates to gifts made by business to colleges and similar institutions, cash prizes, and the like. Another item of $1.7 billion relates to subsidies made by government.

And finally, a sum is added or subtracted simply to make national income as computed by this product method balance income as computed by the sum-of-incomes-earned method. This is the statistical discrepancy we have already noted. In the tables published by the Department of Commerce and available in the *Survey of Current Business,* in the *Statistical Abstract of the United States,* in the *Federal Reserve Bulletin,* and elsewhere, the subtractions from and additions to GNP are listed as shown in Table 8–4.

TABLE 8–4
NATIONAL INCOME AND PRODUCT, 1966

In Billions

Gross national product	$739.6
Less: Capital consumption allowances	63.1
Indirect business tax and nontax liability	65.5
Business transfer payments	2.6
Statistical discrepancy	—0.2
Plus: Subsidies less current surplus of government enterprises	1.4
Equals: National Income	$610.1

When statisticians and economists count incomes, they must be just as careful not to double-count as when they count products. We noted earlier that you cannot say the price of an automobile is $3,000 and then, on top of that, add the price of the tires, battery, light bulbs, etc., already included in the $3,000. In the same way, statisticians are careful not to count incomes received twice. If, for example, during your college years, your father, who earns $20,000, gives you an income of $2,500, you cannot say that together you have an income of $22,500. A more serious problem is involved in the possible double-counting of a businessman's income. Suppose that in the course of a month a small baker takes in $5,000 gross. Obviously, very little of this is income to him. Most of it is the income of others which he must pass on. Part of the $5,000 goes to the landlord, for the baker must pay his monthly rent out of his gross monthly intake. He must pay his wholesalers; he must pay gas bills for heat. The only part of the total that can be counted as income generated by his firm is the difference between his gross take and the sum of his payments for materials and services purchased from other firms. This difference—which, we shall say, is $700—represents the value he himself has added to the goods he sells. The increased value is created because he opens crates, displays wares, weighs out quantities as desired by the housewife, delivers orders, refrigerates perishables, supplies paper bags, and so forth. It is only the value he has added that counts as income created by his firm and contributed to the national total.

Personal Income and Disposable Personal Income

When you read articles in newspapers and newsmagazines about economic conditions, you are likely to run into such phrases as "personal income" and "disposable personal income." An explanation of the meaning of these terms will not add much to our knowledge of how the national income is estimated; but since they are in use, and since they have value to business and economic analysts, we shall discuss them briefly. Personal income measures the amount of income destined for consumers prior to their payment of income taxes. Its calculation is made in two steps. The first step is to deduct from national income those items that are not part of the income of individuals and households. The largest of these deductions is corporate profits. Another is contributions for social security. The second step in the calculation of personal income is to include in it income received by individuals and households but not specifically measured in national income. These additions include government transfer payments (principally, social security and welfare benefits paid to persons), interest paid by the government and by consumers, and corporate dividends. The personal income figure, published monthly, is a useful and frequently available figure that enables business and government economists to determine what the public has available to spend. It is smaller than national income—about 8 or 9 percent less.

Less often published is a figure known as "disposable personal income." This figure, on a national scale, comes close to what, on an individual scale, is the average man's take-home pay. It is equal to personal income minus income taxes. It is, of course, lower than personal income—by about 11 percent in recent years. This figure, even better than personal income, really tells us what the average man can spend on the products and services of private industry—or can save if he does not spend.

Fluctuations of the GNP

The GNP and related figures are characterized by an inconstancy that does not affect many other large numbers of the economy. Population, for example, increases annually and steadily enough to make forecasts fairly reliable. Over the decades the ratio of the labor force to the total population is surprisingly constant. Death rates do not vary from a 10-year average by more than 1½ percent. But the GNP and associated figures have performed erratically. To predict the national income two years hence is risky business. The next chapter will discuss why GNP is erratic. In this section, we shall discuss how it varies.

Table 8–5, in billions, indicates the size of the GNP of the United States during selected years. These figures show two things—

TABLE 8–5

GROSS NATIONAL PRODUCT, UNITED STATES

Year	In Billions
1929	$104
1933	56
1941	126
1950	285
1957	443
1960	504
1962	554
1964	632
1966	740

first, that over the long term, income rises; and second, that there can be vast short-term variations and even sharp declines, as indicated by the great decline between 1929 and 1933. The general tendency of our nation's income is upward, for several reasons. There is a completely fictitious rise resulting from the declining value of the dollar. As everybody knows, prices today are about twice what they were before World Warr II. Thus a more nearly accurate representation could be achieved by cutting in half all figures for the years after 1946. This, of course, would be a pretty rough-and-ready correction because the fraction one half is only an approximation. If we use the most nearly exact fractions available (a different one for each year), with the year 1958 as a base instead of a prewar year, we get the figures shown in Table 8–6.

TABLE 8–6
GNP IN DOLLARS OF CONSTANT
PURCHASING POWER
(Base, 1958)

Year	In Billions
1929	$203
1933	142
1941	266
1950	355
1957	457
1960	488
1962	530
1964	578
1966	631

The figures in Table 8–6 compensate for the spurious growth revealed in Table 8–5. They show relations among the years in dollars of constant purchasing power. Thus, we did really have almost twice as much income in 1962 as in 1941. Table 8–5 tells us that we had about 4½ times as much, and this is not true. But of course, the figures in Table 8–6 are not those collected by fieldworkers and statisticians actually working on the job; they are doctored to enable us to see whether real income rose or fell, and by how much.

Another reason for annual changes in the figures is economic growth. The rise over the period given is approximately a 3 percent cumulative growth annually. Part of this is associated with growth of population, which has increased at a cumulative rate of almost 1½ percent annually. Since there are more mouths to feed each year, an economy tries to produce more things to feed them with, and extra production generates extra income. Every new mouth brings with it two hands which can ultimately become part of the labor force. It is of course possible to imagine a society in which increased population growth does not result in increased income; but under present conditions in the advanced countries of the West, we can assume that increased income goes with population increase. If we take away 1½ percent population growth from the 3 percent general income growth, we still have a small annual increase left over for everybody to share —the reflection of which may be found in more goods, better goods, more services, more armaments, and more men orbiting the earth and shooting for the moon.

Let us now look at temporary declines of the GNP and years of sagging growth rates. Both Table 8–5 and Table 8–6 reveal the great shock of the 1930's, that is, the decline of income between 1929 and 1933. The somewhat larger population of 1933 had considerably less real income than the smaller population of 1929. The depression of the 1930's was, of course, the worst we have ever had. Since World War II, our depressions have been so mild that the annual figures have not always clearly registered a decline of income. Consider the figures listed in Table 8–7, which show the truth of this statement.

The years italicized in Table 8–7 were depression years. Two of them (1949 and 1954) show mild declines of income over the preceding years, and two of them (1958 and 1960) show increases. How can we have an increase of income and a depression at the same time? One answer lies in the fact that the figures given come by calendar years, which depressions do not respect. The 1958 depression really began in about July of 1957; income stayed down during part of 1958; then, by about Labor Day, it rose to its previous high and continued upward steeply to the end of the year. The depression period lasted about a year, but it straddled the last and first halves of two sequential years. The other halves of these two years were quite prosperous and brought the annual GNP totals up to a point that conceals the declines—declines that are quite clear in the quarterly figures. Approximately the same thing is true of the 1960 depression —actually a rather curious one, some of the worst months of which came in 1959, with a rise in the middle of 1960, and a decline again toward the end of the year.

TABLE 8–7

GROSS NATIONAL PRODUCT,
UNITED STATES, 1948–66

Year	In Billions
1948	$259
1949	258
1950	285
1951	329
1952	347
1953	365
1954	363
1955	397
1956	419
1957	443
1958	444
1959	482
1960	504
1961	521
1962	554
1963	589
1964	632
1965	681
1966	740

Other events tend to mask declines of the GNP. One is our almost annual increase in prices, which, barring a few exceptional years, pushes up the money value of the GNP without affecting the actual physical quantity of the product. Another is the upward push of population, which produces a greater total but may award a trifle less to each individual. Finally, a mere arrest of growth should, in our dynamic world, be looked on as an economic setback. In any event, Table 8–7 shows considerable inconstancy from year to year. Annual change varies from roughly —0.6 percent to +12½ percent; this is a wide gap for a period which most of us look back on as being rather uneventful economically—or at least a period free of great depressions or of confiscatory inflation. Changes of this magnitude make for considerable economic insecurity, even if they are not as grotesque as the changes of our great periods of depression in the remoter past.

Incompleteness of the Income Figures

The various measures of a nation's income, as described above, are the result of much human ingenuity, and the figures are gathered at considerable monetary cost. We have evidence that students of the economy have been thinking about measures of income for at least 300 years. It must be said, though, that until the depression of the 1930's, only a few pioneering minds had done much to ascertain the size and composition of the national income or to figure out how reasonably accurate estimates of income could be derived from available figures. Since 1930, the gains in collecting usable figures and in refining concepts and techniques have been impressive; even so, they are faulty.

One considerable omission is the amount produced within the home by the family, particularly by the housewife. If Mother bakes a pie that would cost 50 cents at a store but that costs her only 20 cents in apples, flour, and other raw materials, then the 30 cents that she adds to the national income goes unnoticed by the economists and statisticians. If Father picks up a battered bench put together in 1790 and refinishes it to make a coffee table for the living room, his labor goes for nothing in the national income figures. And if Junior cuts the lawn, his service is not reported to the Department of Commerce, which brings together the figures discussed in this chapter. But if Mother has a cook who bakes pies and a yardman who cuts grass, and if Father sells the restored table as an antique, then the wages to the servants and the value added to the old bench do become part of the national income figures. In short, a pecuniary transaction gets recognition by the economist, but a nonpecuniary action is neglected. Yet even this generalization is violated; for example, the farm family may produce much of its own food and fuel (sawing wood to be used in stoves), and the imputed value of these items *is* included in the national income.

Another frequently mentioned flaw in the national income accounts is the omission of all economic activity in violation of law. Thus the illegal manufacture and sale of liquor is excluded from income and product. Running illegal gambling places, peddling dope, and various other forms of gratifying the baser passions of others for a price are excluded. Interest payments made by the government receive some recognition in the statistics, to be sure, but are treated as transfer payments. When, however, a businessman pays interest to a bank, his payment becomes part of the bank's income and finds its way into the national figures as an addition to income. And so it goes.

Dozens of omissions and inconsistencies can be pointed out, ranging from really serious issues to mere quibbles.

It must not be assumed that the omissions and inconsistencies spoken of above are the result of carelessness or of the indifference of a hard-shelled bureaucracy. The fault lies not in the men who measure, but in the vastness of the motley thing being measured. Any attempt by any group to measure our product or income would require the making of arbitrary decisions and the omission—or at best, the rough estimation—of things that cannot be counted. One does not have to be a very rich man to realize how impossible it is to count one's net worth or to measure one's income. In the autumn of 1967 a man owning $100,000 worth of stocks at 10 A.M. might in the course of the day be worth anywhere between $98,000 and $102,000, depending on the movement of the stock market. A man with the relatively modest income of $20,000 derived from stocks, rental of a house, royalties, and lecture fees actually is unable to compute his income precisely. He can compute something that will stand the most searching scrutiny of the tax collector, but even that is an arbitrary figure. Was the money he spent on house repair a mere repair, or was it an improvement that added value? How much of the wages he paid a typist went for purely personal letters and how much toward his business of speechmaking and writing? When he traveled to Ashtabula, Dubuque, and Kalamazoo to give lectures, how much was spent on necessary travel and how much on personal pleasure? If these problems plague an individual who is only a small-time winner, how can we expect the whole nation to compute its vast income unerringly?

These flaws—forgivable, understandable, and often unimportant for some purposes—do at times have important consequences for economic reasoning. Because they exist, certain kinds of comparisons of national income must be approached with circumspection. For example, between 1929 and 1933 the national income fell from $88 billion to $40 billion—more than half. Does this mean that our actual consumption and well-being were cut in half? For some people, it certainly meant that and worse, but for the average person the figures completely belie the facts. Even if Dad's income was cut in half, Mother still made the beds, kept the house clean, and washed the family's shirts. Junior still cut the grass and emptied the trash. Dad repaired the orthophonic, windup Victrola, and the whole family could continue to enjoy Helen Kane's version of "Button Up Your

Overcoat." People who had a few decks of cards left over from better days could perfect their Culbertson system of bidding. All of these satisfactions are real income, though not counted in the statistics.

We must also beware of drawing unwarranted conclusions when we compare the national pecuniary income of advanced and under-developed nations. A Latin-American nation may have a per capita pecuniary income only one tenth as great as ours. But in any under-developed nation, much economic activity goes on outside the market economy. Neighbors may barter avocados for mangoes. They may listen to the village guitar player instead of paying $500 for a box that enables them to hear and see Dean Martin in gorgeous techni-color with a peacock. In many underdeveloped economies, the people, by knitting, weaving, thatching, sewing, kneading, grinding, pickling, spicing, and salting, can secure satisfactions or utilities that are procurable only with money on the markets of the more highly developed economies. In our own underdeveloped economy of 100 years ago or less, husking bees, turkey shoots, square dancing, tournaments, and evangelical meetings provided recreation and edu-cation which we now buy expensively in nightclubs and amusement parks and through subscriptions to lecture and concert series. In a deeper, philosophic sense the income of a nation really cannot be measured, for income is the sum of incommensurable quantities—health, nutrition, fun, happiness, and miscellaneous satisfactions. Despite this basic fact, the GNP and the other monetary measures we have possess have some usefulness and may even help us to reach the more intangible goals at which we aim.

Conclusion

Our broad conclusions are very simple:

1. Product equals income.
2. We have no single figure that truly gives us either income or prod-uct, but we do have five figures that give us useful approximations; each has its own usefulness.
3. Income fluctuates erratically.

Our next task is to try to find out why income (or product) can fluctuate erratically—remember that in the four short years from 1929 to 1933, it fell from $88 billion to $40 billion.

QUESTIONS FOR REVIEW AND DISCUSSION

1. Define, in your own words, each of the following terms:
   a) Gross national product
   b) Net national product
   c) National income
   d) Personal income
   e) Disposable personal income
   f) Depreciation
   g) Double-counting
2. What productive activities are not included in national income accounts? Why are they not considered? Does their absence destroy the usefulness of national income figures? Explain.
3. Describe fully the two different methods used to obtain national income figures. Why do these methods yield identical results?
4. Which of the following entities would vary least during the course of a business cycle: GNP, national income, or disposable income? Why?
5. What are transfer payments? How are they handled in national income accounting?
6. Smith, a young, well-established executive in an efficiently run profit-making toy manufacturing concern, decides to buy the business from his boss. He borrows $300,000 from a trusting neighborhood bank, pays his boss $100,000 for the company, and uses the rest of the money to pay his workers and purchase raw materials. Smith discovers that he is not a very good toy manufacturer. After six months of production, during which the concern has not sold one toy, Smith claims bankruptcy. The misused plant and equipment, purchased for $100,000, are sold for $50,000, and the unsold toys are distributed to neighborhood settlement houses. What effect has Smith's business venture had on the nation's national income? On the nation's gross national product?
7. By using the following information, calculate GNP and NNP:

Wages and salaries	$100
Unincorporated income	25
Interest income	10
Social security payments	11
Foreign aid	4
Corporate profits	28
Rental income	7
Depreciation	12

Chapter 9

WHY INCOME
FLUCTUATES

Introduction

The last chapter described the concept of national income and examined income fluctuations. In this chapter, we seek to discover why income fluctuates as it does. To meet a variety of deep-seated human values, an economy must maintain stability. We should have neither inflation nor deflation. Our national product, or income, should not decline from one year to another. On the other hand, it is desirable that income should increase annually; thus, when we say that we want stability, what we really mean is that we do not want to backslide but do want steady, healthy, reasonable progress in levels of living. And we want stability of prices as well as of income. If the community is somehow induced to spend money at a faster rate than it is producing goods, as may happen in wartime, then we have inflation —a situation in which "too many dollars are chasing too few goods." The result is, of course, rapid increases in prices. This can be as harmful and disorganizing as depression. Study of these problems may be named "income theory," because we are interested in changes of the national income. The concepts, aims, and entire method of analysis differ from those of price theory.

Modern income theory, as put forward by standard economists dates from the depression of the 1930's. The world was so shocked at the grotesque decline of incomes by 1932 and 1933 that economists had to revise many of their ideas, and the result of that revision is the subject of this chapter. To many young students of economics, it must seem rather quaint that economists talk so much about economic depressions as if they were real and present threats rather than worn-out catastrophes like the Chicago Fire or the sinking of the *Titanic*. Modern college students belong to what is probably the first generation of Americans since 1800 that has not experienced at least a few years of very hard times. Just as their grandparents grew up in an era that believed a world war unthinkable, so their grandchildren are growing up in an era which considers deep depressions to be unreal. But the possibility of depression has not yet been removed from the world, and modern college students may yet discover the reality of hard times, just as their grandfathers learned in 1914 that great wars could happen and as their fathers learned in the 1940's that the great powers had not renounced the wholesale slaughter of civilians as an instrument of policy.

There were many depressions before the 1930's, but the bad years of that decade were the worst in our history. Our physical product was vastly reduced—in industry, cut almost in half. For a while, there were three men for every two jobs; and among the employed, many worked only part of the week and therefore received only thin pay envelopes. Fortunes were lost, hope had fled, and few of us were free from the fear that worse was yet to come. There were so many homeless that in some areas firehouses and jails were turned into flophouses. There were dreadful political consequences. Since the depression was an international phenomenon and covered the capitalist world, significant communist penetrations were made in many countries. And in some desperate areas where communism was kept out, fascism came in. It has been said that Adolf Hitler and World War II can be traced directly to the depression. This is not easy to prove, but most people would agree that the depression was at least a contributory cause to the great political catastrophes of the 1930's and 1940's.

An apparent symptom of depression is that there are goods aplenty but little money to buy them with. The social critics of the 19th century spoke of warehouses "bursting with grain" while men went hungry in the streets. Now, our economy is sometimes beset by a related disease, inflation, the apparent symptom of which is that there is money aplenty but no goods to buy—pockets bursting with cash but no grain in the warehouses. Depression and inflation, though quite different, have the same kind of relationship as have the North and South poles or love and hate. A study of depression (or deflation) leads us eventually to a study of inflation, and comprehension of the one sheds light on the other. We therefore consider them both in this chapter.

Although we have had both depression and inflation in this

country, we have perhaps suffered more from depression. On the whole, the unemployment, bankruptcies, and loss of fortunes resulting from depressions have hurt us worse than have our relatively mild inflations. This is not necessarily true of other countries. Where there have been galloping inflations, as in so many parts of the world, inflation has probably hurt even worse than depression. How confiscatory inflation can be is well demonstrated by the story of the two German brothers who went through the disastrous German inflation of the 1920's together. Both inherited handsomely from their father. One invested his half of the fortune in gilt-edged bonds; the other squandered it on wine, women, and song. But when the inflation had run its course, the empty champagne bottles of the carousing brother were worth more as junk than were the bonds of the sober, solid citizen.

A mild inflation is perhaps more comfortable than a mild deflation from the viewpoint of the majority. Farmers' prices, profits, and wages are likely to rise as prices rise. This means that businessmen, farmers, and workingmen suffer much less than they do in depression, and these three groups account for a large fraction of the population. Debtors also benefit, for they can pay off in today's less valuable money the debts they contracted five years ago when money would purchase more. But certain minority groups are hurt rather badly—those who have fixed pensions or salaries that do not rise easily, such as schoolteachers; their incomes remain the same while prices of the things they buy go up. Creditors—and this includes people who own the bonds of private business or government—are repaid in dollars of less purchasing power.

The basic reason why depressions—in this country, at least—are worse than inflations is that during an inflationary period the goods are there and are being produced and can be bought. What is bad is that the people have to bid so high to get them. Our mild inflations have tended to spur production, giving most people a high standard of living. But in long depressions, goods are simply not there; production is at a low ebb because it is unprofitable to make things that do not sell. This statement seems to contradict what the social critics of the 19th century used to say about "warehouses bursting with grain." Actually, both statements are true; warehouses are bursting with unsold goods, but the factories are closed because businessmen are obviously unwilling to add to the store of unsold goods. Granted, however, that a mild inflation is more benign than depression, economists hold to the goal of stability of prices, that is, neither inflation nor depression. Both are diseases, and what cures have been prescribed will be subject of the next dozen pages.

Development of Theory about Income Fluctuations

Although people throughout history have known floods, famine, and poverty, the thing which we name "depression" is relatively new. It is a phenomenon of capitalism not found under feudalism or under the various other types of economic systems known to the world. It differs from famine or poverty induced by disaster in that all the physical apparatus needed for accustomed abundance is intact, but there is widespread poverty nonetheless. The men are there, the machines and railroads are all there, the raw materials are available; but for some reason, there is no incentive to use them to reasonably full capacity. Some students have said that such an impasse can occur only in a money-using economy, that is, one in which the proximate aim of most economic activity is the making and spending of money incomes and in which few restrictions are placed on how such incomes are made or spent (refer back to a discussion of this same idea on pages 25–27).

Thus, depressions in the modern Western sense could scarcely have occurred in the United States as long as we were largely a country of small farmers, as we were about 1750, most of us supplying our own food, clothing, and shelter directly through our own efforts. Money was used for very few things—for salt, iron tools, and books; the immediate goal of economic activity was to produce goods, not money.

Inflation is an older phenomenon. The value of money has declined, as Paul Einzig, the British publicist, has said, for well over 4,000 years. Kings and emperors have for their own profit reduced the intrinsic value of coins by decreasing the amounts of precious metals the coins contained. Later increases in the world's supply of precious metals caused an imbalance between goods produced and money available; more new coins than goods were produced. Wars have been financed with an excess of printing-press money. But of course, many of the inflations of the longer past had little effect on the underlying population. The medieval serf and even the noble saw but little money over a lifetime. Charlemagne collected much of his taxes in kind. If you produced your own living directly and rarely sold or bought in the market, it scarcely mattered whether prices were high or low or money cheap or dear.

Standard theory was very slow to inquire seriously and profoundly into the subject of depression. It was not until 1936, after we had gone through many depressions for a century and a half, that orthodox economists at last made sustained efforts to study depressions. This does not mean that individuals had not written a few serious pages on depressions, but it does mean that there was no real community of effort among economists to study the unemployment of our productive resources. How could there have been? The model of standard theory, as described on pages 49–53, demonstrated that depressions could not exist, because there was a self-regulating mechanism that always restored the economy after any shock to its normal or equilibrium level of full employment and maximum income. And how can economists put their hearts into a study of what their theory tells them does not exist?

Certain dissenting economists, notably Karl Marx, the founder of modern Communist doctrines, had gone pretty thoroughly into depression theory; but since non-Marxian theorists could not accept his basic assumptions, they could not accept his depression theory. About half a century after Marx, two American noncommunist dissenters, Thorstein Veblen and Wesley Mitchell, handled the issue of depression seriously. Both of them, particularly Mitchell, won some acclaim in this country but did not give the world of economists exactly what it wanted in the way of depression theory. We shall in later chapters return to Mitchell's theory.

In 1936, in the midst of the depression decade, a British economist by the name of John Maynard Keynes, a rather glamourous fellow in his personal life and already known to fame as an economist of extraordinary ability, published a book on depression under the curious title of *The General Theory of Employment, Interest and Money*. It quickly became the center of animated debate, and it has been said that within a decade or so more words concerning it were written than had ever been written about *The Wealth of Nations*, the famous first great book on economics completed in 1776 by Adam Smith, the father of economic science. The Keynesian revolution was on; at last, standard theory had admitted that depressions really existed and required something more than casual study.

Keynes' book electrified the economic world. It had a kind of inspired quality; and although much of it has since been superseded by later economic thinking—superseded in the same way that the Wright biplane has been superseded by modern jets—it has become the basis of modern speculation on the control of the business cycle. We shall describe below the present-day theory of economic fluctuations as derived from the first Keynesian statement.

Modern Depression Theory

A depression may be looked upon as a period in which the national income declines from a previously higher figure. This is a verifiable fact. In 1929, our national income was about $90 billion; and during the worst years of the depression that followed immediately, it was about half that sum. Thus, if you can answer the question as to why income falls, you can solve the question of depressions—a much harder job than may appear on the surface. We do not know whether the job has really been done yet, though we have much more to say on the subject than we did a generation ago.

Inflation is, of course, the opposite, and may be thought of as a sudden and unhealthy increase in the national income. It is unhealthy because the increased money income is not matched by an equal increase in real income, real in the sense of actual things—automobiles, food, clothing, medical services, and so forth. Our real income seems to increase by about 3 percent annually. If our monetary income increases by much more than this, there is an imbalance, and this imbalance we may name inflation.

Now, income generated or produced equals income received, as we found out in the last chapter. Both methods of counting income give the same result. What this means, contrary to some popular fallacies and interpretations of the Marxian theory, is that there is enough income received in dollars to buy back all the things produced according to their dollar value. This fact rules out all naïve under-consumption theories of depression. And yet, handled in a more sophisticated way, the concept of underconsumption does help us to understand economic contraction.

In George Eliot's novel, Silas Marner is described as a miser. He has enough money to buy back his proper share of the national product, but he refuses to do this. He diverts part of the national income to a sterile hoard of gold under the hearthstone. If all of us should suddenly become Silas Marners, hoarding quantities of money, refusing to buy back a large fraction of the goods we have produced, we would precipitate a dreadful depression. Nothing could plunge us faster into hard times than a sudden, widespread, sustained consumers' boycott (assuming, of course, that neither the government nor any other group offsets the effects of the boycott by compensating purchases). Thus, it is possible to cause depression by underconsumption. But of course, most of us are not misers, and even those among us who save a great deal do not hoard money in our humble thatched cottages. We put it in the bank where it can be loaned out to businessmen, or in some other way we try to restore it to the income stream of society. We do not deliberately sterilize it, as Silas Marner did, under the hearthstone. But whether we plan to do so or not, there are times when saving can be just as harmful to the economy as simple hoarding.

To understand how this happens, we must first explore the concept of saving. Most of us, when we save, put our money out at interest somewhere. We put it in a savings bank or a building and loan association, or we buy insurance, bonds, or stocks. In doing these things, we hazily assume that our savings will somehow be used to help keep the wheels of industry turning or to activate commerce. If not, why should we be getting interest and dividends? We feel that somebody will borrow our money through the banker or insurance company and put our savings to productive use, or that the corporation whose shares of stock we buy will invest our savings in machinery, raw materials, and the like. In short, we have the comfortable belief that our money will find some way of getting back into the income stream. But have we any basis for this optimistic faith?

Keynes' greatest discovery, he himself said, was that saving and investing were done by different people. The motives for the two kinds of activities are quite unrelated. We save through habit, against our old age, to send our children through college, for a rainy day, to swell a reserve fund for future plant expansion, for all sorts or reasons that have little to do with investment. But by investment, at least in this context, the Keynesian economist means something special; he attaches a very precise meaning to the word. Popularly, the word "invest" is almost a synonym for "buy": "I invested in a new suit yesterday," or "I invested in two tickets to the hockey game." Less popularly, it may mean to buy any income-producing paper: "He invests his money in municipal bonds." These popular and commercial meanings are totally excluded in the Keynesian definitions.

By investment the economist means buying new capital and putting it into use. It means buying a new concrete mixer or a new punch press, expanding a factory, or building a new building. If you buy 100 shares of General Electric, you as an individual may think you are investing; but from the economist's viewpoint, you are not, because you have not taken part in creating new capital. The stock market is mostly a secondhand market which normally transfers old certificates from person to person. If you pay $6,000 for 100 of its shares, General Electric does not get a farthing of your money. You have not lent that company one cent toward a new lathe or truck or milling machine. You simply paid money through your broker to the fellow who last owned the 100 shares of G.E.

Investing as economists see it is a different matter. Investing is the active buying of real things, not a pushing-around of old documents from person to person or a putting of money into a savings account. The typical investor, Keynesian style, is an entrepreneur who borrows your savings and with them buys new capital goods. He may of course have money of his own to invest; but in our credit economy the typical entrepreneur is a great borrower of idle savings. He, not the saver, puts savings to work by converting them into machines, inventories, and other new capital goods. Saving is passive, precautionary behavior; investing is active and venturesome. Saving and investing, as Keynes said, are done by different people. Provisionally, at least, we can say that there is no intimate connection between saving and investing. Savers may be prepared, in a given year, to save billions; but investors may be prepared to spend only in the millions. And vice versa. In other words, there is no close relationship between Mary's propensity to save and Bill's propensity to invest.

Investment and saving must, however, always be equal. It is

impossible to put steel into power shovels and lathes unless consumers forego (save) the use of steel in autos, stoves, refrigerators, toys. But since saving and investment are done by different people, it would be a very great accident if planned saving and investment in a free economy were ever equal. Thus, we come up with two contradictory propositions:

1. Planned saving and investment are never likely to be equal.
2. Actual saving and investment are always equal.

The resolution of this contradiction between planned and actual saving and investment forms the basis of Keynesian business cycle theory.

What happens is that something in the economy changes, for planned savings and investment must at length equilibrate. The process of equilibration may be cruel; we may have to go through depression or inflation to get equilibrium. But get it we shall. Let us follow the processes.

If savers save too much—which means that they desire to save more than investors wish to invest—then for a while, less is being bought back by the community than is being produced by producers; the business community accumulates an unwanted investment in inventory. We have underconsumption or, what is the other side of the coin, overproduction. The producers respond to this by cutting back production, and a decline of production is a decline of the nation's real income. When the national income goes down, a vast number of individual incomes go down with it, and people with smaller incomes will not be able to save anything at all. Thus, through adjustments in the national income the amounts people plan to save work their way down to equality with the amounts investors wish to invest. It is almost as if some punitive force from a netherworld were threatening: "So you insist upon saving more than you invest. All right, I'll fix you; I'll reduce your incomes. You won't be able to save much when I get through with you." This process may involve heavy human costs. Decline in income means cutting back production. This usually means laying off men, which in turn means unemployment. And this may become cumulative. The men laid off have very little money with which to buy things; demand falls off again; and now there are further cutbacks of production, more men fired, more purchasing power lost to the economy, and so on again in a vicious circle until we have a full-blown depression. And all of this fuss to make planned investment equal planned savings!

Now we look at the opposite process—a process which may lead to inflation. If investors invest too much—which means that they desire to invest more than is saved—then for a while, more is being bought by the community than is being produced. The reader may respond to this statement by observing: "This is a good trick if you can do it, but how do you buy what is not produced—and what do you use for money?" The problem is no problem, for, as we shall see in a later chapter, the banking system can create money to meet needs. For a while, goods are no problem either; there are always more cans of corned beef, beans, and soup on the grocers' shelves than are needed for the day's sales; wholesalers and factories have stocks of goods to keep them going for days, weeks, and sometimes months without replenishment. Thus, what we are saying is not that the community is consuming nonexistent things but that it is "living off the shelf" and is buying with bank-made money at a faster rate than things are being produced. This kind of situation is exactly what businessmen love—at least up to a point. Consuming at a faster rate than we are producing stimulates businessmen to produce more. Increased production keeps up with increased buying. Employers hire new men to produce more; the unemployed, if any, are being absorbed. We are marching toward increased prosperity (assuming, of course, that we were previously in a depression). The national product rises; and with it, individual incomes rise. Higher incomes are accompanied by a higher level of savings because people with higher incomes can afford to save more, and planned saving works its way up to equality with planned investment. This process is one of getting out of the depression.

Though the process as described above is completely beneficent, it can go further—like gentle rain that turns into flood—and become a harmful inflation. If we already have full employment and are already producing to capacity, and if at this point planned investment exceeds planned saving, then the process of seeking equilibrium is accompanied by an increase in prices. And these increased prices do not stimulate an increase in production. We are already producing all we can, for the nation's resources are fully employed. Redundant income is chasing a dearth of goods. Inflation is upon us. This is what happens in a country which, already producing at full or nearly full capacity, goes to war. The extra demands of businessmen for new tools and raw materials to create war goods exceed the rate of saving, and prices go up in an attempt to achieve the necessary balance. Income goes up, too, but in depreciated dollars; you will get $10 for every $5 that you got before; but you will not be better off, for things cost, on the average, twice as much or more.

Applications of Theory to Policy

We shall understand all this better if we now seek to translate these theoretical concepts into public policy. In view of the above discussion, what should be done to sustain an economy on an even keel? In our elementary work, we may assume a rather simple economy—one in which income generated by foreign trade and government is not large enough to take into account at this point.

In such an economy, depression will be averted if consumers and investors spend enough to maintain previously comfortable levels of income (allowances being made for reasonable annual growth). This means that we must have no drooping of expenditures on the part of either consumers of investors; or if one of the parties does resist buying, then the other party will compensate for the dereliction. And to prevent inflation, neither party may go on a wild spending spree; or if one does, the other will compensate by spending less. The essential idea is to find some level of spending and investing which keeps the nation at a comfortable, growing income, and then to hold that level of income by spending neither too much nor too little.

Now, this general guiding statement assumes that consumers sometimes do suddenly reduce or increase consumption and that investors suddenly reduce or increase investment. Is this assumption true; and if so, why? It is indeed true, as various well-publicized figures attest. The "why" is not so clear. If we really knew why reductions and increases in investment and consumption take place, we could more easily solve the problem of economic instability. Unfortunately, we do not have unimpeachable answers, but we can talk around the questions and form a few opinions.

First of all, consumers are, on the whole, pretty reliable people. Apparently, they do not suddenly and unpredictably change their habits radically. When they do change their habits radically and persistently, as most of them were forced to do during the depression of the 1930's, the reason is clear: The national income has gone down, and the incomes of individuals have gone down with it. In quiet and peaceful times, consumers' "propensity to consume" (to use the economist's language) is fairly stable, but it does vary. We do not really know what basic causes or events underlie its variation; but we do know that in rich, advanced economies like ours, consumers do have the choice of saving much or consuming much, and that they do the one or the other. In poor socieites, such a large share of incomes goes for basic necessities that the consumer has little choice as to whether he will consume or not consume; he must buy or starve. In the wealthier nations, no such necessity dictates our behavior, and there is a wide area of choice—the choice of whether to consume luxuries and semiluxuries or not. And of course, underconsuming tends toward depression, whereas overconsuming tends toward inflation. Economists are trying to find out what makes consumers hold up or spend their dollars; but so far, our knowledge is thin. But we do know that people are not likely to make vast shifts in their consuming habits in the short run.

This leaves us with investment as the remaining and principal thing to look into. If businessmen should suddenly reduce their investing by a great deal, income would decline rapidly, and this kind of behavior would tend toward depression. And again, the opposite is true. Exuberant investment would tend toward inflation. Do entrepreneurs in fact expand or reduce investment suddenly? Yes, they do; the propensity to invest is much more volatile than the propensity to consume. Why? Well, when we consume, we buy mostly certain basic necessities of life or things to which we are so much addicted that we can hardly get along without them—food, shoes, shelter, and the like. But investment has less daily importance to us: We can do without or postpone a new steamship or Atlantic cable or steel mill. Businessmen are usually very skittish about new investments. A currency crisis in Latin America may deter a manufacturer in Dubuque or Ashtabula from expanding a factory that makes sugar-mill machinery, but it would not deter Mom from buying meat and potatoes for tonight's dinner. Unexpected strength of either Democrats or Republicans in an important November election might cause a businessman to relinquish plans for building a new hotel in Miami, but it would not prevent his wife from ordering a Thanksgiving turkey. Rumor, fears, or even the illness of a President may cause businessmen to change their investment plans, but would cause fewer changes in consumption plans. In this area, as in the areas of consumption, we know very little, but economists are trying to find out more about entrepreneurial expectations and hope to come up with better knowledge of entrepreneurial behavior.

The next question revolves around the issue of how to combat insufficient or excessive spending. When consumers lag in their consumption, what can we do to make them buy more? When investors see great profit opportunities ahead and invest too much, how can we stop them? Exhortation in these matters has come from American Presidents and other exalted personages with little or no effect. In a democracy like ours, it would of course be impossible to enact a law compelling every consuming John Doe to buy an electric massager or every investing Richard Roe to order a new tugboat. What can we do to make people spend more—or less, if the problem is inflation?

First of all, contemporary economic theorists repudiate the earlier propositions of standard theory which held that a freely competitive economic system automatically seeks equilibrium at the level of full employment. The Keynesians say that this is not true, that though savings and investment search out an equilibrium, the point of balance is not necessarily the point of full employment. In short, there are no self-correcting forces in the economy that bring about full employment; or if there are, they act too slowly. If, then, we want stability, some sort of human and organized action must be taken to get it. This action might perhaps be taken by organized groups in the community—by bankers, the National Association of Manufacturers, and labor unions working together; but it is more likely that this is a proper task of government. Most economists assume that government should at least indicate whatever steps are needed to bring about full employment. Note here, too, that modern economists do not see any benefits from depression as some of the older economists did and as certain publicists and businessmen still do. It is not a "necessary exhalation" after an inhalation or a consolidation of previous growth or a process of "desirable readjustment." To most economists, a depression is an unpardonable failure in our economic system. Thus, governmental intervention is the basic ingredient of any curative prescription.

Now, what is the government supposed to do? In depression the government may be able to increase the rate of consumption or, at least, to keep it from falling further by paying out unemployment compensation benefits, lowering taxes, and in other ways supporting or increasing the purchasing power of the unemployed and of those whose incomes are in danger of being impaired. The government can also encourage private investment in various ways. It may exert its influence to lower the rate of interest. Since so much business is based on borrowed funds, reduced interest rates might be attractive to some businessmen. Corporation and other business taxes might be reduced.

If these and many other ingenious suggestions made by busy economists are not enough to raise consumption or investment or both to the point where income is high enough to sustain full employment, then the proposal has been made that government itself should "invest." The government should engage in public works; it should build roads, schools, hospitals, and dams, or engage in various forms of conservation. In other words, government investment should make up for the deficit of private investment.

We now come to the issue at the other end of the pole of this savings-investment problem. What do we do when investment or consumption or both threaten to raise income to inflationary heights? Well, everything that was suggested above should now be done in reverse. Government can discourage consumption and investment. It can try to dissuade investment by raising interest rates and in other ways discouraging banks from lending money to businessmen. It can raise business taxes. It can raise personal income taxes; this will inhibit consumption. It can, as it did during World War II, make installment buying more difficult by compelling large down payments and a briefer period within which to complete payments.

Some economists have argued that a more nearly equal distribution of income would help to induce a greater degree of economic stability. This is based on the belief that the upper 10th among the income receivers in our economy saves more than can easily be invested. If its income could be cut down—through taxes, let us say—and be given somehow to the lower income groups, many millions of dollars now being oversaved would be spent on the necessities of life and the small luxuries of the poor. It is doubtful whether this would have helped things much during the period of economic exuberance between 1946 and 1958, when consumption and investment were high enough to keep income at the full-employment level most of the time. Perhaps the advice would have been better for the 1920's and might have averted the depressed 1930's. And if we should ever stand on the threshold of a period of sluggish economic activity with high saving and low investment, perhaps we should look into this possibility. Let it be clearly pointed out that "a more nearly equal distribution of income" does not mean an equal distribution. No resposible economist believes that a simon-pure equality of income is equitable or desirable.

The above suggests, in a general way, the drift of modern anticyclical thought originating the work of Keynes. The remedies must of course be applied with discretion and with due attention to timing and to the peculiarities of each special situation. Depressions or inflations are not at all identical. Indeed, it may even be hard to tell whether we are in depression or inflation. In the winter of 1957–58, for example, we were in a most puzzling muddle. Prices were going up as if we were in an inflationary period; unemployment was increasing as if we were heading toward depression. So what were we in? There was a widespread demand for a tax cut. It was argued that consumers would increase consumption (and therefore the national income) if taxes could be freed for the purchase of goods. But some people asked whether giving consumers more money would really increase their spending. Might they not save the tax cut, fearing unemployment or reduced income later on? And if they did spend the tax money, would this not further increase the prices which were paradoxically going up while unemployment was also going up? We were in a quandary, but such quandaries always face the policy maker when he gets away from the simple constructs of theory. One of the more amusing contradictions in the spring of 1958 was that President Dwight D. Eisenhower was urging consumers to buy more things at the same time that the Treasury, through singing commercials, was urging us to save more by acquiring government bonds!

The proper timing of any anticyclical program is always difficult, partly because we know so little about the future. It is always easy to see what should have been done last year—economists, like others, rejoice in 20–20 hindsight—but it is always hard to know what the future holds and, therefore, when to apply remedies.

The reader, pondering some of the preceding pages, may wonder at some of the remedies. How does government pour billions into the economy or reduce taxes without dangerously increasing the public debt? How can interest rates be forced down or up, at will? How do banks create money to permit a rate of investment higher than the rate of saving? These questions must be postponed until we get to our study of banking and public finance in a later section. There, we shall try to answer them—insofar as they can be answered.

The Multiplier

We have not quite finished our theoretical examination of income fluctuation. A rather important thing happens when new money is injected into the economy or withdrawn from it. Suppose a government, in depression, decides to inaugurate a billion-dollar road-building program. This is one kind of injection. The sum of money finds its way quickly to the persons who supply the ingredients that roads are composed of; it goes to labor, cementmakers, owners of gravel pits and sand pits, truck owners, and all the other suppliers of goods and services needed for road building. The money paid to laborers, some of whom may have been unemployed, is passed on to those who cater to family needs; the once jobless now replenish their wardrobes and buy more and better quality food; the grocers and clothing stores, in turn, hand the money over to wholesalers, who spend it again. The cement maker and gravel-pit owner hire new labor, and the newly employed workmen buy new things with their wages. Profits increase for all entrepreneurs associated with the road-building project. They, too, pass their increased income along; they may invest or buy their wives fur coats; in any event, the increased gains are handed on. Thus, in a cumulative process the original billion dollars increases the economy's income several times. A billion dollars injected into the economy may add threefold to the national income.

The cumulative process described in the preceding paragraphs is usually referred to as the "multiplier" or "multiplier effect" or "investment multiplier." Although the value of the multiplier would constantly vary with the ever-changing circumstances of our real and kaleidoscopic world, economists usually assign to it a value between two and three. This means that an injection of new investment into the economy would result in an increase of national income equal to two or three times the original sum. Limits are placed on the multiplier by two facts. First comes time: For practical purposes, three or four years after the first disbursements are made, the lingering effects of the multiplier seem to get lost, as most sound waves get lost after traveling half a mile or so. Second, and more important, is the marginal propensity to save. If every person getting a chunk of the billion dollars being spent on roads were to save one third of it, then the value of the multiplier would be three—the reciprocal of the marginal propensity to save. What happens is that only part of the sum is passed on at each round. If there were no leakages of any kind (the most important of which is saving), the original billion would amplify itself indefinitely.

The multiplier is applicable to other types of sums injected into the economy. If, for example, in depression the government decides to increase its payments to the needy through various forms of unemployment compensation, relief grants, public assistance, and so forth, the new sums paid out will have the same multiplier effect. A large private company's deciding to pay a Christmas bonus of $5 million to its employees will increase the national income by $10 million to $15 million.

The reverse is also true. Any withdrawal from the economy will multiply itself and diminish the national income by two to three times the amount withdrawn. During the depression of the 1930's, for example, many agencies of government cut the salaries of their employees by 5 percent or more. Politically, this had a desirable effect, since almost everybody employed by private business was getting a cut in salary or wages; it seemed only fair that governmental employees should get a cut, too. Economically, it was a very stupid thing to do, however, because it reduced the nation's income by two or three times the budgetary savings. If you decide to save $1,000 more this year than last, you too can diminish the national income by much more than you save.

A Simple Macroeconomic Model

Standard theorists dicusss macroeconomics in a style similar to that used for microeconomics—through the use of mathematical models. To introduce this style of exposition, a rather elementary model of an economy will be developed and then shown geometrically. This model, like all other such structures, consists of a set of simple assumptions about the nature of the economy.

The first assumption delineates the number and nature of the participants in our hypothetical economy. In this model, there are only two—consumers and investors; their activities are similar to those already ascribed to them in this chapter. Next, we must make some assumptions about the forces that motivate our decision makers and the actions they will take under different circumstances. Here the assumptions are simple ones. First, it is assumed that the amount of consumption will be determined solely by the amount of income already generated in the economy. The meaning of this assumption is made apparent by reading the consumption schedule in Table 9–1. If national income is at $600 billion a year, $580 billion will be spent to meet consumer demands; if national income is $850 billion, consumers will demand $780 billion of goods and services, leaving for investment purposes goods and services valued at $70 billion. Second, it is assumed that investors want to add $50 billion of goods to their capital stock no matter what the actual level of economic activity may be.

Two additional assumptions are made for convenience—first, that there is no international trade; and second, that all our discussions relate to a moment in time which we shall call a year. It is not the calendar year you are familiar with, for we do not recognize any year before it or any year after it. It is, however, a convenience for the mind to think in terms of this fictional year when dealing with national income questions, since most government statistics in this field use a calendar year.

It should be clearly evident to the reader how great an abstraction from reality our model is. No recognition is given to the possible effects that advertising, the anticipation of inflation or depression, government hearings on auto safety, or military escalations in the warmer arenas of the cold war might have on the level of domestic consumption or investment. One year is not allowed to influence another, cyclical variation in economic activity is eliminated, and international trade is nonexistent.

There is reason for this. To include all these factors in our model—important though they may be—would render it unworkable. More complex assumptions could be made, of course, and still retain the model's deterministic quality, but no economic theory can include all the complexities and subtleties existent in reality and still meet its primary purpose—the exposition of fundamental principles.

Armed with these assumptions and the definition of "equilibrium" already presented, we can determine the level of national income the economy will tend toward. Reading from Table 9–1, it is

TABLE 9–1

The Determination of National Income in a Hypothetical Economy

National Income	Consumption Expenditures	Savings	Investment	Consumption plus Investment
450	460	−10	50	530
500	500	0	50	570
600	580	20	50	630
750	**700**	**50**	**50**	**750**
850	780	70	50	830
950	860	90	50	910

at $750 billion per year. At this level of national income, saving equals investment, and national expenditure is equal to national income. As long as these equalities exist, there is no reason for the level of economic activity to change.

If, however, for some unknown reason, national income fell to $600 billion, savings would be $30 billion less than investment, and aggregate demand for goods and services would be $630 billion, or $30 billion above the amount produced. This would bring about an increase in economic activity as businessmen employed unused factors of production in an attempt to meet demand. If ample unemployed factors of production were not available to bring production levels to equality with aggregate demand, an inflation would ensue. But whether due to inflation or to an increase in real output, national income will rise to $750 billion a year, and the equality of desired savings and desired investment will be restored.

If by chance the level of national income was at $850 billion a year, a similar process would take place—only in the other direction. The business community would find itself in the unpleasant situation of producing $850 billion of goods and services each year but selling only $830 billion. Desired investment would still be $50 billion, desired savings $70 billion, with $20 billion of output threatening to remain in the inventory held by the business community. To prevent this occurrence, producers will cut back production, releasing factors of production and lowering national income. As national income declines, so will desired savings; and once again, equilibrium will be attained at $750 billion.

The information presented in Table 9–1 is reproduced in graphical form in Figures 9–1 and 9–2. Unlike the supply-and-demand diagrams, in which the horizontal axis represents physical quantities and the vertical axis represents a monetary unit, both axes in Figure 9–1 are in identical units. Each scale measure the total value of goods and services produced in the economy during a given time period, in this case our fictional year. However, each axis measures this aggregate figure from a different vantage point. The horizontal axis represents the income that the members of the nation's households receive for their productive efforts, and the vertical axis is used to present the amount of expenditures made by the two participants in the economy.

An important feature of the diagram is the guideline. Drawn at a 45-degree angle to the origin, it bisects the diagram. All points along it are therefore equidistant to the axes and represent an equality between income and expenditure. It is along this line and only along this line that equilibrium positions can be found, for at any point in the diagram not on this line, national income and expenditure would have different values and so could not be maintained. The C-C line measures aggregate consumer demand at different levels of national income. By adding desired investment of $50 billion to this line, we get the $C + I$-$C + I$ line, which represents aggregate demand for goods and services at different levels of national income. The equilibrium level of national income is found at the point where $C + I$-$C + I$ intersects the guideline.

The determination of national income can also be shown geo-

FIGURE 9–1

NATIONAL INCOME DETERMINATION

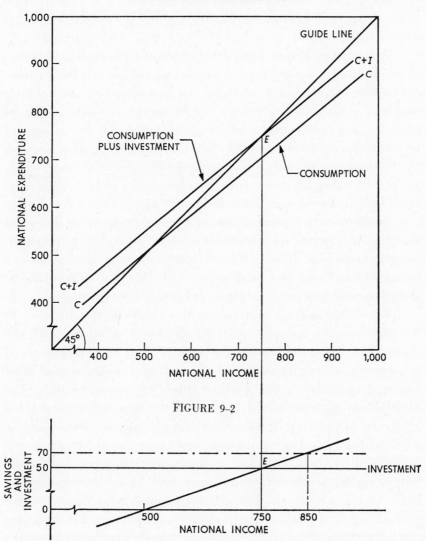

FIGURE 9–2

metrically by employing the savings and investment schedules, since
an equilibrium position can be defined as that level of national income
at which desired savings equal desired investment. This approach is
presented in Figure 9–2. The horizontal axis again measures national
income; the vertical axis now measures both savings and investment.

The intersection of the investment schedule—a horizontal line drawn in at $50 billion—with the savings schedule indicates the equilibrium level of national income, since at that point desired savings equal desired investment.

Among other things, Figure 9–2 can be used to analyze the effect of an increase in desired investment. Let us assume that the business community experiences a wave of extreme optimism about future economic conditions. Expecting a sizable increase in demand for its products, and envisioning celestial profit statements, the community increases its rate of investment to $70 billion per year. This is shown geometrically by drawing a horizontal dot-dash-dot investment schedule at $70 billion. The new equality of savings and investment is at $850 billion, a rise in national income of $100 billion. We can see here the geometric representation of the multiplier effect discussed above: An increase in investment of $20 billion brings about an increase in national income of $100 billion. An identical analysis can be made using Figure 9–1. In this case the $C + I \cdot C + I$ line would be shifted upward to account for the increase in desired investment.

We should remind ourselves at this point that the increase in national income is not necessarily an increase in the quantity of real goods and services available to the population. If all the resources of the economy were fully employed when national income was at $750 billion, no increase in real product would have been possible. The $100-billion increase would have been entirely inflationary. This brings us to the most fundamental concept Keynes contributed to standard theory: The equilibrium level of national income is not determined by the availability of productive resources, but by the level of aggregate demand. Equilibrium positions are therefore just as likely to occur at levels that will leave one out of three workers unemployed as at levels where two jobs chase each man. This observation is the rationale for government action. For if aggregate demand is too small to attain full employment, the government—a participant in the economy unmentioned in our model but of some importance in our national economy—can increase expenditures and so increase the need for economic activity. If the economy is tending toward inflation, the government can lower expenditures, thus reducing the pressure on available resources. It is a simple matter to include government in our model. Instead of thinking of the business community's increasing

investment by $20 billion, assume a $20-billion increase in government expenditures, and the usefulness of the model is enhanced.

Summary and Conclusions

During the 1940's, somebody said that when the United States
sneezes, Europe catches pneumonia. What this meant was that a light
depression here would migrate to Europe, with serious repercussions
on our friends of the West. Depression, like Asian flu, is catching.
Perhaps this is less true than it was 20 years ago, when Europe was
still in the agonies of postwar reconstruction; and since then, Europeans have built defenses against the invasion of an American depression. Nonetheless, it is certainly still true that a deep depression here
would affect our allies unfavorably. But perhaps worse than that, our
inability to maintain steady economic growth without temporary regression would be construed as a basic weakness and would estrange
both our friends and the neutrals. In these days of propaganda
warfare, another great depression would be a serious loss of face. The
Soviet Union does not have depression in our sense, because "boom
and bust" characterize free economies, not planned ones. Our only
hope is that we shall have both will and wit to control depression or
inflation if either seriously threatens our economy.

This chapter has examined the cause and cure of inflation and
depression. The basic theory underlying depression is that not all
savings are invested or, to put it a little more precisely, that the
amounts that savers plan to save or try to save exceed the amounts that
investors are prepared to invest. This causes incomes, and hence
savings, to go down until actual savings and actual investment reach
equality. The unequal rates may arise in the first instance because
savers and investors are different people, and the forces that impel
savings are not the same forces that impel investing.

Inflation is the reverse of this. Inflation comes about because
investors seek to invest more than savers are saving. The only way in
which equality between savings and investment can now be achieved is
through an increase of prices.

The policy implications of the situation described in the above
paragraphs are that means should be found to increase investment
when depression threatens and to decrease investment when inflation

threatens. Government can take steps to spur private investment by taxation policies and in other ways. If this fails, government can, by spending, act as a substitute for private enterprise. It can reduce consumption and investment by increasing taxes.

Expanded spending by consumers is also desirable. Generally speaking, consumers do not hold back on consuming in the same way that investors hold back on investing. If they are spending little, the reason is that they have little money; and they have little money because depression or unemployment of men is upon us. Here the government can help by simply giving consumers more money to spend in the form of unemployment compensation, relief, or public assistance. The increased spending that results will encourage increased investing.

Finally, the effects of increased or decreased spending are cumulative. If one of the monster corporations spends $100 million on a program of expansion, the national income increases by two or three times the new amount spent. The reverse is also true.

QUESTIONS FOR REVIEW AND DISCUSSION

1. Define, in your own words, each of the following terms:
   a) Depression
   b) Inflation
   c) Savings
   d) Investment
   e) Consumption
2. If consumption is $400 billion a year, investment $40 billion a year, and government spending $120 billion a year, what is the level of the national income? If investment should rise by $20 billion a year, will the change in national income be greater or less than $20 billion? Why? If government should lower its taxes but maintain its expenditures, what effect would this have on national income? Why?
3. What would be the probable effect of a cut in the federal individual income tax if, as in 1945, the U.S. unemployment rate were down to 1.9 percent? Why?
4. A thrifty but miserly and suspicious grocer, as a precautionary measure, puts $1,000 annually in his safety-deposit box. Is it correct to say that he is reducing the GNP by about $2,000 annually? Explain. If your answer is yes, how could he return the money to the GNP and at the same time still possess the money?

5. A. H. Raskin, formerly the *New York Times* labor reporter, in an article written for the *Saturday Evening Post* in 1963, stated that a law abolishing all featherbedding at once would result in a serious depression. Do you agree or disagree? Why?

6. If a farmer buys 140 more acres to add to his farm, has he made an investment in the sense in which the word "investment" has been used in this chapter? Explain.

7. Why must savings be equal to investment?

8. "When savings tend to be greater than investment, national income declines; when savings tend to be less than investment, national income rises." What are the underlying reasons for these fluctuations in national income?

9. What effect has Keynesian economics had on the standard economists' view of the relationship between government and the economy?

PART III

Issues of Public Policy

INTRODUCTION TO ISSUES
OF PUBLIC POLICY

Introductory Observations

Public policy, at least as the concept will be developed in Part III, suggests two subconcepts:

1. Recognition of the need for conscious human action to clear up economic muddles that are not being cleared up by "natural" regulatory forces such as the operation of the forces of supply and demand, the seeking of maximum income through self-interest, the achievement of consumers' equilibrium through maximization of satisfaction, and so on.
2. Application of economic theory to the clearing-up of the muddles; use of applied or welfare economics to improve the human condition.

A few words should be said about the first paragraph above. The muddles alluded to take many forms—unemployment, unsatisfactory balance of trade, extensive oligopoly or oligopsony, exploitation of labor or of the consumer, inflation, too much or too little money, slow economic growth, and so on. The forces of competition, laissez-faire, and the behavior imposed upon us by our institutions do much to organize economic life in such a way as to make things bearable for most of us. But sometimes, these forces, often thought of as "natural" regulators, do not work, and we must have recourse to "unnatural" regulators, foremost among which is governmental intervention.

Let us develop this idea of natural and unnatural regulation a little further by imagining a simple case. Scientists discover that a substance now found only in apricots prevents cancer. Soon there will be too few apricots to go around, since everybody will double or triple his intake. Prices soar extravagantly, and both old and new orchardists are now encouraged by high prices to increase the supply. In due course of time, prices recede from their previously fantastic heights to a level near the cost of production, the long-run equilibrium price. No

189

governmental action was needed. "Natural" economic forces took over and solved the problem, namely, the dearth of apricots just after the medical discovery. But now, let us suppose that some barrier prevents this outcome. Many obstacles can be imagined. One is that the Apricot Growers' Benevolent Association, getting wind of the discovery before it was actually announced, had bought up all the good apricot land in America, and now refuses to plant new trees, preferring astronomically high prices per ton on a total crop of 250,000 tons to normal profits per ton on a crop of a million tons. Another is that apricots are overfastidious about soil and temperature and that very little new apricot land is available. Other barriers can easily be imagined.

So now we have a sort of muddle: The possibility of eliminating cancer is almost within reach, yet the needed substance is not being produced. The economy cannot respond to the profound want of a nation. The populace is clamoring for more apricots; congressmen investigate apricots; the mainland Chinese, who have a lot of good apricot land, tell the world that the imperialist, warmongering, degenerate United States would rather bomb Hanoi than increase the supply of apricots by one single willow basket; economists gravely tell their students that the supply of apricots is inelastic, that is, that high price does not call forth a larger supply; all this, but no apricots. Finally, there are apricot riots, calls to impeach the Secretary of Agriculture; James Reston and John Kenneth Galbraith both write articles on apricots and riots; the Presidential election appears to be lost unless something is done. "Natural" economic forces have accomplished nothing, and the government finally decides to act "unnaturally" to appease the now overwhelming demand for apricots. What can government do? Well, many things are possible. If the Apricot Growers' Benevolent Association is really to blame, it can be prosecuted under antitrust and its leaders sent to jail. If a true shortage of special apricot land is to blame, the government can subsidize orchardists who add the proper ingredients to ordinary land and control humidity and temperature under glass. Or the government can open up trade with China and allow the importation of apricots. Or it can inaugurate a crash program to produce the cancer-inhibiting substance synthetically. But these avenues toward the rectifying of the muddle involve the use of "unnatural" means, that is, governmental intervention.

Leaving behind us now our apricot problem and looking forward, we shall soon see that government is playing a larger and larger role in our economy. One sixth of the population is on a governmental payroll; millions besides get welfare or pension checks. The government buys 20 percent of all that is produced. Any substantial reduction of governmental spending would, at least in the short run, be economically calamitous, not only to us but to other nations as well. The public authority regulates in so many areas that any large withdrawal would probably cause the breakdown of transport, communication, and health and sanitation services.

As we go on to discuss regulation and intervention, we shall find that certain values are implicit in much governmental action. Tentatively, we may list them as follows:

1. Full or virtually full employment of the factors of production.
2. Price stability.
3. Economic growth.
4. Relatively high degree of freedom in international trade.
5. Maximum possible freedom of economic action compatible with high performance.
6. Virtual abolition of poverty in the United States.
7. Establishment of a keener price-quality competition than now exists, with full realization that in many lines of business we cannot achieve the perfect competition among many firms postulated by standard theory; we seek workable rather than perfect competition.
8. Protection of the health and safety of the citizenry.

Criteria for Governmental Intervention

Public policy, as we have stated, refers mostly to governmental intervention. If the quasi-utopian dream of an almost pure laissez-faire economy with nearly perfect competition could have prevailed, the question of public policy would have been and would still be a minor one. Competition would have been the economic policeman. Ordinary goods would have sold on the basis of their capacity to fulfill their function, on the basis of such defensible virtues as purity, durability, and beauty; and the goods would have been offered at competitive prices, near the cost of production, uninflated by those advertising costs, often vast, that pay for persuasion rather than fact. Incomes would have been more nearly equal; depressions and unemployment would have been mild enough to cause only small concern: near-monopolies would not exist in their current profusion. But many things intruded to spoil this utopia of the 18th-century mind. First, of course, were human beings themselves, who, although they believed in pure competition for others, steadily sought out sheltered positions in the market for themselves, thus in the end creating an economy of widely imperfect competition. Second (these are not necessarily listed in order of importance) came the unexpected surge of technology which pulled apart the social and economic fabric: Skilled craftsmen became mere factory hands or members of the unemployed army; intelligent consumers were made helpless by new products of untested quality; certain types of factories had to be built huge to use inventions or newly discovered processes efficiently—so huge that the product of two or three of them virtually supplied the market and thus invited digopoly. Third came wars; wars disrupted the channels of international trade and distorted the internal economy; our wars, among other effects, helped give birth to our expensive agricultural subsidies and probably intensified the concentration of industry. Fourth came depressions but particularly the depression of the 1930's, which caused so much suffering and did so much harm to the meritorious ideal of a laissez-faire competitive economy. Last in this brief list, but not last of all the causes that could be cited as spoilers of the 18th-century competitive utopia, came a substitute utopia which, for brevity, we may call the Marxian utopia. In this, we include not only the truly revolutionary ideas of Karl Marx, but also such inventions as consumers' cooperatives or the social insurances, the latter proposed by Charles Fourier and inaugurated on a wide scale by Otto Bismarck in the 1890's. We must also place under this heading some of the nonpolitical concepts of democracy that had begun to take root: economic democracy, the democratic rather than the patriarchal family, equal rights for women, and democracy in education. Literature proclaimed the dignity of man. It was but one step from this rapidly developing humanitarianism to the widespread appeals for better jails, public insane asylums, and hospitals, poor relief, public works for the unemployed, protection of women and children in mill and mine, increased safety on the job, and countless amenities, rights, and freedoms.

Insofar as some of these things required the allocation of resources from one field to another, the problem became an economic problem. Some of them were, of course, not economic, such as extension of the franchise to women or destruction of the patriarchal family. But many of them were, such as poor relief, public works during hard times, and social insurance. Now, under the laissez-faire competitive ideal, almost everything that involved the allocation of resources was to be left to the market. This philosophy was developed and hardened before the great humanitarian surge of the 19th century. But humanitarianism is not often a marketable commodity and hence is not of much interest to private enterprise. If something humanitarian was to be done, the government would in most cases have to do it.

As far back as the last quarter of the 18th century, even the most ardent opponents of governmental intervention saw that some economic goods or services were not among the appropriate concerns of the businessman. One was defense; a second, police and law courts; a third, certain essential highways. To put it differently: Whether any individual John Q. Citizen wanted policemen or not, or protection from foreign enemies, or roads, he would be compelled to pay for his share of these things. He did not buy them on the market; he received them in return for taxes. All this seemed obvious enough, and as long as the list was short and the essentialness of the service or good widely agreed upon, the citizenry was united in support of governmental intervention.

When we come to less obviously defensible matters such as the social insurances, we find unity harder to achieve. Old-age pensions have caused much friction. On this issue, many citizens can say: "Why should I contribute 3 percent of my income toward a pension? I am a well-to-do middle-aged citizen and do not expect ever to need aid when I become a senior citizen." Or "I can save or invest for my own pension—I'm a smart operator and shall be rich at 50." Or "I come from a short-lived family—and anyhow, I don't feel any too good right now and will surely sleep with my fathers before 62, the age I'd

have to reach before getting a penny back of all the money I paid in."
If such objections can arise in a person's mind when the benefits are
destined directly for him, how great are the objections to being taxed
for relief of the poor, or improvement of the care of criminals, or the
increase of farmers' income!

What criteria shall we use to decide how to transfer incomes
from one group to another; or force people to buy what they may not
want, such as public education; or shift steel, bricks, labor, wood, and
copper wire from the building of luxurious private homes to the
building of public psychiatric wards for shoplifters? Certainly, in
a nation of representative government, part of the answer lies in the
demands of the electorate. If, as in the depression of the 1930's, citizens demand, sometimes angrily and threateningly, old-age pensions,
unemployment compensation, or increases in farm prices, then, in
such a situation, government will try to meet minimum demands or
find acceptable substitutes.

When standard economic theory was a little more explicitly
based on the pleasure-pain theories of Jeremy Bentham than they are
today, certain economists, particularly A. C. Pigou, developed the
idea that a philosophy of welfare—and hence one of governmental
intervention—might be based on the concept of the diminishing marginal utility of money. If, for example, my income is $1 million a
year and the government takes away $1,000 of it, my loss is small—
indeed, almost negligible. If, now, this sum is divided among four
very poor families, their gain is great. My loss causes me little distress; their gain causes them disproportionate happiness. The total
happiness or utility or satisfaction of the society is presumably
increased by this transfer.

Another economic criterion for governmental intervention brings
up the question of external effects. The negative side of this is
exemplified by industrially caused air pollution. Paper mills and
plants that generate electricity often reduce their production costs by
troubling the air with poisonous particles or dumping noxious wastes
into our rivers and lakes. The community, through reduced health,
cleanliness, and opportunities for recreation, pays heavily for the
costs saved by the offensive firms. Here, the government may intervene on economic grounds to regulate the companies. In the case of

some public nuisances the monetary costs to the affected community can be computed rather precisely; in others, as in the case of airplane noises, obnoxiousness cannot be so easily measured in dollars. The developing capitalist world, from its early days, has often defended its spoliation by arguing that this is the relatively small cost to be paid by the community for progress. But this defense is losing some of its persuasiveness in our world of poisonous effluence and cubic miles of effluvium.

Certain projects are so devoid of immediate profit-making possibilities that if they are to be undertaken at all, they must be undertaken by privately endowed foundations or by government, or both. Much scientific research belongs to this class of projects. Medical research has been undertaken by private endowments. Two presidents, Franklin D. Roosevelt and John F. Kennedy, spurred on efforts to conquer poliomyelitis and mental retardation through individual donations of money. Other projects, such as space exploration, are simply too vast and expensive to be carried on by anything less huge than the great governments of the world. It is of course possible that some day business enterprise will be able to make money by selling a package trip that takes newlyweds around Venus to the moon for a month of honeymooning in a superluxury hotel, with pink telephones, ice cubes, and TV in every room, but no business firm is prepared to spend money for the basic research needed now. It is easy to understand why only governments can undertake the fundamental and expensive studies, but it is a little harder to understand and justify priorities. Why is it more important to send men to the moon than to abolish poverty, or to study the basis of human aggression and toleration of warfare? In the field of privately endowed research, can we explain why certain diseases have been singled out as subjects of present attack? Should we now devote more money to diseases of the heart than to colds and flu? If so, why?

Many forms of governmental intervention arise out of the sudden dramatization of a latent problem or unrecognized abuse. Our federal food and drug acts, for example, were responses to public indignation inspired by eloquent books or public shock over deaths caused by the diethylene glycol added to an elixir, and over the birth of deformed children exposed to thalidomide. In the mid-60's, dormant concern over automobile safety was awakened by the published studies of Ralph Nader. His work hastened safety changes in Detroit's vehicle industry.

As we shall see later on in the chapter on poverty, the development of technology may often induce governmental intervention. We have already spoken above of the need for the state to intervene when new products come on the market. The housewife of 1850 had to be able to recognize good wool cloth and to tell the difference between linen, silk, and cotton. Today, she has numerous untested textiles to identify under countless brand names. The government could quite properly intervene to insist that sellers describe their goods in terms of durability and resistance to washing or dry cleaning. Technology has caused issues to arise in quite different areas. Our vast capacity to produce has touched off not only a widespread desire for a larger share of the goods and services of our vastly increased productivity but has also stimulated a longing for greater security. Recognition of these things has caused governmental intervention to reduce the swings of the business cycle and to increase interest in the abolition of poverty.

Technology has altered certain agelong situations and relationships. Medical science has prolonged life; thus, we have a large percentage of people over 65 who must be taken care of. The burden of caring for them in an urban and pecuniary society is too great to be borne wholly by their young—hence old-age pensions under social security. Not only that, but even the lighter burden of our yesterdays was still easier to bear in a largely agricultural society where old people could help on a family farm by darning and doing light chores, and where much of the extra food they consumed was home-grown and nearly costless.

Finally, the government has the responsibility of regulating a vast new array of business enterprises. Not only do we have thriving illegal business enterprises in the drug traffic, but we also have the illegal activities of reputable business concerns, such as price fixing, delivered pricing, discriminatory pricing, and all the other devices that restrain trade—a collection of practices tossed into a hopper named "antitrust." Unlike the governments of 1800, we also have to regulate railroads, gas and electric companies, telephone companies, airlines, broadcasting, and urban transport.

We must conclude from this that government necessarily enters economic activity in ways that were never envisaged when the great classical doctrines of economics were laid down. We must also conclude that a firm philosophy of intervention has not yet been worked out—only a few scraps of justification based largely on political expediency and the insistent demands of a technologically dynamic society.

Theory versus Applications of Theory

Up to a point, Part III involves the application of theory, as taught in Part II, to actual human problems. Indeed, a few writers in the field lead their readers to believe that policy is wholly an application of theory. One could wish that this were true; it would simplify things a great deal. There can be no doubt that theory guides us toward the solution of problems as they are found in the real world and that it may give us important initial insights. But for various reasons, problems have a life of their own and are sometimes quite contemptuous of theory.

Some problems have a way of coming at us before the theory exists. The depression of the 1930's is a good example; the nation was severely damaged by an event for which we had no widely accepted theory. The same thing seems to be true now concerning the problem of growth in advanced and underdeveloped nations alike. We are only groping toward theories of growth, and this at a time when the question of growth is linked to the foreign policies of great nations that have the means of killing each other several times over. Indeed, a strong case can be made for the hypothesis that problems always come first and theories about them develop afterward.

Problems are also unmannered enough to come three or four at a time and to demand for their solution contradictory applications of theory. Thus a nation can have a depression and a balance-of-payments deficit at the same time. Curing the first malady may exacerbate the second. What do you do when the solutions are in conflict? One can only reply with another question: What does the physician do when penicillin would cure but the patient is violently allergic to this antibiotic? Or what does the engineer do when he requires a material of great strength and also of low weight? Something intermediate must be improvised; and although a good theoretician may be able to improvise better than an untrained practitioner, new approaches not previously contemplated by economic analysis must be found.

Theory cannot always be applied to a situation that is much more complex than that envisaged by theory. Thus the pure economic theory of the farm problem is absurdly simple: Overproduction takes place when the price offered is above the equilibrium price; the solution is to reduce the support price guaranteed by government. But before recommending this policy, we should give consideration to several other matters, as follows:

1. Farmers—and other groups whom we shall study—have political power; to cut grain support prices drastically is to alienate a strong block politically. Is it not a waste of breath to advocate that either the Democratic or the Republican party take measures to damage its chances of reelection by reducing subsidies?

2. We have built up, not only on the farm, but also throughout our economy, groups that depend and count on subsidies; to cut off suddenly their undeserved incomes may be just but would cause widespread distress to groups whose expectations were suddenly disappointed.

3. Sums paid to farmers reenter the income stream in the form of purchases of tractors, fertilizers, gasoline, paint, barbed wire, and the other needs of farmers—not to mention the sweaters and skirts and lipsticks and hairdos needed by the farmer's daughter. How much employment and how many bankruptcies might be created by a reduction of farmers' income, and hence purchases? It is of course true that the federal funds paid to the farmer through price supports might do more good economically and might better meet our sense of equity if they were used for retraining and rehabilitating the truly pauperized farmer (who gets little if any of this federal money) or or teaching new skills to those unemployed because of automation. But until we could really be sure that funds were switched from an area of lesser need to one of greater need, we had better keep on paying the farmers and continue using one of the acceptable ways we now have for bolstering an economy that seems to need constant support.

Thus, we must conclude that the solution of problems by the application of theory is not enough. Some of our suggestions about the improvement of the economy will be based on empirical and specialized study, on concern for what is feasible rather than for what accords with the strict demands of theory. Even so, some of the policies suggested may seem visionary or require institutional changes that will be resisted by many segments of the general population. Some economic remedies demand the sacrifice of cherished prejudices.

Summary and Conclusions

The capacity of our economy to regulate itself is not nearly so great as might be inferred from the self-regulating model described in Part II. Indeed, the macroeconomic section of Part II made the tacit assumption that equilibrium income rarely, and only by luck, attains the optimum point of full employment. In Part III, we shall study typical situations that require remedy or governmental regulation or intervention in order to make our economy work efficiently and in the public interest. In other words, we shall study public policy.

It is hard to set down precise criteria for governmental intervention. The society as a whole must feel a sense of malfunction—too much poverty, inequitable distribution of income, a too-rapid inflation, an unsatisfactory balance of trade. A few things seem to be clear: What is needed but will not attract private enterprise must be done by government. Our highways, our defense system, our police and judiciary—these are among the things that a capitalist society freely assigns to the public authority. There are other things that only government can do; however, some question exists as to whether government really should do them, but if so, when—e.g., sending men to the moon in the calculable future before solving some obvious problems here below, such as elimination of rat-infested housing.

Among the important forces making for governmental intervention is the development of technology. Technology seems to have an independent life, a life that plays havoc with accustomed ways of doing things and prevents a static adjustment. Automation, for example, destroys existing skills, demands new ones, causes unemployment at least temporarily, increases farmers' crops faster than our ethics of distribution can adjust to the change, makes buggies obsolete, and makes uranium more valuable. Disturbances such as these may require governmental intervention if extreme hardship is to be avoided. The sluggish "natural" forces of the free, competitive, laissez-faire economy are too often too slow and too feeble.

In some areas, technology points out very clearly that something must be done: In TV broadcasting, for example, the relatively small number of channels available gives us the alternative of chaos or governmental regulation. In other areas, as exemplified by programs of public assistance to the poor, we have numerous but also perhaps dubious guidelines—a theory of the diminishing utility of incomes, which justifies taking from the rich to give to the poor; an ethical theory of making available to all the benefits of an increasingly productive economy; a political theory of coming to terms with the revolution of rising expectations.

In general, when we intervene, we do so in accordance with economic theory, as the engineer builds an airplane in accordance with the theories of physics. Sometimes, economic theory is too frail to lean on, and pragmatic solutions must be found, although such solutions cannot bypass economics entirely. Often, political science, psychology, history, cultural anthropology, and the other sister disciplines must be called upon to help.

QUESTIONS FOR REVIEW AND DISCUSSION

1. Is governmental action justifiable in the instances listed just below? Give reasons for your reply.
   a) Maintaining institutions to care for the severely retarded mentally, at no cost (or small cost) to their parents.
   b) Undertaking a project to exterminate rats in cities at governmental expense.
   c) Requiring that instructions for cleaning, laundering, and ironing be permanently and indelibly attached to all garments.
   d) Licensing TV repairmen.
2. In large cities, should the municipality own and operate the major forms of public transportation? Give reasons for your reply.
3. Should government demand that everybody be vaccinated against smallpox and provide free vaccination for those who cannot or will not pay a private physician? Should all citizens be required to present evidence at a governmental office that they have been revaccinated periodically, since vaccination loses its effectiveness after a few years? Give arguments for or against these policies.

4. "I do not share the general belief that government should in principle be allowed to intervene only when no alternative exists; what bothers me, though, is that when government does intervene, the way is open to graft, inefficiency, and delay, and leads to the granite wall of impenetrable bureaucracy." Evaluate the preceding quoted statement.

5. "I can send the soil of my backyard to the Department of Agriculture and get a free analysis of whether to add lime or acid, whether it is good for zinnias or lilies. But to what governmental agency can I send a shirt to ask whether it will shrink, or a camera to test lens and shutter, or a wrist-watch or color TV set?" Does the implied complaint in the quoted sentences seem justifiable to you? Give reasons for your reply.

Chapter 11

DEFINITION AND
FUNCTIONS OF
MONEY

Money and Society

To discuss the significance and importance of money to man is as endless a task as to discuss the significance and importance of the alphabet or of arabic numerals. It is one of the basic instruments of civilized man and has probably played as large a role in shaping his institutions as any single invention that one might think of. Although its chief function is to facilitate the exchange of goods between human beings, one finds it hard to imagine how certain other activities could have sprung into existence or developed very far without money—for example, getting and paying interest, speculation, and bookkeeping. In our discussion of the national income in Chapter 8, we saw how useful it was to convert the value of tens of thousands of goods and services into their money values; these money values could then be added up to give us one single useful figure. A firm would be incredibly handicapped in its bookkeeping if it had to list its assets in kind instead of listing them in the form of money. How else could a dentifrice firm add together such diverse assets as its factory and the name of its internationally famous *Dento-White*, which may be more valuable than the factory? Money permits an exactitude in economic transactions that would not be possible without it. It is infinitely divisible. It makes perfect sense to say that a certain type of bolt costs $0.00376, even if we cannot, in fact, divide a dollar into such small pieces; a hardware merchant, stocking up bolts, can easily pay $3.76 for a thousand. Money is compact and enduring, resists breakage, and can be almost weightless; you can send a $100 bill anywhere in the United States under a postage stamp.

Economists, considering the kinds of things that have been said above, have defined the functions and characteristics of money as follows:

The functions of money are to serve as:
1. A medium of exchange.
2. A store of value (something that represents latent purchasing power).
3. A standard of deferred payment (a standard in which to specify amounts of value to be transferred in payment of debt or other future transfers).
4. A standard of value (for the U.S. the dollar is the unit in which values are expressed).

The following qualities characterize the more desirable kinds of money in modern states:

1. Durability
2. Controlled supply
3. Divisibility
4. Easy portability

Economists of an earlier age underrated the importance of money. If you think of money only as a medium of exchange—a lubricant of what is essentially barter—then money is a rather unimportant subject theoretically, just as oil and grease are quite subordinate to the principles underlying the operation of a gasoline engine. And yet it must be conceded that this early concept of money still has profound validity. The goods and services proliferated by any economic system for the use of man are the products of combining land, labor, and capital. You do not need money to produce. Money would not have made life easier for Robinson Crusoe, and King Midas' ability to turn everything into gold (money) threatened him with starvation. But in a monetary economy like ours, money can do some very important things. Too little money in a modern society may cause depression and, without touching the technical processes of producing goods, cause fewer resources to be engaged in productive activities. At the same time, an excess or deficit of money may enrich or impoverish certain groups in the society through no fault of their own. To return to our analogy of the lubricant in a motor: Oil does not make an engine run, but bad oil can cause it to operate badly. Similarly, money can exercise a vast influence on the economy's functioning. Our discussion of money will try to build up this important fact, namely, that money is a powerful and independent force in the economy, partly determining its rate of production and affecting the distribution of income and wealth.

We might as well, at the very outset, disabuse the reader of the idea that money is composed only of the coins and bills put into circulation by the government. From the economists' point of view—however the law defines it—anything widely accepted in payment is money. Thus, checks are money. If the reader will search his memory for a moment, he will remember that most large transactions in which he has engaged during the past year were settled by checkbook money. A college student's summer wage is usually paid by check. His college fees are mostly paid by check, as is his large September bill at the bookstore. The monthly sums he gets from home are likely to be in the form of checks. A family with an income of $2,000 a month can easily and comfortably get along with only $100 in Uncle Sam's cash. All large items—rent, groceries, utilities, clothing, taxes, car upkeep, and laundry—are paid for by check. Because of the American addiction to checks and credit cards, about 90 percent of the value of all transactions are checkbook transactions; only 10 percent are in coins and bills.

Kinds of Money in the United States

Money in the United States consists primarily of checkbook money, as we have said. This is a sort of private money, made by banks, depositors in a bank, and borrowers. It has a special place in any discussion of money and will receive particular consideration later in the chapter.

The government-made money, a sort of convenience money, is of relatively small importance, and discussion of it can be brief. Our convenience money can be divided into certain categories. First, there is metallic money—coins. Over the long past, these coins had a monetary or face value in considerable excess of their actual worth as metal. At times, however, the commodity value of coins can be greater than their value in exchange. In the last few years the price of silver has risen so markedly that at this time (the summer of 1967) American silver dollars are worth much more than their face value.

The remainder of the money we normally use is paper money. The type of paper representing by far the largest amount of value is the Federal Reserve note. The largest part of our paper money is in this form. Though printed and guaranteed by the government, it is in fact a note issued by private banks, the Federal Reserve banks. Indeed, the early drafts of the bill later amended and passed as the Federal Reserve Act of 1913 made no provision for a governmental imprimatur. The new type of money was to be the notes of a group of nominally private banks.

It may seem strange that private banks would be allowed to create money, but an example from another sector of the economy may indicate that wide acceptance of private money is not so strange after all. Suppose six or seven of our largest firms should decide to pay wages and certain other obligations by issuing uniform bearer notes in even denomination. Thus, if you worked for American Telephone and Telegraph or General Motors or Metropolitan Life Insurance, you would at the end of each week find in your pay envelope not a $100 check, but 10 bearer notes, each for $10. Each note would say something like this: "General Motors will pay $10 to bearer on demand." Chances are you could go almost anywhere in the United States and spend this kind of "money." So long as people had faith in your internationally known employer, so long as it always paid $10 when these bearer notes were presented, so long would such paper be accepted in payment everywhere in the United States and possibly elsewhere.

Federal Reserve notes are partially "backed" by gold, whatever that means. When a Federal Reserve bank issues $100 in its notes, it must be sure that at least $25 worth of gold has been put up as a backing. On the whole, this is a symbolic and ritualistic act, because the value of money can change even though the gold backing is the same. We can buy only about half as much today with a Federal Reserve note as we could in 1945, but the gold backing is the same now as it was then. You cannot convert any part of a store of Federal Reserve notes into gold. Exceptions are made, of course, for fabricators of watchcases, jewelers, manufacturers of medical and dental supplies, and others who may buy gold for fabrication into nonmonetary forms.

Until 1964, when they began to be withdrawn from circulation and replaced by Federal Reserve notes, silver certificates were the next most important kind of money. They constituted most of our paper money under $10 in face value. Silver certificates differ from Federal Reserve notes in that the United States Treasury guarantees their convertibility into silver upon demand. Since the recent rise in the price of silver, silver certificates have had greater than face value. In the summer of 1967, New York coin and currency dealers were paying a premium of up to 30 percent for silver certificates.

There are other kinds of money, rather rare and of small importance; they are gradually being retired. One is the Federal Reserve *bank*note (not Federal Reserve not described above), and another is the National banknote. Their importance is too small to warrant description.

Since the depression of the 1930's, gold has disappeared from view for most of us. Before 1933, gold coins were available everywhere and circulated in noticeable quantities west of Denver. Paper money, named gold certificates, circulated even more widely than gold coins. Any kind of money could be converted into gold coins, but the gold certificates were rather special in that a quantity of gold equal in value to the stated value of the certificate had actually been stored in the United States Treasury. Today, gold is available to the Federal Reserve banks in the settlement of obligations arising out of international trade. Transfers are made, not to private persons, but to foreign banks that play the same role as the Federal Reserve banks do in our country. The gold can be shipped and sometimes is shipped, but often it is not. In underground vaults in the New York Federal Reserve Bank, there are a lot of separate piles of gold belonging to various nations. When we want to transfer gold to England, an employee trundles a few gold bricks from our pile to the English pile. The English leave it there; it is as safe in New York as it would be anywhere. There are two reasons why gold is used as our international money. First, in general, nations do not really want the actual money of other nations; Frenchmen want francs, the English want pounds, we want dollars. Thus, something globally acceptable must be found as an international money. Second, gold is physically one of the best things available to serve as an international money; it is compact, limited in supply, easily divisible, and durable; and because of its position as a centuries-old symbol of riches, it is widely acceptable.

Gold certificates are something like the coatchecks you get in restaurants, except that the object represented by the check is gold—gold in Fort Knox and other storage vaults. This is the ultimate asset of the Federal Reserve banks, but in truth it is an almost meaningless asset. It is true that the gold used in international trade is useful to the United States because other nations are willing to accept it—or may even demand it—in certain types of transactions; but the remaining gold has no real function except a sort of psychological reassurance. The world has for so many centuries associated money, riches, and solidity with gold, and gold itself was for so long used as money, that we would feel uneasy if we did not—even tenuously and illogically as we do—tie our money somehow to gold. History teaches us that some of the worst economic disasters that have befallen this country came while we were on the gold standard, that is, when our supply of money was closely tied to gold and when any citizen could go to any bank and convert his paper into gold. We had a most disturbing peacetime inflation in the early 1900's, interrupted by the famous panic of 1907, one of the sharpest crises in our history; the depression of the 1930's, the worst purely economic disaster of our history, came while we were on the gold standard. This does not of course mean that gold was the cause of all our past troubles; the point is simply that domestically, gold gives us no real economic protection.

Checkbook Money

The most important kind of money is our checkbook money. Checks have greater convenience and safety than government money. They can as easily be made out in uneven amounts, such as $1,871.34, as in even amounts. This saves space in transporting odd sums as well as time required for counting. Since checks are usually, though not always, made out in the name of a person, the theft of a check from the rightful owner is not the complete loss that a theft of other money usually is. A check that is accidentally burned or dropped in deep water can be replaced. All these advantages are real enough, and they may have had more importance in an earlier era when the danger of brigandage was even greater than it is today. But the really great and significant thing about checkbook money is that it permits men, and particularly businessmen, to increase their earning assets substantially.

To understand this rather cryptic statement, the reader must first know that most checks in this country are not written for the purpose of slowly drawing out what we shall name a "primary deposit." The experience that most of us have with checking accounts is that on or near the first of the month, we deposit such items as paycheck or check for allowance or dividend checks in the bank. Then, slowly, by driblets, we pay the butcher, baker, and candlestick maker until at the end of the month there is but a small balance, which is reinvigorated on the first of the next month, and the cycle repeats itself. This is all very well, but it is small-time stuff; it is only part of what banking is all about, and a small part of checkbook money.

The big time in banking is borrowing, and big-time checkbook money is based on loans. Let us take a simple case. John Doe is a solid citizen, well known to his banker, with a good job, a fine house, and $200,000 in stocks and bonds. He learns of a good chance to make 10 percent profit if he can put up $10,000. But he cannot easily lay hands on this sum. He could of course sell some of his stocks; but on some, he would lose, and though he could make money on others, he feels locked in by the capital gains tax and does not like to pay brokers' fees. So he calls his banker and says: "Gordie, I need some money; have you got any of that stuff down there?" Gordie says yes, that they do have a little today, even up to $10,000 of it, and that as soon as John has signed the IOU, which will come in the next mail, the $10,000 will be credited to John's checking account. John will pay back the loan in six months plus interest at 5 percent. Chances are that Gordie will not even ask this borrower to put up collateral, depending, of course, on the general state of the economy, local circumstances, and the personalities of the two men. Within a few days, John has made out a $10,000 check to pay for the investment that will yield him 10 percent. The difference between the two rates of interest is 5 percent. Thus, John adds at the rate of $500 yearly to his income without increasing his possessions but by making them work over-time—for in the final analysis, Gordie granted the loan because he knew that John possessed about a quarter of a million dollars and was an honest and solid fellow.

Although the $10,000 of our example is scarcely big-time money, the pattern is big time. Most of the money in a checking account may be the proceeds of a loan, rather than a credit arising out of a primary deposit. It follows that much checkbook money is based on loans—on a debt. It also follows, at least in the example given above, that the backing of the $10,000 check written by John Doe to pay for his investment was not gold, but his total assets and general probity.

The Basic Issues of Monetary Theory

Now that we have found out what money is and how it comes into being, we can ask the next question: What are the basic problems of monetary theory? The basic problems are price stability and income stability. Money badly handled can cause or at least make possible both inflation and depression, and with this a redistribution of income and wealth. When prices go up, various groups in the society are unable to increase their income. One is the fixed-income group which includes people deriving incomes from bonds, mortgages, and pensions. Creditors form another group; they lose because they are being repaid in money of diminished purchasing power. On the other hand, debtors gain through no virtue or increased contribution to the economy. In a depression, as we have learned, an increased number of firms go bankrupt, profits decline, and unemployment spreads. One of the most useful theories that the economist possesses to aid him in thinking about these issues is the quantity theory of money, in one of its several versions. The quantity theory of money, stated in its simplest and most unqualified form, is that prices vary directly with the amount of money in a society. If this were literally true, it would mean that if you doubled the money in any economy overnight through some miracle, all prices would double the next day.

This business about the doubling (or tripling, or halving if the amount of money is cut in half) needs a little explaining. If, actually, all prices really did double at once, no great harm economically would result, though there might be some inconvenience. If promptly at midnight on June 30, 1964, all prices doubled—wages, cost of postage stamps, payments still to be made on the car, poll taxes, and value of promissory notes—the economic effects would be so small as to be uninteresting to the economist. Something like this, in reverse, happened in France. In 1960 the value of the franc to Frenchmen was by decree increased a hundredfold. The new franc was worth a hundred old francs. Everything—but everything—for which you had formerly paid 100 francs now cost only one new franc. Every debt owed, every payment still to be met, every wage, was to be divided by 100. Except for inconveniences in bookkeeping and occasional misunderstanding and a little awkwardness, there were no repercussions.

What is economically harmful and causes grave repercussions is the kind of uneven price increase or decline that comes with inflation or deflation. When monetary increases affect the price level, there are many lags. Contractual wages, for example, remain the same. Thus, wages as set by collective bargaining or the salaries of teachers and civil servants remain the same, while the prices of things they must buy go up. If prices rose by about 25 percent, as they did between 1950 and 1960, and if I had borrowed $1,000 from you in 1950, you lost about $250 in purchasing power when I repaid the loan in 1960. After the 17-year inflation between 1939 and 1956, when the average of all consumers' prices doubled, a detailed study would have shown that many, many items had tripled or quadrupled while others had gone up very little. A very few prices had gone down or remained the same—indeed, chewing gum cost a penny a stick as far back as 1905, just as it does today. Some forms of taxation in some states did not go up (car registration, dog licenses). What causes trouble, then, is not that prices rise or fall, but that they change unevenly, affecting some groups adversely and other groups favorably.

We must now return to the quantity theory itself. Although our formulation of the theory is oversimplified, as we shall see in a moment, it does possess a certain amount of truth. We do find cases in history in which the amount of money in a society has been increased and the increase has resulted in a rise of prices. But history has also taught us other monetary lessons; for example, price increases have not always immediately and directly followed monetary increases; price increases have not been directly proportional to monetary increases; price increases (or declines) have sometimes come first, and monetary increases (or declines) have followed; price increases or decreases can come about without immediate monetary changes. Thus, various attempts have been made to restate the quantity theory to make it more acceptable.

Restatements of the theory have taken into account a value named "velocity"—the amount of work done by money. Money is passed from hand to hand, and some pieces may do much more work than others. Thus, one $5 bill may conceivably be passed on from spender to receiver (who then becomes a spender who passes it on to a new receiver) 50 times a year. Such a $5 bill does the work of $250 in the course of a twelvemonth. We get the product, $250, by multiplying the amount of money by its velocity. Another $5 bill may have no velocity at all; you put it in a safe place and forget about it for a year. Such a bill performed no work and had no velocity. Money in checking accounts, too, can have high or low velocity. If I write a check for $5, the recipient will deposit it in his checking account; if the recipient soon writes a $5 check in favor of a new recipient, velocity is high. On the other hand, the original check could go into the hands of a man who simply lets the money in his account accumulate; the velocity of money in his inactive account is low. This velocity, an estimated average velocity for all money, is a calculable sum; it is a changing figure but is close to 30 a year. As might be expected, velocity rises in prosperity when business is active and consumption high, and low in depression when the economy is sluggish.

Out of all this, we derive the famous equation of exchange, often written as follows: $MV = PT$. In this equation the symbols mean the following:

M = The amount of money in the hands of the public (mostly in checking accounts).

V = Velocity.

P = The general level of prices (changes in this are often measured by a consumers' price index).

T = Total number of sales or transactions in a given period.

Now, the above equation is not thoroughly satisfactory, and economists have in various ways amended it and even improved it. To go into all this would carry us far afield. It does say enough, however, and contains enough truth to enable us to state that prices will rise if an economy creates excessive quantities of money, through either the government's printing presses or an overactive lending policy on the part of banks—for as we have already seen, a demand deposit can be increased by a loan (as to John Doe a few pages back).

We can go a step beyond the evidence presented above and note that excessive quantities of money may also have other effects on the economy. The rate of interest is also likely to vary—but inversely—

with the quantity of money. When a lot of money is kicking around the economy, we can see that loans should be easy to get; and hence the cost of borrowing, that is, the interest rate, should go down. This will encourage investment and buying. Although many investors and consumers may not be too much affected by interest rates, still, if you borrow to buy capital equipment as an investor or a new car as a consumer, low interest rates may induce you to make the purchase, and increased purchasing tends to raise prices. Thus an excess of money exerts an upward force on the price level directly (quantity theory) and indirectly through a reduction of the interest rate.

The opposite is also true. A decrease of money may lower prices and increase interest rates. Increased interest rates discourage consumers and investors from buying. A diminished stock of money causes prices to fall. Thus, we are in danger of the instabilities resulting from depression if we allow our stock of money to go down.

It should by now be clear to the reader that the aim of monetary policy is to keep the quantity of money stable if we are to guard against price fluctuations, inflations, deflations, and unacceptable rates of interest. When we say that we must keep the quantity of money stable, we do not of course mean that it should remain the same year after year. Money should increase in quantity with real increases in the GNP. The trend of the actual physical product of a growing nation like ours is upward. In 1912, we produced enough food, clothing, and shelter for 95 million people; today, we produce for twice as many. We ought to have twice as much money now as we did then to cover the increased quantity of goods—at least twice as much, for our food, clothing, and shelter should have improved in quality as well as quantity, not to mention the fact that because of increased productivity we ought to have a generally higher standard of living as our developing technology makes us richer. Money should, in quantity, keep pace not only with such long-term trends as we have just described but also with seasonal trends. There are certain busy seasons of the year—Labor Day to New Year, for instance—during which some of our largest crops move to market and during which much money is needed for holiday travel, jollification, and gifts. Our money supply should expand in such a period and contract during the duller months that follow, from January to the Easter shopping period.

It will be asked whether we should not make equal efforts to control the velocity of money. Is it not just as important to control velocity as quantity? The theoretical answer is a decided *yes*. The trouble, from the practical point of view, is that we don't know much about controlling velocity—not as much as we do about controlling quantity. The earlier quantity theorists used to believe that velocity is a constant. We know it is not. We do know that it rises in inflationary periods and declines in depression. Thus, if we could keep the economy on an even keel, maybe the velocity would not change too much, and perhaps we could get a large measure of control by regulating only the amount of money. At least, this is the premise on which policy is being developed.

What Causes Increases in the Quantity of Money?

We have not yet discussed the question of how excess money enters an economy or how it is withdrawn from the economy—as if two pixies and three leprechauns took fiendish pleasure in teasing the human race by now siphoning off money and now pumping it back, thus plunging us into depressions and inflations. This explanation must be discarded in favor of a more realistic one.

When money really consisted of gold or silver—doubloons, pieces of eight, and similar cargo of the Spanish galleons—any newly discovered precious metal was obviously convertible into money. Thus, in the 16th century the gold and silver of the New World increased prices in the Old World. At a later date, when paper money was tied to gold—our status in 1900—discoveries of gold were being made everywhere, and the perfected chlorine and cyanide processes made gold extraction cheaper. This caused prices to rise beginning about 1900, and your grandparents no doubt will remember the vast amount of talk about the "HCL," or high cost of living—the cartoons, jokes, and also apprehension of those days, for steadily increasing prices are disturbing.

Another way to increase the amount of money is to print it. This, of course, is limited to the sphere of government if it is not to be illegal. Governments usually print excessive quantities of money only in emergencies. This is the history of greenbacks issued during the Civil War. Governments may also print bonds instead of money; by a process to be discussed later, bonds can be converted into money. It is, of course, the job of government to print a reasonable amount of money and to increase the quantity as the country grows and needs more money. We may, on the whole, assume that the stable governments of the great and advanced countries will in normal and quiet times neither increase nor decrease capriciously the amount of money.

The third and most important way to increase or decrease the amount of money is to create or destroy checkbook money. The people directly involved in this are private persons—businessmen who want to borrow and bankers who want to lend or to call back the money they have lent. As we have said, most of our checkbook money is based on loans, not on primary deposits. The banking system as a whole can create or destroy checkbook money. And since checkbook money is used for 90 percent of our transactions, the increase can be a sizable one. The banking system can also greatly diminish our stock of checkbook money in a very short time. All of this, of course, is not the result of malice or dishonesty; banks do not try to disequilibrate the economy, and the businessmen who seek loans from them are also without blame. The trouble is that both businessmen and banks, by doing what comes naturally—seeking loans, making profits, protecting loans—can do a lot of unintentional damage.

Because of what has just been said above, banks in most if not all nations of the world are in one way or another tied to their governments, and governments exercise much supervision over them. Some of this supervision is of course designed to prevent fraud and irresponsibility. The aim here is to protect the primary deposits of savers and depositors. With this, we shall not be concerned. Our concern will be with the perfectly honest but sometimes harmful process of making or extinguishing checkbook money and with the policies used to help promote general economic and price stability.

Summary and Conclusions

In this chapter, we have looked at the various types of money and found that the chief money of the United States is checkbook money. This kind of money can be created or destroyed by private individuals and by bankers responding to the needs of businessmen seeking loans.

The quantity theory of money, expressed as an equation

$$MV = PT$$

does not solve all the riddles of monetary theory; but it does tell us that too much money causes prices to rise because we have, in the popular phrase, "too much money chasing too few goods." Too much money also causes interest rates to fall, which—to some degree, at least—stimulates the purchase of both consumers' goods and capital goods. This, too, forces prices upward. And a decline of the money supply does the opposite.

In these days, when gold is a most passive element of our monetary system, and when governments are not hard pressed as in all-out war, the chief source of increased monetary supply, or the chief curtailing agent, is the banking system. How banks can increase or decrease checkbook money, even to the extent of harming or benefiting us, is the subject of the next chapter, as is an examination of banking policy to prevent excessive expansion or contraction of business and banking activity.

QUESTIONS FOR REVIEW AND DISCUSSION

1. Define, in your own words, each of the following terms:
   a) Money
   b) Price level
   c) Value of money
   d) Velocity
   e) Demand deposits

2. "It would be impossible to develop or maintain an industrial economy without having a sophisticated banking system and money supply." Discuss.

3. A nation conquers and occupies another nation; the conqueror issues a new paper money without gold or silver backing. Can this money be acceptable and have value? Explain your reply.

4. Discuss the relationships between the money supply and the price level. Include in your discussion the concepts of velocity and quantity of transactions.

5. Is the *PT* in the equation of exchange equivalent to the GNP? Explain your reply.

6. "Money is a mere lubricant for barter." Defend or attack the quoted statement.

7. Your authors state that about 90 percent of our payments are made with checkbook money. What objects or things of solid value, if any, lie behind checkbook money?

Chapter 12

BANKS AND MONETARY POLICY

Types of Banks

There are lots of banks, and they do all sorts of things. They rent safety-deposit boxes and sell travelers' checks. Some will pay your bills for you in Nigeria or Finland if you are an importer, and some will sell you life insurance. Some will open checking accounts and savings accounts for you. Some will invest and safeguard your children's money in a trust after your death. Banks that do all or most of these things might be named "department store banks." Most banks are department store banks.

There are certain specialized types of banks. One is the savings bank, strictly for savings. Checks cannot be written against accounts in such banks. Others are investment banks, which most of us never enter; they are the kind of banks that lend big money to big business. Then, finally, there is the nation's central bank. Usually, there is only one such bank in a nation; we are an exception in that we have 12. This exception is more seeming than real, for it could be argued that we really have only one, but 12 branches. In any case a central bank is very special. It does not accept ordinary accounts from ordinary citizens. It is charged with the responsibility of implementing monetary policy. Our central bank is the Federal Reserve System (or the 12 Federal Reserve banks).

This chapter will discuss only two types of banking activity: (1) the work of the checkbook division of a department store bank and (2) the work of a central bank, particularly the American Federal Reserve banks or System.

The checkbook branch of a department store bank performs the same job as a strictly commercial bank, few pure types of which exist. Thus, we shall hereafter call the checkbook section of any bank a "commercial bank." To it we turn first.

Commercial Banks

The job of a commercial bank, as seen by its officers, is to make as much money as possible by lending money. It receives primary deposits from depositors on which it pays no interest, and it lends part of their money to borrowers who do pay interest. A commercial banker's heaven would be a place where primary depositors never take out the money they have deposited and where rich, solid businessmen of excellent judgment who never default on a loan borrow heavily and pay high rates of interest. But depositors are constantly drawing their money out of the bank. The commercial banker cannot, therefore, lend out everything entrusted to him by primary depositors. He must keep a fraction—let's say one fifth—of the deposits always on hand, never earning interest, to honor the demands for repayment by primary depositors. One fifth is probably enough, since not every depositor in the normal course of events wants to withdraw all the money he has deposited. This one fifth we shall name a "reserve." It is a sum that the banker cannot lend.

The excess over his reserves he can lend, however. Thus, it is possible for him to lend 80 percent of his primary deposits to borrowers; on this he gets interest, and this is how he makes profits for his firm. But like any other businessman, he may not be able to sell up to the maximum of his capacity to produce. If business is sluggish, few people may wish to borrow; or if plenty of potential borrowers appear, the banker may be wary of making loans to many of them. Some of the would-be borowers may be lacking in business sense, or the transaction they want to borrow for may be unsafe, or they may lack any valuable security. Thus, there may be times when the banker will be able to lend only 40 or 50 percent of primary deposits.

Now, this banker alone, and in the type of transactions of which we have spoken, does not lend sums beyond those deposited in his bank. If you deposit a check for $1,000, and if the bank maintains a 20 percent reserve, it can lend only $800. This fact must be kept firmly in mind, for it is easy in the early stages of one's study of banking to slide into the error of believing that a banker can by some magic take a deposit of $1,000 and blow it up into a $5,000 loan—

still assuming a 20 percent reserve. This most certainly is impossible. But what is equally important to know is that what one banker alone cannot do, the banking system as a whole can do. The banking system as a whole can create a total $5,000 of purchasing power on the base of a primary deposit of $1,000. This is one of many cases in economics in which effects are quite different when one person takes action from what they are when many take the same action. Let us look into this process.

A grocer comes to a bank and makes what we are naming a primary deposit in a bank. He makes this deposit partly for purposes of safety; he does not want to lose the money or to be robbed. He also seeks the convenience of having a reservoir or pool of money which he can tap for the meeting of bills as the mailman delivers them. He does not expect to use all of the $1,000 right away; on the other hand, he does not expect to leave it there for a year or more. If he were truly saving the money for some distant expenditure, say a new delivery truck next year, he would probably put the money out at interest in a savings account or otherwise seek to get an income. Deposits in checking accounts do not pay interest.

Well, our grocer has made his primary deposit and goes away; the banker now takes charge of this money. Both law and practical experience dictate that he can lend 80 percent of this money without getting into trouble, for at no time do demands for withdrawal exceed 20 percent of primary deposits. A small contractor now enters the bank and happens to need $800 to meet a lumber bill in a day or two. He is temporarily short of money, but the banker knows that he is not a poor man and that he is just now building a house for Gotrox, who is also a reliable man financially. A loan is made. Whether or not the contractor puts up security does not concern us; the point is he gets an $800 loan. The form taken by the loan is a deposit in the contractor's checking account. The banker gets from the contractor a 90-day promissory note or similar document—but this, too, is of small concern to us.

What does concern us is that the sum of $800 is almost immediately withdrawn and that it becomes a primary deposit in some other bank. The contractor borrowed the money because he had a lumber bill to pay. Very soon after getting the loan, he writes a check for $800 and mails it to the lumber dealer. The lumber dealer, soon after receiving his check, deposits it in his bank just as the grocer did, and it now becomes a primary deposit in another bank. To be sure, it might have been deposited in the first bank—the bank with which the grocer and contractor carried on their business. But the point we want to make is more easily made if we assume a second bank.

So now the second bank has a primary deposit of $800. Of this, it can lend 80 percent—$640—keeping a reserve of $160. We repeat the process: The fellow who borrows the $640 mails a check for this amount to a man who now makes a primary deposit in a third bank. The third bank can lend 80 percent of $640, or $512. A fourth bank can lend 80 percent of $512—and so on, on, and on. If we add up all the primary deposits it would be possible to make, we would find at the end of the line that the original $1,000 had been puffed up to $5,000. A total of $4,000 has been created by a succession of banking operations.

Readers must not get the idea that this always happens. The above is only an account of what can happen. There are no available figures, but it is quite probable that the process of blowing up money stops far short of potentiality. We do see, however, that it is possible for the banking system to add tremendously to our money supply. Doubling it could be calamitous. This sort of thing needs control lest it become a flood. If the M in our equation $MV = PT$ becomes excessive, prices will rise, and the relationships among prices will be disturbed sufficiently to cause difficulties and inequitable redistributions of income and wealth. We now turn to an examination of the mechanisms of control.

The Federal Reserve System

The ultimate source of control in any nation is, of course, the government, which passes basic legislation regulating banks and money. But in major capitalist nations the government has delegated authority for day-to-day management to a controlling organization known as a central bank. In the United States the nearest thing we have to a central bank is the Federal Reserve System. It may be described as a vast banking cooperative or league to which half the banks (holding 85 percent of the demand deposits) belong. This vast federation, organized in 1914, maintains a dozen regional banks—the

Federal Reserve banks found in major cities such as Boston, New York, Chicago, Dallas, and San Francisco. In other words, we have not one but rather 12 semiautonomous central banks. At the top of the structure is the Board of Governors, selected by the President of the United States and the Senate.

The Federal Reserve banks—often called "Feds"—perform a large number of service functions for the 6,000 commercial banks that belong to the system (about 7,000 banks are not members, but they do only 15 percent of the nation's banking business). We are not much concerned about most of these services, which only simplify the running of machinery. What is of real importance is that the Federal Reserve banks can exert significant controls over the amounts of checkbook money in the economy.

Perhaps it is time to drop the rather unfledged phrase "checkbook money" and to use instead the phrase "demand deposit," a rather more grown-up term for a checking account. We saw earlier in this chapter and in the first chapter on money that a demand deposit could be created either by a primary deposit or by the banker's granting a loan. And we also saw that granting a loan was equivalent to creating new money. We also know that creating too much or too little money may affect prices by causing rises or declines in prices. These may affect the economy adversely. Over the years, as economists and government and banking officials have studied both our banking system and the operation of our economy, certain policies have been formulated to give us control over our money supply; and these controls are designed to increase the stability of prices and to improve the performance of our economic system. A discussion of the controls by the Fed follows.

Alteration of Reserve Requirements

A commercial bank must maintain a reserve. It cannot lend out all of its primary deposits, as we have several times noted above. It must maintain a fraction of its deposits in liquid form to meet the demands of depositors who want to draw out money. This money could be kept in the bank's vaults in cash form, or it could be deposited as an account in some other bank. We have consistently spoken of a 20 percent reserve; but of course, this figure was selected at random. A safe reserve would depend on a bank's experience over the years; it might be 2 percent or 50 percent. The laws regulating Federal Reserve member banks do not, however, permit member banks to decide where they will keep their reserve or what its form or amount will be. They prescribe that member banks must establish an account with the Federal Reserve Bank; this and cash in the till are the only legal reserves. Any other sums the bank has not lent do not count. The Federal Reserve Bank also sets the minimum percentage figure for the bank's reserve. By law, the Federal Reserve Bank is given flexibility in this matter. For large city banks, minimum reserves may be set between 10 and 22 percent; for town banks, between 7 and 14 percent.

It is obvious that if the rate for big cities is set at the minimum of 10 percent, a bank can lend more than if reserves are set at 22 percent. If we take a $1,000 primary deposit as our unit, the bank can legally lend $900; but at 22 percent, it can lend only $780. Thus, it is pretty clear that the Federal Reserve Bank can, by changing reserve requirements, increase or decrease the amount of demand deposits. This means it can increase or decrease the amount of money and hence exert a force against high or low prices. Or it can discourage and encourage business activity by cutting or increasing the volume of loans to businessmen.

This is a powerful instrument of control, particularly in booming times when businessmen can find lots of ways to make money and want to borrow actively. At such times, commercial banks are able to lend all the money they have, except their reserves. If, now, reserve requirements go up, loans will have to go down immediately. The alteration of reserve requirements is not often used as a method of control.

The Rediscount Rate

A second method of control is alteration of the rediscount rate. The rediscount rate, better known as the discount rate, is the interest rate charged by Federal Reserve banks to member banks who borrow from them. As was said at the beginning of this chapter, the purpose of a commercial bank is to make money; and since, in the popular phrase, "you need money to make money," the more money you have at your disposal, the more money you can make. One way in which a businessman can dispose of more money than he has is to borrow it, and the same is true of a banker. Through the operations of his bank, taken in isolation, a banker may be restricted to lending only $10 million a year at 6 percent. But if he can borrow several million more, he will be able to relend several millions at 6 percent—something that increases his revenue. We have assumed, of course, that the banker has plenty of customers (borrowers), that his problem is not demand but limitation of his ability to supply funds. The obvious lender to a bank is the Federal Reserve Bank. That is why we call it a banker's bank. Now, the Federal Reserve Bank is *not* in business to make money. It *does* make money, as a matter of fact; but whatever it makes above a certain minimum, it has to turn over to the government. And this minimum is not very hard to make. Thus, when it sets a rate of interest for member banks, it is not motivated by the profit motive but by the general welfare of the economy. Whether it gets 2 percent or 10 percent for its loans is, from the viewpoint of revenue, not very important to the officials of the Federal Reserve Bank. What is important is that the rate oef interest should tend toward damping inflationary trends in an exuberant economy or stimulating a laggard economy.

If the Federal Reserve Bank should set a very low discount rate—say 2 percent—and a member bank could relend at 6 percent, the member bank would be making a rather pleasant gross profit of 4 percent (gross, because from this the member bank must deduct clerical services and other expenses incidental to making loans). If, however, the Federal Reserve Bank's discount rate were 5 percent, and the member bank could relend at only 6 percent, lending might be quite unattractive to the member. The differential of 1 percent might be absorbed in clerical and other costs, and the bank might even lose money.

But losing money is not the only thing at stake. When the Fed sets a high and discouraging rate, it is also warning all banks and businessmen and the country at large that something is wrong in the economy, that expansion of loans—and hence of business activity—is going on at an unhealthy rate of speed. Even banks that are not borrowers heed the Fed's signals and may put a tougher lending policy into effect, thus reducing demand deposits or slowing up their growth. The Fed set the high rate deliberately to discourage borrowing, overexpansion of loans, and hence the creation of demand deposits and of money. It is, in effect, calling attention to the equation $MV = PT$ and saying that M or V or both are going up too fast and that therefore there is danger that P will rise.

Commercial banks are not legally obligated to heed the Fed's signals; and if the discount rate, though high, is not high enough to discourage borrowing, the member banks can continue to lend anyhow, enlarge loans or demand deposits, and increase the money supply; but there is a strong tendency for the Fed's action to be discouraging. It is still possible, however, for firms to go on enlarging their plants by spending sums of money that they themselves have accumulated. This increases demand for goods and may contribute toward further price increases. The discount rate further loses some of its possible effectiveness because of the fact that commercial banks are not great borrowers from the Fed. In practice, they borrow mostly when their reserves are low, and to borrow too often might arouse the suspicion of the officers of the Fed who, among their other duties, are on the lookout for unsound banking practices. And yet the Fed's influence throughout the economy is such that a high discount rate is generally believed to be fairly effective and to help in retarding inflationary tendencies.

The Fed may also lower its discount rate, hoping to achieve the opposite effect during a deflation or depression. If a member bank can lend to businessmen at 6 percent and borrow from the Fed at 2 percent, the member bank will welcome any sound opportunity to lend, that is, to create demand deposits. The trouble is that when business is dull and expectations of profit dim, businessmen do not want to expand their firms and therefore do not need to borrow money. If you own a motel and can now rent only half of your rooms every night, you will not want to add a new 20-room unit even if you can borrow the money at 3 percent, which is a bargain rate of interest. Thus, we conclude that the interest rate, though it may be very effective in slowing up the hyperactivity of inflationary times, is not very effective in depression. Still, interest rates should be low in depression; if only a few businessmen want to invest—and a few do, even in depression—they should be encouraged.

Open-Market Operations

The third great lever that the Fed can pull to control or affect the supply of demand deposits is named "open-market operations." This refers to the buying or selling of bonds, mostly government bonds. The Fed always has a backlog of government securities in its possession. If it wants the public to buy some of them, it lowers the price; and since the Fed cares only for small and limited profits, it is not too much concerned about offering bargains. Latent demand is always there because banks, insurance companies, and other business organizations like to place funds in government bonds even if only temporarily. Since these operations are of considerable magnitude, they have an effect on the money supply. The effect is produced by a diminution of bank reserves. The buyers of bonds pay the Fed by check. These checks are drawn on commercial banks, most often on member banks. When the Fed gets these checks, it pays itself by reducing the accounts that member banks must hold with the Fed; the reader will remember that member bank reserves are kept in the form of accounts in the Fed. The reduction of accounts reduces reserves and thus impairs the power of member banks to lend.

If the Fed wishes to make lending easier, it pursues the opposite course. It buys bonds, luring sellers, if needed, by offering high prices. The Fed pays sellers by checks which, barring exceptions, are deposited in member banks. The members deposit them in their accounts with the Fed; this increases their reserves and hence their lending capacity.

The raising and lowering of bond prices exert an influence on the interest rate. If, for example, the Fed is buying bonds, and if as a result the price rises from $1,000 to $1,020, the rate of interest on bonds declines. Bonds pay a fixed sum in the form of interest regardless of price—let us say $35 a year for a bond with a face value of $1,000; this is interest at the rate of 3½ percent. If, now, the bond goes up to $1,020 and continues to pay $35, the rate of interest has declined from 3½ to 3.431 percent—not a vast decline, to be sure, but a decline in an important sector. Buying bonds is done to make lending easier, and the accompanying decline in the rate of interest is a movement in the right direction. And again, of course, the opposite is true. When a $1,000 bond yielding $35 a year actually sells at $980, the rate of interest rises from 3½ to 3.571 percent. We can restate the above explanation loosely but perhaps helpfully by saying that when the Fed buys bonds, it showers the community with money; and when it sells, it sucks money away from the community.

Open-market operations are almost continuous. They are used much more often than changes in the discount rate or in reserve requirements.

Some Observations on Controls by the Fed

It must not be assumed that the controls discussed above work miracles or that they are easy to apply. Nothing is easy in a complex society where crosswinds are forever blowing and where the Fed's policies, though helpful to John Doe, are harmful to Richard Roe. Timing is always a problem. A recession which in retrospect may have begun in May of 1963 is not recognized for what it is until September of 1963. Four precious months will have been lost in the application of controls.

Important public objectives may be in conflict. For example, in the summer of 1963 the Fed raised the discount rate. The purpose was to dissuade Americans from lending abroad and to entice foreigners into lending money to Americans—activities that would tend to prevent an outflow of gold (we shall discuss this more fully in Chapter 14 on international trade). But 1963 was also a year of high-level stagnation, a year in which public policy aimed at encouraging increased business activity. Increased interest rates are not encouraging. Things like this happen all the time. There was a period before 1951 when the Treasury wanted low interest rates because the national debt had grown enormously and the burden of interest payment was becoming heavy. The Fed, however, wanted to stem inflation through high rates. Obviously, it is impossible to go in opposite directions at the same time.

Another problem lies in the fact that banks are not the only source of funds. Although a period of inflation, if long continued, will ultimately be harmful to all business, for many businessmen the earlier part of the period is a period of solid profits and prosperity. It is hard to discourage them from expanding their businesses and bidding up prices of land, labor, and capital. If commercial banks refuse loans to optimistic businessmen, other sources of money can be found. Many large companies have lots of money (often in the form of government bonds) and are self-financing. In September of 1963 *The Wall Street Journal* reported that the joke making the rounds in Detroit was that "General Motors is saving up to buy the Federal Government." The corporation was holding liquid assets of $2.3 billion. This sum is larger than the assessed property valuation of 18 of our states. The businessman, even if he is too poor to pick up a dozen or so of our smaller states, may go to money-holding firms other than commercial banks, such as insurance companies. As for the consumer, one has only to look around as one walks down the street to see how many finance companies are clamorously offering to lend. An old-timer was once heard to remark to a friend in a small town in New York: "There are now more finance companies on Main Street than there were saloons before 1919; that's progress for you."

The V in our equation $MV = PT$ presents difficulties. The Fed can do something about M, but less, if anything, about V. Even a professional or salaried man can quicken the velocity of money—that is, make it do more work—and it would be hard to stop him. Suppose a physician keeps an average checking account balance of about $2,000 monthly. If he could get only 2 percent on his money from a savings bank, it might not occur to him that it would be worth the time and energy to cut down this sum. But if he can get 5¼ percent in a California building and loan association, he might try to manage on an average checking account balance of $500 and put $1,500 to work earning interest. He has increased the efficiency of his checking account, which is an increase of V. A corporation, too, by managing its much larger funds more carefully, can increase the efficiency with which it uses money.

The last difficulty to be discussed here—but by no means the last difficulty in existence—is that monetary policy is, to say the most, only a passive encouragement in depression. In an extreme year— let's say 1932, one of the worst years of the last Great Depression— many businessmen would not borrow at any rate of interest much higher than zero. Even putting money in a savings bank was an unsafe investment during that year, for banks were failing right and left. Pessimism was so deep that some people went so far as to wonder whether government bonds were safe. This, of course, is the extreme case. When the prospects for profits are bad, low rates of interest are insufficient bait to induce businessmen to snap up an opportunity to make a new investment.

Summary and Conclusions

This chapter has described how the major components of the banking system are tied together into the Federal Reserve System. The reserves of banks doing 85 percent of the nation's business are held by the Fed, and the Fed requires banks to keep minimum reserves. By making higher or lower reserves mandatory, the Fed can cause a decrease of demand deposits or set the stage for an increase. The Fed has two other major tools to stimulate or permit the increase or decrease of demand deposits, namely, open-market operations and the discount rate.

Periods of depression and inflation are obviously complex affairs, and their root causes cannot be attributed to an excess or deficiency of money (demand deposits). Still, if demand deposits can be curtailed in an inflationary period and increased in a depression, the economy will operate on a more nearly even keel. The Fed can and does make a contribution to stability by its monetary policy, though sometimes other goals of public policy may nullify the Fed's attempts. On the whole, the Fed is probably more competent to get out of inflation than out of depression.

If the Fed were the only lending agency in the nation, its policies, particularly its anti-inflationary policies, might be more effective than they are. The springing into existence of other lending agencies in recent decades and the Fed's inability to control the V of the equation of exchange subtract from its power.

QUESTIONS FOR REVIEW AND DISCUSSION

1. Define, in your own words, each of the following terms:
    a) Reserve requirement
    b) Rediscount rate

c) Excess reserves

d) Government securities

2. John Doe deposits $6,000 in the Centerville Bank. On the basis of this deposit alone, how much can the bank lend if the reserve requirement is 25 percent?

3. The Market Street National Bank has $2 million in demand deposits. Its account with the Fed amounts to $450,000. Assuming a 20 percent reserve requirement, how much can it lend?

4. How does the granting of loans by commercial banks increase the money supply? When a commercial bank calls a loan, what effect does this have upon the money supply? Why?

5. Analyze in detail the effects of each of the following Federal Reserve actions:

a) Lowering the rediscount rate

b) Raising reserve requirements

c) Selling government securities

d) Buying government securities on the open market

e) Raising reserve requirements

f) Raising the rediscount rate

6. In times of recession, which of the possible Federal Reserve actions listed under question 5 would be used? Why?

7. In times of inflation, which of the possible Federal Reserve actions listed in question 5 would be used? Why?

8. A bank is a privately owned business that has the potential of being a social benefactor or a miscreant. Because of this, governments have placed certain constraints on banking operations. What are these constraints? What effect do they have on bank operations?

9. Does the President of the United States or any member of the executive branch have the power to order officials of the Federal Reserve banks to alter interest rates?

10. The Federal Reserve note is the note of a bank that is not owned by the U.S. government. On the face of the note, the following statement appears: "The United States of America will pay to the bearer on demand ten dollars"—or whatever the denomination of the bill. Why should the United States assume this obligation, since it is a banknote? Suppose you were to take the note to the U.S. Treasury and demand $10, what would they give you in return?

Chapter 13 TAXES AND THE PUBLIC DEBT

Introduction

People have never ceased to complain about taxes. Especially is this true in the United States today, when rates are so very high and the sums collected are being used for purposes that violate the deepest instincts of the "virtuous" middle classes (as John Stuart Mill described us). It is probably through our system of taxation, budgeting, and public finance that the most sensitive economic nerves of the lower-upper, middle-upper, and upper-upper classes are touched and the most exquisite pains produced. What fur coats we might buy our ladies with the sums we give bureaucrats to fling away for us! What extensions of our business establishments? What cushions of safety when embarking on new ventures! Not only are large sums taken away from us; but also (it is widely thought) these staggering amounts are being used to undermine the pillars of American society and the moral fiber of its citizens, and to drain the very springs that made the large sums possible in the first place. The seed corn is being destroyed. The hardworking and thrifty are being penalized while a devitalized population seeks soft security. Meanwhile, heresies are spreading: Impractical idealists are saying that the government might as well print the money as collect it by taxation; that budget balancing is old-fashioned; that a good budget is an unbalanced budget; that a public debt is only a debt we owe ourselves, so what does it matter how large it is, and why not cancel it anyhow? Can economists be serious when they recommend a Yo-Yo tax system, that is, one which permits the President to raise and lower taxes at will, depending on his whim, or what he thinks is good politics, or on his weird opinion of what makes sound economic policy?

Are things really that bad? Are our fiscal policies as unsound as they appear to be, and do modern economists ridicule such axioms as are contained in the notion that expenditures of government must not

229

exceed income of government? Well, our taxation and budgetary situation is not perfect. One could wish things were otherwise, but let us suspend judgment on the state of our fiscal system until we have taken a look at it and at some of the theories that underlie and inform it.

To keep within reasonable bounds, we shall have to lay major emphasis in our discussion on the federal government's budget and taxation policies. From the viewpoint of the general economist, what the central government does about taxes is vastly more important than what state governments do. All the states and subdivisions together collect in revenues about half as much as does the federal government. In depression or inflation, it would be most unlikely that the 50 states could act together to rescind or increase taxes as countercyclical measures. The federal government, on the other hand, can within a month increase or decrease the take-home pay of almost every employed person; this gives it tremendous power to fight depression and inflation. The federal government can, as it did during the Civil War, print money to finance emergency needs—and if not money, then bonds which can be metamorphosed into money. State governments lack this kind of power. Washington alone has greater fiscal strength than have all the states combined. We shall therefore devote most of our time to seeing what Washington does and can do, and shall make short work of the state and local problems of public finance.

Increase of Governmental Expenditure

At the turn of the century the federal government was spending about $0.5 billion a year. Since then, population has grown about 2½ times, and prices have quadrupled perhaps.[1] We may reasonably expect changes in these two areas of the economy to have their effects on governmental expenditures by increasing them. If we multiply the $0.5-billion budget of 1900 first by 2½ for population

[1] The reason for the "perhaps" is that there are difficulties in the way of comparing consumers' prices over a period as technologically dynamic as was the period between 1900 and 1967. We use quite different things today. In 1900, consumers bought horseshoes and oats to keep their buggies rolling; we buy tires and gas. Women in those days used more cloth for their dresses; men wore stickpins in their ties; housewives bought Welsbach mantles to brighten gaslight. Among things they did not buy were aspirin tablets, cellophane, Kleenex, nylon, vitamin pills, and zippers. We cannot accurately say that the cost of living has doubled (or quadrupled) when the items consumed have changed so radically.

growth, then by 4 to account for price increases, we get a budget of $5 billion. There is, therefore, every reason to expect that current annual governmental expenditures should amount to at least $5 billion.

But we have also become wealthier. Our "real income"—that is, income expressed in terms of what we can buy rather than in terms of dollars—has probably tripled. Since the rest of us are living three times as well, so should government. Its employees should be better paid. Its soldiers should enjoy the same expensive foods and medical care that civilians have come to expect. President Theodore Roosevelt drove to his steam-drawn, nonair-conditioned railway car in a horse and carriage; presidents now have helicopters, planes, and automobiles. This is fitting and proper, and brings the $5-billion budget up to $15 billion because we multiply by 3 to take account of the tripled standard of living.

Thus, we can easily work governmental expenditures up from $0.5 billion in 1900 to $15 billion in the present. But governmental spending has recently been near $125 billion, or 8½ times as much as can easily and reasonably be accounted for. How explain this enormous increase? The explanation is largely war—past, present, and future. We are in an armaments race. We are fighting in Asia. We are paying for a host of benefits to veterans of both world wars and the Korean War, not to mention benefits to soldiers of the Spanish-American War and possibly even a few pensions to widows of Civil War soldiers. Around 1900 the Army, Navy, and Marine Corps numbered a little more than 100,000. In recent years the armed services have totaled about three million; they are 30 times greater than they were. And of course, the equipment is incalculably more complicated and expensive. Finally, the wars of this century have left us with a large public debt on which the annual interest alone is more than $13 billion.

But war and defense are not the only things that have caused such large budgetary increases. The concept of government as a mere umpire in domestic affairs has given way to the concept of government as a service agency, as a protector of certain groups in the community. The creation of the Department of Labor in 1913 and of the Department of Health, Education, and Welfare in 1953 are two large symbols of this change, but only two. Many new agencies, commissions, and bureaus have been created to perform service functions ranging from mediation in labor disputes to guaranteeing minimum prices for wheat, tobacco, and various other crops. We are subsidizing business enterprise in an increasing number of ways: Governments spend a lot to maintain airports and to build roads that get hard use from trucking companies; advertising is being carried in the mails at subsidized rates.

The upshot of all this is that the federal government is responsible for spending about 20 percent of the national income today; in 1900 the figure was nearer 2 percent. This makes the government a rather decisive force in economic affairs. If the government should suddenly decide to cut down its expenditures vastly, to stop buying jets, guided missiles, and uniforms, and to cease subsidizing farmers and industry, we could be plunged into a devastating depression. Of course, things might not be too dreadful if at the same time taxes were cut deeply to allow citizens to spend the money instead. Even so, the period of conversion and transition would be difficult. However you look at it, a government that controls nearly one fifth of the nation's income is a much greater economic force than one which controls only one fiftieth of it. The rate at which great modern governments spend may make all the difference between stable prosperity, depression, or inflation. And it is on this basic fact that most of the economists' theories of public finance are built.

The Budgetary Outgo

Each year, in January, the President of the United States submits to the Congress a budget, estimating income and outgo of the federal government for the next fiscal year. This means that the budget he submits in January, 1968, applies to the period between July 1, 1968, and July 1, 1969, and it is referred to as the budget for fiscal 1969—that is, the budget for a twelve-month period ending in the middle of 1969. Thus, it will be seen that the President is in a sense predicting events almost 18 months in advance. He predicts in January income and outgo for a 12-month period that will terminate about a year and a half later.

In January of 1967 the President made the innovation of submitting to the Congress a budget which stressed the "national income accounts" approach to governmental budgeting. Although the concept was not new to economists or to governmental officials concerned, it was new to many well-informed persons. Readers of headlines with good memories were rather shocked because the 1968 budget appeared suddenly to demand $169 billion compared to a sum closer to $100 billion in preceding years. We were of course prepared to spend more because of the Asian war, but not $169 billion. The jump was not so great as all that, since the larger figure belonged to the new national income accounts budget, while the smaller figure went with the administrative budget of recent years, and the former is always larger than the latter. As submitted in January, 1967, for the fiscal year 1968, the two Presidential budgets proposed the following:

	Expenditures	*Receipts*	*Deficit*
Administrative budget	$135.0 billion	$126.9 billion	$8.1 billion
National income accounts budget	169.2 billion	167.1 billion	2.1 billion

Thus the reader can see that although the national income accounts budget provides for larger expenditures, it also takes account of larger receipts than the administrative budget and reduces the deficit almost 75 percent. The reason for the difference between the two budgets is that the larger includes certain items not present in the smaller, particularly the income and outgo of certain social security funds.

The federal government makes two types of payments to the public: First, there are payments for goods and services to be used in the conduct of governmental affairs. Expenditures for flamethrowers, schoolhouses, cement, and carbon paper come under this heading. All such expenditures are listed under the administrative budget. Second, the federal government makes payments to the public that do not reflect the purchase of materials and services for governmental use. Instead, these payments are simply a transfer of purchasing power from the general public to a specific segment of the public. Social security payments are of this type. Most members of the labor force and their employers pay social security taxes. These taxes are then placed in a trust fund, controlled by the federal government, out of which payments are made to that segment of the public entitled to social security benefits. This is considered a transfer payment, for the government does not make these payments to purchase material and labor. All such payments are listed under trust fund expenditures and become part of the national income accounts budget.

Though trust fund expenditures have become an important item in our economy, it is the administrative budget expenditures that will occupy most of our attention, for it is this budget that indicates the ways in which the federal government uses a large part of our national product.

The budget message is normally greeted with dissatisfaction the nation over. Some say that it leaves out estimates for important projects; others, that it is again the dismal and perennial example of the extravagant spending of irresponsible and power-crazed bureaucrats. And this happens under both Democrats and Republicans, for it is human nature to feel that the government should spend more on what we consider important and less on what the other fellow wants. Now, this budget is neither an executive order nor a bill to be passed nor the writ of a court. It is merely a working paper, a guide to Congress as to how much money the President thinks the government ought to collect and how to collect it, what he thinks the government should spend and how the sums should be allocated. Only Congress can tax or appropriate money, and the budget is never adopted as a whole.

Many expenditure items in the budget are rigidly set by previous law or contractual agreement. For example, various forms of aid or pensions to veterans are already being paid out on the basis of existing law, and interest is paid on government bonds according to a contractual arrangement. Our federal government has the power, of course, to amend pension laws and to repudiate contracts, but such things are not undertaken lightly. Thus, many items in the budget are for all practical purposes unchangeable. The same is to be said for income. Congress cannot undertake the vast job of rewriting all of our tax legislation every year or so. It would be too large a task and would be impossibly confusing to the taxpayer. Thus, from year to year, except in wartime, one budget very closely resembles another whether the government is under control of Democrats or Republicans.

The ordinary citizen may be startled to learn this, since it is his opinion that spending policies are vastly different in the two parties. Actually, both have to meet realities when faced with the responsibilities of office, and both of them do just about the same thing. But both make a great to-do about irresponsibility. Each accuses the other of extravagance. Franklin D. Roosevelt in 1932 accused Herbert Hoover of fiscal recklessness. Dwight D. Eisenhower accused Harry Truman of incautious spending. And in 1957 the Democrats accused Eisenhower of heedless imprudence; in 1959 the Eisenhower administration ran a deficit of $12 billion, the biggest yet on record in peacetime.

The reader may wish to know whether, from an economist's viewpoint, such charges have any basis in fact. This is an extremely difficult question to answer. Almost every family wastes some of its money in the course of a year and makes certain unwise and thoughtless expenditures. This is a human failing, and there is no reason to believe that governments have overcome this human weakness. It is quite probable that under more rational controls, better supervision, less junketing and graft, a few billions might be saved annually. This is something and well worth saving; but relative to the whole budget or the American income, it is not a huge sum. On the whole, economists worry less about expenditures and deficits than do average citizens; the reasons for this will be discussed toward the end of the chapter.

To get a substantial reduction in taxes, the American nation would have to give up many things that it now appears to want. Everyone favors expenditures that benefit him but considers wasteful many expenditures that benefit others. Let the Postmaster General economize by proclaiming a reduction in the number of daily mail deliveries, and massive protests will be heard from Newport, Rhode Island, to Newport, Oregon. Trade unions are willing to bear the burden of cuts made in the budget of the Department of Commerce but are less philosophical about cuts made in the Department of Labor. The southern congressman from Magnolia says that dredging the Sweetbrier River would contribute to the national defense and welfare, but he believes that flood control in Maine is a way of throwing money down a rathole. There would be no problem about reducing federal expenditures if we were all willing to give up something that we care about. But few of us are; and if we defend our favorite expenditure vehemently on the grounds of the public good, we may expect others to do the same.

This is a particularly bad time to write about the budget, since the situation is very dynamic during the summer of 1967. Because of

TABLE 13–1
PAYMENTS TO THE PUBLIC*
Fiscal Years (in Billions)

Function	1966 Actual	1967 Estimate	1968 Estimate
Administrative budget expenditures:			
National defense	$ 57.7	$ 70.2	$ 75.5
Excluding special Vietnam	(51.9)	(50.8)	(53.6)
International affairs and finance	4.2	4.6	4.8
Excluding special Vietnam	(3.9)	(4.1)	(4.3)
Space research and technology	5.9	5.6	5.3
Agriculture and agricultural resources	3.3	3.0	3.2
Natural resources	3.1	3.2	3.5
Commerce and transportation	3.0	3.5	3.1
Housing and community development	0.3	0.9	1.0
Health, labor, and welfare	7.6	10.4	11.3
Education	2.8	3.3	2.8
Veterans' benefits and services	5.0	6.4	6.1
Interest	12.1	13.5	14.2
General government	2.5	2.7	2.8
Allowances:			
Civilian and military pay increase			1.0
Possible shortfall in asset sales			0.8
Contingencies		0.1	0.4
Interfund transactions (deduct)	0.6	0.8	0.7
Total Administrative Budget Expenditures	$107.0	$126.7	$135.0
Trust fund expenditures:			
Health, labor, and welfare	$ 26.4	$ 31.5	$ 37.1
Commerce and transportation	3.8	3.7	3.7
National defense	.8	1.1	1.4
Agriculture and agricultural resources	1.2	1.4	1.2
Housing and community development	3.2	3.0	1.0
Veterans' benefits and services	0.6	0.8	0.6
All other	−0.2	0.1	0.3
Interfund transactions (deduct)	0.8	0.7	0.7
Total Trust Fund Expenditures	$ 34.9	$ 40.9	$ 44.5
Intragovernmental transactions and other adjustments (deduct)	$ 4.0	$ 6.8	$ 7.1
Total Payments to the Public	$137.8	$160.9	$172.4

SOURCE: *The Budget of the United States Government, Fiscal Year Ending June 30, 1968* (Washington, D.C.: U.S. Government Printing Office, 1967), p. 18.
* Columns may not add up to total given because of rounding.

the war in Vietnam, the deficit in the national income accounts budget is already being estimated by governmental officials and economists at approximately $25 billion (instead of $2.1 billion) unless there is a tax increase soon. The President did of course propose increases

TABLE 13–2
FEDERAL CASH RECEIPTS FROM THE PUBLIC*
Fiscal years (in Millions)

	1966 Actual	1967 Estimate	1968 Estimate
Administrative budget receipts:			
Individual income taxes	$ 55,446	$ 62,200	$ 73,200
Corporation income taxes	30,073	34,400	33,900
Excise taxes	9,145	9,300	8,800
Estate and gift taxes	3,066	3,100	3,100
Customs	1,767	1,980	2,100
Miscellaneous budget receipts	5,231	6,015	5,837
Total Administrative Budget Receipts ..	$104,727	$116,995	$126,937
Trust fund receipts:			
Employment taxes	$ 20,022	$ 26,445	$ 28,392
Deposits by states, unemployment insurance	3,067	3,000	3,000
Excise taxes	3,917	4,514	4,946
Federal employees' retirement systems	2,269	2,361	2,360
Interest on trust funds	1,908	2,268	2,685
Veterans' life insurance premiums	511	517	515
Other trust fund receipts	3,159	5,793	6,245
Total Trust Fund Receipts	$ 34,853	$ 44,898	$ 48,142
Intragovernmental and other noncash transactions	−$ 5,100	−$ 7,231	−$ 6,973
Total Cash Receipts from the Public	$134,480	$154,662	$168,106

SOURCE: *The Budget of the United States Government, Fiscal Year Ending June 30, 1968* (Washington, D.C.: U.S. Government Printing Office, 1967), p. 58.
* Columns may not add up to total given because of rounding.

TABLE 13–3

	Billions
National defense	$57.7
Space research and technology*	4.2
Veterans' benefits and services	5.0
Interest†	12.1
Defense Total	$79.0

* Some readers may feel that this item should not be classed as a defense item but should go elsewhere; other readers will agree with the authors.
† This is the interest on the national debt, most of it to service war deficits, but not all.

in the income tax, social security tax, and postal rates. To what extent increased taxes will reduce the $25-billion deficit remains to be seen. At any rate, Table 13–1 and Table 13–2 suggest objects of outgo and sources of income for recent years. Examination of the figures in

Table 13-1 reveals clearly the fact that expenditures for defense monopolize the budget. Even if we took the relatively peaceful year 1966, when military expenses were much lower than in 1967 or 1968 (projected), we find that the administrative budget devotes about 75 percent for wars—past, present, and future. The computation of the defense total goes as shown in Table 13–3.

Now, according to our calculations, only 25 cents out of every tax dollar remains for all the nondefense items of government. This pays for many functions that none could reasonably question: salaries to congressmen, the FBI, weather prediction, engraving and printing of our money, federal highway aid, building of post offices, and the paying—often underpaying—of our postmen. When the cost of these and other widely accepted services and functions are deducted from the 25 cents per dollar, precious little is left to argue heatedly about. But it is in this remaining area that public controversy is most explosive. Shall we pay the farmer more or less than 90 percent of parity (see Chapter 17); shall we cut out school lunches or serve more and better ones? If we think about these things calmly, we must come to the conclusion that Uncle Sam is not throwing money around quite so indiscriminately as is often charged. Much of the major portion goes for defense; next come needed services that any government should supply; after that, a few pennies of each dollar go for the reasonably debatable services. John Kenneth Galbraith, a well-known economist, in a delightful little book entitled *Economics and the Art of Controversy*, maintains the thesis that the violence and vigor of our national debates on economic questions are never proportional to the magnitude of the points involved. A 2 or 3 percent difference on some issue is likely to create a debate as unrestrained as if the participants were separated by differences of 90 percent. There seems to be great truth in Galbraith's thesis, and much of the sound and fury of fiscal debate goes into attacking a few pennies in each budgetary dollar.

It will be argued that some of the most extravagant and debatable expenditures are made under the least debatable heading—defense in all its forms. Lush swimming pools are built for American officers stationed in Shangri-La; a pint of ghee is shipped daily to make a dubious friend of every dweller in Lahore, Mysore, and Bangalore. Former Senator Paul Douglas, when chairman of the Senate Sub-committee on Defense Procurement, noted that Secretary Robert

McNamara, by better procurement policies, was able to save the
taxpayer $1 billion in fiscal 1963 and stated that even greater savings
were planned and possible for the future.[2] If this could be done in
fiscal 1963, why was it not done in 1962 or 1961 or 1958? As
taxpayers, we obviously have a right to ask these questions. But it is a
long step from these savings that involve only 1 to 5 percent of the
total to the view-with-alarm editorials and other propaganda which try
to make the ordinary citizen believe that half of his taxes are being
squandered by irresponsible officeholders or starry-eyed do-gooders.

The Budgetary Income

Where does the government's money come from? In a typical
year of the early 1960's the share of each type of tax might have been
about as shown in Table 13–4 (payroll social security taxes are not
included, since they do not form part of the administrative budget; the
complete story is to be found in Table 13–2). The 1969 estimate is not
very much different, but income taxes are scheduled to bring in more
and excise taxes less.

Each one of these taxes has a special personality and has its own
special effects on the economy. Let us look more closely at the first
three, for they are the most important. The first to consider is the

TABLE 13–4
PERCENTAGE RECEIPTS, EACH TYPE OF FEDERAL TAX

Individual income taxes	54.0%
Corporate income taxes	26.0
Excise taxes	11.5
Estate and gift taxes and all others	8.5
Total	100.0%

individual income tax, which is the one almost everybody gripes
about. For most regularly employed persons, it is subtracted from the
paycheck; the self-employed send the money in on certain dates. The
tax contains a provision which, though now long and widely accepted,
still arouses controversy. It is the progressive character of the tax. This

---

[2] *Report of the Subcommittee on Defense Procurement to the Joint Economic Committee of the Congress* (Washington, D.C.: U.S. Government Printing Office, 1963), p. v.

means that people of higher incomes not only pay more but pay a higher percentage of their incomes. The figures in Table 13–5 suggest what the head of a typical four-person family pays and how the percentage of income paid in tax varies with size.

TABLE 13–5

Income Received	Amount Paid	Approximate Percentage of Income Paid
$ 5,000	$ 290	6%
10,000	1,114	11
25,000	4,412	18
100,000	37,748	38
500,000	284,000	57

Many people believe that the upper levels of the income tax are too high; that they reduce incentives to take chances, to make progress; that they damp entreprenurial enthusiasm; and that the big bites into income encourage dishonesty or at the very least foster an ingenious search for loopholes. It is hard, on the evidence, to agree wholeheartedly with all of these strictures. We have been strong and prosperous and have grown reasonably fast since adopting the moderately high tax levels of World War II and after. We have had more progress than you could shake a stick at. This is the period of the wonder drugs and polio vaccine, of television and frozen foods, of widespread air conditioning, of reliable transoceanic plane service, of satellites and astronauts. We have entered the age of automation and of atomic power. It can of course be argued that we might have done even better had we had a less rigorous income tax, but we have done much even with a heavy burden. It is, however, quite probable that the tax does encourage dishonesty and frantic lobbying to create loop- holes, but this sort of thing went on in the 1920's when taxes were absurdly low by current standards. Studies of taxation reveal that some persons with fabulous incomes pay no income taxes at all and that countless others, from $25,000 upward, are able to find ways of paying 10 to 40 percent less than is demanded by the scheduled rates. This is not illegal. This is loopholes.

Most economists would hesitate to go on record as saying that an income tax is "too high" or "too low." Too high for what? Too low for what? For a period of inflation such as we had in the 1950's, tax rates might have been too low. For a period of high-level stagnation such as we were experiencing in the early 1960's the tax rates were probably too high. What is important about a tax is not whether it is too high or too low to please the individuals affected, but whether it brings about desirable results in the economy as a whole. And let us remember that what pleases individuals taken in isolation does not necessarily please them taken as a totality. Thus, we may all, as individuals, be delighted that income taxes are reduced; but if this results in inflation, we may all be very sorry.

The income tax is not only countercyclical but it is, to some degree, automatically so. It has, therefore, a stabilizing influence on the economy, whether Congress takes action or not. Thus, if our incomes go down, as they do in depression, our tax load becomes absolutely and proportionately less. This releases a larger percentage for consumer spending and lends a degree of stability to our purchasing power. And the opposite happens during inflation. The government takes proportionately more away from us—something that also makes consumption more nearly stable.

When we consider a tax, we are always interested in where the burden of payment finally falls. The issue is this: The person who actually pays the tax to the government or its agent is not necessarily the person who finally pays it. Taxes can be shifted, at least in part; nobody dreams, for example, that distillers pay the major part of federal liquor taxes, even though they buy the stamps. The consumer is usually looked on as the ultimate taxpayer here, even though he pays nothing directly to the government. Now for our question: Can the income tax be shifted? Ask any householder about April 14 when he is feverishly working on his tax return and wondering whether he'll ever be able to find the money he owes. Just ask him! Obviously, *he* pays, and he cannot foist the bill onto anybody else. Economists agree in a general way that income taxes cannot be shifted, but they do wonder whether this is invariably true. Do not high corporation executives clamor for various fringe benefits because income taxes are so high? Do not labor unions tend to think of take-home pay and bargain in these terms—that is, in income-tax-free terms? Perhaps there is more shifting than we used to think there was. But is it shifted back just to the employer? Can the employer shift it forward to the consumer? The questions are good ones, but at the present stage of economic wisdom the answers have not been perfected. There is some reason to believe that some part of our income taxes may be borne by the consumer.

The second most productive tax in our battery of taxes is the corporation tax. Like the income tax, it is popularly supposed to soak the rich. It is a tax on the net income of corporations. It has varied in recent years and has absorbed about half of what is legally defined as net corporation income. In some ways, this federal corporation tax— there are several taxes on corporations, but a tax on their incomes is the most important—seems to be the product of confused thinking. It treats a corporation as if it were an individual. If Joseph Doakes has a net income of $1 million a year, we can safely say he has a high income, and we may with some justice argue that he should be heavily taxed. But if a corporation has a net income of $1 million, we cannot on the basis of that fact alone determine whether its income is high or low. We would have to know more about the amount of capital involved. A taxable net income of $1 million would be very little for a steel company that owns a few blast furnaces, a railroad, a coal mine, a rolling mill, and a couple of ore-carrying vessels. But a $1-million income suggests unreasonably high profits for, say, a small contracting firm. The corporation tax does not take all this into account. It just taxes the $1 million.

But the corporations are probably not hurt too badly. Actually, a part of the corporation tax is quite likely passed along through higher prices to the consumer, though the owners of the corporation must also meet part of it. What really happens has not been clearly determined by the economist. Some of the burden certainly falls on stockholders; yet it is hard to believe that stockholders would get twice their present dividends if the 52 percent tax were lifted. Perhaps tax reduction or repeal would make entry and survival of small firms easier. This would increase competition; profits and prices of established firms would perhaps decline—and with them, dividends.

As in the case of the progressive income tax, it is held that the corporation tax discourages risk taking, stifles small corporations, and threatens to block economic progress. There may be some truth in all this. It might be desirable to exempt corporations from some of their tax if they would agree to expand countercyclically, that is, to spend impounded funds for new plant and equipment when hard times threaten.

The remaining important federal taxes are often named consumption taxes. They are regressive in that many of them demand a larger share of income from low-income persons than from high-income receivers. Thus, if each of two men smokes a pack of cigarettes a day, the $2,500-a-year man pays 1 percent of his income in cigarette taxes while the $20,000 man pays one eighth of 1 percent. When such taxes are laid on the impecunious man's daily needs and small luxuries, such as beer, movies, and sugar (tax laid through the tariff), they have the effect of soaking the poor.

These taxes are not always levied directly on the consumer. They are like transportation charges. Sometimes the seller pays the express company, sometimes the buyer. But the buyer pays in the first case just as surely as in the second, for prices are high enough to cover transportation. And so with many taxes. The manufacturer pays cigarette and liquor taxes initially, but we consumers pay them in the end, at least in part. To be sure, the manufacturer, even if he can pass along the whole tax, feels it, too, for he could sell more of his goods if the tax did not increase the price. No manufacturer likes to see his product taxed, though he can shift the burden, because sales tend to go down when the price to the consumer goes up.

What Kind of Tax Is Best?

There is no really final answer to the question of what kind of tax is best. Some are better than others for purely technical reasons, but not for reasons of equity. For example, a tax, however equitable, is a stupid one if it costs so much to collect it that the yield is scarcely greater than receipts. This was an argument made against excess-profits taxes in war; they cost too much in proportion to yield. Taxes are bad—technically—if dates of payment are not precise or the basis of taxation is not or cannot be known clearly and unequivocally. Our federal income tax is often a little hazy, and lawyers are sometimes in dispute as to whether a certain sum is taxable or not.

On the side of equity, we quickly come to a dead end. One principle of equity would be that taxation should be proportionate to benefits received. The gasoline tax is one of the few taxes which might be worked out pretty neatly on this principle. If you use up the highways a lot, either because your truck is heavy or you drive your passenger car 30,000 miles a year, you automatically pay a gasoline tax proportionate to your wearing-down of roads. But use of the road is not the only benefit. People who don't own cars or use buses will benefit from the overall prosperity generated by a good system of transportation. Roughly the same thing might be said of education. If you make only the parents of school-going children pay the school taxes, you get a sort of naïve equity; but we all benefit from a literate population. As for the benefit system in matters of defense or soil conservation or flood control, it is all but hopeless to search out specific beneficiaries.

Another principle of equity would be capacity to pay. This may be a principle of some ethical systems or a principle on which a majority agree, but it is not a scientific principle. Even if there is widespread agreement, an issue presents itself in a difficult form when we consider a flat income tax rate as opposed to a progressive rate. Table 13–5 told us that a family receiving an income of $5,000 pays $290 in taxes; but it also told us that a family receiving $500,000 does *not* pay a mere $29,000. This sum bears the same relation to $500,000 that $290 bears to $5,000. But the scheduled amount is much greater. This would be one way of interpreting the concept of capacity to pay. Actually, the family of higher income pays not only more, but at a higher percentage rate. Here, "capacity to pay" escalates itself upward to the high figure of $284,000. Is this wrong? There is no answer based on equity.

Deficits as a Source of Income

We now discuss another great source of governmental revenues —borrowing, our resort when we live beyond our means. Confronted with expenditures greater than can easily be met by taxation, a government could, as ours did during the Civil War, print money and put it into circulation. This has certain merits over borrowing, since interest need not be paid on printed money but must be paid on loans. There are, however, certain disadvantages to printing money; and modern states print IOU's, or bonds, instead, which do require interest. On the basis of these, banks can create checkbook money. The bonds are the form that the borrowing takes; they are the loan; they are the deficit; and they serve to swell the public debt.

Economists are sometimes under attack in the public press and elsewhere as perverted wastrels who take demoniacal pleasure in seeing the public debt increase. This is arrant nonsense. They feel about the public debt as they would feel about a private debt—that it should be contracted or increased only when circumstances justify going into debt. If money will cure the breadwinner's hepatitis, then the family should go into debt, if necessary, to get the money. If borrowing will send a gifted child through college, then the family should borrow. There are at least two public emergencies which, from the economist's viewpoint, justify increasing the public debt.

The first is war, and for this there is widespread agreement with the economist that borrowing is desirable. When a catastrophic event like a war occurs, there is no time to hold long hearings about the equitable taxation measures needed to pay for it; and let us make no mistake, it could be paid out of current taxation—from the merely mathematical viewpoint, at least. The line of least resistance is to borrow. The real costs of a war are current costs; and if real costs can be met, then financial costs can also be met. By real costs, we mean the amount of labor required to make a gun or a jet; the loss of resources by the removal of coal and iron ore from the ground; self-denial by civilians when they reduce their consumption of gasoline, prime cuts of meat, or sugar; and most important, of course, the very great sacrifices of the armed forces. These things cannot be borrowed from future generations; and since these and other real costs must be met during the war itself, a war is a pay-as-you-go affair as far as real costs go, and could be made pay-as-you-go financially. But we do not do this, for various reasons. We are not quite prepared to tax too heavily as we go; we feel that the economy will function more easily if we meet only part of the costs by taxation and borrow the rest. We feel that under a very great load of taxation, monetary incentives may be too low and that the public morale may decline precisely at a time when morale needs to be high. So we borrow and leave it pretty much to the postwar years and fate—but not necessarily the next few generations—to decide who profits or loses by having invested in war bonds which, as we have said, are the form that the debt takes. If Smith buys a $5,000 bond during World War II and holds it until

1965, the purchasing power of the $5,000 has been cut in half, and he loses.

The second emergency that may justify borrowing is depression and its variant forms—recession, high-level stagnation as in 1962 and 1963, low rates of growth, and the like. All are similar, in that the resources of the economy are being underutilized. It has been estimated that the shortfall in production between 1953 and 1959 (both years inclusive) was about $199 billion.[3] If this figure is valid, it would mean that every family might have had, on the average, about $600 more in the form of goods annually during that period. In human terms, it would mean finding jobs for over two million unemployed, a disproportionate number of which include young people and Negroes—something that might ease the tensions now taking the form of juvenile delinquency and racial disturbances.

In the Keynesian view, as we learned in Chapter 9, depression comes about when investors are unable to invest at the same rate that savers are trying to save. In such an event, government can, by injecting new purchasing power into the economy, act as a substitute for private investors. And these sums injected are multiplied, as we have seen, so that an injection of $5 billion may raise the national income by $15 billion. But of course, this must be "new" purchasing power. Such new purchasing power, on any massive scale, is likely to arise out of borrowing and to swell the public debt. It does little good to collect it first in taxes and then reintroduce the same purchasing power back into the economy.

Thus, to summarize, budgetary deficits are tolerable if the reasons for borrowing are sound. Most economists believe that certain emergencies or unhealthy situations provide justifiable reasons. War is one of the major emergencies. Chief among the unhealthy situations is a slowdown in the economy, like the era of high-level stagnation in the early 1960's.

The Public Debt and Public Obfuscation

To many readers the above paragraphs will not seem convincing. Their comment may run something like this: "I agree that you may

[3] Conference on Economic Progress, *The Federal Budget and the General Welfare* (Washington, D.C., 1959).

have to borrow in wartime when our whole national life is threatened, but is it really necessary to borrow in order to increase our prosperity? I know that if my own income were cut in half, I'd be pretty miserable; but I would refuse to borrow—at least, to borrow as a way of life. I'd move to low-rent quarters as soon as possible. I'd lay down the law to my wife and kids: no new dresses or hats, no spending of $2 or $3 week-nights at Tony's Pizzatorium, no more expensive hairdos. Myself, I'd move down to those 5-cent cigars I hear about on TV; it would be Ping-Pong in the playroom instead of golf at the club, and a family game of Old Maid instead of bridge at a penny a point. Why can't we, as a nation, tighten our belts and simplify our lives the same way? Why should my daughter get shampoos at Henri's—her grandchildren will have to pay for that—when we have branch water at home and good old Ivory soap?"

Translated into more abstract terms, this citizen's observations might be summed up as follows:

1. There is no difference between a public debt and a private debt; both have to be repaid. If not, they impose unjust burdens on future generations.
2. Private poverty (or a reduced level of living) is like public poverty (or depression); in both cases the thing to do is to tighten your budget and wait for better times.

The reader will by now be able to find the fallacy in the second proposition. Nothing could more quickly bring on a depression or deepen one already here than a sudden cut in the consumption expenditures of a nation. The first proposition is a little harder to refute, but it also contains several fallacies to which we shall address ourselves in the next few paragraphs.

Most people are dreadfully anxious about the public debt. Adam Smith, in about 1775, predicted that European nations, too much addicted to borrowing, would all go down in ruin fairly soon if they did not mend their ways. The British debt at that time stood at £129 million sterling. Most of this anxiety is misplaced and has its roots in ignorance, superstition, false analogy, and the ceaseless propaganda of those who oppose the alleviation of poverty by public action and who believe that unemployment is an individual sin. It is true, of course, that a nation can be damaged by an irresponsible and demagogic government if it relies on heavy borrowing rather than taxes.

And it is also true that some hard-pressed governments after wars—international, civil, or revolutionary—have relied too irresponsibly on the printing press for either money or bonds and thereby have caused unmerited suffering among certain groups in the population. But there is nothing on the horizon of the countries of western Europe or North America to suggest that any such fate is a proximate danger.

Let us take up one by one a few of the major myths about a public debt. First is one that arises out of a false analogy between balancing the books of a household or business firm and those of the government of the United States. The analogy is almost worthless because the debts of a household or business firm are external debts; that is, families and businessmen owe money to landlords, suppliers, gas and electric companies, and others outside the family or firm. We owe the public debt to ourselves mostly—a few citizens of other lands do possess some of our government bonds (the form that the IOU's of the public debt take), but only a few; the percentage is unimportant. There is a great difference between owing to ourselves and owing to others. In a large firm, analysis of accounts would probably show that the shipping department owes money to the maintenance department, and the sales department to the production department, and so forth. But such internal debts are quite different from the debts owed by firm A to firm B. It is alleged that 15 or 20 years ago some responsible economists said that since we owed the debt only to ourselves, it did not matter how large the debt was; and so, what the heck, let's cancel it anyhow. No responsible economist argues this way today, and its size does matter; still, it is true that a domestically held debt is less onerous than an external debt.

The second myth arises out of our belief that the debt is fantastically large, that if it were laid end to end it would reach from the moon to Betelguese and back to Guadalajara. This numerical acrophobia, in turn, stems from our incapacity to deal with large numbers. Untutored savages are said to be able to count up to only 3 or 4; after that, any number is simply "a great many." The average citizen of modern civilization does not easily visualize figures above a million or so. Between 1960 and 1965, our public debt increased by $31.4 billion. This means an average annual deficit of $5.2 billion. Now, in the same period the average national income was $475 billion. This means that our debt increased at the rate of 1.1 percent of our national income a year. To make things still more concrete, let us cut this down to the size of a typical American family. The median family income during this period was about $6,145 a year. If such a family had overspent by the same percentage, it would have overspent only $67.60 a year. It is true, of course, that no family should regularly overspend even a dollar a year if it wishes to remain solvent; still, the sum is not huge. The reader should be reminded again that the family's $67.60 becomes an external debt; our overspending of 1.1 percent of our national income adds to an internal debt and is therefore less threatening.

The third myth is that we are living extravagantly by increasing the public debt and that we are making our children and grandchildren pay for our extravagance. Before answering this one, we must digress for a moment to ask why we think so much of our children and grandchildren when we talk about public debt and pay so little attention to their welfare when we pollute air and water, allow our cities to develop into monstrous ghettos, disembowel our natural resources, and fill the welkin with a million firkins of radioactive dust. But to return: Our descendants will not repay the debt unless they should want to. The internal debt of a government can stand indefinitely. Nobody demands that it be repaid. The creditors are the people who hold government bonds. Those who wish to have cash instead of bonds can sell them on the market or, depending on the type of bond, turn them in to the Treasury through their banks. The Treasury can handle this small demand without strain, or it can simply issue new bonds for those turned in. There is nothing unusual about this even in private business, where debts are external. Some railroads issue perpetual bonds—bonds that the railroad does not promise ever to repay. This is not customary; but look at the list of bonds on the New York Stock Exchange. Some of them are not due until almost the middle of the 21st century; and when they come due, new bonds can be issued in their place that may run until the middle of the 22d century. Letting debts run indefinitely is not the act of an irresponsible gang of politicians. All governments and many corporations will probably stay in debt until the crack of doom. New England mortgages on farms used to go with the property and were inherited from father to son through several generations. Our children and grandchildren will not be called on to repay the debt.

And yet there really are some burdens in connection with the public debt; and the bigger the debt, the greater the burdens to ourselves and posterity. The interest is running around $14 billion a year, or something over $70 a head. Many of us, of course, are getting all of our share back in the form of interest on our government bonds, provided we own enough of them or invest in them indirectly through our insurance companies, trusts, and so on. But of course, if we had had this money invested in stocks or bonds, we would not be paying it out in taxes before getting it back in interest. Many of us do not own bonds; we pay interest to those who do. The public debt of the United States cannot be such a dreadful thing; the bonds are held by banks and rich men; many of us would be delighted to have a million dollars' worth of it and to enjoy the $30,000 annual income that would come to us. But however you look at it, the payment of interest is a burden, and to pay less is better than to pay more.

Another myth—though this one is only a half myth—is that increases in the public debt bring about inflation. This can be true under certain circumstances. The danger should not be overlooked, but it should also be made clear that the danger is not always present. When the government borrows, it prints bonds. The bonds are in large part bought by banks. Banks are legally permitted to enlarge their loans on the basis of the bonds they hold. These loans are checkbook money. This new money is released to the public, which uses it to buy and bid up prices; and now we may have inflation. But we are not likely to get inflation if there is any appreciable slack in the economy, that is, if we have underemployment of resources. Or to put it differently, government borrowing leads to inflation only if the economy is at the stage of full employment. But in prosperous times of peace, with a fully employed economy in an advanced nation, governments should not borrow. Actually, under such circumstances, there is no reason for them to borrow. The only major reason for large borrowing in peacetime is to fight depression and restore prosperity. If at full employment a government needs more money, it should increase taxes.

A few minor items of clarification and reassurance can be added. Both private and public indebtedness, if sound, bear a direct and appropriate relationship to income. A young couple in their 20's struggling along on $6,000 a year, can ill afford to support a debt of

$3,000. To their successful parents, earning $30,000 a year, a debt of $3,000 should be a bagatelle. In the 15-year period between 1945 and 1965, the national debt increased at a (cumulative) rate of about 1⅛ percent yearly. The GNP has increased at the much more rapid rate of 6 percent.[4] Since population has increased while the debt has remained more nearly static, the amount of the per capita debt is declining regularly. The passage of the years should reduce the importance of our public debt relative to the other large figures of our economy, and also the burden of interest. But the war in Asia may change all that.

One final observation. All the way through this discussion, we have tacitly been accepting as gospel truth a lot of figures which are really questionable: The debt is so much, the deficit is so much, the government spends this and that, and so on. Well, the figures were correct enough, but what were they figures of? We should spend a few minutes on this question. Whatever the government spends is counted as irretrievable outgo, whether it be for carbon paper, which soon finds its way into the trash, or for a post office or bridge or dam, which may last 100 years. This is quite different from the bookkeeping procedure of a business firm or private family. If General Electric builds a new plant in Cicero Falls, its books will show that it spent $1 million on land, building, and equipment; but they will also show that it owns a valuable piece of property. Some governments (Sweden for one) divide their expenditures into two categories—current and capital. Current expenditures include sums spent on salaries, paper clips, soap, interest on the public debt, and so forth. Capital expenditures might be used for flood and erosion control, airports, and other permanent items, some of which are salable, and some of which make long-term contributions to economic productivity. No less an authority on these matters than Harold M. Groves has noted that if German budgetary accounts were managed like ours, they would reveal greater deficits than ours. Yet Germany is widely reputed to handle her fiscal affairs with exceptional prudence.

The point to be made here is that the budget of the United States, with its deficits, looks much worse than it really is, for we do not use a

[4] This overstates the actual U.S. growth rate in the period because no correction has been made for the inflation that had taken place. Since, however, no correction was made for the public debt either, the two percentages given correctly suggest the relationship.

method of bookkeeping that takes account of the long-range benefits of permanent installations; it does not even take account of the actually salable assets the government is acquiring every year.

Fiscal versus Monetary Policy

In the chapter preceding this one, we spoke of how manipulation of credit, interest rates, bank reserves, and allied entities might help to maintain stability; and now, in this chapter, we have discussed fiscal manipulation to achieve stability. The reader may very well be wondering which to use and which policy is better—monetary or fiscal.

A direct answer to this question is impossible. So many ingenious schemes are in use or have been proposed in the capitalist world that merely to enumerate and describe them adequately would probably require a book of this size; and to evaluate them, another one. Inventive economists proliferate new ideas almost daily. Moreover, the circumstances under which the stabilizing schemes are to be applied are never the same. In some depressions, retail prices go down; in others, up. Our balance of payments was fine in the depression of 1949; but in 1959, it looked rather bad. Sometimes, our unemployed are just unemployed; in 1963, unemployment was "restructured because of automation." Sometimes, we don't even have depression; in the early 1960's, they were calling our slow growth "high-level stagnation." Economists have the same troubles as doctors. Patients never break their legs the same way; each depression differs from the last. Patients who ought to have penicillin are allergic to it; if you reduce the rate of interest to cure one thing, you get into trouble somewhere else.

On top of all this, we have the politicians—on the whole, a most able and even noble 600, but containing also in House and Senate some who represent interests that are not hurt by depression or inflation and who, therefore, may prefer things the way they are. A few others favor a certain amount of unemployment because, they say, it disciplines the working force. A few are governed by sheer and almost total ignorance or unshakable prejudice against any kind of governmental intervention. Legislation to meet the motley and contradictory interests of this group too often terminates in battered and contradictory policies.

One thing seems to be rather clear. Monetary policy is probably more useful in combating inflation than depression. Making credit hard to get does eventually discourage business expansion and hence controls inflation. But making credit easily available to a businessman in depression does not seem to encourage him to build up inventory or expand his plant; the lot of a solitary man in a life-boat after shipwreck is not much improved by the dozens of life preservers stored under the seats or by the three extra pairs of oars. So, too, redundant credit may be useless.

Most economists believe that fiscal policy works better in depression. Reducing tax rates is a remedy that has wider support. But even this has possible difficulties, and the details of working out the broad principle are not clear. One trouble is that we know little about the consequences of tax reduction in depression. The question is: Whose income taxes should be cut? The corporations'? Well, maybe, but it is on the individual income tax that attention is focused. And here the issue is whether there should be an across-the-board cut or a selective one. If we reduce the tax on the great incomes, we may stimulate investment. But shall we really? What is there to invest in during depression? If we reduce the tax on low incomes, we shall certainly increase consumption, for families living at levels of $5,000 a year or under have many unsatisfied wants. But by how much shall we do so? The poor have precious little income to tax. Those who are up one step higher on the ladder may not spend their released money after all and will take it out of the income stream by saving it. They save because they see people being laid off all around them and fear that they too will be laid off soon. In depression, money saved does not contribute toward cure.

The real answer to our question about the efficacy of fiscal policy over monetary policy is that there is no answer except, perhaps, that abundant credit does not cure depressions. Applied economics is still an art, and a more primitive art than healing the sick. Depressions do not come in standard sizes or shapes, like clothing or doors. Policy will always depend not on a mechanical application of a formula, but on a creative appraisal of each situation in all its complexity.

State and Local Taxes and Expenditures

A few terminal words about state and local finances: State and local governments in 1965 collected about $55 billion in taxes. The states took in a little more than half of this and the local governments a little less, but the inequality was not great. As additional revenue, the states received $11 billion in grants from the federal government. Since the receipts of the federal government in the same year amounted to $93 billion (administrative budget), the reader can see that Uncle Sam alone runs a show that is nearly twice as big as all the state and local divisions put together. And if we include social security taxes and a few other items, the federal government takes in considerably more than twice as much.

For their revenue, states rely heavily on sales taxes, including taxes on motor fuels, alcoholic beverages, and tobacco. The automobile is a fairly large source of income to state governments: The aforementioned fuel tax, plus licenses, accounts for a quarter of the total taken in. Individual and corporation income taxes are pouring steadily increasing streams of money into the state coffers. Local units within the states get most of their revenue from property taxes. The property taxed consists largely of land and buildings, though levies are made on other property, fitfully and capriciously. Objects taxed include jewelry, cattle, furniture, stocks and bonds, and bank accounts.

The great reliance placed by state governments on sales and excise taxes, and the lesser but still considerable reliance of the federal government on this form of revenue, clearly introduce a moderately large regressive element into our total tax system. The property tax, the incidence of which will be discussed presently, also opens the door to regression into the total tax edifice, but less decidedly so than sales and excise taxes. The very high brackets of the personal income tax on the federal level have for a generation made us feel that the rich turned most of their income over to the government. Actually, all of us, rich and poor alike, pay a great deal; and though the poor do pay less as a percentage of income than the rich, the differences are probably less than is popularly believed. See Table 13–6.

TABLE 13–6
PERCENTAGE OF INCOME PAID IN FEDERAL, STATE, AND LOCAL
TAXES, BY INCOME CLASS, 1958*

Income Class	Percentage of Income Paid in Taxes
$ 0 – $ 1,999	21%
2,000 – 3,999	20
4,000 – 5,999	21
6,000 – 7,999	22
8,000 – 9,999	21
10,000 – 14,999	22
15,000 and over	34

* Adapted from studies made by the Tax Foundation, Inc.

The property tax, the only form of taxation not previously discussed, is the well-known tax on land, homes, and other buildings. The homeowner is not likely to be able to shift the tax onto the shoulders of anybody else; but the owner of apartment houses, office buildings, and the like will probably be able to shift at least part of the tax forward to the tenant. One big trouble with the property tax is that it makes a constant demand on a person's income, which is often inconstant. If my income is cut because of depression or loss of job or old age, or if I must retrench because of large medical expenses, I can avoid paying some of my income taxes; I can even, by reducing my consumption of gasoline, tobacco, and liquor, cut down the amount I pay for sales taxes; but unless I sell my house, I cannot avoid the fixed, relentless cost of the property tax. The property tax was probably introduced in an era when the amount of tangible property possessed by a man was a genuine index of his capacity to pay. This is less likely to be true today. One may own hundreds of thousands of dollars' worth of stocks and bonds without owning a square foot of land. The stocks and bonds usually are not taxed, though the income from them is, of course.

Where does the money collected by states and local governments go? That is an easy one. Local taxes go mostly for schools and highways, in that order; and state taxes go mostly for highways and schools, in *that* order. Moderately large chunks of both state and local funds go for health, welfare, and unemployment compensation. Most police and fire protection is paid for locally; a small share is borne by the state. The rapid population growth of the United States has put a large strain on local units of government. They spend about 30 percent of their income on schools and derive most of their income on the rather rigid property tax. Thus, we have a very dynamic phenomenon yoked to a very static one.

State and local governments have in recent years felt the squeeze of an increasing population, on the one hand, and increasing demand for welfare and similar services, on the other. This has caused anxiety not only for the present but also for the immediate future. The Tax Foundation, Inc., has made a most thorough study of this problem and finds that, overall, the rate of increased expansion will decline. Pressures on spending at an increasing rate will diminish, partly because education and highway building will slow down their rates of expansion. On the other hand, expenditures for welfare and health will grow at an increasing rate. But the whole picture is reassuring.

Economists do not have much hope of using local fiscal systems countercyclically. The amounts are much smaller, and countercyclical policies would have less impact on the total economy. States have a sort of sovereignty, and even a semisovereign is likely to be balky. If a President were to request all 50 states to stop building schools during an inflationary period when public activity should be reduced, some governors, for political reasons or even out of sheer defiance, would refuse. Many state and local activities, such as collecting garbage or maintaining police and fire protection, cannot be turned on or shut off during prosperity or depression. Rapid and steady population growth has left local communities small choice about scheduling the building of new schools. The same thing is true of bringing in more water or piping out new sewage. All public work involving construction, whether federal, state, or local, presents inherent difficulties as a stabilizing force. It takes a long time to get work started on bridges, roads, dams, and schools; by the time the preliminary work is finished, the depression may be over, and the structures will have to be completed in a period of prosperity or abandoned at great loss. Yet something could be done, and the nation might benefit from a more thoughtful countercyclical planning of public works by the states.

One important exception must be noted to the above. A major stabilizing force in the economy is the system of unemployment compensation, a system which gives to the unemployed up to about 40 percent of the wages lost by joblessness. Although this is technically a state operation, standards are set by the federal government; and in other ways, Washington is deeply involved.

Summary and Conclusions

This chapter first discussed the federal budget, the taxes that nourish it, and the expenses that dissipate the funds collected. The taxes were evaluated, and we tried to find out whether they could be shifted and, if so, how. It is widely believed that because of high rates applicable to upper income brackets, the rich pay punitive taxes and that a major redistribution of income is constantly going on in our society. This is false, for two reasons: First, many loopholes and exemptions reduce the taxable incomes of large fractions of the very rich; second, most remaining forms of taxation are regressive.

In view of the sound and fury that surrounds discussion of the public debt, which grows when the proceeds of taxation are insufficient, we tried to look at it dispassionately. The conclusion was that the debt is not nearly so dangerous as is popularly believed. On the contrary, in depression an increase in governmental spending—and hence in the public debt—is likely to be beneficial. The danger of inflation arises only when deficits are created in periods of full employment.

Since fiscal policy may be used to stabilize the economy, the question was raised as to whether fiscal policy is superior to monetary policy. Fiscal policy seems, on balance, to be superior to monetary policy if the problem is to restore prosperity. But our experience in the conscious use of fiscal policy prevents us from being dogmatic.

State and local taxes are of small importance on the national stage. The 50 states collect much less than the amount collected by the federal government. Since, on the whole, state and local governments cannot and perhaps will not, acting in concert, do much toward correcting inflation or deflation, their fiscal systems and problems are of small interest to the student of general economic policies and issues. The state-administrated unemployment compensation system is an exception to this rule, but it has unique ties to the federal government.

QUESTIONS FOR REVIEW AND DISCUSSION

1. Define, in your own words, each of the following terms:
   a) Fiscal policies
   b) Real income
   c) Income tax
   d) Progressive tax
   e) Regressive tax
   f) Proportional tax

2. What effect does a progressive income tax have upon the distribution of income? Why does this effect take place?

3. "The public debt is to the nation what private debt is to the household." Discuss critically.

4. If a mother were to say that every time she made beds, the family owed her 50 cents; if every time the son emptied the trash, he claimed 10 cents; if every time the daughter washed dishes, she would demand a credit of 25 cents—if the individual members of a family constantly entered claims against the family as a whole in this fashion, a large family debt would soon be built up. Would such a debt be comparable to the public debt of the United States?

5. Your authors state that a war can be fought without increasing the public debt. Try to imagine what might have happened if the United States had fought World War II without borrowing.

6. The individual income tax is thought to be valuable as an "automatic stabilizer." What is this attribute, how does it work, and why is it desirable?

7. Under what conditions would an increase in the public debt enhance the nation's economic performance? Under what conditions would it hinder it?

8. Why is monetary policy easier to put into effect than fiscal policy?

9. What are some of the loopholes in federal income tax law?

Chapter	INTERNATIONAL
14	TRADE

The Basic Mechanism of Foreign Trade

Foreign trade is often symbolized in magazine pictures and elsewhere by a freight steamer at dock, with a cargo net full of merchandise being swung down into the hold. As a symbol, this may be good enough, but it does fail to suggest the whole complex. An American in Dubuque buying new shares of a Canadian oil company through his local broker is carrying on an international transaction and therefore international trade. Every American passenger on the *Mauretania* and every non-Hollander flying KLM airplanes is engaged in foreign trade. If you, as a tourist, buy a ticket to go from Paris to Chartres, you have imported a ride; if, in a French nightclub, you buy a bottle of champagne, you have imported it as surely as if you were a wine importer sitting in your New York office. If, like United Fruit or Anaconda, you develop banana lands or copper mines in Guatemala or Chile and then bring the bananas and copper to be sold here, you have engaged in complex crisscross import-export activities. If you sell French francs "short" in the hope of being able to buy them cheap later on, you are engaged in a form of foreign trade.[1]

Thus a congeries of operations comes under the heading of foreign trade. Their common bond is that in all of these transactions, the money of one nation must be converted into the money of another. If you buy a meal in a French restaurant, you must do one thing more

---

[1] To sell short means to reverse the chronological order of buying cheap and selling dear. A simple example would be as follows: You sell a man a piece of land which you do not yet own for $5,000; you do this because you are quite sure you can buy it next day for $4,000. Of course, you are taking a chance; you may not be able to buy it so cheaply. If you can't, you are stuck; but if your judgment was good, you make $1,000. Obviously, in many short sales, you must get around the problem of immediately delivering the thing you have sold before owning it. In stock market transactions you can borrow shares of stock for a while and deliver those immediately; eventually, you must of course buy and return the stock you borrowed.

than you do when you buy a meal in this country; you must, before you enter the restaurant, convert your dollars or travelers' checks into francs. To be sure, a restaurant accustomed to tourists will do the job for you; but somebody must do it. In the United States, you can buy passage on a French steamer without converting dollars into francs, but at some point the French Line will want to convert at least part of your money into francs.

The word "convert" is not really a good word to use, because in a literal sense conversion is impossible. Nobody can convert apples into pears, and nobody can convert dollars into British pounds. Sometimes, we speak of "buying pounds" or of "exchanging dollars for pounds," and peerhaps these expressions are more nearly exact. The process comes close to offsetting, or clearing.

We pay for the things we buy abroad by an elaborate system of clearance or of transferring debts. International trade is carried on without actual dollars, francs, pounds, or pesos—at least, without the transportation of much actual money across the borders. If we lend the British $4 billion, the "money" all stays here in American banks. Then the British buy American goods; in payment, they proffer checks written in dollars, payable at the banks that carry the British accounts. In due course of time the accounts are exhausted; what has moved to England is goods, not money.

Let us follow the process in a simplified transaction. If you buy a few cases of champagne in France for $150, you owe some Frenchman that amount or its French equivalent (let us call it 750 francs). If I sell some Frenchman an adding machine for $150, he owes me 750 francs. Accounts can be squared in this fashion:

1. You pay me the champagne money (thus, I get my $150).
2. I tell the French adding-machine buyer not to try to pay me, but instead to give 750 francs to the seller of champagne.
3. The adding-machine buyer follows instructions and pays 750 francs to the champagne seller (thus the champagne man gets his money).
4. The French champagne seller informs you that he has been paid, that everything is in order.

In such a transaction, everybody has what he wants; you have your champagne, one Frenchman has an adding machine, the other his 750 francs, and I have my $150. The only question left to consider is how to get four people so neatly together every time a foreign sale is made.

The agency that gets people together is a broker of some sort with a correspondent abroad, often a bank. We shall now, with simplifications, trace the same transaction through two such brokers—a broker in the United States, who will be named Elmer, and his partner in France, Pierre. If I do not know you and therefore do not know that you are buying champagne, I can go direct to Elmer for my money. I present to him documents as evidence that I have made a bona fide sale, that an adding machine is being shipped, that it is insured, and so on. Elmer takes my papers and gives me $150 minus a small commission for his service. Of course, I authorize Elmer to collect, through his partner Pierre in France, the 750 francs that the French buyer of the adding machine has agreed to pay me. Not only collect but keep. I have no further interest in the transaction, for I have been given my money. The deal is over for me. Now, Elmer has paid me out of a kitty which would soon be exhausted if he dealt only with exporters like me. But he also deals with importers and knows that somebody like you will come along presently and that you will want to pay money *into* the kitty. That is, you will want to give Elmer $150 for your champagne on the understanding that Pierre will pay 750 francs to the French seller of champagne.

As long as total transactions among all importing and exporting Frenchmen and all importing and exporting Americans approximately balance each other, our brokers will get along all right. But this does not always happen. Americans may sell much more to Frenchmen than Frenchmen sell to Americans. Let us see what happens now.

If, by excessive sales in France, Americans are constantly taking dollars away from Elmer and rarely paying dollars into his kitty, then there is trouble. When this happens, our transatlantic Pierre is being uncomfortably deluged with francs. Frenchmen are buying a lot of things in the United States and not selling much. Pierre's kitty of francs is becoming huge. Unless something happens to change the trend, our partners will soon have to give up their brokerage firm. When Elmer has run out of dollars to give to American exporters, he is unable to perform the very service for which he is paid commissions. There is no point in his staying in business; he has nothing to offer. Pierre will go out of business, too. They are not bankrupt. They simply have nothing to offer potential customers. There is a stalemate, as when a newsboy has no papers left to sell. Pierre has all the money; that is, he has both kitties—not only the fund Elmer started out with but his own as well. But all the money is now in francs! In the absence of any other mechanism or firm that can "convert" francs into dollars —and we have been tacitly assuming that the Elmer-Pierre firm is the only one—Elmer will, if he wants his money back, have to move to France, claim his portion of francs out of the firm's combined funds, and live there until he has consumed his share of the partnership's assets. The firm has run into the same problem that plagued most of Europe during reconstruction after World War II: It has a "dollar shortage." Indeed, we can go a step further. We have assumed that all Franco-American trade is funneled through the Elmer-Pierre firm. If this firm has a dollar shortage, then all of France has a dollar shortage! In its simplest terms a French dollar shortage only means that Frenchmen would like to buy more from us than we are prepared to buy from them (or that Frenchmen are not able to tempt us with the quality and price of their wares in sufficient amount); they are therefore unable to build up credits in this country to pay in dollars for the things they would like to buy here.

There are, of course, ways of preventing so untoward an outcome under favoring conditions; in wartime, deep depression, or postwar periods, nothing may avail. Under a gold standard, when too many francs begin coming in and too many dollars going out, Pierre could fix Elmer up with gold. Pierre might buy gold with his excess francs and ship it across the ocean to Elmer. The American partner can then convert the gold into ordinary dollars, which he can use to build up his faltering kitty. This operation may place slightly heavier costs on the firm. It costs money to transport and insure gold; if the sum is large, interest forgone amounts to a tidy figure. Loss by abrasion is another cost. But the firm can charge a higher commission to offset these costs.

Why gold? Why cannot Pierre buy up and send French gloves or perfume or some other French product instead? On the surface, it may appear that Pierre can as well convert his excess francs into demijohns of *Arpège*, and that Elmer can convert that famous perfume into dollars by selling it in the United States. One answer is that gold is less speculative. Normally, the selling price and buying price of gold in different currencies are figures you can rely on, while the prices of merchandise normally waver, particularly if large lots are dumped on the market. But the more basic reason is that we Americans have shown—and the clear evidence is the unbalanced kitties of the partnership—that we simply do not want or cannot afford the things that France has to offer. In short, the reason Pierre has all the francs is that Americans cannot absorb any more champagne, cognac, gloves, perfume, gowns, or anything else at the prices the French are prepared to sell them for. Gold, because of its special position in the economic system, we are always ready to take.

Another way to prevent a stalemate is to alter the rate of exchange. This can be done without using gold. When the kitties begin to reveal imbalance, Pierre can tell his French customers that hereafter they will have to give him 6 francs for every dollar of debt they want to settle in the United States. (The rate first used in this example was 5 francs to the dollar.) This new rate will make Frenchmen pause before buying here, for to them it is equivalent to an increase in the price of American goods. Elmer, at the same time, will inform American clients that they can now settle 6 francs' worth of French debt for every $1 they pay in. This encourages American importers to buy in France. In terms of dollars, they can buy French goods more cheaply. Soon American importers will be paying dollars into Elmer's kitty again, while French exporters will be withdrawing francs from the futile and excessive hoard of Pierre. Thus, equilibrium will be restored.

We have suggested above the basic mechanism and have worked out the structure of international trade on the premise that the importers of any given nation, by use of brokers, pay the exporters in the currency that both customarily use. But of course, the real-life mechanism is much more complicated. Most banks will do what only Elmer and Pierre did in our first approximation—even United States post offices will arrange to pay your debts abroad. Our rudimentary firm handled only the Franco-American business; our large banks will handle transactions almost anywhere in the world; there are brokerage houses to which you can pay dollars and receive in return the currencies of many nations—the financial pages of large newspapers list the prices of some 40 of them daily. Our simplified example took into account only the trading of tangible goods. But foreign trade, as we have already said, in its broadest sense includes the tourist trade, remittances sent by immigrants or foreigners to their families abroad, investment abroad, and so on.

The great banks in New York, London, and other money centers hold checking accounts abroad in the actual currency of the foreign nation. Thus, instead of Elmer, we have the New York Iron Exchange Bank, which has a checking account of 10 million francs in the *Crédit Beaujolais* (instead of Pierre). And the Sussex Downs Bank of London will have a checking account in the form of dollars in a New York bank. The New York Federal Reserve Bank also has an account expressed in pounds with the central bank of England. This account serves as a reservoir from which private American banks may buy British pounds when they want to increase their accounts in British banks. If the foreign account of the New York Federal Reserve Bank should run too low, the bank is legally empowered to transfer gold to the British bank, which will then credit the American bank with an equivalent in the form of pounds.

All the high-powered machinery described above should not obscure the basic fact that importers (or those engaged in importlike transactions) pay exporters (or those engaged in exportlike transactions). Without this, international trade could be carried on only on a basis of barter. It would be quite possible for the United States government to trade a million tons of steel for 300 million pounds of coffee from Brazil. Each government could resell to its citizens. It would also be possible to arrange private bartering transactions, but this would make international trade quite awkward.

Demand and Supply and the Value of Foreign Exchange

The reader will already have recognized the action of our two brokers as merely another manifestation of the ubiquitous law of supply and demand. The desire (demand) of French importers to pay debts in the United States became so great in our example that to prevent a stalemate, the brokers had to charge them more for dollars. Or as businessmen and economists prefer to put it, the demand for "dollar exchange" was great enough to send up its price in terms of francs. The other side of the picture was that the American desire to pay debts in francs was so small that the price of that currency went down. If the new rate of six to the dollar undercorrects or over-corrects, the rate of exchange can be altered again and again until an acceptable figure is reached.

A real-life example may be taken out of the newspapers. On June 27, 1957, *The Wall Street Journal* stated that the Canadian dollar had risen to $1.055 in terms of the U.S. dollar, highest since 1933. It went on to say that the apparent reason for this increase was heavy U.S. purchasing of Canadian corporate and municipal secu-rities. In other words, many of our citizens rather suddenly wanted very much to invest in Canada; to pay for those investments, they had to buy Canadian dollars; so great was the demand for Canadian dollars that their price rose.

It may seem rather astonishing that the actions of private citizens can change the value of a national currency. Do not governments set the value of their monies? How can just ordinary people, by buying heavily in a foreign country, exert such a strong influence on money, something that is so jealously guarded by all the powers of a govern-ment? It is a crime to print counterfeit money. Is it not also a crime, though perhaps a lesser one, to change its value? Well, that depends. Suppose I want very much to call my wife, 100 miles away, to tell her that I have a flat tire and shall be home late. I am at a lonely roadside pay-telephone station and have only dollar bills. You pass by, and I ask if you have change for a dollar. You search your pockets and can find only 90 cents in nickels, dimes, and quarters. But I gladly accept your 90 cents and give you $1 in return; it is more important for me to be able to make the call with the coins you proffer than to get full value for my paper dollar. You have bought $1 for 90 cents, thus tampering with Uncle Sam's valuation of American money. But we have done nothing illegal.

Strong, well-balanced countries whose economies are in good shape domestically and internationally do tolerate at least small changes in the international value of their money, as determined by the forces of supply and demand. The figures in Table 14–1 suggest the ranges within which the prices of foreign monies moved over a short period during 1963.

Some nations have a pegged rate of exchange and do not permit their money to move in accordance with the forces of supply and

TABLE 14-1

Currency	April 30	July 2	July 5
Canadian dollar	$0.9295	$0.9277	$0.9274
English pound	2.8006	2.8013	2.8016
Australian pound	2.2405	2.2415	2.2415
Swiss franc	0.2310	0.2313¼	0.2312¾

demand. Others prevent large fluctuations by engaging in what might be named counterspeculation. If supply and demand cause wide fluctuations in the value of a foreign currency, healthy trade is inhibited. Between 1920 and 1925, for example, the British pound would sell at $3 one week and $5 the next. This, of course, discouraged foreign trade. Importers are not keen about trading with England when, having contracted to buy tweeds at £1 sterling per yard, they do not know whether they will have to pay $3 or $5 to honor the contract. In the interests of maintaining relative stability of the value of their sometimes erratic currencies, many governments use a formidable battery of countermeasures—that is, they try to frustrate the law of supply and demand.

The simplest device, in principle, is manipulation of an exchange equalization fund. One way to envisage how such a fund works is as follows: The British government, not unlike our two brokers, Elmer and Pierre, of a few pages back, would keep a few scores of millions of dollars on deposit in New York banks and a similar sum in pounds in London banks. Now, if the pound starts to nose-dive, the British government buys pounds, paying for them with its New York account in dollars. Unless the economic situation is desperate, this will cause the pound to stop falling, just as any large purchasing operation is likely to halt a decline in price. And if the pound starts zooming upward, the British government can reverse the operation, buying dollars with its London pounds.

In obstinate cases, such a fund is not likely to be sufficiently potent medicine. In this event, some form of exchange control is used. This means, at least in its ultimate form, that government exercises enormous control over foreign trade. It buys up all the claims to foreign currency earned by private traders and rations them to those importers who buy the most vital foreign goods needed in the public interest—such things as food in countries which, like England, are nonagricultural; or armaments; or fuels for nations that lack coal or oil. By doing this, the government may discourage or even prohibit the importation of such luxury goods as furs, sports cars, private airplanes, and yachts, or even such minor mass luxuries as nylon stockings, coffee, and American cigarettes. The small amount of foreign currencies earned by past exports is used for those imports that the government considers to be in the public interest. In short, a country which finds that its currency is losing value abroad simply chokes off demand for imports by prohibiting, or virtually prohibiting, all but the most essential imports. This sustains the international value of its own currency by suppressing the demand for foreign goods and, therefore, for foreign monies.

There are still other ways of attempting, at least in the short run, to conserve the value of a currency in the international market, for governments are most ingenious at things of this sort; but only one other will be mentioned here. Among the specialized agencies related to the United Nations is the International Monetary Fund. By making loans to countries whose currency is falling in value, the governing body of the Fund may help to maintain stability in the international exchanges, though certain other means are available to it. Its early history of achievement in this respect was not very brilliant. For this, there were several reasons: One was that the economic and political dislocations of World War II lasted so long; another was that the world was divided politically into two hostile camps. But the Fund has been having more success in recent years.

It may be helpful to make a demand-and-supply list of transactions that, in their immediate effect, do the following sets of things:

1. Either increase the American demand for foreign monies, or decrease the supply of foreign monies available to Americans, thus tending to increase the price of foreign monies or to lower the price of the dollar to foreigners.
2. Either decrease the American demand for foreign monies, or increase the supply of foreign monies available to Americans, thus tending to lower the price of foreign monies or to increase the price of the dollar to foreigners.

If Americans do the following things, they will achieve the results described in the first paragraph above (the list is not exhaustive). In the balance of payments, to be described presently, the transactions listed below give rise to debits:

Import goods.

Buy passenger or freight transportation on foreign boats or planes.

Insure cargoes through foreign insurance companies, like Lloyd's.

Spend money as tourists in foreign countries, or as government officials living abroad.

Build American branch factories, or maintain offices abroad.

Buy stocks and bonds from foreigners.

Pay foreigners interest or dividends arising out of investments made by foreigners here.

Send gifts to foreigners.

Lend to foreigners.

If Americans do the following things, they will achieve the results described in the second paragraph above (the list is not exhaustive). The following give rise to credits in the balance of payments:

Export goods.

Sell passenger or freight transportation to foreigners on American boats or planes.

Sell insurance to foreigners.

Sell things to European tourists, travelers, or diplomats.

Sell materials and labor to foreigners who build branch factories here.

Sell stocks and bonds to foreigners.

Receive from foreigners dividends or interest arising from investment made by Americans.

Receive gifts from foreigners.

Borrow from foreigners.

The above covers the normal business transactions, mostly between businessmen and between banks. In recent years the government of the United States has created an important category which, if neither new nor unique in the annals of peacetime commerce between nations, has come to assume considerable importance in the Free World's foreign trade figures and in ours, particularly. This is the category of U.S. military expenditures abroad. The item runs into billions. Like imports, this type of expenditure is a debit and increases the demand for foreign exchange (foreign monies). It includes sums spent for supplying our troops with foreign goods, and the money they themselves spend overseas.

In trying to memorize the above lists, a mnemonic aid is to follow through any transaction in concrete terms to see what happens. For example, a gift to a foreigner would work out like this: You send an English friend a $5 bill as a birthday present (gifts to foreigners); to spend this, he must go to a bank and convert it into pounds, shillings, and pence; this has the same force as buying English money with American money. The transaction creates demand for English money and tends to increase the price of British pounds. To be sure, it exerts too small a force to affect value, but the tendency is there. Your action has the same effect as an import; if you import from England, you must buy pounds, too, in this case to pay the British seller in the only currency he wants. Transactions involving loans and investment follow the same principle but are not quite so easy to follow through; here, another aid to memory is available. The trick is to focus on the direction in which the IOU moves. Thus, if you lend to a British firm or buy its stock or bonds, the IOU moves from England to the United States, like an import of goods. Imports of IOU's, like imports of goods, increase the demand for foreign currency and create debits.

The Balance of Payments

The value of credits and debits in the two lists (and of all similar and related items) will always balance. There is nothing magical about this. It is, fundamentally, not very much different from saying that the assets and liabilities of a firm or household must be in balance. It must not be inferred, however, that when accounts are in balance, whether in foreign trade or in the home or in business firms, everything is going well. Countries, like individuals, may live beyond their means. But the accounts even of a person who lives beyond his means must balance. He may be throwing away his capital, but this is not spending something he does not possess. Some items in his balance sheet may not be very pretty ones. They may reveal such practices as excessive borrowing, defaulted debts, and, in extreme cases, a touch of blackmail or polite swindling. But even an unscrupulous person who lives beyond his means cannot spend more than he possesses or can earn, beg, borrow, or embezzle. And so it is with nations. Some make their accounts balance by "uneconomic" practices, such as paying for their imports with excessive quantities of gold, which resembles an individual's dissipation of his patrimony. Others may default on their foreign debt. A few nations have used political blackmail to secure loans—something that helps them to balance their international accounts. A balanced account has nothing to do with economic health or probity.

The United States government and most other governments hire a corps of men and women to quantify the two lists given above. They find out, with as high a degree of accuracy as is possible, the actual dollar value of exports, of imports, of loans, gifts, gold shipments, and various other foreign-trade items that were suggested by the above two lists. When properly worked out, and when compensations are made for short-run discrepancies and unavoidable error, the two lists balance. They ultimately become a document known as the "balance of payments." Study and analysis of the trends in the balance of payments is a basic guide to foreign-trade experts whose job it is to suggest policy either to governments or to large banks or corporations.

How to analyze a balance of payments presents difficulties and requires special training and knowledge of a country's general economic status. It is still popularly believed that a "good" balance of payments should reveal an excess of exports over imports. This is nonsense. It is true that when physical exports exceed physical imports, we still speak of a "favorable balance of trade" (*trade*, not payments), but this is a carry-over from the age of mercantilism which ended 200 years ago. It has in itself small meaning as far as a nation's economic health or welfare is concerned. As this is being written in 1967, the United States has a favorable balance of *trade*, but an unsatisfactory balance of *payments*. That is, we export more tangible goods than we import, but other items in our balance of payments cause anxiety to businessmen and government officials. To describe our presently unsatisfactory condition, popular writers and newspaper reporters say that we have a "deficit" in our balance of payments. But this, too, is figurative and is impossible, for no balance of payments, however unsatisfactory, can show a deficit. What it can show is an excess of unsatisfactory items or a dearth of favorable items, taking into account the nation's stage of development, its previous situation, its types of industry or agriculture, and similar matters.

The item which has caused most concern in our recent balances has been our loss of gold. Although gold is, from a purely functional viewpoint, rather valueless except to satisfy certain minimal medical, scientific, and industrial needs, it does have great conventional and putative value. It is the only good that central banks will always accept to even up accounts that cannot be settled in normal trade. Our Federal Reserve System can, when need arises, send it to the central banks of England and France, for example, and receive pounds and francs in return. These can be transferred to private U.S. banks; now they become available to American importers and other businessmen engaging in international transactions. Thus a continued drain on our gold over a period is an unhealthy sign, partly because our limited store can be exhausted, partly because the outflow indicates that we are unable to tempt foreigners, at our prices, with enough goods and services to achieve a healthy balance.

Another unhealthy symptom is the excessive size of the short-term loans item in our balance of payments. These consist of bank accounts, U.S. government securities, and the like, owned by foreigners. As long as they remain in such forms, they are no problem; but they are highly liquid assets, and foreigners can easily convert them into gold if they should choose to do so. The threat constantly overhangs us that foreigners will suddenly want to convert these assets into U.S. gold through their central banks, which they have a right to do.

Balance-of-payments difficulties often reflect deficiencies in the economy. Much of western Europe had such troubles as an aftermath of World War II. Our problems in the late '50's and early '60's, as is well known, are not attributable to any glaring defects in the economy. It is perhaps true that some of our industries have fallen behind technologically and need modernization, but our basic distress arises elsewhere. What really causes trouble in our balance of payments is our commitment to give foreign aid and to help in the defense of many of the world's areas. Gifts to foreigners are debits. President John F. Kennedy recognized the essence of our predicament in his speech and press conference on March 7, 1962, when he said: "The balance of payments problem could be settled overnight if we withdrew our security efforts around the world." And now, of course, we have the Vietnam conflict.

We were such avid exporters during most of the first 60 years of this century that the experience of losing gold is new to us, and perhaps we are overly frightened at the phenomenon. We had so much of the world's gold after World War II that some economists feared we might dry up the springs of world trade, in somewhat the same way that a poker game must come to an end if one of the players wins all the money. Others were complaining that we were sending good things abroad—wheat, cars, steel, coal, and oil—and in return getting nothing but gold, useless gold.

The situation is quite different now. Just how we shall get out of our present unsatisfactory situation is not clear. A few small measures have been taken to decrease imports and stimulate exports. Withdrawals of "security efforts around the world," to use President Kennedy's phrase, seem unlikely. In July of 1963 the Federal Reserve Board raised interest rates for short-term loans. Foreigners like to lend money here, at interest, for short periods. This causes a foreign demand for dollars and tends to improve the quality of our balance of payments. But these foreigners are always on the lookout for the highest interest rates. If they can get a higher rate in Japan or England or Italy, they will switch their loanable funds from us to the nation that pays the most (compatible with safety). Switching drains off our gold. To preserve our gold, we have limited investment by Americans in foreign countries; we have reduced the amount of duty-free goods that American tourists may bring back from abroad.

Automatic Equilibriums of Foreign Trade

Standard economic theorists are never happier than when they find that disturbances in an acceptable situation tend to right themselves automatically without governmental intervention or other interference. The automatic restoration of equilibrium demonstrates that natural law is at work, as it is when a boat, without human aid, unceasingly searches to find an upright position among the waves. Several theories of foreign trade are particularly satisfying in this regard. The first one, though outdated, is a model of elegance. In the old days of the gold standard, when paper money could be freely converted into gold coins and gold could be shifted all over the world as if it were simply another metal, the amount of paper money available in any nation was closely geared to the amount of gold it possessed. If a nation acquired a lot of gold, its total supply of money could and did increase; and in accordance with the quantity theory of money, prices rose.

In these circumstances, if England bought too heavily from France without selling much, thereby worsening her balance of payments, she would have to ship gold. The shipping of gold reduced her total supply of money, and her prices fell in accordance with the quantity theory, as we explained a few sentences ago. In France the opposite was taking place: She was getting too much gold, her supply of money was expanding, and her prices were rising. France's increased prices now discouraged British buying of French goods; but England's lower prices encouraged French buying of English goods. Soon, gold would begin to flow westward again, away from France. The return of gold to England increased her money supply and her prices; the French loss of gold caused her supply of money and her prices to decline. And so it went, back and forth, like a gently rolling ship, always near the point of balance, never quite at rest, but always tending toward equilibrium.

The above analysis, applicable not merely to two nations, but also to any group of nations that traded among themselves, explained how they were able to maintain satisfactory balances of payments without governmental intervention or other conscious guidance.

A second discovery of a self-equilibrating situation applies to more recent times and comes out of the Keynesian analysis. In Chapter 8, when we were discussing the national income, we said that it could be represented by the following equation:

$$Y = C + I + E + G$$

E was the excess of exports over imports. Now, E can be either plus or minus, depending on whether or not exports exceed imports. Thus, national income can be diminished by our export-import situation, in which case we can write: $Y = C + I + G + (-E)$. This means, in simple terms, that a nation's income may be seriously affected by its successes or failures in foreign trade. Like other items on the right-hand side of the equation, E has a multiplier effect, both upward and downward. A sudden loss of a billion dollars' worth of trade might result in several billion dollars' loss of national income, and the opposite would of course be equally true. Since the total of our exports of goods and services is only about 6 percent of our GNP, the net E for the United States is not large, and its power to exert a determining force on our national income is not crucial. Or at any rate, a large and positive E is much less important for us than it is for nations like the United Kingdom, Holland, and Belgium, which are much less self-sustaining than we are, and which depend for their national income on a relatively more vigorous trade with other nations.

The fact that E affects national income favorably or unfavorably gives rise to an interesting theory of automatic regulation—or equilibrium—of foreign trade between two nations or between one nation and the remainder of the world. Let us return to the Elmer-Pierre firm spoken of earlier in this chapter. In that illustration, we assumed that France was overbuying in the United States, and we found that by shipping gold or changing the value of the franc, trade could be maintained in a situation which would otherwise have resulted in an impasse. An additional corrective is the income effect of foreign trade.

If France (or a group of nations—but we shall, for simplicity, use only France) keeps buying excessively from us, its E will decline, and ours will increase. As France's E declines, its national income decline also; but as our E increases, our national income increases. This sets the stage for a process which tends to correct the imbalance in our trade relations with France (or any group of overbuying nations). Using our increased income, we can buy more *Arpège*, champagne, berets, and the other products of France. But the French, with their diminished income, will buy less office equipment, machinery, and agricultural products from us. Thus the income effect of foreign trade has an equilibrating tendency.

The same concept can be used to prove that any nation will increase its income by diminishing its imports, thus achieving a higher E. In plain words, this means usually that in a depression a nation may erect a tariff barrier, keep out foreign goods, and buy more things produced at home. No one questions the workability of such a program, provided that other nations do not retaliate. But other nations will retaliate. If we should try to keep out Canadian or English goods in order to pull ourselves out of a depression, we can be certain that they would promptly respond by erecting a higher wall against our goods. We would therefore lose exports, and the excess of exports over imports would go down again. In 1930, after the great stock market break that ushered in the depression of the 1930's, Congress passed the Hawley-Smoot Tariff Act. The protective level was the highest in our history. It was well timed to get us out of a depression; but the depression continued for years, and nation after nation adopted retaliatory tariffs while our foreign trade languished.

Few governments are willing to rely upon "natural forces" to resolve their nations' balance-of-payments problems. For to attain equilibrium in the balance of payments without recourse to direct government action, a nation must be willing to endure a highly unstable economy. If the gold standard were relied upon, continual changes in the domestic money supply and price level would occur; if the national income approach were followed, trade-induced recessions and inflations would be commonplace.

In recent years, there has been much discussion among economists of an equilibrating process that would not interfere with domestic economic activity, namely, freely fluctuating exchange rates. Under this system the price of a nation's money in terms of foreign currencies would be determined solely by supply and demand, with absolutely no intervention on the part of governments. This mechanism would correct balance-of-payments difficulties without disrupting domestic economic activity, except, of course, those domestic activities tied to international trade. But even such an automatic mechanism might not be desirable. One reason is that fluctuating exchange rates increase both the uncertainty and the risk of conducting international business transactions, and would therefore tend to decrease the volume of international trade. A more important reason, however, and one that is relevant to all automatic mechanisms, is that governments do not want to relinquish the great degree of control they now have over international trade, since trade is often an important factor in the foreign, domestic, and defense policies of nations.

Paper instead of Gold

Until now, we have said that gold is the only acceptable international currency. But at this point, we shall have to backpedal a little and state that as early as 1900, some forms of paper money began to be nearly as acceptable as gold in foreign transactions. At first, it was the British pound, and the nations that took it as willingly as gold were members of the British Empire. Part of the inducement was that paper pounds could be deposited in the bank and would draw interest, while gold continued to maintain its sterility.

Since World War II the United States dollar has become equally acceptable in foreign trade, if not more so. Thus, any nation, or its central bank, making an inventory of its foreign trade reserves—that is, of its immediately available purchasing power abroad—could count three forms of money: gold, dollars, and pounds. This has been an informal development, not sanctified by legislation or multilateral treaty.

It is not too easy to explain exactly how this all came about. Perhaps the evolution of international payments is not unlike the evolution of domestic payments. In medieval times, only the precious or semiprecious metals were acceptable as payment to sellers. Slowly, paper money displaced metal domestically; and today, personal checks are the chief means of payment, in the United States at least. To be sure, the acceptability of paper in international trade is sustained in part by the knowledge that normally dollars and pounds can be converted into gold, not by the average man on the street or even by the ordinary bank, but by central banks or other special agents. It is, however, widely known that the world does not possess enough gold bullion or coins to meet all the obligations that might be presented for conversion into metal. Thus, in a fundamental way, international trade is carried on in the atmosphere of mutual trust, or at least something that resembles trust. In 1966 the gold stock of the United States was worth $13.2 billion; claims from abroad amounted to exactly twice as much. If all foreign banks and governments had presented their claims at once, we should not have been able to meet them; but as long as claims dribbled in slowly for relatively small amounts, the problem was only potentially serious.

It is not surprising under these circumstances that economists and bankers have begun to wonder whether we might not create— perhaps only for the Free World—a paper currency, about as acceptable anywhere as pesos, francs, dollars, and pounds are in their native lands. In the summer of 1967 the finance ministers of the 10 largest industrial nations of the Free World reached agreement on a plan to create an international money. If their proposal is ratified by the necessary number of member nations of the International Monetary

Fund, "paper gold" will join—but not replace—gold, dollars, and pounds as an international monetary reserve by 1970. This money, already named "standard drawing rights" or SDR's is to be regulated by the IMF. Member nations in need of foreign currency reserves will be entitled to borrow, within predetermined limits, SDR's from the Fund. These SDR's will then be used to settle international debts. It is not anticipated that the new money would be entirely cut off from gold. British pounds and American dollars, as well as gold, would continue to form part of the reserves of most nations. That gold will have to play a dwindling role in international trade seems quite clear, since the volume of trade is increasing faster than the production of gold.

An international money, like an international language, can be defended on rational grounds, but the barriers to acceptance are powerful. The League of Nations and the United Nations have existed for half a century, yet in their deliberations nobody speaks Ido, and both the oratory and documents of the U.N. are presented laboriously in several languages at great cost in hours of work, typing, printing, and paper. Whether we shall be driven by the exigencies of international economics to use a form of money as rootless and contrived as Ido is in the sphere of language remains to be seen.

The Law of Comparative Advantage

One of the issues that has been of great interest to standard economic theory relates to the reasons for international exchanges. We can best approach this question by taking an extreme case—bananas. It is obviously cheaper for North Americans to buy Latin-American bananas then to grow them in Vermont hothouses. The advantage of hot countries in producing bananas is absolutely and clearly visible. Therefore, we import Nicaraguan bananas, and one need not go into the economic blue to understand why such a transaction takes place. Many imports offer less extreme examples but conform to a similar principle—the great wines, perfumes, and dresses of France; Russian caviar; tweeds from the Isle of Harris; and Hungarian Tokay. These things simply would not be what they are if they came from Ubangi or Texas; therefore, they are imported from the originating countries.

When we consider something like plain muslin, mystery begins.

Two or three dozen countries can make muslin quite cheaply. Should all make muslin for export? Should all make at least enough to meet their own needs, or should some cheap-muslin countries import muslin from other cheap-muslin countries? One answer is that in quiet and normal times, importers never ask such questions. If they find such bargains in muslins across a border that they could, with importing expenses, be put more cheaply on the domestic market than muslins made at home, then the importer buys the muslins abroad without bothering his head as to who should, could, or would produce what quantity of muslin for which market. No doubt, many international transactions are just like that: A bargain is picked up here, there, or elsewhere with scant regard to economic laws. Still, there are certain economic principles of standard theory that seek to explain the larger drift of foreign trade.

David Ricardo was the first economist to discuss this matter fully and to give an answer that is still accepted in essence by standard theorists today. His answer has a historical background. During the Napoleonic wars, wheat growing in England had been a most profitable occupation, since there had been little competition from foreign grain. After the wars, landowners took steps to win back, through a wheat tariff, the monopolistic position thrust upon them in wartime.[2] They argued that it was absurd to import wheat when England could grow it quite as advantageously as any other competing economy. Ricardo was interested in the progress of manufacture and the decline of landlordism. He found an answer to the landlord's argument of equal advantage in the doctrine of comparative advantage. "Granted," he said, in effect, "that we can grow wheat as cheaply as Russia or Poland; but what really matters is that we can produce textiles *more* cheaply than they. Let us make textiles for them and let them grow wheat for us. The final result will be that they will benefit by getting more textiles than they would otherwise get and the English will have more wheat." He clinched the argument with the following:

Two men can both make shoes and hats, and one is superior to the other in both employments; but in making hats he can only exceed his competitor by one-fifth, or 20 per cent, and in making shoes he can excel him by one-third

2 Much of the material in this section follows the position taken in Charles Gide and Charles Rist, *A History of Economic Doctrines* (2d English ed.; New York: D. C. Heath & Co., 1948), Book VI (by Rist).

or 33 per cent. Will it not be for the interest of both that the superior man should employ himself exclusively in making shoes, and the inferior man in making hats?[3]

The Ricardian theory is still widely taught in American textbooks. It has, however, been somewhat amended by subsequent writers, particularly the Swedish economist and cabinet minister Bertil Ohlin (still living). Ohlin objects that Ricardo's theory of international trade is based on the labor theory of value, which, as we saw, has been abandoned. Secondly, the force of demand may cause things to sell above or below their cost of production and, therefore, determine in part the direction of the flow of goods. The amenders of Ricardo also lay stress on the fact that trade arises out of the different relationships among the prices of goods in trading nations. Ohlin's most telling argument is that varying relationships among national price structures, the basis of international trade, arise out of the basic economic pattern of trading nations. Each country has its own pattern: Some have much labor, some relatively little; in some, special arts have been handed down under a tradition of high craftsmanship; some have much virgin soil, others a highly developed industrial plant. Out of these differences of pattern, some historical and some natural, arise the price differences that make foreign trade profitable. In the final analysis, one wonders whether much more has been said than that importers buy where goods are cheap and sell where they are dear.

Free Trade and Tariffs

If, according to standard theory, the governments of the world would foster international freedom of trade, each nation and region would soon specialize in the things in which it has the highest degree of advantage. The international division of labor would then be most fully realized. The entire globe would presently be organized to produce most efficiently; the standard of living everywhere would be the highest possible under our institutions and technology. It has even been argued that such a world, a world without tariffs, import quotas, export bonuses, exchange control, blocked currencies, and all the other fancy devices used to balk freedom of trade, would have such a

[3] David Ricardo, *Political Economy* (London: Everyman's Library, 1911), p. 83, ftn.

strong community of economic interest that wars would be unthinkable. To all this the modern economist has new arguments to add. Greater freedom of trade would do much to reduce the power of the great oligopolies. We saw in the 1950's how much the importation of small European cars did to disturb the American automobile manufacturers. The public welfare would presumably be served if the complacency of a larger number of our huge firms could be unsettled. A greater freedom of trade might also help us to get rid of some of our farm surpluses—something that would reduce the size of our farm problem and, with it, our taxes.

If all this is true, or only partly true, or even plausible, why do nations build artificial barriers in the form of tariffs and other impediments to trade?

Well, obviously we are saddled with some of our tariffs by the political power of pressure groups which are permitted to operate their firms either inefficiently or too profitably, or both, under the shelter of tariff walls. Once they have established themselves, they can use the argument that if the tariff were removed, thousands of workmen would be unemployed. Makers of public policy must decide whether they are prepared to inflict hardship on thousands of families to get rid of the parasitic industries. The harm, of course, is that prices of the goods produced by sheltered industries are higher than they would be if they had to meet foreign competition.

In response to this, tariff advocates often say: "But the reason that foreign goods are so cheap is that foreign labor is paid so little. America is a land of opportunity for workingmen; they do not labor for a mere pittance as workers do in Italy or Japan or India. To maintain the honest American workingman's high standard of living, we must keep out the goods made by cheap Oriental labor." What about this argument?

There may be some truth in this sometimes, for some specific commodities; but as a general argument, it is clearly open to question. First of all, tariffs may help to protect American wages, but they also increase the prices of what the American worker buys; thus the gain, such as it is and what there is of it, is not unmixed with loss from a higher cost of living. Second, in many operations the American worker is one of the lowest paid workers per unit of output. He may get $2 per hour, and his opposite number in Tokyo may get only 20 cents an hour. But Joe Doaks may produce more than 10 times as much as Hiro Oshiro. Per unit, the cost may be lower on a vast list of goods, though in some things, no doubt, foreign labor is cheaper per unit.

But the real point in the low-labor-cost argument is this: What is foreign trade all about, anyhow? If it makes any sense at all, it is that every region should produce what it can produce cheaply; and what it does not need, it should send out of the country, to receive in return what other regions can make cheaply. Thus, everybody—including the American worker and the foreign laborer—is better off.

There are nonetheless a few valid arguments for a tariff. One is the infant-industry argument for underdeveloped nations. During part of the period that the United States was underdeveloped, we had a high tariff behind which our industries could develop, sheltered from the keen competition of the more industrially advanced countries—England particularly. It is important, however, that the infant industries do not continue to be protected when they become giants. The industries to be protected in underdeveloped countries must of course be wisely chosen. It would have been absurd in the United States to use the infant-industry argument for bananas, natural rubber, or pineapples. The argument makes sense only for those industries that have some hope of producing efficiently; in this country, these included metal manufacturing, furniture, steelmaking, and similar industries.

Another acceptable argument—or at least partly acceptable—is the national defense argument. We may, for example, have to protect the synthetic rubber industries in order to have domestic rubber during wartime when imports of natural rubber are cut off. Since synthetic rubber costs more than natural rubber, its manufacture could not long continue in peacetime on a standby basis unless it were protected somehow. But it is not necessary to use the tariff to get this protection. Such protection should probably be done by subsidy, that is, by paying the synthetic rubber people to stay in business. This might turn out to be a cheaper way of doing the job, much cheaper than making every user of natural rubber pay something extra for tires and a host of other rubber goods.

Perhaps we should, before going on, stop for a moment to look at the height of the American tariff wall. It has declined a good deal in the past 35 years. Expressed in dollar value, about 40 percent of imports entered for consumption came into the country duty-free in 1964. On the remainder, we paid an average 12 percent. Duties per capita in 1961 came to $5.68—for the typical family of four, the bill was $22.72.

In the late spring of 1967 the United States government announced that the tariff had been cut on thousands of items. This was the result of four long years of negotiations among the representatives of 53 nations. The cuts were reciprocal; that is, for each cut made by us, some other nation or nations made matching cuts in their tariffs. This was perhaps the most gigantic step ever taken in world history to reduce the trade barriers of nations. It was named the "Kennedy Round." The name arose out of the fact that President Kennedy had requested and been given authority by Congress to reduce tariffs. The executive had to stay within certain percentage limits, of course. The enabling legislation, known as the Trade Expansion Act of 1962, was not a radical change of American trade policy, but rather successor legislation to the Trade Agreement Act of 1934. The Kennedy act contained, however, several novel provisions which strengthened the hands of our negotiators and which were geared to some of the problems posed for us by the European Common Market (see a few pages below).

But tariffs are not our only way of keeping out goods. The United States and other nations also have recourse to import quotas; under the quota system, we simply refuse to accept from abroad more than a limited number of tons or pounds of some good. We have applied quotas to sugar, lead, zinc, peanuts, and almonds. Quotas help to keep prices up by restricting supply. Finally, we keep exports out by various administrative policies that discourage importation. Importers complain that if a thing can be classified—even at times unrealistically—into either of two classes, it will always be classified in the category that bears the higher tariff. Thus a garment that is held up at the waist by a wide elastic band might be classified either as shorts or rubber goods, whichever carries the higher tariff rate. Various other arbitrary and ungenerous rulings impede the importation of goods, even if the actual tariff barrier is not very high. The Kennedy Round, spoken of just above, did very little to remove barriers outside the realm of tariff cuts. Business groups, government officials, and other interested persons are now saying that new multilateral bargaining sessions should soon pick up where the Kennedy Round left off, and seek to lower the nontariff walls.

The Common Market

Perhaps the most interesting thing in the sphere of foreign trade in the 1960's is the development of the European Common Market. France, Germany, Italy, and the geographically smaller Benelux countries have agreed, through the 1957 Treaty of Rome, to collaborate economically in a variety of ways. These nations propose to establish by 1970 a common market in which trade restrictions among them will be abolished. In short, they plan to form a free-trade area like that of the United States. But they also propose to insulate themselves from outside trade by keeping out many goods produced in the remainder of the world. The treaty is a little more complex than has been suggested above; and outside its terms, greater political union is invisaged—but we do not need to go into this. The tariff barriers are not of course to be knocked down all at once in 1970. The process has begun and has been under way for several years.

The progressive lowering of tariff barriers has already given these nations the appearance of prosperity. Whether the prosperity visible to the tourist results primarily from increased freedom of trade is, of course, a thesis that cannot yet—if ever—be proved.

Theory concerning a customs union is not very useful in estimating the rewards or penalties of creating such a free-trade area. Something depends on elasticity of demand for imports; something else depends on whether the nations involved have complementary or competitive economies. Something depends on the evolution of the policies of the union—what their relationship to the outer world will be. The United States is a customs union of 50 states; but despite popular statements to the contrary, this may not be the fundamental basis of our prosperity. Without going into detail, it can be argued that our Civil War resulted from the fact that an agricultural economy (the South) was joined in a customs union with an industrial economy (the North). The German customs union of 1834 resulted in the exploitation of the working classes.[4] The Common Market cannot be unqualifiedly defended.

An argument favoring the Common Market is that local monopolies will be destroyed by free trade, and that small industries, having access to a larger market, can expand to produce more economically. This may be true, but one wonders whether there will be any such effect on the already huge automobile, oil, and electrical equipment companies of the Common Market nations.

Against this possible benefit is to be pitted a possible disadvantage. Suppose that the United States produces office machines cheaper than any other nation and that France, before the Common Market, admits them free of duty. Suppose, now, that Germany produces good but more expensive machines. France, as a member of the Common Market, now erects a tariff barrier against the United States but abolishes barriers (if any) against German machines. It will be cheaper for her to buy the more expensive German machines than to buy ours with duty added. The French will certainly not benefit from such an arrangement—nor, indeed, will any other member of the Common Market except Germany.

Whatever aid the customs union may or may not bestow on its members, the existence of such an exclusive club will have repercussions on world trade and may harm the United States. Our government and our businessmen have not been unaware of the problems involved. Our businessmen, fearful of barriers to be erected against our products, have been busy building branch plants within the Common Market countries. Thus, their products will not have to climb over the customs fence. Our government in 1962 passed legislation that has made it procedurally easier for us to bargain with the Common Market nations on tariffs, as has been stated a few pages back.

The final result to be hoped for would be the creation of a vast free-trade area, including western Europe and the United States. If the United Kingdom should also join this wide trading area, the most powerful nations of the Free World would be united by freedom of trade. The common benefits of creating such a large tariffless area are more clearly visible than are the benefits arising out of the limited

---

4 See Charles P. Kindleberger, *International Economics* (rev. ed.; Homewood, Ill.: Richard D. Irwin, Inc., 1958), pp. 317–18.

Common Market of six European nations. With such a vast expanse of free trade, we might reasonably hope for the efficient worldwide division of labor that has been the consistent goal of economists for 200 years.

Summary and Conclusions

The concept of international trade embraces all business and financial transactions between citizens and governments of one nation and those of another. Certain problems arise out of this form of economic activity that do not arise out of transactions between members of the same nation.

One of the problems is that of paying sums owed in an acceptable currency. American sellers want dollars, and the British want pounds; a French or Dutch buyer can offer only francs or guilders. Gold would be acceptable to all and is, as a matter of fact, used by central banks for certain special kinds of transactions. But gold also has disadvantages—bulkiness, loss through abrasion in transit, and irrevocability of loss by shipwreck (a document could always be replaced). Hence a vast and ingenious superstructure for payment by paper has been developed by the banks of the world and other financial houses. What they do, reduced to its simplest terms, is this: They get the importers of any given nation to pay the exporters of the same nation in the currency that both use in common.

Another issue arising out of international trade as compared with national trade is the seeming attractiveness of selling to others without buying from them. It has been argued that this will do everything from protecting high wages to curing depressions. Sober analysis indicates, however, that though some exceptions may sometimes be desirable, free trade is the norm to strive for.

A third problem arising out of foreign trade is the possibility of a nation's getting into balance-of-payments difficulties. The United States is now in this situation. What this means is that we are unable to pay for all of our business and governmental transactions abroad by selling goods and services to foreigners or by drawing on other resources (for example, interest or dividends due us from previously made overseas investments). Thus, we have to sell them gold—something that will always be bought by nations that do not want anything else from us. Since our stock of gold is limited, this method of balancing accounts cannot long be used.

The value of our money abroad and of foreign exchange here is basically dependent on the forces of supply and demand. We demand a foreign currency whenever we want to pay money to a foreigner, whatever the reason; this is the basis of demand. Supply is determined largely by the foreigner's desire to pay us for goods and services bought or investments made here. Since, however, the free play of the forces of supply and demand may cause excessive fluctuations in the value of foreign exchange, the governments and central banks of the world try to keep fluctuations within a narrow range by placing various controls on trade and by counterspeculation.

The European Common Market is an interesting experiment in the creation of a large free-trade area. At this writing, it is hard to foresee what lies ahead. Dissension among its present members may stop it dead in its tracks. The exclusion of the British may mean the fragmentation of the Free World into two or three competing blocs. The inclusion of the British and the breaking-down of tariff walls between the United States and the expanded Common Market may bring into existence the largest and most powerful free-trade area the world has ever known.

QUESTIONS FOR REVIEW AND DISCUSSION

1. Define, in your own words, each of the following terms:
   a) Imports
   b) Exports
   c) Balance of payments
   d) Balance of trade
   e) Free trade
   f) Tariff
   g) Quota
2. Modern nations have managed to reduce the amount of gold used in modern monetary systems, so much so that it is doubtful whether any gold at all is needed within the boundaries of nations like Holland, France, England, Switzerland, and the United States. Could this be done internationally? Is gold really still needed as an international money? Give reasons for your reply.

3. Would you, by subscribing to the English magazine *Punch,* act in such a way as to contribute toward a further decline of the U.S. gold supply? Explain.

4. What effect would the placing of a 50 percent tariff on Canadian goods by the United States have on the Canadian economy? On the American economy?

5. Describe and discuss the policies a nation can use to improve an unfavorable balance of trade. Which of these policies has the United States used in its attempts to solve its balance-of-trade problems?

6. "International trade permits a nation to attain a higher level of national income than would otherwise be possible." What economic law is this statement based on, and how does this law operate?

7. Assuming that Belgium has a comparative advantage over Switzerland in the production of a certain grade of muslin, what evidence do we have to have to demonstrate that fact?

8. Discuss two processes which, without governmental intervention, might correct a nation's unsatisfactory balance of trade.

9. How could the United States be hurt by the Common Market?

Chapter 15

THE LABOR PROBLEM

Introduction

Many things flock to mind when the phrase "labor problem" is pronounced—strikes, pickets, wage spirals, unemployment, automation, collective bargaining, trade-union power, safety, child labor, minimum wage, industrial poisoning, labor parties, trade-union racketeering, and fringe benefits, to name a few. It is not easy to define the labor problem, but it is very easy to list many of its components. They form a conglomerate, spilling over the field of economics and into the fields of psychology, law, government, engineering, medicine, sociology, criminology, and yet others.

The labor problem is a relatively new problem to mankind. It is true that in ancient regimes of slavery or serfdom, problems arose in the labor force; history records slave insurrections and peasant revolts. But the day-to-day management of labor, the almost continuous collective bargaining that now prevails, the establishment of personnel departments—all this is new. One never reads of peasant-relations advisers to the Thane of Glamis or a slave-relations adviser to our own southern plantation owners. If difficulties arose, the master was free to use the knout or the lash. But what really kept down labor trouble was the long, undisturbed tradition of status and servility. A slave was a slave; he could usually be recognized by the color of his skin, his accent, or his head shape; and the entire society conspired in countless ways to keep him a slave. There was no hope for him to rise. The serf, too, was a marked and recognizable man; and he, too, lived in a world where for centuries a serf was a serf with no hope for improved status, for he lived in an unchanging society with rigid class lines.

Labor problems arise out of the vast changes that have been made in the social life of the past few centuries. Most important is the acceptance of democracy and a belief in the dignity of man—ideas that animated the American and French revolutions and several waves

288

of reform in England. In the advanced parts of the Western world, slavery, peonage, and serfdom are no longer tolerated. The belief that all men are created equal, however interpreted, means in part that the servant may call the master to account; indeed, it means the virtual disappearance of the invidious words "master" and "servant," and the substitution therefor of such colorless words as "employer" and "employee."

The right of men to rise in their stations in life is a denial that the stations are fixed. It creates a restlessness and a striving in the masses of the population that did not exist in earlier ages. In modern times, avenues of advancement have been opened to the working classes; and even those who are unable to progress along them—and there are many—may at least dream that their sons and daughters will be able to move forward.

In the agricultural eras that knew villein and master, slave and owner, there was, of course, an urban working population that had escaped the bonds of servility and caste. Like the Dick Whittington of legend, a few rose from orphaned scullion to great riches and influence among the ruling classes. But even among the city people the labor problem did not arise until about 1775. The probable reason is that in the cities there were relatively few dependent workers in the modern sense. What is today the worker was then the independent artisan owning his own tools. Artisans were self-employed; they were small businessmen. Weavers, bootmakers, tinkers, and smiths had not yet become time-clock punchers with numbers instead of names. When large numbers of men are trained in the aspirations of a democratic society, work with tools and machines belonging to others, and delegate the marketing functions to others—only then does the labor problem emerge. Unemployment, too, is a new phenomenon, and one of our most stubborn economic problems.

The tensions developed in modern society are greater than those in earlier economic systems. Modern society is dynamic and free; it encourages class mobility; it is often disturbed by depression, inflation, and threats of war. New methods of discharging tensions (for example, strikes) are tolerated; and new means of seeking security (for example, union membership) have been made legal. Capitalism offers great hope for individual self-improvement as well as for raising the general level of living. The fact that there is hope today—

there was little under feudalism—stimulates labor to active and sometimes belligerent pursuit of its hopes.

Part of the freedom encouraged in the great capitalist societies takes the form of fighting for what one wants, within the law and the canons of mature behavior. But sometimes the parties commit themselves so fully that they fight beyond the boundaries of law or of mature behavior—and perhaps one of the major components of the labor problem is the search for techniques that keep both parties to a dispute within the limits of legal and civilized action.

It is hard to divide the labor problem into neat classifications of parallel significance and logical interrelations. One reason is that the labor problem belongs not only to economics but also to politics, social psychology, law, and the arts of applied psychology. Any plan of discussion we may make will leave out something important. If we can shed a little light on the topics listed below, perhaps we shall have done well enough. The topics are:

1. The important statistics on the labor force and union membership
2. The special disabilities of the hourly paid worker
3. Collective bargaining
4. Automation and featherbedding
5. The government and labor
6. Wage increases and the public interest

The Statistics

First, the statistics. Almost every adult "labors" in our society, from the meanest charwoman to the most glamorous movie star, from the shoeshine boy to the college president, from the garbage collector to the millionaire. Yet the word "labor" is used in a special sense to include manual workers or "bossed" workers. In the special sense, all workers are employed by somebody else, but not all employees are "workers." For example, the chief managers of the great corporations are "only" employees—and so are generals and ambassadors and members of the President's Cabinet; yet none of these is "labor" in the sense that they are eligible for union membership or that they need protective legislation (minimum wages, maximum hours, overtime, or factory safety). On the other hand, the line of the labor problem is not always to be drawn at the manual level, since many high school teachers, musicians, and entertainers are union members, and union activity is an essential sector of labor-problem study.

Though one could long debate the meaning of the word "labor," for ordinary purposes the problem is not too difficult. The U.S. Census Bureau makes recurrent studies of the size and composition of the U.S. labor force and has developed a set of classifications that are satisfactory for all but unusual needs. Under the Bureau's definition the armed forces are not included under "labor." The gainfully employed categories as given by the Bureau may be divided by us into independent classes and dependent classes, the latter being "labor" as used in such phrases as "the labor problem." The figures for 1966 are as shown in Table 15-1.

TABLE 15-1

	Numbers (in Millions)	Percentage
Independent classes	18.9	26
Dependent classes	53.9	74
Total	72.8	100

The independent group contains executives, owners, farmers, professionals, and the like. The dependent group (meaning dependent on an employer, or "bossed") includes all employed manual workers, plus employed clerical workers, salespersons, and the like. This is the group that is organizable into trade unions. Certain classes in this group are not easily organized, to be sure, and have no strong unions —for example, farm laborers, domestics, and the lowlier white-collar people. But on the whole, it can be said that this group of 53.9 million workers is the theater of union activity.

American trade unionism today includes about 18 million members; roughly, every third "dependent" worker is a trade unionist. Or to put it differently, one third of the organizable group is organized. Though this fraction is very large compared with American figures of a generation ago, it is less striking if compared with current European figures. Whether this one out of three represents a point of saturation remains to be seen. Between 1936 and 1946, American unionism grew at a tremendous rate; then the rate of growth decelerated. In very recent years, there has been a slight increase in the growth rate of union membership.

American trade unionism is not spread evenly, either geographically or industrially, throughout the dependent classes. It is, on the contrary, quite strong in certain areas and occupations, and quite weak in others. Unionism is moderately strong in all manufacturing industries and very strong in several—important exceptions being nonalcoholic beverages; confectionery products; cotton, silk, and rayon textiles; and dairy products. In the nonmanufacturing industries, unionism holds some very strong positions, but also some weak ones. Almost every form and aspect of transportation—air, sea, truck, bus, railroad, and longshoring—are strongly unionized, the exception being intercity bus-line transport, and even that is not weak. Coal and metal mining are almost completely unionized, but quarrying is not. Telegraph employees are more strongly unionized than telephone employees. Construction and entertainment, almost at opposite poles, are both highly unionized. Among the fields least organized are agriculture, beauty shops and barbershops, laundries, taxis, and crude petroleum. Geographically, the South is the area of least union activity. Unions are stronger in cities of 50,000 or more than in small towns or cities. The greatest number of union members may be found, as one might expect, in the most populous states, the order by union members of the first five being New York, California, Pennsylvania, Illinois, and Ohio.

There are about 185 unions in the United States, each with an average membership of about 97,000—though this average is meaningless, really, since it is distorted by many small unions at one end and a few monster unions of half a million or more at the other. A median or "typical" union would probably have about 30,000 members. The largest American unions, in order of 1964 size, were as shown in Table 15–2.

TABLE 15-2

Teamsters	1,507,000
Auto, aircraft, etc.	1,168,000
Steelworkers	965,000
Machinists	808,000
Electrical workers (IBEW)	806,000
Carpenters	760,000

Most of the 185 unions are affiliated with the large, loose federation of labor known as the AFL–CIO. The remaining unions are unaffiliated and include primarily the teamsters, the independent coal miners, and the independent railroad brotherhoods.

Disabilities of the Hourly Paid Worker

Our second topic revolves around the special disabilities of the hourly paid worker. What problems does he have that are a little tougher than those of the remainder of the community and that put him in an especially disadvantaged class? To many readers, this may seem to be an absurd question, since the working class is often depicted in popular magazines as the most favored class in our society. They have a 40-hour week, and no attaché cases to take home after work, as do professional men and business executives. They have fringe benefits and pensions, unemployment compensation and social security. In popular articles, they are alleged to get more pay than schoolteachers and clergymen. The mass magazines tell us that chemical engineers average $6,500 a year, but that rollers in steel mills, sitting in their air-conditioned pulpits, make $1,000 a month.[1]

It is certainly true that labor has been doing better in recent years than it did in the great preceding era of prosperity, the 1920's, and obviously much better than in the depressed 1930's. But it is easy to single out spectacular cases of high earnings in certain special jobs and to hold them up as being typical of all workers. In 1965 the gross average weekly earning of production workers in manufacturing industries was $107.27. At 52 weeks a year, this means an annual wage of $5,578.04, which is considered to be within the "deprivation" class for a family of four.[2] No doubt some young mechanics can earn $7,500 and, if unmarried, can afford to buy a Jaguar or an imposing motorboat to flaunt before their former teachers and former schoolmates getting their Ph.D's and M.D.'s and living on something close to nothing at all. But Jaguars and inboard motorboats, it may be stated categorically, are not in the budgets of American working-class fam-

[1] See "How Does Your Income Compare with Others?" *Collier's*, November 23, 1956, p. 56.

[2] As defined in Conference on Economic Progress, *Poverty and Deprivation in the United States* (Washington, D.C., 1962), p. 14.

ilies. Numerous classes of workers earn less than $90 weekly—sometimes down to $40. These include many of the clothing trades, food canning, confectionery manufacturing, farm labor, and many other types of jobs.

By comparison with even the ill-paid clergy, many hourly paid workers suffer special disabilities. Generally speaking, their work exposes them to greater hazards of accident and industrial disease. Every day of illness requiring a work absence is a day of lost pay; but clergymen and college professors are not docked for small illnesses. The worker tends to be laid off at intervals when orders are slow; professional men and women are not. We generally think of most professional men, executives, and the governing classes as still young at the age of 45; but in industry and in most of the other manual and lowly clerical occupations a person is through at that age. He may not be fired from his job promptly at 45, but if he does lose it, he may have difficulty finding a new one.

There are, of course, a few mitigations. Unemployment compensation helps those who are laid off; workmen's compensation is a payment to those who are injured. These are usually inadequate—and in some states of the union, almost negligible—remedies. Not all workingmen are covered by these forms of compensation. There is no legal mechanism, except through our public welfare legislation, to take care of those who find it hard to get jobs at the ripe old age of 45—though they may be entitled to an old-age pension 17 years later.

There is at least one other major disability. Much of the work of labor is deadening; it is often repetitious; it leads nowhere; it does not, as in the professions, contribute toward personal growth and development. A few promotions are, of course, open to workingmen; but it is the rare employee who is able to leave his class behind, though in a land of opportunity he often does have the satisfaction of seeing one of his children rise to high position in a profession or in government.

From all this, we must conclude that a second look at the status of American labor reveals a variety of working conditions both good and bad; and some of the bad ones impose very real burdens on many of our citizens. It is not surprising that through union action, sometimes even militant action, they seek to remove some of their disabilities or at least to support programs of mitigation.

Collective Bargaining

Our next topic is collective bargaining. Where this complex thing does not exist, each employee is hired under an individual contract, oral or written. Usually, there is no real contract of any kind; the employee simply decides he is willing to work at the hours and wages offered and under the general rules of the company—many of the last being unwritten or even unthought of as yet. In many small plants a rule is what the boss happens to think up today. Under the system of individual agreement, particularly in a large establishment, the individual employee may experience great difficulty in getting a wage increase or in the adjustment of a misunderstanding of which he has been the victim—such as the unjustified accusation by the foreman that he was smoking in a no-smoking area of the factory, with resulting dismissal from the job. This is especially true if some degree of unemployment prevails in the labor market, a situation which has been a fairly chronic one. The busy employer with 1,000 or 20,000 men under him has little time to consider individual grievances, and his attitude is likely to be "If he doesn't like it here, let him go somewhere else; there are plenty more men where he came from." Thus, any complaint or even reasonable request may be met by dismissal. This cannot happen under collective bargaining between union and management. There is no individual bargaining. The union, through its officers, asks for pay increases or handles complaints of victims of alleged injustices.

The union members, in short, bargain collectively with the employer. The employer can no longer ignore even the most ridiculous wage demand or the most baseless complaint of the least of his employees, for the whole union stands behind any aggrieved member until a satisfactory adjustment has been made. If a satisfactory adjustment is not made, the union may go to the length of striking, usually a costly process to the employer. Under the system of collective bargaining, any individual contract of employment for union members must conform to the collective written agreement signed by union and employer. It is a very definite document and often even a very long one. Many persons deplore this state of affairs, believing that labor, when so unionized and protected by government, has an overwhelming advantage—greater perhaps than the employer ever had under the older system of individual bargaining. The pendulum, they feel, has swung the other way, and now trade unions are in a position to coerce employers. No doubt this is true in some cases, when large and powerful unions can dictate to small firms. On the other hand, it is doubtful whether unions in telephone, motors, and steel can exert more economic power than the great companies in those industries. By law and otherwise, the government, too, has various powers to intervene and to curb some union excesses. We shall discuss the government's role in labor relations presently. No final answer can be given as to whether unions are or are not too strong, since in a last analysis the reply belongs to the realm of values. Some people feel that a democratic society needs powerful labor unions; others believe that in the public interest they should be shorn of some of their present power. Answers to questions of this sort lie outside economics.

But we must go back to the question of how collective bargaining works, from which we have digressed. Since collective bargaining is the heart of trade unionism, and since the union contract is the heart of collective bargaining, let us look at some of the principal types of clauses of a well-drawn document. The following issues are usually covered:

1. *Wages* (in all its complications, such as overtime, pay for waiting time, vacations with pay, etc.).

2. *Hours of Work.*

3. *Seniority.* This relates to rights and privileges of various kinds enjoyed by those longest employed by the firm, department, or plant. Employees of longer seniority have first rights in promotions, desirable transfers, choice of good shifts, etc. Most important is the right of the longer employed man to be laid off last when there is a lull in operations and to be rehired first when full activity begins again.

4. *Grievance Procedure.* This outlines the procedures to be employed when the parties are unable to agree on the interpretation of a clause in the contract, when a dispute arises over the facts, and in similar matters. Grievances, if not settled within the plant by employer and union representatives, are often settled by an outside arbitrator. Grievances are usually small matters, often involving only one employee; they differ from *issues* in a dispute, which presumably affect

the entire plant and involve matters of grave concern to the parties. A typical grievance would be the complaint of an employee that somebody of less seniority than his and of only equal skill and ability had been promoted to first fireman in the boiler room.

5. *Union Security.*   The problem here, from the union viewpoint, is to try to get the employer himself to help preserve or strengthen the position (security) of the union. This may be done by getting him to agree to hire or to retain in his employment only union members; or to induce those who are now members to continue membership, partly by automatic deductions, made by the employer, of union dues. The employer turns the sums deducted over to the union officials. This is the so-called "checkoff." One of these forms of union security, the closed shop, has been made illegal by the Taft-Hartley Act, though this clause of the act is in fact being circumvented. The closed shop means that the employer must hire men who are already union members; thus the union becomes, in effect, the agency that recruits new workmen. The union shop is a variant of the closed shop. The employer may hire whom he will, but the new employee must within a given period—30 or 60 days—join the union. The union shop, though permitted by the Taft-Hartley Act, may be forbidden by state law; at the present writing 19 states have laws barring the union shop. Those who approve of such laws speak of them as "right-to-work laws" because they enable men to hold down jobs without belonging to a union. The unions think of them as union-busting laws, since the security of a union is often endangered if it cannot get the union shop.

6. *Miscellaneous.*   Even the simplest contract is likely to have a no-strike agreement to remain effective during the life of the contract. Strikes are likely to come after the expiration of the contract, not during its life. And of course, any well-drawn contract should state the exact coverage (all employees of Plant No. 3, or only carpenters in Department C); it should also contain the dates of taking effect and expiration. These are not always minor matters or matters of procedural detail. In the summer of 1956, one of the major issues in the five-week steel strike was the length of time the contract should run. The companies wanted a five-year contract, the union a two-year contract.

When collective bargaining breaks down, we are likely to have strikes. Strikes, like fires, are exceptional and are newsworthy. A strike involving an experienced union and a responsible employer is usually the product of a long period of patient negotiation—even though futile—for no responsible group wishes to engage in such a contest. A typical strike begins to develop visibly about a month or two before the expiration of a contract. This is the period when the parties meet to amend the agreement and to negotiate for the wages, hours, etc., that are to obtain during the next year or two. The union members typically present their "demands" for the new contract. Their list may contain as many as 100 demands—indeed, even more—some of which are inconsequential, some of which the union will not seriously press for but will use as bargaining counters. A few really serious demands remain, usually exaggerated, also for bargaining purposes (for example, the union will demand a 20-cent hourly wage increase, will settle for 10, but will strike if the employer refuses this).

If compromise is impossible, state or federal mediators, or both, may be called in. These men have no power to settle the dispute (as arbitrators do in grievance cases), but mediators often do aid in reaching agreement by skillful exercise of their peacemaking roles, by bringing fresh and unbiased formulas into a tense situation. If they fail and the date of contract expiration arrives, the strike may begin. Strikes may be peaceful or bloody, generous or vindictive in temper, on either or both sides. An employer who is determined to keep his mill in operation by the hiring of new men will meet strong opposition by pickets, that is, men stationed by the union to prevent new employees from reporting to work. The right to picket is, to the union, of prime importance. If the union cannot prevent new men from going to work in the struck mill, the strike will be ineffective, and the employer will suffer only minor inconvenience. Effective picketing is therefore an integral part of a strike, not just something added to annoy. Because it is so important, it can sometimes turn into a violent affair, with police clashes or the stoning by pickets of men who try to go to work.

In recent years in some large strikes a fraternal spirit has pervaded the dispute which seems almost incredible to one who remembers the bitterness of strikes 30 or 40 years ago. Employers make no threat to bring in new employees—strikebreakers or "scabs," as the union would call them; the picket line in such cases is a mere formality, and there is no violence; in a very few cases the company has even displayed friendly hospitality toward the pickets, allowing

them to use company wires so that the bored men can listen to ball
games over the radio. Although this has not yet become the norm, it
does suggest an acceptance if the union and of collective bargaining
which would have been almost inconceivable a generation ago.

Certain types of strikes are considered to be against the public
safety—for example, railroad strikes or steel strikes in a period of
war or fears of war, extended longshoremen strikes, and the like. Such
strikes may be halted by the federal government for a period of many
weeks during which various procedures may be used to try to bring
about a settlement. The President of the United States may intervene;
Congress may be given an opportunity to settle the problem by
passing legislation. If, however, no high-level mediation avails and no
legislation is passed, the strike may recommence. We have no legally
prescribed answer as to what comes next in such a case.

Strikes do not occur haphazardly. Certain underlying and general circumstances seem to precipitate them. In a period of rising
prices, revival from depression, and increasing employment opportunities, strikes are frequent. They are sometimes epidemic in depression, however, when work is sporadic and slack. In this event, neither
side has much to lose. Thus, both sides may be willing to allow any
dispute to degenerate into a strike.

Automation and Featherbedding

During the 1960's, many strikes and threats of strikes have been
characterized by issues which, though not new, have recently received
a new emphasis: automation[3] and—to use a word that unions abhor
and avoid—featherbedding. In a majority of cases, these two issues
merge into one. What happens is that an employer installs labor-
displacing machinery; the union, fearing the consequent unemployment, demands the retention of redundant workers. The union may
demand that five men do the work that, in the employer's opinion, can
be done as well by four. Or as in the case of diesel locomotives, the

---

[3] The word "automation" will be used rather loosely in this section to include ordinary laborsaving machinery. Strictly speaking, automation should be reserved for the
name of processes that include mechanical self-regulation, or feedback, as in the case of
a heating system controlled by a thermostat. Our interest in this section is in loss of jobs
through machines, electronic equipment, and better techniques of management, as well as
automation in the strict sense.

union insists that firemen be retained even though the fireman's job—
to shovel coal into the firebox—no longer exists. The employer argues
that since oil flows automatically into the diesel engine, the fireman is
not needed. The union agrees that nobody is needed to shovel coal;
but it says that a diesel in motion needs frequent adjustment of parts
beyond the reach of the engineer, that locomotives are now more
powerful and faster, and that therefore a sort of copilot or lookout is
required for safety's sake. Out of such conflicting interests, disputes
arise.

It is part of the American credo that any kind of labor-displacing
machinery, though it may abolish some jobs, also creates new ones;
that a waning demand for labor here is compensated for by a waxing
demand elsewhere; that therefore technological unemployment does
not really exist; and that unions which seek by featherbedding work
rules to stretch out employment are hindering progress. This credo is
a mixture of truth and error that we must inquire into.

If one takes a really long-run view—say 100 years—the above
statement of the situation is substantially correct. The percentage of
unemployment in the past 20 years is probably no greater than it was
in any 20-year period since the Civil War. An economy that grows fast
enough will of course provide more jobs each decade. Even so, there
will be much hardship. A skilled glassblower, aged 50, unemployed
because of the introduction of bottlemaking machines, can scarcely
meet his bills by philosophically reflecting that somewhere else in the
growing economy a young man of 21 is being taken on, or that his
grandchildren will have the convenience of no-deposit, throwaway
cola bottles. For all practical purposes a jobless 50-year-old member
of the working class is an unemployable; and even if he does manage
to get a night watchman's job somewhere, this would be a heartbreak-
ing comedown for a skilled artisan. We must remember that unemployment has become a little more unendurable with each passing
year. In 1870, when 80 percent of the population lived on farms or in
small towns, it was often possible for the industrial discard to go back
to his homestead and earn his keep by chopping firewood. Now, only
about 30 percent of the population lives on farms or in small towns—
and firewood is out of style, except to create a decorative effect in the
living rooms of well-heated houses and expensive apartments. But the

point to remember is that economic growth is the force that has kept employment stable, not the shuffling-about of the same labor force.

We must also beware of accepting the idea that if a large earth-moving machine displaces 100 men, the manufacturers of earthmoving machines will hire 100 additional men to make the new or additional machines. A machine is not a laborsaving device if it does not save labor. If the number of man-hours required to make a machine equals 10,000, then it will have to be able to save more than 10,000 man-hours before an entrepreneur would even consider buying it. We assume, of course, that all hours of labor under consideration cost about the same, and that price and number of labor hours required to produce a machine vary together—something that does not do violence to the actual facts.

There are certain periods in which our rate of economic growth is slow and in which other developments place a particular burden on workmen unemployed because of innovations. Such a period existed in the late 1950's and early '60's. American growth was slow; besides, the number of young people entering the work force—or trying to enter it—was great because of the increase in the birthrate, beginning in 1940, zooming in 1945, and in high orbit until recently. Even without the current trend toward automation, we often face a difficult task trying to create enough jobs to absorb the newcomers.

In these circumstances, unions are making desperate efforts to keep their members on company payrolls or to reach some sort of compromise solution. Almost every great national labor-management dispute in recent years has involved the issue of work rules, that is, of rules relating to the limitation of the employer's freedom to install new procedures and machines and to discharge employees affected. One approach is to get the employer not to discharge anybody, but to rely on normal attrition to reduce the working force—attrition by deaths, retirement, or quitting. This often means retraining of employees; the employer may lose a welder through death, but his new machinery freed a loader. The employer now has the problem and expense of converting the loader into a welder. Another compromise is to require that the employer pay a dismissal wage—that is, a moderately large lump sum—to every man discharged. Akin to this is early retirement.

Not all employers are able to reach acceptable solutions, for all such solutions or compromises cost money, and marginal firms in highly competitive industries cannot afford the luxury of recompensing their employees. But the real trouble and, in a sense, the real injustice in making either the employers or the workers, or both, bear the burden of automation is that technological progress is a matter of national concern. At stake are such things as our national security, our position of world leadership, our level of living and that of our descendants. The costs of progress—for there are costs as well as benefits—should be borne by the entire community. There are various ways of distributing the burden—greater public support of retraining programs, more generous unemployment compensation, increased tax benefits to employers who introduce new machinery, and many others, no doubt. But perhaps most important of all is a greater sense of responsibility on the part of the community to speed economic growth and to maintain full employment.

An interesting result of the widespread introduction of labor-saving devices and of automation is the fact that some establishments can continue operations during a strike. The managers and supervisory personnel, who do not strike, are often capable of running the plant for a few weeks or so. How this will affect labor relations in those industries that can temporarily dispense with ordinary labor remains to be seen. It is perhaps too early to say that the strike has become obsolete, but this has not deterred journalists from raising the issue frequently in Sunday magazine sections.

The Government and Labor

If one were to venture a sweeping and almost reckless generalization about the relations between American governments—federal, state, and local—and the working classes, it might be as follows: Until 1932, American governments were moderately helpful to the working classes in most things except encouraging the spread of unionism, at which point they were unfriendly; since 1932, governments have continued their general helpfulness to labor and have besides encouraged or at least tolerated unionism.

American governments have been helpful to the working classes in various ways. Earlier than in several other democratic nations, property ownership as a voting qualification was waived by a large number of American states. Thus, by about 1830, most American male workers except slaves were permitted to vote. Though a free system of good public education came much later, the record of our state and local governments has been pretty good. And this has been more helpful to workingmen and their children than to any other group. Free land, though perhaps less of a boon to the working class than was once widely believed, was nonetheless a measurable benefit. On the other hand, the various agencies of government not only did little to help unionism but also tended to take sides with the employers, who were understandably in favor of curbing it and even abolishing it. The United States was also behind most other nations in establishing systems of social insurance—the earlier name for what we now call social security. Even today, our system of compensation for job accidents and occupational illnesses is rather wobbly in many states. Our unemployment insurance and old-age pensions are somewhat better for the workman but have not kept up with the cost of living.

Governmental attitudes toward unionism changed radically in 1932. The depression had encouraged working-class militancy. The antiunion action of many local governments, and particularly of the courts, had become something of a national scandal. To correct this, an act was passed, the Norris–La Guardia Act, which limited the issuance by courts of injunctions in labor disputes. Without going into technicalities, the act permitted workers to organize or strike without being in contempt of court, something that had often not been possible before. This was the beginning of a vast organizing movement that was to continue for 10 years or more. In 1933 the New Deal administration of Franklin D. Roosevelt came into power. Additional laws were passed permitting labor to organize freely (particularly the famous Wagner Act), and hence to bargain collectively and to use the weapons of the strike and picket line. An essential clause of the new legislation was that an employer was denied the right to fire an employee simply because he was a union member or helped to organize a union.

Of equal importance were decisions of the Supreme Court which put many labor matters under the jurisdiction of the federal government. Until 1937, Washington kept out of labor diputes unless interstate commerce or national emergency could be proved. In other words, only in such cases as war or when railroads were involved did the federal government step into a labor dispute. Legislation concerning child labor, the work of women, minimum wages, compensation for injuries—all of this was left to the states; and to this day, we have some 50 labor codes in addition to what might be called the federal labor code. But in 1937 the Supreme Court placed a large number of firms under federal jurisdiction by its interpretation of the Interstate Commerce Clause. As things now stand, any firm that does a considerable business of selling or buying in other states is covered by the interstate concept. And it is therefore responsible to the federal government.

During World War II, this friendly attitude began to change, partly because of a widespread feeling that labor was getting too powerful. To the New Deal legislation and the favorable interpretations of the courts must now be added the excellent business conditions that prevailed after 1940. Labor is always stronger when two jobs are chasing one man than when two men are chasing one job. In the course of the war the mounting political and economic power of labor inspired Congress to pass a law that very modestly curbed trade-union activity. On the other hand, the policies of the National War Labor Board were mostly advantageous to labor, and unions gained rather than lost in this period. In 1946, American labor reached a peak of power never before attained. It had both economics and politics on its side. A really serious reaction now set in; and in 1947 the Congress passed, over President Harry Truman's veto, the Taft-Hartley Act, a law to curtail some of labor's powers. The closed shop was outlawed, as was the union shop in those states that had passed laws against it (that is, state law was allowed to take precedence over federal law). The employer was permitted in minor but often effective ways to take certain steps to curb unionism that he had been denied for a decade. Certain types of strikes could be halted by injunction. The union's proselyting activities in political campaigns were hedged about with restrictions.

A new blow, from organized labor's point of view, came in 1959 in the form of the Landrum-Griffin Act. This was the reply of Congress to an investigation it held concerning corruption and racketeering in various unions, particularly the Teamsters. The underlying assumption of this law was that a corrupt union was a union deficient in democratic processes. A group of self-perpetuating union leaders armed with dictatorial power was more likely to be corrupt than a union in which the leadership was subject to the ordinary processes and controls of democracy—such as being voted out of office through a secret ballot, frequent submission of issues to the whole member-ship, publicly available financial reports, and so forth. The law calls for these and other instrumental aids to democracy. Such provisions can hardly be considered blows to unionism, but some leaders have argued that much litigation may arise from the act's detailed pro-vision and that litigation takes time, strength, and money. There are, however, other provisions in the act that are more obviously onerous to labor. One outlaws some forms of picketing; another stringently limits the secondary boycott.[4] Labor feels that, all in all, the Landrum-Griffin Act makes organizing efforts harder.

Employers, of course, feel that the postwar legislation expresses the will of the people, and they would hold that a greater degree of equality of economic power has been restored. However these things may be, there will for a long time, no doubt, be a jockeying back and forth on the part of each side to gain advantages; and as time goes on, we shall continue hearing in one decade that labor has the advantage, and in another that the employers hold the trumps. But one thing appears to be certain: As long as we remain a democratic nation, the basic right of collective bargaining and union organizing activity will be defended by law. Until 1932, we were in doubt as to whether a free trade-union movement should be supported as part of a democracy. Apparently, that decision has been made for good and reinforced by the law of the land. The question that remains is how to secure a parity of bargaining power.

Wage Increases and the Public Interest

This section inquires into the economic effects of wage policies. A body of economic theory has long held that neither society as a

---

[4] The secondary boycott is complex and multiform. One simple example may, how-ever, be given here. A is an electrical contractor who installs neon signs. The union has no complaint against him until it learns that A buys his electrical supplies from B, who is "unfair to organized labor." The union warns A to stop buying from B. A refuses. The union goes on strike. This is a secondary boycott and is illegal.

whole nor the working class itself benefits from wage increases. In the early 19th century the Malthusian doctrine, of which we have already spoken in Chapter 4, could be made to say that increases in wages, by enhancing the well-being of labor, would permit a larger population to survive; this larger population would press on a limited food supply, with the result that ultimately the working class would have less to eat per capita, and so would be worse off than it had been before its high-wage fling. After Thomas Robert Malthus, the wages-fund doctrine held that a certain fixed fund existed for wages; any group of workers who could get more than its proper share of this fund through unionism or otherwise would be securing a temporary and selfish advantage that would only impoverish others in the working force. In the popular mind the idea is firmly implanted that many wage increases are against the public interest and, indeed, bad for labor itself.

It is widely believed today that high wages are largely responsible for the inflation of the period 1940–60 and for the balance-of-payments deficit. In the first case, the argument runs, the great, powerful unions jacked up wages, and hence costs, to such a degree that prices were forced upward. Increased prices reduced the real gains anticipated by labor; this encouraged the unions to demand new wage increases whose only logical result would be still higher prices. And so on in the vicious circles, spirals, and merry-go-rounds that newspaper cartoonists so often use to symbolize the process. In the second case, it is held, American manufacturers must compete on the world's markets against manufacturers in Japan, Germany, England, and Italy, where wages are 50 to 90 percent below ours. Both beliefs are examined below.

Wages and Inflation

There are two kinds of inflation, which economists have inelegantly described as "demand pull" and "cost push." Demand-pull inflation is an increase of prices resulting from an increase in demand. Two typical situations bringing on this type of inflation are war expenditures and heavy business spending toward the peak of the business cycle—spending on new plant, increased inventories, and the like. Obviously, inflation of this kind has nothing to do with wages or the assertion of labor union power. It is true, of course, that if unions in such a period press for higher pay, the movement toward an increased cost of living proceeds at an accelerated tempo. If, however, wage earners do not seek or get higher wages, their share of the national income will go down. To put it differently, their wages will remain the same, while prices rise; they will therefore be able to buy fewer goods, and this at a time when both real and monetary rewards to other factors of production are increasing. Thus, labor, in its attempt to live as well as it did before, may add momentum to a movement that it did not initiate.

Cost-push inflation is different. It is set off not by increases in demand, but by increases in costs unaccompanied by enlarged demand. If, for example, some basic industry, such as steel, should secure sufficient market power to increase prices, then all steel-using industries would increase their prices—automobiles, tractors, refrigerators, stoves, "tin" cans, office cabinets, and so forth. In the same way, labor unions possessing great market power could increase costs that would affect the entire economy. If such great unions as those in steel, autos, and transport were simultaneously to get wage increases, they would affect virtually all prices of finished goods. (For the moment, we disregard productivity increases, which will be discussed presently.)

There is ample evidence that much of the inflation that took place in the period 1940–60 is traceable to demand-pull inflation. The wars and boom periods between Pearl Harbor and the Korean settlement provide sufficient explanations for the rise in the Consumer Price Index from 63 to 114 (1953). It is harder to account for the increase from 1953 to 1960 (114 to 126). There seems to be little doubt that the 12-point cost-of-living increase of the latter period stems to some degree from the substantial wage increases of 1956–58. Other cost-push factors, however, probably contributed to the price increases—possibly oligopolistic price increases in one or more basic industries and, quite likely, farm-price increases.

We must conclude that wage increases are not the fundamental cause of the inflation that has cut in half the value of our dollar between 1940 and the present. Or to put it differently, demand-pull has been a more potent force than cost-push in the recent past.

But we must probe a little deeper into this wage inflation business. Not only American labor but also labor generally in the Western world has enjoyed real wage increases of 300 percent or more over the past 100 years—sometimes with, and perhaps oftener without, the aid of trade unionism. It is doubtful whether anyone deplores this fact; on the contrary, we applaud the benefits that Western capitalism has conferred on the working classes. It is perfectly proper, we feel, that they should share in the increased productivity of the society and in the improvement of commodities and services. As earners, they can share in this increased and improved production through wage increases; as consumers, through lowered prices, for many goods are cheaper today than they were a generation ago—certainly in real and constant dollars and often even in our depreciated dollars.

This process of passing on to the working class its share of increased production can take place and has taken place without cost-push inflation. Each year, except in depressions, our economy produces a little more than the year before, perhaps 3 percent on the average. If wages rise in conformity with these increases in production, the cost of living need not rise. The reason, of course, is that each dollar of increased wages (which increases demand) is matched by an increase of goods (which increases supply). When demand and supply rise together in appropriate relationship, prices are unaffected.

The principle stated just above appears to be the basis of a national wage policy as outlined by the former Secretary of Labor, Arthur Goldberg. In his speech of February 23, 1962, he stated that the government would not thereafter merely mediate crucial disputes but would define and assert the national interest. Subsequent statements by administration spokesmen indicated that the government would use all its efforts to prevent wage increases from exceeding general productivity increases and, looking at the other side, that it would tolerate increases within the limits of enhanced productivity. In recent years the guideposts have been abandoned. Whether they will be reinstated is a question to be answered in the future.

From any realistic point of view, increases in productivity are the only substantial source of increases in the worker's purchasing power. One other source remains open, to be sure, but its use has two serious defects: First, it is a meager source; second, tapping it would risk the dangers of social upheaval. We have previously said that the share of labor in our society is around 75 to 80 percent of the national income. This leaves 20 percent or more to be divided among the three other factors of production—land, capital, and entrepreneurs. By aggressive and militant action, organized labor might conceivably secure for itself this additional 20 percent or a large part of it. Thus, if other things remained equal—and obviously they would not, since a society with low or nonexistent property incomes would be a form of communism—labor could increase its income by appropriating 20 percent of the society's income. But this is not very much to divide among some 70 million workers; and in any case, it would be a once-and-for-all affair. Thereafter, increases would again come only as a result of increased productivity.

How futile such a program of encroaching on the incomes of the other factors would be is brought home by the realization that a 3 percent annual increase very quickly becomes a large increase indeed over a relatively short period of years. We can use compound interest tables to demonstrate that a worker, assuming 3 percent growth, will double his income in the relatively short space of 23 years. Thus, if he joins the working force at 18, his income will be doubled at the age of 41. Just before he retires at 65, he will have doubled his income again. This does not take into account increases he may get through promotions to higher skilled work or supervisory jobs.

Such as they are, the figures we have indicate that for perhaps 100 years or so—and more demonstrably for 60 years—American labor has as a matter of fact encroached but little on the incomes of the other factors of production. Statistical proofs are not easy to supply, partly because the figures collected by the government and other agencies do not conform to the economists' categories of pure wages, rent, profits, and interest, and partly because we have had vast migrations from independent proprietorship and entrepreneurship into wage earning (for example, farmers have left the farm in huge numbers and have gone into occupations rewarded by wages or salaries rather than interest, rents, or profits). What figures we do have indicate a considerable stability in the wage and nonwage relationships, though labor does seem to have gained a little at the expense of receivers of rent and of interest.

This does not mean that there have not been considerable shifts within groups. From the economists' viewpoint, the college professor and the household servant both are workers, and their rewards are wages. Thirty years ago a senior professor could on his salary (wages) alone afford a full-time maid. Today, he cannot. According to Lloyd G. Reynolds, a distinguished student of such matters, there is good reason to think that the most important form of income transfer now going on in the economy is a transfer from white-collar worker to blue-collar worker.[5] But this is not a transfer from the so-called "property incomes."

Before leaving this section, we must clarify the meaning of the phrase "increased productivity of labor." This phrase may suggest to some readers the concept that labor itself is somehow responsible for general increases in productivity, that workers take shorter coffee breaks or rush around more or accept stricter discipline on the job. This concept is erroneous. Increases in productivity of a society as a whole happens to be measured in terms of output per worker or per man-hours worked. The reasons for this are historical rather than logical. The increased productivity of labor is only partly the result of any efforts exerted by labor. It is the result of improved processes, application of new machinery, better education of all groups in the society (including the working class), the progress of science, and so forth. In short, the determinants of productivity—or increased productivity—are mostly beyond the control of any single group within the society.

Wages and Foreign Trade

We have already touched on the question of wages and foreign trade in Chapter 14, but it may be desirable to turn again to the issue in a different context. In about 1958, Americans began to see that the U.S. balance of payments was in an unhealthy state, and this unhealthiness has continued. Among the causes put forward is our high-wage economy. How can we, it is asked, sell textiles abroad when our average textile wage is $1.90, whereas rates in Japan and Hong Kong are 40 cents or less? Well, now, it is certainly true that if American

[5] Lloyd G. Reynolds, *Labor Economics and Labor Relations* (3d ed.; Englewood Cliffs, N.J.: Prentice-Hall, Inc., 1959), pp. 470–71.

labor were to accept a wage cut of 50 percent across the board, and if this action did not shake our entire economy to its foundations—as it would—then we could compete more favorably in foreign markets. In this sense, it is true that high wages make difficulties for us in selling abroad. But it is also true that high wages are one of the character- istics of the American economy to which we point with pride and which favorably distinguish our form of capitalism from other forms.

The fact is that many of our goods can be sold abroad more cheaply than can competitors' goods, despite our high wages. For various reasons, we have considerable superiority over other nations in several fields. Our farmers, more highly mechanized than else- where, can produce grains and tobacco at competitive prices. We have no trouble selling industrial machinery, automobiles, aircraft, and their parts and accessories in foreign markets. Part of the reason for this is that we are relatively more efficient in these endeavors than in, say, textiles or in pottery, porcelain, and china. Over a long period of years, we have usually sold more goods abroad than we have im- ported. This situation has not suddenly changed in the sense that American wages have recently zoomed skyward while the wages of our customers have remain anchored.

Many studies have clearly established the fact that in many types of business, unit labor costs are lower in the United States than abroad, despite the higher hourly wage rate. And even in some areas, such as steel, where our unit wage costs are higher, other costs are lower—interest rates, fuels, iron ore, and scrap.[6] It has also been noted widely that our most successful export industries are those in which wage rates are highest.

Now, all of this does not mean that in a balance-of-payments crisis, wages should be allowed to rise unchecked or that national wage policy is of no importance when foreign-trade problems arise. It does, however, suggest that high American wages are not the major cause of our difficulties. And when they are, as they probably are in the case of certain textiles, we ought to reconcile ourselves to the fact that we have no business producing them. We do not try to produce pineapples, bananas, and coffee in the continental United States. Why textiles and pottery?

[6] Louis Lister, *Europe's Coal and Steel Community: An Experiment in Economic Union* (New York: Twentieth Century Fund, 1960).

Can Unions Really Increase Wages?

The preceding discussion on wages and public policy was partly based on the popularly accepted assumption that unions can raise wages at will. If a union strikes—or threatens to strike—for a 10-cent wage increase and gets it, then it would appear that organized labor can use its allegedly monopolistic, bludgeoning, or blackmailing strength to raise wages whenever it wants to. This assumption—if it is not to be ridiculous—must of course be qualified at the outset. Obviously, unions cannot make such excessive demands as to bankrupt all their employers wholesale. As we saw in Chapter 6, even the most perfect monopoly has nothing to gain by charging so high a price that sales would hover around the zero mark. In the extreme case, no jobs would be open for union members to fill. Besides, high wages could be countered, and are countered, by substitutes—that is, by labor-displacing machinery or plant reorganization. There are, obviously, realistic limits to what a union can get, even if we postulate great monopoly power.

The question still remains, of course, whether within broad limits unions are able to force wages upward. Several careful studies of this have been made by competent economists. The studies are not conclusive. They suggest that when an industry is newly unionized, wages tend to rise rather rapidly. In long-unionized industries, wages seem to rise no faster than in nonunionized industries. In recent decades a few dramatic wage increases have taken place in nonunionized industries—domestic service, for example. Some economists have wondered whether high wages do not foster union organization, rather than the other way around. Some have ventured the opinion that the unions most successful in raising wages are found in industries where labor productivity is highest, thus suggesting that productivity is a more potent factor in wage determination than overweening union power. The field is only half explored. The data are difficult to handle. The only safe conclusion to draw at this point is that one cannot with dogmatic confidence assume that unionism has sufficient power to get wage increases in defiance of the forces of supply and demand or of the principle that larger rewards must be sustained by enhanced productivity.

If unions are but feeble instruments to secure wage increases, it must not be assumed that they are worthless to the workingman. Through the collective bargaining agreement and the union power behind it, he gets many benefits that go well beyond the gifts he might expect to get through the operation of the forces of supply and demand. He is protected from arbitrary dismissals, from the brushing-aside of legitimate complaints, from suddenly invented ex post facto rules, from favoritism in layoffs. Some employers, of course, would handle these things as well as the unions do, and some unions rule their members as harshly as bad employers would; but both are exceptions rather than the rule, and good unions fill a great need between the extremes. The best of them supply welfare services, offer educational opportunities, and help to give their members a sense of dignity and worth. In this country, in Europe, and in Asia, American unionism has through its domestic and foreign efforts been a buttress against communism. It would be an overstatement to say that union-ism has favorably affected every American workman down to the least Negro laborer employed in a southern turpentine still, but unionism has spread its benefits far beyond its confines—if for no other reason than that one way for an employer to ward off unionism is to do a better job than unions themselves do.

A Word about the Future of Unionism

Beginning in 1963, we have been hearing predictions that union-ism is dying. Many facts have been adduced in proof: The rate of union growth is slowing down. The merger of the old AFL with the CIO, far from bringing unity, has degenerated into a most unsatis-factory relationship—"We've moijed, but we ain't happily married," a local union official is alleged to have said. The leadership, con-fronted with automation and unemployment, appears to lack re-sourcefulness. So many things have been won and taken for granted (such as grievance procedures) that union officers cannot find new causes for members to rally around. Walter Reuther, leader of the auto workers, has hinted that he may withdraw his large union from the AFL–CIO because the national federation's leadership has, Reuther suggests, become complacent and smug.

In addition to all this, the federal government and circumstances are narrowing the issues in collective bargaining to such a degree that bargaining has sometimes become almost a farce. To prevent inflation, the Kennedy administration, it is charged, placed on organized labor the moral responsibility of keeping wage demands within productivity limits; and many employers are prepared to meet such minimal demands anyhow, without the goad of the union. Before World War II—that is, before the atom bomb, the transoceanic airplane, and the intercontinental missile—the oceans gave us adequate safeguard from attack by an enemy. Now, that kind of safety is gone. We must test everything by the standard of defense; and this means that steel strikes, longshore strikes, and rail strikes cannot be tolerated—not to mention stoppages in the defense industries themselves.

Not only automation but also the expanding service industries demand more and more white-collar people and fewer blue-collar workers. The white-collar people will not join unions, at least not unions of the AFL–CIO type. They will join various types of associations (such as the American Association of University Professors), but these tend to be rather pallid groups, lacking in militancy. (It should be noted that this is not always true and that certan of these professional groups are quite aggressive, as is evidenced by the teacher's strikes of 1967.)

It is hard to assess current statements about the weakening of unions. We cannot yet say that they have sufficient validity to form the basis of a prediction that unions and collective bargaining are doomed to disappear. It is possible that they will decline as an economic force but take on renewed strength as a political force. In any event, the answer belongs to the future.

Summary and Conclusions

The labor problem, though basically an economic problem, is also a complex social problem, parts of which fall into the realms of sociology, psychology, law, and similar domains. It is a modern problem that has developed in step with the evolution of democracy, humanitarianism, and industrialization. Perhaps the essence of the labor problem is the attempt of a traditionally disesteemed and disadvantaged class to move toward the social and economic levels of the middle classes.

Although only about one third of the working class belongs to trade unions, any discussion of labor problems is likely to emphasize unions and their activity because these organizations do express many of the aspirations of the working class. Trade unions, like corporations, seem to be divisible into two groups numerically—one small group of very large unions, and a second large group of relatively small ones. The top 6 percent embrace about 40 percent of all union members; the remaining 94 percent include about 60 percent. Some degree of union activity is to be found almost everywhere in the nation, but unions are much harder to find in small cities and rural areas than elsewhere. The large, heavily populated industrial states obviously contain the largest number of union members.

The most important function of unions is to bargain with employers about wages, hours, and working conditions. Apart from wage fixing, the settlement of grievances has perhaps been the second most important function of the union—a process which guarantees a hearing to aggrieved employees. With the spread of automation, and indeed even before the present flood of laborsaving devices and practices, another major union function has been to ease the cost of job loss to individual workmen, or even to prevent their dismissal altogether.

In a democracy like ours the local, state, and federal governments have over the long run been moderately generous to the working class in various social and economic matters, with, however, one important exception: Until 1932, they took a strong legal position against trade-union growth and activity. It is true that unions were not forbidden and strikes were not proscribed; but both were at the mercy of court orders which, in effect, permitted local judges to stem union growth. The Norris–La Guardia and Wagner acts changed all this insofar as the federal government has jurisdiction over interstate commerce. Numerous state and local governments followed suit. The Supreme Court generously interpreted the concept of what constitutes interstate commerce. As a result, trade unionism has been given the explicit right to live in the most populous and industrially advanced areas; some jurisdictions still exist, however, where unions and their activity can be proscribed by law and court order. The large benefits just described above, a gift of the 1930's, have been to some degree withdrawn in the past quarter century, but the basic protection remains.

The man on the street often believes the popular notion that trade-union power begets high wages which beget inflation or prices high enough to affect our balance of payments unfavorably. The line or lines of reasoning used to reach these conclusions are quite dubious. First, unions do not really have as much power as is here assumed, for wages are not entirely exempt from the so-called "laws of supply and demand." Second, the forces of demand-pull inflation are given too little recognition in such an analysis. Third, the role of administered prices by oligopolies should be recognized as a possible force in price increases, as well as governmental influence on farm prices. Finally, in foreign trade the important figure is not the hourly wage but the unit labor cost, which, in some of our more efficient industries, is the lowest in the world.

The function of trade unionism, at least as we now know it, is in some danger of declining in importance. Collective bargaining, spurred by the overhanging threat of the strike, may have to change its character in a strikeless society. And strikes may virtually disappear for three reasons: First, in a nation which seems to be almost perpetually at war or at the brink, as ours seems to be, interruptions in the process of defense will be considered intolerable. Second, we are becoming so interdependent and so urbanized, that failure to produce anywhere may cause disorganization almost everywhere. Finally, many strikes, unless they last a long time, will not do much to disorganize production, since the machines will continue to produce with minimal attention, and that minimal attention can be given by the nonstriking executive force. If this happens, the economic pressures of the past may change into political pressure.

QUESTIONS FOR REVIEW AND DISCUSSION

1. Define, in your own words, each of the following terms:
   a) Dependent classes
   b) Union shop
   c) Seniority
   d) Fringe benefits
   e) Featherbedding
   f) Grievance procedure
2. "American trade unionism is not spread evenly, either geographically or industrially." In what industries and geographic regions in the United

States are you most likely to find a high degree of unionism? What historical, cultural, and economic reasons can be given to explain this distribution of union power?

3. Recent labor problems in the newspaper-publishing industry and in the railroad industry have brought about increased public criticism of collective bargaining. Many claim that collective bargaining, though effective in the past, can no longer be relied upon as the major instrument for resolving labor disputes. What is collective bargaining? What changes in labor conditions, unions, and industry have altered the effectiveness of collective bargaining? What alternative methods for resolving labor disputes can be used?

4. Discuss the changing attitudes of the federal government toward organized labor.

5. Describe the difference between "cost-push" and "demand-pull" inflation. What types of government policies can be used to combat a cost-push inflation? Are these policies different from those designed to combat a demand-pull inflation? Explain.

6. There is a growing concern in the United States that the social and economic problems caused by automation will be virtually impossible to solve. What is automation, and what problems is it creating? What benefits can automation yield? Are there any private or public policies that will help guarantee that automation's benefits may outweigh its disadvantages?

7. What economic forces limit a union's ability to raise wage rates? Discuss.

8. Discuss some of the forces that lie behind increases in labor productivity.

9. What evidence would you present to support the contention that "the American trade union is more a social than an economic organization"?

10. What is "automation" as contrasted with "laborsaving"?

Chapter 16

PRESERVING

COMPETITION

Introduction

Although the Constitution says nothing about it, a basic principle underlying the American belief system is that competition shall prevail in our economic life. On this point, we are clear. But just what we mean by the word "competition" is less clear. It is one of those difficult words, often heavily freighted with emotional overtones, which signifies different things to different people. It is almost in a class with such words as "liberty," "justice," "truth," and "love." In any event, we object to monopoly in our free society. Competition, we feel sure, is the standard to strive for.

We have defined pure competition on pages 45–47, but this definition is so aseptic that we hardly expect to meet its fulfillment in real life. The problem is to determine how far competition may deviate from the ideal and still remain within the realm of reasonably active and workable competition.

When we speak of economic competition, we obviously never think of competition so intense as to countenance assault and battery, as in competition for food in the animal kingdom. On the other hand, we are not sissies about competition. You may open a restaurant that competes successfully with another on the same block. If, without malice or the use of unfair methods, you put the other one out of business, you have performed a meritorious act. If your success has serious repercussions, such as driving the owner to suicide and the wife to insanity, and denying educational advantages to the children, you are still blameless—though you may regret that you started such a melancholy chain of events. The law prohibits a pursuit of gain that involves threat and direct physical injury, but is heedless of the consequences of fair competition.

We expect a little rowdiness in competition, and we hardly expect businessmen to play the game as if nothing were at stake.

Business is not like a set of tennis between college chums. We scarcely hope to find in commerce the high standards of latter-day chivalry that are said to prevail on the playing fields of Eton and Harrow. We do not countenance some of the business violence of the 19th century, but even today rival soap companies have been known to tear down each other's drugstore and chainstore displays, and a certain amount of industrial espionage is considered to be part of the game. If competition can conceivably range from chivalrous sportsmanship to conquest red in tooth and claw, where do we in our business culture draw the line? At what point do we begin to penalize our economic players because they are unnecessarily rough? At what point does our moral sense begin to condemn the behavior of businessmen as we condemn the baseball player who files his spikes?

We condemn overvigorous competition, but what shall we say of lethargic competition? Sometimes the trouble is not that firms compete against each other with an excess of zeal, but that they seem to respect one another's preserves with immoderate diligence. The large cigarette companies appear to fight one another with nothing more offensive than singing commercials, though the Big Three in tobacco during the 1930's showed a capacity to act together with great economic violence against small competitors. We condemn the dirty player in any game or race, but we can scarcely admire a horse race in which the jockeys bring their horses to a walk near the finish line and invite one another to cross the finish line first or, to use a better analogy, in which three of them decide that they will share the first three places by mutual aid and by shooting down all the other contestants. Yet something like this does go on in some fields of business enterprise.

The issue is not entirely a moral one. It is also an economic issue. A completely ruthless competitor may not only offend our ethical sense; he may also be inefficient, or the repercussions of his work may be uneconomic. Both the ruthless and the sluggish competitor may be taking early steps toward monopoly or undue market power. We have already learned in Chapter 6 that the monopolist is likely to charge more for his product than he would get under competitive conditions and that this leads to a misallocation of resources. According to standard theory, the greatest good to the greatest number is served by the most nearly perfect competition. In day-today living, we must obviously settle for something far short of perfect competition; but we must try not to backslide too far away from a reasonable ideal.

It will be the purpose of this chapter to study a few typical situations in which our society is trying to solve the question of workable, lively, and fair competition.

Large Size: Pro and Con

Because it usually attracts the most interest, we shall first open up several questions clustering around the concept of bigness. Is a very big business always efficient? Is big business always monopolistic? Is it necessarily opposed to the public interest? Does it restrain trade? What do the courts say about all this? These are among the issues.

Americans have long been ambivalent about bigness. We belong to what Oswald Spengler names the "Faustian culture," which is enamored of far-flung operations, large numbers, hundreds of miles per hour, and billion-dollar corporations. Having no kings toward whom we may yearn, we identify ourselves with the captains of industry and such great names as General Electric, General Motors, Procter & Gamble, American Telephone and Telegraph, and Radio Corporation of America. Presidents and their cabinets may come and go, but Ivory Soap and Coca-Cola go on forever. We cosset ourselves with the electric blankets of the great corporations and with their deep-cushion auto rides; and we joyfully endanger our health with their cigarettes. We allay our anxieties by gossiping with our neighbors through the instruments they provide or sit in comfortable hypnosis watching their television sets. We rationalize their size by saying that they survive because they produce the best or because great size is required to produce cheaply or because only large firms can carry on research. We even endorse their self-praise by humming the singing commercials they perpetrate or incorporating their misspelled and ungrammatical lyrics into our humor.

At other times, we free ourselves from this romantic adoration of size and shake off the corporation's capacity to ingratiate. We are shocked that some huge firms squeeze their dealers unmercifully and compete homicidally with small ones. We are disillusioned by high General Electric officials' going to jail for price-fixing.

If we look into the matter systematically and with detachment, we find that almost everything we have uncritically accepted as characteristic of the giant company is subject to qualification. First, we look at the argument about the alleged efficiency of size. Joe S. Bain has made important studies of optimum size. In 11 out of 20 industries studied, he found that to produce at lowest unit costs, each firm would need to produce for only one 40th of the total market, or less. In other words, there could, with efficiency, be 40 or more firms of about equal size where now some four to five plants often supply as much as 90 percent of the total. In the automobile industry, efficiency could be secured by firms producing only about 500,000 units; since we sell 10 to 11 million cars a year, this would leave room for about 20 companies of equal size instead of the Big Three and a few minor ones. George Romney, formerly president of one of the minor companies (American Motors) and now governor of Michigan, informed a Senate committee in 1958 that the manufacturing facilities for an efficient automobile company plus other financial requirements would demand the investment of $576 million.[1] In that same year, General Motors was listed as having assets of $7.5 billion, or about 13 times the size of an efficient competitor as described by Romney; Ford, with $3.3 billion, was about 5½ times larger than efficiency demanded; and Chrysler, with $1.5 billion, was 2½ times larger.[2] It is well known that vast size contributes to inefficiency at times. The corporation becomes unwieldly. Supervision is more difficult. The use of computers, however, and the transformation of the art of leadership to the science of management may steadily increase the size of the efficient firm.

Many large firms, as in the bread-baking industry, are not technologically integrated: Each baking plant is a separate bead on a string, independent, self-contained. The average (median) *plant* capacity of the largest baking firms, such as Continental and General, is

[1] U.S. Senate Subcommittee on Antitrust and Monopoly, *A Study of Administered Prices in the Automobile Industry* (Washington, D.C.: U.S. Government Printing Office, 1958), p. 16.

[2] These figures, particularly for General Motors, include assets used for the production of things other than passenger automobiles. A proper subtraction could be made, but it would not change the significance of what has been stated above.

no larger than that of the average independent wholesale baker. Household liquid bleaches, in modest quantity, can be made efficiently in plants that cost $100,000 or less. Yet one firm alone, in recent years, made and sold nearly one half the U.S. total. The "efficiency" of many large or mammoth firms in many industries is not based on their technological superiority, but on their financial power—their capacity to preempt expanding markets and raw materials, and, finally, to engage in coercive and predatory activities[3] and to enjoy other nonindustrial advantages.

It is also often argued that great size makes possible the spending of large sums for research and that this research is ultimately beneficial to the consumer. No informed person denies that some large firms spend much for research that is of ultimate advantage to consumers. But not all large firms engage in research, and not all of those that do carry on research use it to improve their products. One of the well-known studies in this field of inquiry concludes that only half of the 60 most important innovations of recent decades came out of corporation research, and only part of these were the fruit of research carried on by very large corporations.[4] A typical case history of a major improvement is that it is pioneered by a small firm. We are all aware that the great work of Marie and Pierre Curie, Jonas Salk, Alexander Fleming, Albert Einstein, Niels Bohr, and Enrico Fermi is not to be associated with corporation research. The U.S. government is paying approximately two thirds of the cost of all research being done in this country.

The question as to whether the mammoth corporations make the best products and therefore, grow huge because millions of customers flock to the brand that offers the best buy is a hard one to discuss objectively. Best for what? Here, we run into the thorny question of the advertising copywriter versus the technically trained people. Two face powders may be equally good (or bad) from the viewpoint of the dermatologist, toxicologist, informed beautician, and skilled olfactor. But if one of the powders, named *Languorous Lady*, has a better

---

[3] For confirmation of this and above statements on size in the bread industry, see U.S. Senate Subcommittee on Antitrust and Monopoly, *A Study of Administered Prices in the Bread Baking Industry* (Washington, D.C.: U.S. Government Printing Office, 1960), pp. 5, 6, and *passim*.

[4] J. Jewkes, D. Sawers, and R. Stillerman, *The Sources of Invention* (London: Macmillan & Co., Ltd., 1958).

copywriter than its rival, *Peachy Girl*, then *Lady* will outsell *Girl*, and the test of superiority will really be a test of copywriters' ability to evoke fantasies of easily acquired charm, not a test of functional qualities. And what is true of face powder is, with appropriate variation, equally true of automobiles, breakfast foods, and almost every other differentiable commodity on the market. The commodity that gives us extra pleasure because it has been made to seem superlatively desirable by Madison Avenue may be the best for us, even if its functional values are just ordinary or even below the ordinary. One who reads the evaluations of consumers' organizations finds that "best buys" are not always the products of the largest corporations. The copywriter may make you yearn for the "pinpoint carbonation" of a soft drink; but one of the great chemists of his generation, Linus Pauling, told a group of acquaintances that he had tried for years to find out what the phrase meant, and had failed.

Some firms are large—or larger than they would otherwise be— because they bring under one roof a number of unrelated plants. Thus, Radio Corporation of America has acquired Hertz, the auto rental firm. Colgate-Palmolive once considered merging with National Biscuit. International Telephone and Telegraph operates subsidiaries in life insurance and book publishing. Several airlines run chains of hotels. It is perhaps not always true that some of these conglomerate mergers find their rationale in lower advertising costs, but some of them do. It was quite probably true of the Procter & Gamble–Clorox merger of 1957, recently annulled by the Federal Trade Commission.[5] Many such firms gain little in efficiency as viewed by the engineer; their bargaining power is, however, enhanced.

The fact that the largest corporations sometimes do not produce at lowest cost or do not always manufacture the best buy or do not always sponsor research may be looked upon as a mere peccadillo rather than a cardinal sin. In an affluent society, is there really anything very wrong about the giants?

We shall first dispose of a noneconomic matter before we examine the economic issues—the political power of our large corporations. By political power, we mean the ability of money to maintain lobbies; to get the sympathetic attention of newspapers, radio, and TV, which they help to support by their advertisements; to hire public

[5] See "The Clorox Case," *Consumer Reports*, July, 1967, pp. 360 ff.

relations experts who create a favorable public image. The large corporations have something akin to diplomatic relations with foreign corporations and at times with foreign governments. They have not always served the best interests of our country. Adolf A. Berle, Jr., lawyer, scholar, and diplomat, feels that American corporations have, however, been more circumspect in their foreign relations in recent decades than they were in the 19th century; in any event, considerable power for good and evil over foreign events lies in their hands. Berle feels that they are now exerting their power constructively, but we have no way of knowing whether the sense of responsibility which he found to exist in 1954 will continue to mark corporate activity.[6] What is particularly objectionable here is power divorced from responsibility. The President of the United States and Congress have power, but they can be held responsible—that is, they can be thrown out of office. A vast corporation can, through its propaganda, exert considerable power over our minds; but unlike the teacher whom we can discharge, we cannot do much about a corporation's officers if they decide on a propaganda program that is contrary to the public interest. We can easily enough get away from much of the propaganda of other social groups, but we can scarcely cut off the vast amount of what tumbles out of our radio and TV when we try to look at our favorite performers or to listen to our news programs. But we must leave the question of political power to the political scientists and return to the ways in which corporations can exercise economic power against the public interest.

If the corporation's power is great enough to permit it to raise prices above the competitive level, the corporation is misallocating resources. In simpler terms, what this means is that factors of production are not being used as the consumer would most like to have them used, and the reason is that the price is higher than is required to meet costs (including normal profit). A firm does not have to be a monopoly to allow it to raise prices above the competitive price. Indeed, it

---

[6] Berle, in his books, *The 20th Century Capitalist Revolution* (New York: Harcourt, Brace & Co., 1954) and *Power without Property* (New York: Harcourt, Brace & Co., 1959), expressed the idea that a "corporate conscience" as a protector of the public interest has been evolving during the 20th century. However, in his latest work, *The American Economic Republic* (New York: Harcourt, Brace & World, Inc., 1963), there is, says one reviewer, "apparently . . . a diminution in his enthusiasm for the rectitude of corporate management." The review was by John W. Blair, *Washington Post*, May 12, 1963. Blair is an economist who has long studied the large corporations.

does not even have to be a monster firm. A rather small giant—or at least, an oligopoly composed of several little giants—can achieve remarkable results, as the bread-baking industry attests.

The larger wholesale bakers of the United States are all little giants, none having assets appreciably in excess of $175 million, a sum equal to about one 75th of the assets of General Motors. But by various tactics, such as selling cheap in one market and later raising prices when competition has disappeared, they have succeeded, in West Coast cities particularly, in increasing prices 10 to 12 percent above the national average (allowance being made for high costs on the West Coast).

Through administered prices and price leadership, an oligopoly in which none of the members controls as much as half the market may set fairly high prices. An administered price is one that is not set by competition in the market (to which the firm adjusts), but a price set by the firm itself. It is characterized by being changed infrequently. In this, it differs from a price set on a nearly perfect market, such as the stock exchange, were prices of individual stocks often fluctuate by as much as 3 percent a day without eliciting much attention. A price leader is a firm, often the largest in an oligopoly, which sets a price to which other members of the oligopoly conform. If the price movement is upward, they conform, partly because they like high prices. If a smaller firm does not act in accordance with the leader because it prefers to get a larger share of the market at the old and lower price, it may become the victim of various predatory practices. One might be the punitive and preemptive buying-up of raw materials by some of the larger oligopolists; this would cripple the smaller firm, which would not then know where to turn for its supplies. If the price leader decided to reduce prices—something that has not happened often in recent years—the other firms must follow; if not, nobody would buy from the independents who hold out for the higher price.

There are, of course, limits as to how high a price leader can raise his price. Obviously, prices cannot be exorbitant. Few people would buy steel at $5,000 a ton. Apart from this kind of absurdity, the price must not be high enough to attract new competition. Pricing must be done "within the wall of difficult entry," to use Gardiner C. Means's phrase. In some industries the difficulties of entry are greater than in others. To manufacture automobiles, for example, you must be prepared to lay about $750 million on the line. Such a sum is hard to get together, and this partly explains why General Motors can make an average profit of about 25 percent on invested capital without attracting new entrants. In other industries of administered prices the price leader may have to set his profit goals at a lower rate. The lower the profit, the less attractive it is for newcomers to enter.

Unfair Competition

It was suggested above that an oligopoly might discourage serious competition by preempting raw materials. This is only one of many ways in which a powerful firm or an oligopoly can punish or even rid itself of a smaller independent. One of the commonest weapons is geographic price discrimination. A chain grocery might cut its prices low enough, for example, in Hannibal Falls to run the independents out of business. When it stands alone, it can charge higher (monopolistic) prices. This is illegal, of course; but so is driving 70 miles an hour in many states, yet thousands do it.

Another coercive measure is to favor pliant dealers at the expense of difficult ones. For example, the Cyclops Company makes cameras and film. The film is standard and fits several other types of cameras. One dealer handles the Cyclops camera and film, but no other type of film. Another handles both of the Cyclops products but also handles the standard films, Kodak and others. Cyclops does not like this and may do several things in reprisal. It may deny the second dealer either Cyclops cameras or film, or both; and if Cyclops is a popular brand, this may be damaging. Or the pliant dealer may be rewarded by prompt shipments or advertising displays that increase sales and place the other at a disadvantage.

In the bread industry an interesting form of punitive action has been used, named "stales clobbering." Stales clobbering grows out of two practices in the baking industry. First, the wholesaler who sells bread to grocery stores agrees to take back next day all the unsold (stale) loaves and to credit the grocer with their cost; second, the retail customer, usually a housewife, seems to buy the brand of bread that is piled highest on the grocery store shelf. Thus, the wholesaler wants to overpile his bread on the grocers' racks, not only for its psychological effect on the customer, but also because the shelf room he occupies subtracts that much space from his competitiors. On the other hand, overpiling is costly. Half the pile may be unsold; the wholesaler has agreed to take the bread back and to reimburse the grocer. A giant bakery company operating in hundreds of areas can afford to "stales-clobber" in Halbrook Center, even to the point of losing heavily and consistently. What he loses here, he presumably can make up in the areas in which he is already well established and need not be overly aggressive; he can even make up his losses in Halbrook Center itself, eventually, if these and other tactics drive out serious competition.

A few forms of unfair competition have been suggested above. Many more could be described, some adaptable to the economies of one industry, some to another. In addition to these, there is also, of course, the classic price-fixing conspiracy. This involves the coming-together of all the sellers—at least all the important sellers—to agree on a price; and obviously, this price is higher than the competitive price, or else there would be no need to meet and come to an agreement.

All of the practices spoken of above are illegal and can be prosecuted. The penalties may be serious, but usually are not, involving fines and possibly imprisonment—as in the famous General Electric–Westinghouse *et al.* case of 1961. Considering the capacity of the firms to pay, fines are usually small; as for imprisonment, this is so rare that it is doubtful whether, for strictly business crimes, all violators together have spent as much as a total of five years in jail since 1890, when the Sherman Antitrust Act was passed.[7]

The Question of Bigness without Badness

The practices spoken of above may be considered unfair or unreasonable restraints of trade or conspiracies to monopolize. But what of bigness—sheer bigness—uncomplicated by misdeeds or intent to take advantage of size? Is it illegal to be a good-natured, well-intentioned Gulliver in Lilliput? Certainly, Gulliver was a dangerous fellow to have around, however benign.

---

[7] There have been some convictions of labor leaders and gangsters under the law. These are excluded under the phrase "strictly business crimes."

Here we get into difficulties. A mammoth firm may be a monopoly. But what is a monopoly? Control over 100 percent of the market? Such control rarely exists. Well, then, what is it? Ninety percent? Sixty? Even if there were 100 percent control, would the monopoly always be damaging to the public interest? Suppose you had complete control over a device that would automatically tip a gentleman's hat every time he nodded to a lady of his acquaintance on the street. Since the human male arm and hand make a completely acceptable substitute, this sort of monopoly would be meaningless. Similarly, can any firm have a 100 percent monopoly of aluminum, since steel, copper, tin, plastics, cement, and plywood—all these and many others—can be used as substitutes? What about cellophane? Here we have many close substitutes, such as waxed or glassy paper. There are, indeed, many substitutes for almost everything, yet at some point people want the real thing—aluminum or cellophane—not a substitute. At what point do we say: "This is a monopoly because substitutes are not acceptable, even though they exist?" These questions are by no means academic. Actually, the courts are required to make decisions for and against large firms, and some criterion is needed to define a monopoly resulting from sheer size.

There has been an interesting evolution of the judicial theory of monopoly by size. The first famous case to come to the attention of the Supreme Court was the United States Steel case of 1920. The company at that time was a merger, resulting from a combination of 180 smaller companies that merged first into 12 and then into one, the United States Steel Corporation. At the time of its court appearance, it controlled half the supply of steel, though it had, a decade or so before, controlled about two thirds. The company had, at an earlier date, engaged in price-fixing and was still engaged in a rather complex form of price discrimination (presumably not well understood by the court). But these questions were not at issue. The real issue was whether a huge company controlling half an industry stood in violation of antitrust laws. The Court found that its actual present behavior was exemplary. It resorted to none of the "tyrannies or brutalities" to which some other companies had resorted. It created no artificial scarcity of steel. The company was admittedly big and powerful, but not predatory, and the law presumably does not make mere size an offense. United States Steel was found not guilty. Thus was born the doctrine of the "good trust," which cannot be punished; and the inference was made that antimonopoly legislation applied only to unfair practices.

This position was reaffirmed seven years later in the International Harvester case; the company then controlled 64 percent of the output of agricultural implements and machinery. Like Steel, it was a good trust; and like Steel, it was found not guilty. An interesting sidelight on this case was that the company was the price leader in its field. The economist, if not the judge, is likely to look upon price leadership with a suspicious eye, as pointing to quasi-monopolistic practices. But the Court, apparently less suspicious, stated: "The fact that competitors may see proper, in the exercise of their own judgment, to follow the prices of another manufacturer, does not establish any suppression of competition."

Five years later (1932) the Court stated in the dictum concerning the Swift and Company case that mere size is not an offense unless magnified to the point at which it amounts to a monopoly. It went on to say that size carries with it an opportunity for abuse that is not to be ignored when the opportunity is proved to have been utilized in the past. Though this was merely an observation by one member of the Supreme Court, it proved to be a turning point in antitrust doctrine.

Thirteen years of depression and war passed, during which, for various reasons, including those attributable to the troubled times, antitrust activity was at a low ebb. But in 1945 a landmark decision was handed down in the government suit against the Aluminum Company of America. In this case the Court of last resort (not, in this special case, the Supreme Court), ruled that bigness in an industry does constitute monopoly, and the principle underlying the Steel and Harvester cases was reversed. The Court held that a firm which expanded to meet the market was in fact a monopoly, whether it wanted to be one or not. The following quotation from the decision is of particular interest:

It was not inevitable that it [Aluminum Company of America] should always anticipate increases in the demand for ingots and be prepared to supply them. Nothing compelled it to keep doubling and redoubling its capacity before others entered the field. It insists that it has never excluded competitors; but we can think of no more effective exclusion than progressively to embrace each new opportunity as it opened, and to face every newcomer with new capacity already geared into a great organization, having the advantage of experience, trade connections, and the elite of personnel.

The Court went on to say that one of the purposes of the antitrust laws was "to perpetuate and preserve for its own sake and in spite of possible costs, an organization of industry into small units which can effectively compete with each other." The result of all this was that the Aluminum Company of America was ordered to rearrange its affairs in such a way as to reduce its power. Its production of new aluminum was within a short period reduced from 90 to 50 percent of the total.

Several other decisions have been handed down on the issue of size. They have suggested a slight retreat from the firm position taken in the Aluminum case. Although the Court has been a little less strict since 1945, on the whole the principle has been established that being big relative to the industry is enough to arouse suspicion of antitrust violation, particularly if the acts of expansion and the search for new customers have a preemptive flavor. In other words, there is no such thing as the passive possession of power. If you have power, you exercise power actively. We do not yet have a definition of "big," though it appears that a firm must control more than 60 percent of the supply before it is accounted too big. Here is what the Court said in this connection: "That percentage [90] is enough to constitute a monopoly; it is doubtful whether 60 or 64 percent would be enough; and, certainly 33 percent is not."

The last statement, that 33 to 60 percent is not enough to constitute a monopoly, raises serious problems for those who believe that many oligopolies are not in the public interest and who can find no way under our antitrust laws to prosecute them. For example, in automobiles, even the giant, General Motors, has never controlled appreciably more than half the market, and often a little less than half. But with Ford and Chrysler, the Big Three have consistently controlled 90 percent of the market, give or take a few points. The typical situation in industries that lend themselves to vast operations is not that one firm controls most of the output, but rather that two to eight companies control 75 to 95 percent of the total product.

The government met this problem in part in the famous American Tobacco et. al. case of 1946. In this case the Big Three of the tobacco industry were tried together. They constituted an oligopoly, of course, and not a merger. Together, they controlled more than 80 percent of the sales in their price line. They raised and lowered prices together and to the same levels. They seemed to march in lockstep in their purchases of tobacco. They bought preemptively the kinds of tobaccos used by their rivals, who, during the depression of the 1930's, were successfully selling a very low-priced cigarette, and no explanation was offered as to how or whether this tobacco was disposed of. The Court noted that when such vast sums were spent for advertising as were spent by the Big Three, a powerful weapon was being used to combat entry of new firms.

What was really important in this case was that no direct proofs were submitted of conspiracy to fix prices of tobacco bought or sold; no written agreement was produced; no witness overheard a price-fixing conversation. The evidence was circumstantial; the Court was persuaded that there was a conscious parallelism of action; it believed that the evils of monopoly may come about without a conspiracy to monopolize; and the defendants were found guilty.

Now, obviously, the question arises as to whether the Tobacco case can be used as a precedent for other cases of oligopoly in which the lockstep is found. For example, could the Big Three in automobiles be found guilty of monopolization if it could be demonstrated that their prices rise and fall in concert and that their prices are virtually identical for competitive models? Viewing these cases and other material as well, it may be that the time has come, as the Senate Antitrust Subcommittee has stated, when "sheer power alone, without further misdeeds, should be argued as enough to violate the antitrust laws, particularly where such power has been deliberately maintained."[8]

How to Break Up Monopolies

A few pages back, in connection with the Aluminum case, the Court was quoted as stating that United States policy was "to perpetuate and preserve for its own sake and in spite of possible costs, an organization of industry into small units which can effectively compete with each other." The word "small" must be interpreted relative to markets and technology, and might mean about $0.5 billion per

[8] U.S. Senate Subcommittee on Antitrust and Monopoly, *A Study of Administered Prices in the Automobile Industry*, p. 169.

firm in steel but only $1 million for shoes, for in these magnitudes efficient firms are possible. Assuming that we are prepared to follow the policy of tolerating only the small yet efficient units, how do we go about achieving this end?

Here, prevention is easier than cure. Our battery of antitrust laws contains a provision to prevent mergers of competing corporations if merging has the effect of substantially lessening competition. Thus, no big fish can swim around in economic waters swallowing—or merging with—all the little fish, if the law is enforced. Also, a great variety of unfair practices that cause the disappearance of competitors are illegal. Some of these have already been mentioned—price discrimination, exclusive and tying contracts (the Cyclops case, page 326), and, indeed, almost any unfair practice not specifically described in the law, such as stales-clobbering (pages 326–27).

If the full force of law had been brought to bear on all American business since 1890, we should have nipped in the bud the vast agglomerations of capital which distress us so much today. But it was not. Various hampering decisions of the Supreme Court in the first quarter of the century, public apathy, unwillingness of Congress to appropriate adequate funds for enforcement, conflict of responsibility among governmental agencies—these and other causes allowed some corporations to grow up to be giants and some to become monstrous.

Now, we are faced with 15 corporations that exceed $7 billion in size, and 165 that exceed $1 billion. How do we go about cutting them down to size? First of all, we must of course find which are guilty of being in violation of our antitrust laws. Then the Court must order the guilty ones, somehow, to break up. This is authorized under the three D's of antitrust: divorcement, dissolution, and divestiture. These three measures are similar, and each results in fragmentation, though there are small differences among them. Courts are reluctant to use any of these remedies, for, in doing so, established rights of property may be violated. However, the remedy has been used to break up about two dozen firms. The first two companies dissolved were Standard Oil and American Tobacco, both in 1911. In the case of Standard Oil, the breakup was mostly a paper affair. The same men who had previously held a controlling interest in one company now held a controlling interest in several companies. Each of the new companies remained supreme within its sales area for at least 40 years afterward.[9] Dissolution of American Tobacco was not much different. Knowledgeable observers at the time thought of both attempts as rather good jokes. In more recent times (1943) the National Broadcasting Company was forced to sell its Blue Network (now ABC). The Aluminum case was a rather special one. During World War II the government built aluminum plants. These were ultimately disposed of by sale to Reynolds and Kaiser. Thus, competition—or at least potential competitors—sprang up about the time that the Aluminum Company of America was found to be a monopoly. The American company was, however, required to surrender control of its Canadian subsidiary, Aluminium Limited, and to license some of its patents on favorable terms. A rather curious aftermath of the case is that the Aluminum Company of America has been ordered not to set some of its prices too low, for fear that very low prices might injure small fabricators of similar products. The case of United Fruit reminds us of the father who orders his son to bring the switch with which he is to be chastised. The company was given 12 years to create a competitor large enough to import 35 percent of the bananas brought into this country.

In a nation which permits almost any gimcrack to be patented—as we shall see a little later—one method of promoting competition is to place a monopolist's patents into the public domain. This does not necessarily mean that anybody can use a company's patents gratis, though it may mean that. But it does mean that a company may be forced to license its patents to anybody who would like to use them, sometimes royalty-free, sometimes for a reasonable payment. This has been the fate of a whole galaxy of blue-chip companies—General Electric, Eastman Kodak, Radio Corporation of America, International Business Machines, and still others.

On the whole, the record is not an imposing one. About the best that the three D's have been able to do is to break monopolies up into oligopolies, or to force oligopolies to include a larger membership. It should not be concluded from the above, however, that the Sherman Antitrust Act, the Clayton Act, and other legislation seeking active competition and punishing restraints of trade have been completely ineffective. The record is better than that. Almost any agreement to fix

---

[9] No very recent authoritative study of this question is available; they may still be the dominant companies.

prices, when discovered, has consistently been declared illegal since 1899. The laws have dealt effectively, on the whole, with exclusive dealing, tying contracts, discriminatory pricing, and restrictive use of patent rights. Despite the frailties of our antitrust policies, we can safely say that American business is better organized in the consumer interest than it would be without antitrust legislation. We are ahead of Europe, which has not done much about antitrust, though reports state that the Common Market countries are attacking the problem and are following the American pattern.

Is Competition a Lost Cause?

Many economists and other students of the problems discussed above seem to feel that the creation or re-creation of a competitive economy composed only of many small and equipollent firms is both impossible and undesirable. We still have, of course, many small firms—millions of them, literally—but the point is that the assets of a million of the smallest would approximately equal the assets of only one company such as Prudential Insurance or Metropolitan Life Insurance, and fall by several billion dollars under those of American Telephone and Telegraph. To advocate the multiplication of small firms and the atomization of the gargantuan is widely looked upon as regressive and utopian, and as quaint as the poems of Henry Wadsworth Longfellow.

The Marxists were perhaps the first to take this position. They believed that bigness, progress, and industrial efficiency went together; that the small businessman—the *petit bourgeois*—was doomed by an ineluctable historical process; and that attempts to maintain competition among the many were ridiculous. From the viewpoint of the practical revolutionary—we go back nearly a century —it would be easier, they taught, to capture an economy in which the Marxian leadership would have virtual control of the productive apparatus after dealing with only 100 very great firms than to take over a system made of many millions of *petits bourgeois*, none of whom had a dominant place. Thus, although the Marxians always joined those who denounced business, big and little, they also thought that the concentration of industry into a few mammoth firms was a step toward socialism—a convenience, indeed, to the architects of the cooperative commonwealth.

To many of our contemporary non-Marxian economists, some of them dissenters from standard economic theory, or at least backsliders from the pure doctrines of Adam Smith, disillusionment with 19th-century competition has set in. They tend to look for regulation in the public interest from sources other than competition or antitrust legislation. John Kenneth Galbraith thinks he sees some sort of countervailing power at work. Mail-order houses, for example, have vast buying power. They can bargain rather effectively with suppliers in an oligopolistic industry and pass their savings on to the consumer. Or farmers, if they must sell on an oligopsonistic market, may seek relief in governmental subsidies. Gardiner C. Means, who has long been studying corporations and their economic impact on the economy, has suggested a plan of regulation. The essence of it is that the very largest corporations affected with a public interest—perhaps the first 100—be limited to a reasonable profit, around 8 percent. Since this might lower the incentive of corporation managers, he has devised an ingenious incentive plan for them. This is tantamount to saying: "Stay as large as you like, as long as you submit to a degree of public regulation."

Other approaches might be effective. One would be to lower tariff barriers in protected industries. Both automobile and steel have in recent years had a taste of foreign competition, and the public interest has probably gained thereby. Another would be the overhaul of our patent system. The use of government-owned and competing enterprises has been tried through TVA; elsewhere, notably in Sweden, the yardstick idea has been applied to such things as galoshes. This is contrary to our belief system and tradition of free enterprise, but so is monopoly. Federal, rather than state, chartering of corporations has been suggested as a remedy, and the suspension of the charter if their power is excessive or used in ways that are contrary to the public interest. The government might pay more attention to buying more of its supplies from small rather than so much from large corporations.

Regulation of Utilities

We now take up a totally different aspect of the preservation of competition—the case of recognized monopolies which are subject to governmental regulation.

Some monopolies are inevitable—"natural monopolies," they

are often called. It is patently uneconomic to have three competing telephone companies in the same city, and quite a nuisance to the customers. The same sort of problem arises in the case of firms that supply electricity, gas, water, bus and rail transport, and other services. Here, it is pretty obvious that to avoid duplication of expensive equipment and the constant digging-up of streets to lay mains, only one firm should serve an area of appropriate size. In such cases the government, federal or state, protects the private monopoly, but regulates it. What in effect happens is this: The government says to a telephone or electric company or similar firm: "You may have the exclusive right to sell your service in this area; but in return, you must give good service, insure safety, and charge the prices we fix; and you must sell to all who can pay without unfair discrimination." Briefly, the government, by regulation, supplies the benefits that competition is expected to supply.

The firm is then put under the supervision of a public utilities commission, which fixes prices to consumers and engages in other regulatory activities. The usual formula in price regulation by commission is that the firm is permitted to charge a rate that yields a fair return on a fair valuation of the investment. This sounds precise, but in fact it is not. Usually, the price of any investment—a piece of land or a stock certificate—is based on the income it produces (either current or prospective). If two apartment buildings, in most respects alike, yield different incomes, then the selling price of the one yielding the larger income will be higher on the market than that of the lower-yielding apartment house. In other words, income determines value of investment. But the formula applied to natural monopolies is the reverse: Determine value first, and then derive income from that. This creates an initial problem of considerable magnitude for the commission. How does it go about doing the job of valuation in reverse? Well, one might suggest going to the open market to find out what other similar utilities are worth—how much they are selling for. This works if I grow peonies to sell; I set my price by finding out what local greenhouses are charging. Why not utilities? But few of us want to buy a gas company, and there is less homogeneity in gas companies than in peonies. The market therefore is an imperfect one, and the price-fixing process in such a market depends partly on bargaining ability or power. How, then, to determine valuation by the market process? It cannot be done. The result is that valuation is thrust into the realm of legal controversy and is subject to the arts of bargaining.

Assuming now that value has been finally agreed on, by guess and by gosh, by threats, political pressure, and bluff—it has sometimes been named the "trance method," because everybody concerned goes into a trance and finally comes up with a value—the next thing to do is to determine a fair rate of return on whatever valuation was arrived at. Actual practice seems to fix this figure at 5 to 8 percent. A difference of more than $1 million of income a year may ride on a 2 percent spread between upper and lower rates. But again, somehow, a suitable percentage figure is at last arrived at—and again by the arts of bargaining. The utility is now allowed to charge rates which are estimated to produce a net income appropriate to the value of the property. Since the Court decision in the famous case of the Hope Natural Gas Company (1944), the ultimate test (in the event of litigation) is not whether values and rates have been set precisely or whether the method for arriving at the figures was the best possible method, but whether the utility's rate of return is enough to enable it to operate successfully and to compensate investors adequately. The Court stated:

If the total effect of the rate order [issued by the regulating agency] cannot be said to be unjust and unreasonable, judicial inquiry . . . is at an end. The fact that the method employed to reach the result may contain infirmities is not then important. . . . Rates which enable the company to operate successfully, to maintain its financial integrity, to attract capital, and to compensate its investors for risks assumed certainly cannot be condemned as invalid, even though they produce only a meager return on the so-called "fair value" rate base.

Sometimes the rate estimate turns out to be a bad guess. The utility may sell much more or much less of its service than had been estimated, either because the community is growing faster or slower than had been calculated or because inflation or depression has ensued or because demand elasticity had not been accurately taken into account. Whatever the reason, if the utility loses money, it is not entitled to a refund, though it may petition the commission for higher rates. And if it earns more than a fair return on fair value, it may keep the excess. When this happens, customers, particularly large industrial customers, may petition the commission for a decrease of rates, and the request may be granted. But it usually takes a long time to make such changes, and the utility may go on losing money or earning excess sums for several years before a proper adjustment is made.

Regulation of public utilities gives the consumer more protection than he would get under unregulated monopoly, of course, but there remain laxities beyond those spoken of above. One is that the regulatory commissions are often passive rather than aggressive representatives of the consumers' viewpoint. It must be said that consumers themselves are often inert, rarely well organized or alive to their own interest; they often are unable or unwilling to make the sustained effort that would be required to keep the commission on its toes. Many commissioners are untrained; their terms are often not long enough to permit learning the job. Appropriations are so small that only in a few states can a sufficiently large force of staff workers be maintained. Regulation is surrounded by a legal and courtroom atmosphere of wrangling, objections, technicalities, delay, and appeal, with the result that there is often a great lag in rate changes—a lag that may be unfairly advantageous to either consumer or company. The managers of the utilities often complain that regulation is too severe. There may of course be many cases of overly severe regulation; but on the whole, the utilities do not seem to be too hard pressed, and many investors' "growth" portfolios contain liberal quantities of utility stocks.

Commissions have few general supervisory powers over the efficiency of the campanies they regulate. It is at least theoretically possible for an inefficient firm to collect its 6 or 7 percent even though its facilities are antiquated and its management lazy and overpaid. If there were no guaranteed return, and if competition existed, such firms would have to go out of business. This, however, does not in fact describe utility firms as a whole, many of which are reputed to be technologically excellent. Whether they would be still better if they could operate under competition we have no easy way of knowing.

Thus far, we have been talking only about intrastate regulation and about areas of such size that one firm would be enough to supply local needs. The same kinds of problems, but with important variations, arise on a national or regional scale. It may be desirable to have only one gas company in Chillicothe; but it may be quite desirable to have several railroads, airlines, or bus lines between such great and important cities as Detroit and Chicago or New York and Washington. On the other hand, it would be extremely wasteful to have 10 or 20. Here, of course, state commissions have no power to act, and the federal government may intervene, since only the federal government has jurisdiction over interstate commerce.

There are five federal commissions and several major departments of government that are authorized to exercise some sort of regulatory control over a long list of interstate business activities from oil pipelines to airlines, from ships to stockyards, from railroads to sellers of investment securities, from certain kinds of toll bridges to television. One can without much trouble count some 20 areas of business enterprise in which federal regulatory commissions are expected to intervene on behalf of the public because some degree of monopoly exists or because the industry is affected with a public interest.

As has already been suggested, it is not the province of these federal commissions to regulate one firm in a limited area, but rather to regulate railroads in general, or airlines in general. They may, among other things, fix rates as do the state commissions, regulate entry of new firms, forbid or permit mergers within the regulated industry, or fix standards of safety. The last is under extremely close government control in aviation, where the Federal Aviation Agency issues takeoff clearance to pilots and guides them in landing by radar. It is beyond the scope of this book to describe this kind of regulation in detail. We shall have to leave it with the brief summary that many types of businesses affected with a public interest are constantly being supervised by governmental agencies.

Preserving the Competitor Rather than Competition

Another type of governmental regulation makes its appearance in markets in which competition is too keen. The idea underlying this form of regulation is that competition, if it becomes intense, can be disastrous to the competitors and may open the way to monopoly—to the survival of the fittest in a jungle sense. In some ways, this is the other side of the problem heretofore discussed in this chapter. It is recognition of the principle that unbridled competition can be as harmful as competition that is too lethargic. An example may be found in major branches of farming, such as the growing of wheat, corn, tobacco, and cotton. Here, with government aid, the farmers all band together, as it were, to fix a price higher than would be obtained under competition. Similar action is taken in other industries. The government aids fruit growers and dairy farmers to organize into combinations that restrict supply or dribble it into the market slowly; the rate of production of crude petroleum—gift of a highly competitive industry—is reduced by governmental action.

In retailing the government has aided firms to keep prices high through resale price maintenance laws. Such laws, often known as "fair-trade laws," both state and federal, have in their extreme forms the effect of forcing all retailers to sell well-known products at a price established by the manufacturers. This means that some cut-rate merchants and discount houses operate illegally where the laws apply. Fair-trade legislation had rough going in the Supreme Court during the 1950's; and it is possible that because of adverse decisions, resale price maintenance is on the way out. These laws have the apparent effect of protecting a manufacturer who wishes to set a national price. This is partly true, of course, but their real supporters are small retailers, particularly druggists. In 1962, Edward F. Denison of the Brookings Institution estimated that fair trade cost us 1 percent of our national income—about $25 per capita for that year.

Patents and Monopoly

The last form of regulation of competition we shall discuss—but not the last kind that might be discussed—relates to patents. No type of monopoly seems to be better founded or more deserved than a monopoly based on a patent. Our history books tell us about the great benefits conferred on mankind by such inventors as Eli Whitney, Robert Fulton, Thomas Edison, and Guglielmo Marconi. Surely, economists are not prepared to take potshots at them for being monopolists! Weren't they entitled to whatever money they may have made through their great inventions? Of course they were. Economists do not question the right of great inventors to the economic fruits of great inventions; but they do question, as leading to monopoly, certain parts of our patent legislation and the procedures associated with it. The right to patent can be abused, as we shall see presently, and may be the basis of socially undesirable business practices.

Perhaps the best place to begin this discussion is to call attention to the fact that patent protection may in fact last half a century rather than the 17 years fixed by law, because of a rich variety of procedural loopholes. Thus—under certain circumstances, at least—the protection afforded by government to a monopoly has lasted almost three times longer than that envisaged by the basic principle of the legislation.

Few patents cover inventions of the Fulton-Marconi-Edison type. Indeed, many of them protect something even lower than low cunning:

Patents have covered an indentation on the head of a screw, an eraser on the end of a pencil, rubber hand grips on bicycle handlebars, a bosom or dickie sewn onto the front of a shirt, the use of flat cord instead of round cord in the loop at the ends of suspenders, and the use of an oval rather than a cylindrical shape in a roll of toilet paper. . . . The patent that gave the Johns-Manville Corporation a monopoly of the business of insulating previously constructed buildings by blowing mineral wool into the space between the outer and inner walls was one that applied, not to the manufacture of the wool itself, nor to the machinery used in blowing it, but to the process of "providing openings to afford access to the air spaces" in existing structures . . . ; in short, it was a patent on the idea of blowing through a hole.[10]

Thus the possibility of making huge sums of money is legally protected by legislation that confers monopoly rights on those who operate on the nether levels of mechanical ingenuity. It should, however, be added that the Supreme Court has not always validated such flimsy patents when the matter came before it in patent infringement cases. Justice William O. Douglas has stated that a patent should "reveal the flash of creative genius" and has deplored the fact that it was possible for miserable little cases on trifling patents to acquire enough dignity to reach the Supreme Court. But few patent cases are taken to the Supreme Court. In the meantime, the Patent Office, pressed by low budgets and inadequate power, grants patents on the most piddling excuses for inventions; the patentee then automatically gets a legally protected monopoly. It may be 10 years—or never—before somebody catches up with him and some court invalidates his "invention" as a triviality. It should be added that Congress, revising the patent legislation in 1952, repudiated the flash-of-genius doctrine and allowed the standard of patenting to remain low.

---

[10] Clair Wilcox, *Public Policies toward Business* (Homewood, Ill.: Richard D. Irwin, Inc., 1955), p. 144. This section relies heavily on Wilcox' discussion of the patent problem in the book cited, though he obviously is not responsible for what appears here.

One of the greatest abuses of the patent is patent warfare. A typical situation in this kind of cutthroat competition would be where two companies, one large and one small, are manufacturing milk bottles. Both produce with slightly different equipment, some or all of it patented. One day the large firm decides to destroy or acquire the small firm. An easy way of doing this is to sue the small company for patent infringement. It does not matter much whether the large company has a real case or even, indeed, whether it wins or loses. The charge of infringement has plausibility, since the product is the same, and since, it may be inferred, there must be some similarity in the machines and processes. The point is that to the large company the legal expenses are only a fractional part of income; to the small company the expense may be everything. Often the only real choice left to the small company is to sell out disadvantageously to the large firm or to expire. Litigation has often been used coercively in business, and patent litigation is a particularly good field for economic combat of the strong against the weak. Some of our important companies have developed part of their present power through patent warfare, among them National Cash Register, Eastman Kodak, and United Shoe Machinery.

Allied to this sort of practice is that of building up a monopoly of patents in some specialized industrial field. Some large corporations own thousands of patents relating to the scope of their operations. Thus, almost anything a competitor does may infringe on some patent held by such a company. A few firms own almost nothing but patents and derive their income mostly from royalties.

There is occasional danger that a patent may sometimes become the basis for illegally extending the monopoly legally conferred by a patent. Suppose you patent a new kind of light bulb and start manufacturing it, but at the same time find that your factory is only large enough to supply the middle western states. You therefore decide to license your patent to manufacturers on the East and West coasts. This means that they agree to pay you a penny, let us say, for every bulb sold. So far, so good. Now, as a manufacturer, you want to sell your own bulbs in the Middle West at 50 cents apiece. Your licensees on each coast, however, are able to sell at 40 cents. You fear their competition. Thus, you stipulate in your agreement with them not only that they shall give you royalties of a penny apiece but also that they must charge 50 cents in order not to spoil your market. The penny royalty is clearly legal. But is the agreement to charge 50 cents an illegal practice? It is hard to say what the courts would do if this case were actually brought up. The Supreme Court has ruled both ways on similar cases; no two cases are ever identical, and the Court does not always rule in 1960 as it did in 1926. Whatever the law, economists would, in vast majority, rule against you and in favor of your East Coast, West-Coast licensees. Economists would say that each manufacturer in a competitive society should be free to sell at prices that reflect his ability to keep costs low and that each should be free to judge what quantity-price ratio is best for him.

There are other ways of extending a monopoly beyond the original patent, but enough has been said to indicate that our patent system may be manipulated to do more than reward the deserving inventor. In our interpretation of patent rights, we are more likely to be overgenerous to the owner of the patent than to think of the public welfare. This is a shift in our thinking, for the rights of the inventor were apparently not uppermost in the minds of the founding fathers when they drafted the constitutional clauses on the basis of which our entire patent structure was set up. They wrote: "The Congress shall have power to . . . promote the progress of science and useful arts, by securing for limited times to authors and inventors the exclusive right to their respective writings and discoveries." The emphasis is apparently on promoting the arts and sciences, presumably for the welfare of the whole society, rather than overprotecting the writer and patent owner—who is not always the inventor.

Summary and Conclusions

Business enterprise, modern and ancient, large or small, has always had to be regulated. Deceit, unfair competition, a tendency to monopolize, and similar practices, many of them identified in the Middle Ages as regrating, forestalling, and engrossing, were frowned upon by guild regulation, common law, and church law. The modern equivalent of medieval business regulation is our antitrust legislation —the Sherman Antitrust Act, the Clayton Act, and a spate of minor acts and major court decisions—all of which can be lumped together as "antitrust."

Antitrust has performed several functions well, particularly the abolition of collusive price-fixing. It has, however, done little to prevent the growth of oligopoly or to hinder the development of mammoth corporations—though it might be interesting to speculate on how much more monopolization and concentration would now characterize the American economy if pure laissez-faire had prevailed.

One of the thorny issues of antitrust is whether bigness is inherently bad. Bigness has been defended as technologically required for efficiency and for research. Reasonably large size is often needed for efficiency, but it is doubtful whether any industrial firm needs to exceed $1 billion in size to operate at peak efficiency; and many—such as makers of bread or household laundry bleaches, to take only two cases—work with utmost efficiency in plants that are almost microscopic. As for research, a few large firms in a few industries deserve blue ribbons for their research, but much of what the man on the street believes under this heading is wrong. It is hard to see what substantial benefits we get from the behemothian firms. They are, on the other hand, capable of exercising antisocial political and economic power. That they sometimes do is undeniable; it is also undeniable that they often do not. At best, the mammoth firm is a mixed blessing.

Some monopolies are desirable in the public interest, if regulated properly. One class of monopolies is named "public utilities." These are regulated under the theory that they should receive only a fair return on a fair valuation. The governmental commissions that do the regulating perform their works unevenly. On the whole, it is generally believed by impartial observers that commissions are not zealous in their efforts to protect the consumer. Another type of monopoly is that conferred by patents. One can scarcely quarrel with this sort of monopoly; but when the privilege of patenting is abused, and when the standards for granting patents are low, the public interest is not well served.

Sometimes, competition appears to be too keen. The governments sometimes protect small retailers and growers from the full force of competition by "fair-trade" laws and various kinds of farm legislation.

One need not be a very reflective person to emerge from this chapter with a sense of confusion. In one decade the Supreme Court tolerates a huge firm because, apparently, it is a good giant; in another, the Court says that no giant can ever be wholly good. In one decision the Supreme Court states that, to be patentable, an idea must reveal a flash of genius, whereas other agencies of government grant patents for such paleolithic discoveries as holes to blow through. Everybody favors competition, yet we cartelize several groups of producers in order that they may escape the rigors of competition, and we prosecute retail merchants who undersell others. We create commissions to regulate natural monopolies in order that they may serve the public interest as well as they would if competitive, and then understaff the comissions and otherwise prevent them from doing a good job. The appropriation for the Antitrust Division of the Department of Justice during the first 45 years of its existence was below $300,000 annually—about what one topnotch corporation lawyer might have earned. Though the Division has been getting nearly $4 million in recent years, even this sum is sadly inadequate to its huge task. To the ever-rational visitor from another planet, our adventures in maintaining competition must appear to be a comedy of errors rather than the sincere efforts of intelligent men.

Part of the confusion, of course, is accounted for by the passage of time. The "good giant" theory of big business goes back many years; and as the years pass, intelligent beings may reverse their former beliefs. But not all contradictions can be so explained. Some of the trouble arises out of the kind of human beings we really are. The willing of inconsistencies is a very human trait. We roundly criticize big business, and yet feel immature pride in the shiny, unsafe automobile we have just bought from one of the Big Three. We have the same sort of reverential awe of General Motors or American Telephone and Telegraph that an English cockney has of his Queen. We pass laws that make criminals of price fixers; yet when we do send two or three of them briefly to jail, we feel that these fine, civic-minded men should not have to submit to such indignity. We want keen competition in production, but no competition so keen as to exclude certain classes, like farmers and small retailers, from the high American standard of living. We feel that any business affected with a public interest needs regulation, but we deplore invasive supervision by the public authority and do little to support the regulators.

It is no easy task to reconcile all of these contradictory emotions and desires. The average citizen is less likely to try to resolve the conflicts in his mind than to fall back on prejudices acquired in childhood. In some families the tradition is to hate big business; in others the tradition is to believe uncritically all the nice things that corporations say about themselves. To absorb either of these attitudes irrevocably is to weaken one's effectiveness as a good citizen. To call for competition and laissez-faire in all circumstances, and as sacred principles, is to be ignorant of the fact that under some conditions these principles do not achieve the results we want. And to depend on governmental intervention to solve all of our difficulties is equally self-defeating.

There is no secret formula for maintaining the workable competition that will bring us a proper balance between economic liberty and governmental intervention, between the rights of individuals and the rights of society. Our only hope is that as democratic capitalism broadens its base of educated men and women—as it is most successfully doing now—the average man will develop more mature ideas than he currently has on the subject of workable competition and be better able to communicate them to his elected and appointed governors.

QUESTIONS FOR REVIEW AND DISCUSSION

1. Define, in your own words, each of the following items:
    a) Efficient size of firm
    b) Technological integration
    c) Merger
    d) Cartel
    e) Price-fixing
    f) Patent

2. A basic principle of the American belief system is that competition should prevail in our economic life. How is the term "competition" defined in this context? What are the differences between this definition and the definition of competition used in standard theory?

3. What is a public utility? Why is monopoly allowed in public utilities but not in other forms of business enterprise?

4. Government agencies responsible for the regulation of prices charged by public utilities attempt to guarantee the owners of public utilities a fair

return on their investment. Before a government agency can decide what prices will yield this fair return, it must compute the capital value of the public utility (determine the size of the owners' investment). Why not find out how much the buildings, equipment, etc., cost in the first place and then subtract for depreciation? Would a value so arrived at be fair to the utility? To the consumer?

5. "We cannot afford competition in many of our most important industries. The existence of many independent firms in these industries would raise the cost and lower the quality of the good produced." Under what conditions would this statement be valid? Invalid?

6. The Supreme Court has changed its views on the relation between bigness and competition. Discuss the views the Supreme Court has held and the Court decisions in which these views were formulated.

7. Discuss the nature of "monopoly based on patents." Under what conditions is this type of monopoly justifiable?

8. Many Americans would like to reduce the quantity of imperfect competition in our economy, but few methods are available for doing this. What methods have been used to limit the pervasiveness of imperfect competition? What difficulties are encountered when government attempts to destroy imperfect competition?

9. What is the difference between a firm and a plant, as those terms were used in the early pages of this chapter?

10. How can advertising reduce rather than stimulate competition?

11. "Patents really do not encourage invention. Among the greatest inventions of mankind were the wheel, fire, boats, the alphabet, gunpowder, windmills, and harness for oxen and horses—all invented before the patent system." Do you agree with this quoted statement? Why? Why not?

Chapter 17

THE PROBLEMS OF AGRICULTURE

Introduction

The American farm problem is as confusing a problem as any in the realm of economics. First, there is no single farm problem; there are many problems. Beginning at the bottom, we have the rural poor who eke out some kind of subsistence from the soil and who will never—miracles excepted—have enough capital, land, or skill to produce a measurable crop. What to do with them is a challenge to the Department of Health, Education, and Welfare rather than to the Department of Agriculture. This group has always included a large fraction of southern Negroes, many of whom are moving northward and bringing their poverty and problems with them to the urban ghettos—but plenty of them still languish on their barren acres.

Second, we have the middle-sized farmer. He is not without skill, land, or capital; but he competes lamely with the big boys (to be described in a moment); and the question is: Is he worth helping out and, if so, how? He is the yeoman, the head of the family farm, the resourceful, independent American beloved by all true Jeffersonians. But his relatively weak position as a producer makes him vulnerable and his survival dubious. Competition from the large, highly mechanized farms is getting to be rather tough on him.

The third group is composed of the owners of really big farms—of the haciendas of the Southwest and California, of 8,000-cow dairies (the average Wisconsin dairy, 20 cows), of chicken farms with broiler houses as long as the Washington monument lying on one side, of feedlots for cattle that nourish 40,000 head, of far-flung agricultural enterprises that require the supervision of airborne overseers.

And the above is only one way of classifying them. Another would apply the criterion of the crop. There are wheat farms, corn farms that sell their feed and corn farms that feed their grain to their own pigs and cows, apple orchards, citrus groves, cattle ranches, truck farms, tobacco farms, dairy farms, and mushroom caves—each type with its own economic and technical problems and with its particular complaints. Then there are farms which are only secondarily farms, and primarily land held for speculation, for possible ventures in oil, or for reducing the income tax of the prosperous owner. And for the operator who really knows his way around, the farm may be the basis for pecuniary gain by exploitation of the contradictions and loopholes of agricultural and tax law. Perhaps the labors of Billie Sol Estes in the early 1960's would stand as the peak of achievement in this realm had he not landed in jail. We may reasonably believe that other men are carrying on his work, less grandiosely but also less dangerously.

And this is still only part of the story. In farming, all of the headaches of the ordinary entrepreneur are compounded by the dynamism of rapid technological change, with associated changes in the structure of management, control, ownership, and financing. A good example is found in the broiler industry. To be a top producer of broilers, one must, according to the testimony of Edward Higbee, employ a geneticist and a statistician to maintain and improve strains. And to be able to afford this, one must produce in the hundreds of thousands. For the small farmer who lacks quantities of capital, the choice is to leave broiler growing or to go to work under contract for some feed dealer or chain store. The little man can get credit more easily if he has a contract with the A & P or some similar buyer. The battle for control of the poultry business is killing off thousands of independents, and some observers are saying that in the 1970's our nation will be supplied by a mere 25 companies.[1] Contract farming is moving forward in other areas, Higbee notes, as in pork, beef, and milk production. Crops that can be frozen or canned lend themselves to this type of organization.

This is but one aspect of the dynamism of agriculture. Probably no large economic sector has increased its productivity so rapidly in recent years, that is, has so much reduced inputs of land, labor, or capital without subtraction from output. Thus, in the broiler industry, 3 pounds of feed were required to produce 1 pound of chicken in 1955; since then, the University of Georgia has been able to produce 1

[1] Edward Higbee, *Farms and Farmers in an Urban Age* (New York: Twentieth Century Fund, 1963), pp. 27 ff.

pound of meat out of 1.88 pounds of feed. In 1880, it took 20 man-hours to produce an acre of wheat; now two hours will do the job—which means that a bushel can be produced with about five minutes of work. A bushel of corn takes less. One could go on citing these *gee-whiz!* figures indefinitely, and they would apply not only to labor requirements but also to land requirements—24 bushels of something per acre in 1950 and 52 bushels of the same something today, and so, and so on.

A further example of dynamism is to be noted in the need of the farmer to adjust to synthetics and similar substitutes. Margarine has obviously hurt the dairy industry; housewives have virtually stopped buying wool blankets because the new textiles are easier to wash and do not attract moths; oats, once the chief feed for the mules or horses that pulled our plows and carriages and fire engines and brewery trucks, have been supplanted by gasoline. Detergents have reduced the demand for the soapmaking fats; paints no longer require turpentine or linseed oil; plastics replace leather. The freezing of fruits and of the preferred green vegetables has reduced the demand for the old root vegetables that were our winter mainstays—potatoes, turnips, rutabagas, winter squash, and the like.

Perhaps the next big problem to face the farmers is higher wages. The farmers' employees have been systematically overlooked by minimum-wage legislation and by laws to guarantee freedom of association. Though headway toward these forms of protection has not gone far, the beginnings are here. Labor costs have been low for the farmer until now; but the future is not bright as demands for higher wages become increasingly insistent.

In this rapidly changing world stands the small farmer, still at the mercy, as was his ancestor, of drought, insect plagues, flood, frost, and animal and plant disease. No wonder he has problems. His numbers have diminished appreciably in recent years. In 1919 the farming population amounted to 30 percent of all Americans; in 1965 the farming population accounted for only 6.4 percent of the total. It is estimated that this last figure will drop to 5 percent in 1975. The number of farms has diminished, too. It has fallen from 6.5 million in 1919 to 3.4 million in 1965. But the size of each farm has jumped surprisingly in the same period, from 150 acres to 340. The figures do more than suggest that farms have passed from weak to strong hands.

And they point toward the conclusion that the small Jeffersonian farm lives in nostalgia rather than in the future.

Farm Income

At the heart of the farm problem—as of so many other economic problems—lies an insufficiency of income, or rather a *feeling* that income is insufficient. The facts are a little elusive here, and we must be careful in our statement of the issue. At the bottom of the pile, we find about 1.6 million "farm" families that do not form part of the farm problem at all. Many are hobbyists or retired persons who putter about on the land and whose product is low, but who are not necessarily poor and whose plight need not detain us. However, about one third of a million Mexican and Negro families, in the South and Southwest mostly, are seriously trying to make their wretched livings by husbandry. They were classified in the preceding section as the proper objects of rehabilitation effort and poor relief rather than as objects of agricultural concern.

After subtracting this whole group of 1.6 million, we have about two million farm families left, with gross farm incomes of $2,500 or better. As a rule of thumb, it may be said that net farm income runs about one third of gross income. Thus the farmers at the low end of this upper group get net incomes of only $833 from land cultivation. The upper end of this group includes farms that net around $0.5 million or more.

In between the destitute and an upper crust of about 100,000 farms lies a middle class that numbers some 1.8 million farms— about half the total. They produce about 63 percent of the entire value of farm crops.

Counting the upper crust and the middle class together, the average income of this combined group during most of the 1950's ranged between $4,000 and $5,000 a year from farm income alone. But from other sources, such as investments or work off the farm, the members of this class were able to supplement their incomes by sums that averaged about $1,200 a year. Hence the plight of this group is not really bad; yet in some of their worst years, such as 1957 and 1959, their average family income was about $2,000 less than that of nonfarm families. In their best year, 1951, they actually were ahead of the nonfarm families; after that, their relative position deteriorated sharply. All farm incomes spoken of above include in them the supplements provided by the government in the form of price supports and other forms of aid. Thus, we come to a rather important generalization: In the 1950's, even after disregarding the families at the bottom of the ladder, the incomes of farm families were appreciably lower than those of nonfarm families.

This generalization is, however, subject to a few qualifications and comments. First, in years of extreme demand, such as 1951 (Korean War), farmers do very well, even better than their city cousins. Second, farmers are in a favorable position to avoid reporting income and hence to avoid paying taxes on it; annual undeclared farm income has been estimated at $4 billion—about $1 billion of unpaid taxes. Third, the incomes cited may have a downward bias; some competent observers believe that income in kind derived from the farm (garden vegetables, for example) is appraised at too low a figure in estimating income. Fourth, this qualification may itself be qualified by noting that farm people usually do not have as good schools, medical care, recreational opportunities, art galleries, and so forth as city people. Finally, this generalization, though limited to the 1950's, applies to many other decades as well; the farm family has a lower income over the years than the nonfarm family.

Now, standing back and looking at this group of about two million families, which are the true concern of farm policy and whose members are constantly declining, as the 1970 census will no doubt show, we can see that there is indeed a low-income problem, but not a very desperate one. Low incomes abound in our economy, even among entrepreneurs—among retailers, among independent repairmen, among hairdressers, realtors, and morticians. Why does everybody "have kittens" about the farmer, while calmness reigns elsewhere about the thousands of small entrepreneurs who stand at the verge of poverty?

There are many answers. One is a blend of sentimentality and romanticism. We attribute vast integrity to countrypeople. They are the salt of the earth. If they complain, their murmurings must be more honest than the complaints of other groups. They and their virtuous daughters have been exploited and leered at by villainous, ugly mortgagers, who are animated by the spirit of business enterprise in its greediest form. It is hard to feel as much sympathy for realtors or morticians and their daughters.

Next, we feel that they do have unusual economic problems. A century ago, they began making us aware of their exploitation by bankers who charged high interest rates; by railroads that absorbed their profits in freight charges; by buyers who formed oligopsonies (before the word was invented); by the meat trust, sugar trust, and other trusts that sold on monopolistic markets while they, poor things, sold on competitive markets. How much of this is true is open to question, though not all of it can be completely false. Many economists point out that other groups in the community have had to contend with the same costs and types of markets, and have asked for and received less countervailing aid than farmers.

Economists are rather unanimous, however, on one great economic disadvantage of the farmer, namely, his vulnerability to both inelastic supply and inelastic demand. This means, looking first at demand, that a small decrease in price does not pick up many new customers. The reason is, of course, that we can eat only limited amounts; these amounts most of us eat anyhow, and relatively few of us would buy appreciably more of such staples as bread, ground beef, milk, and the like if the price fell a penny or two. Thus, when crops are abundant and prices begin to fall, they have to fall rather far before buying support makes itself felt in the market. Looking now at the supply side, what we find is that farmers tend—within limits, of course—to grow as much as they can, regardless of price. If prices are high, they grow a lot for the usual reasons; but if prices are low, they still produce heavily, since they can do little else with their land, labor, and machinery. There are few alternative uses for these factors of production. Because of their special circumstances, farmers are sluggishly responsive to the supply-and-demand thermostat, which, in so many cases, calls forth a large quantity when prices are high and a smaller quantity when prices are low.

This inelastic demand-and-supply situation can of course work in favor of the farmer as well as against him. It can send prices up rather far in years of great demand, as in wartime. And as a matter of fact, farmers do very well in such emergencies. But these years of great demand are relatively few, though wars are distressingly frequent. Besides, the farmer learns each year how to produce more. His productivity has increased fantastically over the years, without much regard to demand. When he sets out to produce as much as he can, he produces more than the market will absorb at rewarding prices. Farm output per man-hour increased threefold in the period between 1940 and 1960 and almost doubled between 1950 and 1960.[2] With tractors, new fertilizers, better seed, and other improvements in technology, agriculture has become one of the most progressive sectors of the economy. But the farmer's recompense has not kept pace with his physical productivity. It has been estimated that a 5 percent increase in supplies "results in farm prices dropping 15 to 30 percent or more."[3]

Inelasticity of demand and supply is not the farmer's only problem. The fact is that few promising new outlets are visible to him. All advanced countries are learning to produce more food on less land with less labor. We cannot appreciably increase our rate of exports to them. And the backward countries, though still hungering, cannot pay for the food they need. But even they may be expected to increase their own production of foodstuffs eventually, not import more of ours. To be sure, in some lines where our technology excels, we may be able to capture a few markets. At the moment, we seem to have a great advantage in poultry production and are exporting broilers in vast numbers. The world's population of domestic animals is increasing, and this stimulates our sales of feed grains. But when all is said and done, the outlook for increasing rates of exports of farm products is not bright.

We have frequently been urged to use our surpluses constructively, as gifts to improve the health of our own poor and to win friends among the undernourished abroad. In both areas, we are already doing about as much as our institutions and our foreign policy objectives will permit. But let us first note that, unprocessed, many of our surplus foods are scarcely edible. What is a young American widow on relief, with three small children, expected to do with a bushel of surplus oats or 100 pounds of parched corn? Oats are not Cheerios, and parched corn is not cornflakes. Most surplus

2 *Economic Policies for Agriculture in the 1960's* (Materials Prepared for the Joint Economic Committee, 86th Cong., 2d sess. [Washington, D.C.: U.S. Government Printing Office, 1960]), p. 4.

3 *Ibid.*, p. 14.

"foods" must be processed before we recognize them as foods, and processing is expensive and would be resented by the taxpayer. Our most persistent surpluses do not take the form of apples, beans, lettuce, celery, and other crops that can be eaten directly. To a lesser degree, this would be true of gifts to backward foreign nations; what we have to give them is not always what they need most, but what we least want. There are, moreover, other problems. Backward nations are deficient in facilities for transport and distribution and would be overwhelmed by great quantities of food dumped on their docks. American public opinion is outraged when it learns that our surplus food sometimes falls into the hands of unscrupulous speculators who withhold it from its intended beneficiaries. Backward nations would like to receive our surpluses if they could be counted on—so many tons each year for a stipulated period, say six years. They would then be able to integrate their own plans for production and disposal with their receipts from us. But our system of government, with its frequent elections and weathercock policies, is not hospitable to long-range commitments.

In short, then, almost the only safe place to look for new outlets, whether by sale or by gift, is among the newcomers in the world, that is, our growing population. And the trouble is that as far as our own country is concerned, agricultural productivity is rising at a much faster rate than our population.

How Government Increases Farm Income

Our next problem is to find out what the government does to help the farmer overcome his handicaps. Let us first take note of the fact that the government is particularly sensitive to the difficulties of farmers—indeed, surprisingly so, when one considers that there are less than four million farm families in the United States, representing less than one 10th of the total population. As is well known, however, rural areas are overrepresented in the state and federal legislative chambers. Supreme Court redistricting decisions of the early 1960's may in due course of time remedy these inequities, but in the meantime the rural areas possess greater legislative power than their numbers warrant. Besides their own multiplied strength, farmers have powerful allies in various nonfarm groups. Obviously, everybody who sells to farmers, from small-town merchants to the giant chemical companies that make fertilizer, will consider sympathetically any legislation that increases the farmer's purchasing power. Many urban congressmen vote for farm measures; most agricultural legislation would be defeated if their passage depended on the farm vote alone. Finally, the farmer has had the benefit, as the factory and construction workers have not, of a compassionate public.

For several decades the government has done many and contradictory things to help farmers. It has undertaken research and given advice through its agents; in recent years, it has given farmers $0.25 billion worth of limestone and fertilizer free. One is sometimes amazed at how various agencies of government conspire to increase production at the same time that other agencies seek to restrict it.

The systems of restriction are many. One is the "marketing order." When this method is used, the government suspends the operation of the antitrust laws in order to allow producers and shippers of certain farm products to determine how many bushels or barrels or crates will be sent to market. The people involved thus form a cartel (a combination to further the members' economic interests) which receives the benediction of the Secretary of Agriculture. The cartel is not used for any of the principal farm products except milk. Most of the marketing orders are used for fruits, vegetables, nuts, turkeys, and similar minor crops.

The Soil Bank is another restrictive device. As is widely known, the Soil Bank is composed of acres formerly productive of crops which the government now rents and does not use for the growing of foodstuffs. One difficulty with this system is that it involves the withdrawal of only one of the factors of production. The farmer can—and does—after renting land to the government, concentrate more labor, capital, and entrepreneurial skill on his remaining fields; his total crop may be as large as it was before turning over some of his land to the government. Another trouble is that aimless, random, and sporadic renting of a few acres, though profitable to the farmer, does little good to the nation as a whole. If large, contiguous areas were permanently acquired and turned into forests, parks, water storage sites, and the like, the program would make more sense. Actually, such attempts have been made in some areas; but in 1957, less than one fourth of the total number of 28 million acres in the Soil Bank was put to long-run constructive and conservation uses. Payments that year averaged about $25 an acre, and a little more the following year.

The best-known and most widely publicized system of farm relief is the support price. Basically, the way this works is that the government guarantees a certain price per bushel, bale, or pound. If, when the crop is ready, the farmer can get more than the government support price on the free, open market, he may sell it on that market. But if the free market price is lower than the support price, he can sell to the government. Actually, the process is a bit more involved, since a system of government lending before buying figures in the procedure; but essentially, the process is as described. In return for the privilege of selling to the government, however, the farmer must previously have agreed to cut down the acreage planted.

Support prices are usually set high enough to be attractive to farmers; therefore, they produce abundantly under their guarantees. Acreage limitations, unless extreme, do not prevent them from growing huge crops. They simply pile on the fertilizer to compensate for their acreage cutbacks. This has been the typical situation in wheat and the feed grains. In tobacco, however, the cutback system worked for a while. Cotton, too, fared moderately well under the price support program. In the autumn of 1961, cotton experts were saying that the current cotton stocks were a reasonable reserve rather than a surplus, and that the 1961 crop would be half a million bales below needs. However, as recently as the summer of 1967, we had a large surplus again.

In recent decades, we have had various programs for agriculture, but basic to them all was the overpricing of wheat by the government and the inevitable overproduction of wheat by farmers despite acreage cuts. Between the late 1940's and the early 1960's, acreage was reduced from 70 million acres to 52 million, but bushels per acre increased from 17 to 26. During part of this period, it was estimated that the support price of wheat was overpriced by at least 20 percent.[4]

The situation in corn is basically the same. Here, too, we have overpriced and fantastically increased yields per acre—from about 35 bushels in the late 1940's to 53 in the early 1960's. But there are

[4] T. W. Schultz, "A Guide to Better Policy for Agriculture," *Consumer Reports,* April, 1954, p. 186.

differences, too: The acreage decline has been smaller, the over-pricing has not been so high, and the surplus is relatively smaller. The number of bushels produced is much greater—two and three times as much—but corn as feed is the basis of many animal products. Much of it never reaches the market, for it is used by farmers as the raw material for the products they sell—hogs, milk, and beef.

Before leaving this subject of overpricing, we should say a word about one of the well-known pricing formulas used, often designated by the word "parity." It is not really very important for a beginner's purpose to understand the word, but since it often appears in discussions of agricultural problems, it will be safer to describe it here. The concept of parity harks back to the period 1910–14, the best peace-time years the American farmer ever had. Let us assume that in those years the proceeds of the sale of 100 bushels would have bought for the farmer an assortment of goods and services as follows: six pairs of socks, two pairs of shoes, a dress for his daughter, a subscription to a magazine, a ton of coal, a visit to the doctor, and a six months' supply of coffee, salt, sugar, flour, and tobacco. Now the current parity price of wheat is a price such that the farmer today will be able again to get an equal assortment of goods and services through the sale of an equal quantity of wheat. The idea has been more pithily summarized in this statement: "If a bushel of wheat was worth a man's shirt in 1910, then a bushel of wheat should be worth a man's shirt today." Governmental statisticians calculate the parity price; in the summer of 1963, it was $2.50 a bushel for wheat. But the support price, set by the Congress or some other agency of government, is not always equal to the parity price; it is lower—20 percent lower for wheat in 1963. Thus the support price does not guarantee the present farmer a living as good as his father's or grandfather's 50 years before; the parity price does, however, keep before the eyes of the Congress and of the executive a figure with which they must not completely lose contact.

Recent Developments in the Farm Problem

A review of farm developments during the past few years, ending in the summer of 1967, will suggest the sort of wonderland in which agricultural policy resides. In April of 1965, President Lyndon B. Johnson proposed a new farm bill extending the then current farm bill for two years, but also making certain modifications which were designed to reduce costs, raise farm income, place greater reliance on the free market, and withdraw 40 million acres of land from production. Some of the costs were to be passed on to the consumer (which, basically, is no change at all). Various other highly technical changes were to be made, which would take us further into the details of the farm program than most of us would care to go.

Six months later, in October of 1965, the reports from Washington stated that the United States was running out of surplus foods! But not cotton or tobacco, where we still had bothersome surpluses. The chief reason for this was that we had been able to ship more food abroad than before. Some of it was sold in the usual way; some of it was disposed of under a variety of generous terms to poor nations.

In November of 1965 the President signed the new farm bill. It followed many of his April recommendations. The old Soil Bank now became the "Scenic Soil Bank," since much of it was to be used for parks and other forms of rural beautification. *The Wall Street Journal* described it as an act "to tighten the reins on farm output and spur exports"—both, obviously, means to reduce surpluses or prevent them. These goals were to be achieved again by rather complex arrangements, including the old one of withdrawing acreage from production and the new one of lower guaranteed prices to the farmer —prices close to market prices. In the bill, before passage by Congress, one provision had called for a limit to the amount paid to large farmers in the form of benefits. Since a few government price support loans have approached and even exceeded $1 million and many have been made in the $50,000–$100,000 bracket, it is pretty clear that agricultural aid is not confined to the "Momma, Poppa, and son Hank" family farm. To be sure, these loans are not outright benefits. Some are paid back if the price of the produce is high; if not, the government keeps the produce and sells it for what it can get. The point to note is whether the taxpayer is trying to help large operators or the small, industrious, virtuous family farmer. But to return to the bill; it was passed without the provision limiting payments to large operators.

About six months later, in the spring of 1966, as farm news began making seasonal headlines, the business and financial journals wrote pleased and purring articles about the farm problem. "Natural" prices were close to support prices; surpluses were dwindling; eastern

Europe and Japan were eating more and hence buying more American produce; the United States was expanding aid to underdeveloped nations and thus absorbing surpluses. The picture was rosy—so rosy in the fall of 1966 that the government began to call into production farmland that had previously been taken out of production. Emergency reserves of some products were low.

Then came another winter. In the spring of 1967, strange new stories began to appear in the papers. At the end of March (1967) the president of a large farm organization said that farm unrest was at its highest point in years. Milk producers were "striking" and dumping milk as a gesture of protest against low prices. A *Wall Street Journal* headline (April, 1967) ran as follows: "High Costs, Low Income Dash Farmers' Hopes for 1967, Stir Anger." With subsidies, farmers could get $2 a bushel for wheat, but they could also get $2 in 1951 when costs were lower. They regretted their large plantings of the previous year, when prospects had been so bright. The government had been increasing purchases of meat to sustain price. Foreign aid programs were less generous than had been forecast. Farm prices were declining. In the latter part of the spring, May 10, 1967, *The Wall Street Journal* reported a huge and stubborn surplus of cotton. One trouble with this surplus is that it is composed largely of short-fiber cotton, which has difficulty finding markets even in Japan, Hong Kong, Taiwan, and Korea. New textile machinery rejects the short fibers. The Department of Agriculture would like to stop accepting short-fiber cotton or, at least, reduce support prices for the inferior cotton, but political considerations must be taken into account: Much of the short-staple cotton comes from Texas, a most important state politically.

In midsummer 1967, corn prices were dropping as observers noted that good weather was assuring a record crop. Soybeans, too, were declining in price, but they did not threaten to become an unmanageable surplus. Farmers in the nonproblem crops were doing well—tomatoes, potatoes, and eggs. But farm prices in general were 4 percent lower than they had been a year before.

On August 18, 1967, President Johnson held a press conference and, among other things, spoke of the farm problem. He said that the farmer is on the short end of the stick; that the farm price situation is one of the most serious problems we have in this country. He urged collective bargaining for farmers. On the same day, members of his administration called for quick action by Congress to raise falling grain prices. The Under Secretary of Agriculture urged passage of a bill allowing the government to stockpile millions of bushels of wheat, feed grains, and soybeans. This would cost $200 million the first year, perhaps more.

And this ends our story of the recent past. It can perhaps be summarized by saying that things have not changed much despite the comprehensive farm act of the early winter of 1965, which was supposed to benefit everybody, reduce the need for governmental intervention, and increase farm income. Things had not changed much in a quarter century.

Proposed Solutions

As the account given above suggests, agriculture in the United States is in an untidy condition. One third of our farmers are among the lowest people on the income ladder. The other two thirds are appreciably below the nonfarm average despite the various forms of aid given them, and we have mentioned only a few. Space forbids our going into the issues involved in the milk, sugar, and wool programs. Examining them would open up other vistas of economic inefficiency. A basic inefficiency of most of the programs is, of course, that the valuable resources of land, labor, capital, and entrepreneurship are being used to produce things we do not want—indeed, some things we cannot even give away. Another is that our technology has moved forward more rapidly than our knowledge of how to cope with abundance. Besides this, crops eventually spoil in storage; we have paid as much as $1.5 million daily simply to store what is not needed. We are, however, storing less now, and things are better. The professed goal of saving the family farm is not being attained—if by "family farm" we mean establishments of relatively small size and modest capital. Finally, the various programs leave loopholes for graft or sharp practice, as the famous Billie Sol Estes case of 1962 indicates. Agriculture seems to be an activity that responds neither to the undirected forces of supply and demand nor to human planning.

What can be done? It would be rather easy for any fledgling economist to lay down a general plan: Lower support prices, and let the government guarantee to buy only a certain number of bushels (or bales or tons), not the produce of a certain number of acres. Half the textbooks of America contain diagrams to clarify the truism that if a price is arbitrarily set above the equilibrium price, producers will supply more than would be supplied at a lower price. The seemingly obvious conclusion is to lower support prices. But it is not too easy to lower support prices and limit production rigidly. The considerable political power of the farmer, of the organizations he belongs to, and of his suppliers is opposed to both lower prices and stringent control of the amount of produce the government will buy. Serious proposals seeking to limit acreages drastically, at least in the wheat and feed grain sectors, are described as "regimentation." In June of 1962 the Kennedy administration sponsored a bill that was intended to impose strict controls on grain production. It was roundly defeated. Press comments from Newark, New Jersey, to Portland, Oregon, ran like this: "Its defeat is a victory for freedom of action on the farms. . . . The old law of supply and demand should be given another chance. . . . President Kennedy's farm bill was a monstrous bill. . . . It was as close to socialism as any farm proposal has ever been."[5] President John F. Kennedy himself, commenting on the bill, said:

On the farm bill, when we got defeated . . . there were powerful interests against it. . . . There was the opposition of those who store surpluses. They like to have additional surpluses built up. There are $9 billion of them now, but they want more because they make money out of them. Then there were those who want cheap feed . . . the more surpluses there are, the cheaper the feed is. So that those who feed livestock, they do not want it.

Then there are other parts of the country who want to plant corn, and who figure that if there are restraints on production, they won't be able to plant it. So there are powerful interests built up.[6]

Others have suggested that slowly all (or nearly all) of the farm program be allowed to die and that agriculture be left to the operation of the "law" of supply and demand. As a matter of fact, several sectors of agriculture seem to get along rather well without price supports or detailed governmental intervention. Livestock, vegetables, fruits and nuts, and poultry and eggs, which account for about half of the farm income, are virtually unsubsidized. However, most of these

[5] "Opinion of the Week: At Home and Abroad," *New York Times*, June 24, 1962, Sec. 4, p. E 9.

[6] President's press conference of June 27, 1962, as reported in *The Wall Street Journal*, June 28, 1962, p. 10.

products are of elastic demand and are therefore better regulated by market forces. It has been argued by those who would like to see agriculture returned to laissez-faire that the various support programs are legacies of the depression of the 1930's and of the war of the 1940's. Since, presumably, we are now living again in quiet and normal times, agriculture should be returned to the forces of supply and demand.

This last argument is not quite valid. It is of course true that direct price supports and controls date from the 1930's; but since the Civil War, and barring a few periods of war or rising prices, the American farmer has considered himself to be a grade B citizen, deprived of his share of the increasing income of the nation. The Populist party of the 1890's grew out of the agrarian discontent that had been generated by the depression of the 1890's. A doughty female orator of the day achieved transitory fame by urging the farmers to raise less wheat and more hell. William Jennings Bryan's famous "Cross of Gold" speech may be looked upon as a proposal to increase farm prices by inflation. The 1920's, which in retrospect seem to be a period of overflowing prosperity and gaiety, were a period of increasing poverty and gloom for the farmer. Many people believe that, other things being equal, a return to free enterprise in cotton, tobacco, and the grains would be economically disastrous. We should also perhaps take note of the fact that supply and demand work better in a relatively static situation. Agriculture has been so dynamic in recent years that other forms of regulation must be sought.

Research done by Walter W. Wilcox for the Joint Economic Committee of the Congress of the United States indicates that if present programs were dropped and not replaced by others, farm income "would drop several billion dollars." He goes on to write:

Projections of farm production, prices and income for 1965 indicate a drop in net income of 36 percent from 1959 and 45 percent from 1958 if production controls and price supports are discontinued. Prices of the price-supported crops of cotton and wheat would drop 30 to 50 percent. Prices of the uncontrolled feed grains and livestock would drop 10 to 30 percent below recent levels. The index of prices received by farmers would decline 21 percent from 1959.[7]

[7] *Economic Policies for Agriculture in the 1960's.* Materials prepared for the Joint Economic Committee (86th Cong. 2d sess.) (Washington, D.C.: U.S. Government Printing Office, 1960), p. 14.

The chief reason for our difficulty in finding a cure for our farm problems is that we are not clear as to what we really want to achieve. For example, it is easy to say that we must adjust supply to demand, but this leaves out important social, political, and international issues. To take a case, should we make this adjustment without regard to the survival of the "family farm"? It can be argued that this socio-economic unit is valuable to American civilization and should be preserved. But the opposite can also be argued, namely, that it is an expensive luxury. The "factories in the field" are not only more efficient producers, but they probably also have sufficient reserves to tide them over the bad years, years of insects or drought or abnormally low prices—for the larger problems of the farmer include the smaller problem of occasionally vast income fluctuations. Another unclarified goal is whether we really want to improve the diets of our schoolchildren through the school lunch program and of our unemployed through weekly food packages or some sort of enlarged stamp plan—a plan to issue scrip which may be used by recipients of welfare checks at any grocer's for food and which the grocer can then redeem for real money. In that case, we must plan for surpluses of milk, eggs, meat, and vegetables, not hold surpluses of corn, wheat, and cotton in storage. Somewhat the same observation may be made concerning aid to backward nations. If we really want to help them, we must produce the food and fibers and seeds that will strengthen their economies and then gear our production to their requirements over the whole period of their dependency on us. If we really want to move the lowest 350,000 families off the land and into industry or the service occupations, then we must not only carry out efficiently the programs of retraining and rehabilitation which we now so falteringly have put into execution, but we must also see that our economy is one of growth and full employment. A southern Appalachian hillbilly or coal-mining discard, living on a wooded hillside in his picturesque but tumbledown cabin, getting a relief check and surplus commodities, probably feels that he is better off than he would be as a member of the urban unemployed in a city slum. Actually, the problem of getting people off the land is not too difficult if there is any place to go. Even under present circumstances, with considerable unemployment in the cities, young people are leaving the farm. Contrary to the romantic notions of some, farming is not a delightful way of life or a preferred occupation.[8] Finally, we must make a choice between freedom and regimentation; or rather, we must test out whether stricter controls on production do deprive farmers of essential liberties. In any event, we have here a problem of values—control versus freedom—which is not entirely a problem of economics.

If we really were looking for a one-shot solution of the farm problem, it is quite probable that full employment combined with a high rate of economic growth would come closer to providing the solution than any other single thing. Getting jobs easily in factories or the service occupations would lure excess farmers off the farm at a rate even faster than their current rate of migration. Increasing purchasing power by full employment would not only increase consumption of farm products, but it would also shift demand toward the proteins, and from mere protein to the more desirable ones, such as steak and chops. This would increase the market for the feed grains. Filet mignon is corn in its finest hour. To say that full employment would cure all problems instantly would of course be to claim too much. There are no specifics in economics as there sometimes are in medicine. The unresponsiveness of some of our great crops to the forces of supply and demand will continue in good years and bad. But there can be no question that in an economy of full employment, what now bulks large as the "farm problem" will assume lesser proportions.

Summary and Conclusions

Governmental aid to the farmer takes a bewildering variety of forms from subsidies for research to the encouragement of cartels exempt from antitrust legislation. The programs of aid are so numerous and so diverse, and are changed so often by federal and state legislation, that it is doubtful whether any but a relatively few specialists possess more than a smattering of knowledge of what is being done. These bounties, aids, and subsidies, though perhaps unusual in that the sums involved are large, do not really conflict with the American policy of subventions to politically powerful minorities.

Many reasons and rationalizations have been given to explain the existence of our far-flung program of farm aid. The chief one is that

[8] Schultz, *op. cit.*, p. 186.

farmers are by low incomes denied access to the generous American standard of living. It is certainly true that a million or more people living on our worst farms are among the poorest Americans. But surely, our farm subsidies are not primarily for them, since they are able to profit but little from the chief benefits of subsidy. If this group is classed as a problem of human and community rehabilitation rather than as a problem of agriculture, farm poverty is not nearly so great as it is sometimes made to appear. It is true that in normal peacetime years the incomes of the middle and upper group are less than those of their city cousins; it is true, too, that many of the lower middle group facing the competition of the huge mechanized farms may feel insecure about the future, but this is also the plight of many independent retailers and many small manufacturers. When all is said and done, however, farmers' incomes are low and fluctuating.

Other reasons and rationalizations would lay emphasis on the fact that farmers without aid would operate under conditions of perfect competition, whereas they are forced to buy on markets that are largely oligopolistic. Moreover, they would sell under peculiarly difficult competitive circumstances—on markets characterized by inelastic demand and inelastic supply and sometimes oligopsony. Some students lay stress on the fact that the farmer was hit particularly hard by the depression of the 1930's; he had become almost a ward of the state by 1934. Depression was followed by war, which required active encouragement of the farmer if our needs and the needs of our allies were to be met. The net effect of this backing is that the farmer has become so much accustomed to aid that governmental withdrawal now would be ruinous to him. Other students of the problem would call attention to the farmer's political importance. Though his numbers are dwindling and his political power is doomed to disappear, we still have a rotten-borough system that causes disproportionate farm representation in our state and national legislative halls. This situation obviously results, it is argued, in laws that have the effect of taxing the city folks so that their country cousins may enjoy a fuller life. It is not easy to assign precise weights to the reasons given above—and others that might be advanced—but it is likely that they all contain a little truth and serve to justify farm subsidies.

The most expensive and most spectacular of our farm subsidies relate to cotton, tobacco, wheat, and the feed grains. The basic system of subsidy here is that the federal government asks growers to decrease the acreage planted and then rewards those who curtail the amount of land cultivated by guaranteeing to buy the whole crop at prices that are generally favorable to the farmer. These support prices may be lower than those subsequently set by the forces of supply and demand, in which case the farmer may sell where he pleases. Withdrawal of the one factor, land, does little to curtail the size of crops, because a currently dynamic agricultural technology teaches growers every year to raise more bushels on fewer acres. Surpluses develop, which the government acquires and for which it finds relatively few outlets.

In the final analysis, there is probably little we can do to remedy this situation until we can make migration away from the farm more appealing than it now is. Farms are being abandoned by the young, and even by older persons, in large numbers, for farming is less attractive than the romantic imagination pictures it to be. But the land is not being abandoned fast enough. If more jobs were open in the manufacturing, trade, and service industries, migration from the farm would increase and probably bring about, with much smaller subsidies, a better balance between town and country. Full employment would also cause a greater consumption of farm products and might stimulate desirable shifts from the production of cereals for human consumption to the more desirable foods, such as beef and lamb.

QUESTIONS FOR REVIEW AND DISCUSSION

1. Define, in your own words, each of the following terms:
   a) Agriculture
   b) Oligopsonistic market
   c) Marketing order
   d) Soil Bank
   e) Support prices
   f) Food stamp plan
2. "There are two farm problems in the United States. One is a problem of plenty, the other of paucity." Discuss.
3. Describe some of the methods employed by the federal government to limit farm production. What results does the government expect to attain through the use of these policies?

4. "The major enemies of the American farmer are inelastic supply and demand." Analyze this statement by drawing supply-and-demand diagrams.

5. A government policy of price supports and production controls for agricultural products will not eradicate poverty from agriculture. What types of government policies could help to eliminate poverty from agriculture? Are these policies different from those that can be designed to eliminate urban poverty?

6. America has avoided using the "free market" as a means of handling its farm problems. How would the free market go about solving our farm problems? What arguments can be given in support of using the free market? What are the arguments against it?

7. One of the most formidable blocks to the creation of the European Economic Community (Common Market) was the difficulty of combining the agricultural policies of the six member countries in one uniform program. By using the resources available in your school library on the Common Market countries, gather information about the different agricultural problems faced by these countries and the policies by which they have attempted to solve them. How will the agricultural program of the Common Market affect the agricultural situation in the United States?

8. Why is our policy of giving away surpluses to underdeveloped nations often ineffective and sometimes little appreciated?

Chapter 18

POVERTY AND ITS ALLEVIATION

Recognition of the Existence of Unnecessary Poverty

Human history has not concerned itself much with "the short and simple annals of the poor." Taking the form of slaves, of serfs, or of dirty, smelly factory hands, or repulsive Bowery bums, or sweaty field Negroes, the poor have been virtually denied recognition as full-fledged human beings by the more opulent classes. Not all of this neglect can be put down as heartlessness. After all, most of us are rather ignorant of the subcultures of other groups in the same community. F. Scott Fitzgerald believed—probably rightly—that the rich really think and act differently from other classes; and most of us in the middle classes have only a glimmer of what goes on in the more exalted circles of government, wealth, and power. Café society understands little of the social life or aspirations of atomic scientists. Businessmen do not fully comprehend academic people. It may be a convenience to the guilty conscience of prosperous America that the very poor do such a good job of concealing themselves, but beyond this lies a sort of ethnocentrism which dims our view of any group unlike our own.

In recent years, however, we have become increasingly aware of the American poor. We seem to be more willing—or able—than we were a generation ago to give recognition to the least prosperous group of this nation. Several forces have combined to bring this about. One of them is certainly the audible cry of the Negro as he has marched through our streets demanding equal civil rights. Beneath this demand for equal rights lies entreaty for greater economic opportunity and for jobs. Most of what we knew authentically about the lower depths before World War I was dredged up by rather unusual investigators who went down into the slums, as if they were diving in the darkest and most forbidding waters, and brought back amazing stories from the murk: Jack London, Jacob Riis, Upton Sinclair, and, in England, Charles Booth. But since then, we have accumulated much information; and in addition, we possess statistics on income distribution, property ownership, and the like—statistics that only began to be collected during the great depression of the 1930's. From these, we can make inferences about how poor people live even in their invisibility. Our changing attitudes toward crime are causing us to wonder whether we cannot attack evildoing more successfully by reducing poverty than by increasing penalties. Urban decay multiplies our glimpses of destitution, and these glimpses are sometimes shocking. Automation and its power to rob men of jobs are matters of growing concern. Many other forces could be named, but perhaps the most important of them all is the increasingly obvious gap between technological capability and institutional stability. This perhaps cryptic sentence refers, first, to the widely known fact that in the United States, at least, there is no very serious technological problem about how to produce enough to supply all citizens with sufficient goods and services to raise them above the present dividing line between poverty and genteel adequacy; and second, it means that our traditions, laws, court decisions, and belief system do not easily permit us to lift the poor out of their poverty. We shall develop this idea more fully a few pages hence.

What proof have we that it is possible, technically, to produce enough to lift everybody out of poverty? The answer is that not only is it possible, but we are actually doing this now. The per capita income of the U.S. citizen in 1965 was approximately $2,770; or for the typical family of four the income would, if all income had been distributed equally, have been $11,080, not a sum to allow for a backyard swimming pool, two cars, orthodontia, college for both children at once, and psychoanalysis for Mother; but it does allow a fairly comfortable life for people without special problems. So much affluence for so many people was simply not possible 50 years ago, when our productive capacity was much inferior. But the arithmetic average of $11,080 is not a typical income; the median income is less than $7,000.

The possible income of $11,080 for every family is proof of the adequacy of our technology. It is true that it also conceals several problems. If every family did have such an income, the demand for certain goods and services might rise so high as to create no end of bottlenecks. Medical and dental services might be deficient; and until a satisfactory balancing of supply and demand at new levels could be achieved, many families might have more trouble getting medical service than $11,080 families have today. Decent housing would also be in short supply; and for a long time, even with this five-figure income, many people would not be able to move out of the slums. But the point is that we do have the long-run capacity to produce abundantly. Given time, we could shift resources from the production of polo equipment, mink fur, and penthouses to the production of more medical services and rat-free housing.

The reader may at this point wonder whether we propose that income be divided equally in order to attain the goal of abolishing poverty. If so, how? Will not such a proposal be resisted by all who now receive incomes above this figure? And anyhow, is it a good thing to divide income equally? If we do, what incentive can be held out to the gifted members of the population to develop their endowments and offer their services? We shall try to answer these and other questions in later pages. We have only sought in the paragraphs above to indicate that the abolition of poverty is technically feasible.

Let us now survey the problem of poverty without looking for solutions—simply inquiring into its dimensions. Later in the chapter, we shall try to see what can be done about it.

Poverty: What Is It?

No definition of poverty is entirely satisfactory. No definition can long possess validity, since poverty is related to the nature and state of the cultural milieu. For example, in the United States, nylons are worn by most women, rich and poor alike; yet in India, China, Egypt, and other poor countries, a pair of sheer stockings with a life expectancy of a fortnight is only for the well-to-do. Sixty years ago in this country a really poor man, seeking work as yardman, floor polisher, window washer, and the like would not be expected to have an automobile. If he traveled from neighborhood to neighborhood, he used the streetcar, the interurban trolley, or his bicycle, or he walked. The same man today must often own a car; the old methods of public transport may no longer exist for him. The automobile has driven out virtually every other means of travel. Donkeys, mules, spavined nags, and bicycles are now out of the question. But today, such an odd-job man could be poor and yet could, by performing miracles with rubber cement and a left-handed monkey wrench, manage to keep a four-wheeled vehicle running from one part-time employer to another.

Thus, if, in the United States, you are working out a kind of minimum budget to carry a family just above the poverty line, you may have to include items that would not be included anywhere else in the world or, for that matter, in the budget of a relatively affluent American family 60 years ago.

Assuming that this question can somehow be settled and that we agree that minimal income is imposed by the culture, the next question is to try to find a figure that cuts off geniune poverty from a tolerable level of living in this culture. Widespread agreement among experts in the mid-'60's places the average or basic figure around $3,000 for an urban family of four. A family of six in the more expensive areas (such as Boston, New York, Los Angeles, and San Francisco) should get proportionately more; a three-person family in a town in Mississippi could get along on appreciably less. But this figure is not really very generous. The United States Department of Labor has, for 1959, estimated that the total cost of maintaining a modest but adequate level of living for the standard family of four was as follows in selected cities:

Atlanta	$5,642
Boston	6,317
Chicago	6,567
St. Louis	6,266
San Francisco	6,304
Seattle	6,562

We shall nevertheless accept the rather mingy figure of $3,000 as the cutoff point for poverty, assuming always that this must be thought of as a base to which additions or from which subtractions are made for extra children, fewer children, inexpensive areas, or expensive areas (note, just above, that it costs $1,000 more to live in Seattle than Atlanta).

How Many Poor: Who and Where?

In 1966 the Statistical Abstract of the United States reported (for 1964) that 17.6 percent of all "families in households" received

incomes under $3,000. The total number of such families in early
1965 was 57.25 million and the average size 3.31. These figures
suggest that at least 33⅓ million persons out of our total population
of about 195 million (in 1965) are really poor, or about one person
in six (17 percent). But this figure is only an approximation. Poor
individuals, not forming part of families, are omitted; no correction is
made for the fact that poor families are often larger than middle-class
families, that is, exceed the average size of 3.31 given above. On the
other hand, many of the poor live on the land and can, especially in
the South where seasons are long, grow a fair crop of potatoes and
mustard greens and perhaps even some chickens, or can do a little
catfishing and crabbing. Different experts have made different estimates, most of them larger than the figure of 33⅓ million given
above. The President's Council of Economic Advisers has counted 35
million; Michael Harrington, one of the most eloquent writers on
American poverty, accepts Leon Keyserling's estimate of about 45
million. We shall certainly have to have more agreement on the
figures than this if we are to make serious plans and appropriate exact
sums of money; but in the meantime, we can at least conclude that the
figure of 35 million is by no means excessive, though 50 million
probably is.

What kind of people are these poor? Joseph A. Califano, Jr., an
aide to President Lyndon B. Johnson, has given us a very detailed
answer to account for 7.3 million of them—those who are on public
welfare. As summarized by *The New York Times* on April 20, 1967,
the following figures have been presented by Califano:

1. Of the 7.3 million, 2.1 million are in the old-age class, with a median
   age of 72, mostly women.
2. Seven hundred thousand are blind or severely handicapped.
3. Three and a half million are children whose parents cannot support
   them.
4. About one million are left over, 90 percent being mothers of those
   children and about 10 percent being fathers. One may surmise that
   most of the mothers in this group are either deserted wives or the
   mothers of illegitimate children, or both.
5. Of this entire group of 7.3 million, only about 50,000 are capable
   of working or of absorbing instruction that will make them employable. Presumably, the mothers, some of whom are employable, must
   stay at home with their children because they cannot find or cannot
   afford sitters.

So much for a close-up of the 7.3 million on the relief rolls. But most of the poor are not on public welfare. What about the broader picture? Specialists in this subject often speak of poverty-linked characteristics. Oscar Ornati lists these characteristics as follows: nonwhites; families with no earners; female-headed families; families headed by men 14–25 years of age, or over 65; families whose members have less than eight years of education; rural families; large families; and residents of the South. These attributes do not invariably cause penury, to be sure. Some large families—Senator Robert Kennedy's, for example—are rich; many residents of the South are millionaires. One should also be careful about another type of cause-and-effect relationship—this one, for example: A person may be poor because he has less than eight years of schooling, but it may be equally true that antecedent poverty prevented him from going through eight grades. He may have had to work (this happens despite child labor laws); he may have had such poor clothes that he was ashamed to go to school; his home may have been so barren of such primary amenities as warmth, light, quiet, and space in which to study that he could not easily do his homework.

The case of the nonwhites is notorious. It is widely known that Negroes form a disproportionate percentage of the very poor and of the unemployed. They possess many of the poverty-linked characteristics spoken of above. Their educational achievement is low; their numbers bulk large among the female-headed families; many are rural, and many reside in the South. It is true that a strong movement to northern cities is pulling Negroes out of the rural South, but many of them are still there.

When Ornati speaks of families with no earners, he probably includes the involuntarily unemployed. The number of unemployed has, between 1950 and 1966, fluctuated from about 2.6 million to 4.2 million. Not all of these are to be counted among the poor, since a period of temporary unemployment accompanied by the payment of benefits does not always plunge a person into poverty. On the other hand, unemployment can cause that plunge; and in a period of rapidly expanding technology, when fewer inputs of labor are followed by equal or greater outputs of goods and services, the danger of permanent unemployment increases. Automation increases poverty for some, though it may increase the well-being of others; just where the balance sheet now stands is not clear.

Do the Poor Deserve Their Poverty?

Many people will say that any war on poverty must be rather hopeless, since the poor are—to put it courteously—devoid of productive capacity or lacking in industrial quality. A less polite way of describing the poor is to say that poverty falls on misfits, whether they be 14-year-old girls embarking on a career of producing illegitimate children, or bums, drunks, junkies, and petty thieves whose refractory conduct disbars them from jobs. It will also be said that the poor are poor because they are shiftless, unambitious, extravagant, or at least uneconomical when they do have a week's pay. The partial answer to this is that obviously many of the poor are—like many prosperous members of society—feebly endowed with the more austere middle-class virtues. They pay greater penalties, however, than the middle classes for their aberrations from middle-class standards. The college student's parents often can, with the money needed for psychiatric aid and legal advice, cover up the peccadilloes, crimes, and sins of their sons and daughters. Some of the familial problems of the Negro, from illegitimacy to desertions, are among those most resented by the socioeconomic classes above them, who are taxed for the relief checks. The program of aid to dependent children—which often means aid to illegitimate children—includes a disproportionate share of Negroes. The reason for this arises partly out of poverty and partly out of the fact that the ideal of a close-knit family was not fostered by the whites during two centuries of slavery, as even a cursory reading of *Uncle Tom's Cabin* will suggest. The tradition of monogamy is not yet established. The 14-year-old slum Negro girl has no expectation of a large church wedding, walking down the aisle on her father's arm (who is her father, and where is he?), a husband regularly employed, and so on through all the pleasant and attainable fantasies of a middle-class adolescent. If the young slum Negress does entertain such fantasies, she knows that they cannot come true for her; and she settles for what, by middle-class standards, is rather sordid romance—romance which, because of low educational attainment and low incomes, is engaged in without contraceptives. It should also be noted that many mothers with children on welfare lose their checks if a husband shows up and tries to assume fatherly responsibilities.

The middle-class virtues do not thrive in an atmosphere of

frustration and absence of rewards, of hopes for getting ahead dashed by undeserved unemployment or by the quick exhaustion of resources in case of illness, even minor. Apathy because of unfruitful and unrewarded attempts to better one's lot becomes redoubled apathy and sheer hopelessness. We should, finally, recognize that poverty has its own culture. One can hardly expect the poor to belong to the middle class and to accept its standards when they are denied access to that class and often do not really know what its standards are. The poor are not merely middle-class people who happen to have very little money; they are outsiders. Poverty for the poor is not a temporary thing, as it is for young graduate students. Poverty is something that in a large proportion of cases was known by the parents of the present poor, experienced by the current generation from birth to death, and transmitted to their children.

The poor suffer many kinds of disabilities that go beyond mere poverty. Many poor neighborhoods are infested by the lower orders of crime and vice, representatives of the numbers rackets, procurers, and purveyors of drugs. Students of this aspect of the problem should read Claude Brown's *Man Child in the Promised Land* (Harlem) to understand the paradox of how gambling and drug using—both expensive —can go along with poverty. The males are more likely to be drafted, for they lack the thousands of dollars that are needed yearly to go to college. The accused is more likely to go to jail because he has access to only inferior legal aid; he is even more likely to suffer capital punishment because he cannot afford appeal after appeal and, finally, make credible a plea of insanity or self-defense.

The homes of the poor (such as they are) often reflect the inherited cultural aridity of several generations of poverty—homes that have lacked magazines, books, record players, pianos, cameras, games such as monopoly and Parcheesi, and chemistry sets. Families with incomes of $3,000 or less often cannot provide the apperceptive basis their children require to go to school. There are slum children who scarcely know what a lawn is, or a farm animal; a Negro bean-picker's son of 12, slightly injured on the road while walking home, was brought into a nearby $40,000 house for first aid; he later wandered around and asked the owner: "Where are all the people?" He had never seen so much living space for one small family. The children of the poor are often unlikely to know the nursery rhymes of

the middle class; they are handicapped by not knowing certain childhood games such as pinning the tail on the donkey, by not quite
understanding such concepts as "taking your turn," or by not having
bred in them such chivalrous concepts as punching girls on the nose
more gently than boys. Observation suggests that proficiency in standard English speech—up to a certain point, at least—is positively
correlated with income. If poor young people are to survive the
standard American education, they will have to start more or less at
the same post as middle-class children. If they are to compete for jobs
paying over $6,000 annually, many of the stigmata of the very poor
will have to be erased by special education. Apparently, the suddenly
wealthy business classes of the 17th century felt a similar cultural
inferiority; but they were able to hire tutors to teach them acceptable
speech and manners—as did M. Jourdain in Molière's famous comedy. But to return: The poor will need to be reclaimed from the
culture of poverty if they are to take their part in the mainstream of
American society.

The poor have few ties with the organizations of the community
that bring people together in a cooperative and civic mood. Their
children are not really welcomed among the Brownies and Cub Scouts
and Camp Fire Girls. They can scarcely afford to give or buy at bake
sales. They are not made sponsors or board members of libraries,
hospitals, art centers, marching bands, or Little Leagues.

What often happens to the poor, as Gunnar Myrdal observed
about the Negro, is that the middle and upper classes exclude them
from many opportunities for self-development and self-improvement,
often allowing them, over several generations, to live in a substandard
atmosphere and then saying to them, in disgust: "Look how substandard you are, how underdeveloped and unimproved; aren't you
ashamed of yourselves?"

Programs for Reducing Poverty

Any realistic program for the reduction of poverty will be costly
and will entail a redistribution of income. This can mean several
things—higher taxes on the larger incomes, lower taxes on the smaller
incomes, and perhaps higher taxes on the really great luxuries such as
yachts, country estates, fox-hunting horses, and private airplanes. It

may also mean higher minimum wages. The taxes would form the basis of transfer payments to the poor. But transfer payments are probably not enough. Certain services will probably have to be inaugurated or diffused more widely or pressed more energetically if we are to lift the poor out of the culture of poverty. Some of the services needed will probably demand techniques that have not yet been developed, such as returning chronic dropouts back to regular school attendance. Many of the poor, especially from the South, speak in unintelligible accents. Speech of this sort not only chains them to local jobs where they are understood, but also prevents them from accepting white-collar jobs where ability to communicate clearly is more necessary than in the tobacco fields or slums. Special instruction will have to be developed.

Two kinds of goods, at least, seem to be so expensive that unless the $3,000 basic annual income of which we have spoken earlier in this chapter were doubled or tripled, many families could not afford them. One is housing; the other is medical care. For some reason, private enterprise seems to be unable to provide decent housing for $3,000 people. And the same is true of medical care. In both fields, some progress has been made in recent years, but we still have a long way to go, and Medicare is only for the aged. Urban renewal is widely acknowledged to be something close to failure as a means of supplying low-cost housing.

It will perhaps be objected that we are doing enough of this sort of thing already. We have old-age pensions, relief for farmers, unemployment compensation, and the like. Actually, some of these programs are decidedly wayward. Farm relief does not go to poor farmers—not the really poor—but rather to the middle and upper income farmers. Actually, some of the very poor are taxed to increase the income of already prosperous farmers. Old-age pensions are totally denied to some of the very poor; and for the rest, they vary directly (up to a point) with income earned during the working life. And in any event, the federal old-age pension program comes at least as close to a paid-up old-age pension program as to a transfer from the rich to the poor. Unemployment compensation is defective in coverage, amount paid, and duration of payments—defective, that is, if the goal is to make a big dent in real poverty.

Some will argue that poverty can be eradicated simply by the nation's growing productivity. If, indeed, we are capable of producing so abundantly, the rich can be rich, and the poor can overcome their poverty just by getting their present proportionate share of a greater abundance. Hence, there need be no radical redistribution of wealth. Even today, many of the poor have television sets or radios or can avoid smallpox and other diseases through immunization, often available at no cost at free clinics or county hospitals. This was something that the most powerful king could not buy 200 years ago. Technology has reduced pain through anesthesia for rich and poor alike—indeed, even for animals, since veterinarians invariably use anesthetics when they operate on pets. Women on relief can wear nylons; the men can smoke the same cigarettes as college students; the youngsters can eat peanut butter just like the Rockefeller children. Though all these things are true, they are not always true, and they do not apply to all commodities and services. Housing, for example, reveals vast gaps between the affluent and the poor. One cannot by any stretch of the imagination see much similarity between a slum dwelling and even so low a grade of housing as a college dormitory. The poor man's home crowds as many as a dozen in one room; heat and hot water are likely to be inadequate; insect and rodent control are sketchy; toilets are chronically stopped up; community services are often at a low level. Police protection is of inferior quality, as are street lighting, garbage disposal, snowplowing, and public school buildings and the teachers in them.

It will be said that all these things are getting better and that our constantly increasing productivity will ultimately destroy poverty in the United States. This brings us face to face with an interesting and important question: Is not poverty merely a relative question? If today's American welfare families live better than modestly successful Chinese peasants, if life is richer for most of the poor today than it was for the British textile workers of 1800, then are we not justified in saying that poverty can never be abolished because it will always be defined as the lowest third or fourth or sixth of the population? If in a far-off day of the fantastic affluence that is bound to come through vast technological progress, the very poor wear Brooks Brothers shirts and drive Cadillacs, will they not be considered underprivileged because the class next above them wears individually tailored Christian Dior shirts and drives Rolls-Royces? Where does all this stop? The only answer to make is that that great day is not here yet. The issue now is whether—in a society that already produces enough to make possible dignified living for all—one fifth of the population should live in slums, receive only minimal medical attention, and be forced onto diets which, if they sustain life, are heavily weighted with starches, chitterlings, dried beans, bread, and other vitamin-loaded gourmet delights.

We have suggested that any serious program for the abolition of poverty now requires a redistribution of income. By redistribution, we do not mean equalization. In everything that has been said above, the implication has been that the maximum guaranteed income would, under current conditions, not go beyond a basic $3,000, though certain services—some of them rather expensive—from Medicare to decent housing, would increase the amount to be redistributed. We are, moreover, through existing welfare payments and in other ways, already paying a substantial part of the cost of programs similar to the ones suggested in this chapter. However, since increased benefits of whatever sort will require more money, let us look into the broader repercussions of income distribution.

Redistribution of Income: Some Economic Repercussions

War on poverty will require a redistribution of income which in one way or another takes more than we now take from higher income receivers and transfers this surplus to the poor, either through a guaranteed annual wage or through provision of certain goods or services to the poor, from public housing to remedial speech classes. Our belief system tends to disapprove of this on ethical grounds, since we make the assumption that barring outright swindling, robbery, and the like, all persons with large incomes are entitled to them because of their recipients' intrinsic worth, large natural gifts, or superior economic productivity. This is an ethical matter which we shall not pursue here. But it is also felt that any appreciably increased taxation of the higher brackets will somehow bring about economic disaster. The gifted and productive will cease putting forth their best efforts; investment in new production facilities will decline; the rewards for successfully gambling on consumers' acceptance of new products will be too small to attract the venturesome.

Such fears do have a certain validity; and for this reason, we should look into some of the possible economic repercussions of a more nearly equal distribution of income. But one widely diffused bit of misinformation should be cleared up before we proceed. It is generally assumed that the rich are already being "soaked" unmercifully. In the chapter on taxation, this issue was clarified, and the student is referred back to Chapter 13. The fact is that, what with the low taxation of capital gains, stock options, tax-free bond income, depletion allowances, and other loopholes, rich people pay surprisingly little income tax, and what with regressive sales taxes, the poor pay surprisingly much. It is true that some persons with fairly high incomes do get stuck pretty badly if their high pay comes exclusively in the form of straight salary payments without stock options or generous entertainment allowances or other arrangements that put them in favored tax-sheltered categories. These are the unlucky ones in our disorderly taxation system.

Well, now, if income really were distributed more evenly, the economy, looked upon as a total organism, might in some respects function more smoothly. In the simplest Keynesian model, namely, scheduled $C + I = Y$, the C would, under a regime nearer income equality, increase. And if I remained the same, Y would rise—that is, the national income would increase with consumption.

The reason C would increase is that the persons who received the greatest transfers of income would be the poor, and they would probably still not save much because, even under these circumstances, they would not yet be getting enough to carry them much beyond the sum needed for ordinary necessities. At \$3,000 a year, you can scarcely save if you meet the basic biological needs as dictated by our culture.

It can be argued that I will go down and perhaps compensate for the rise of C, thus keeping Y stable, or even reducing it. Support for this argument will come from the belief that the rich, being too much taxed already, will not save; and if they do not save, the streams of new investment in plant, research, and inventory will slow down to a mere trickle. This is the seed-corn argument, so often made in the editorials of our large newspapers—that if the seed corn is used up to feed the populace, to give them bread and circuses, then we shall decline and fall as did the Roman Empire.

But this is not strongly supported by modern theory. Current experience and theory both indicate that new investment takes place when consumers are spending briskly. The entrepreneur's expectations are highest when the average propensity to consume is high. A vast flow of demand from the poor, transferred to them from the rich, will encourage entrepreneurs to invest and produce. The reader may, however, say: "Granted, but if the rich must pay in taxes what they might have saved, then where will the money come from for new investment?" Well, one answer is that new investment can be made through bank loans. But another answer is that the question betrays the fallacious thinking of the last generation that individual saving is the sole source of investment—or that savings and investment are the same thing. Individual saving may give individual savers command over (ownership of) capital, but the process of (new) investment is nothing like the 18th- and 19th-century process in which a thrifty businessman saved and then invested his savings in new or enlarged plant. Modern theory holds that heavy investment calls forth savings —not the other way round. And again, investment is profitable when purchasing power abounds. The majority of economists now believe that a greater equality of income, far from bringing about disaster, may strengthen the economy by stimulating consumption and investment and keeping the economy more nearly stable.

There are perhaps more economically dangerous repercussions in a regime of greater income equality than those alluded to above. We can find several really troublesome issues related to a guaranteed base income of $3,000. One is the radical effect it would have on the labor market. Who would eviscerate broilers or launder other people's clothes if he could collect $3,000 at a governmental office? Obviously, wages for hospital orderlies, agricultural workers, certain hotel employees, and similarly low-paid workers would have to rise and, with them, prices where productivity could not be made to increase. Another objection is that $3,000 would not spur various kinds of unemployables to make themselves employable. Why should a wino change his habits or seek rehabilitation if he has an assured income? We can only reply that perhaps half the winos are driven to their unworthy use of leisure time by the despair of great poverty; and we can have faith that when this generation of wine bibbers dies out, the next—not driven by extreme penury—will embrace a smaller fraction of dipsomaniacs. Some students of economics have wondered whether even ambitious, gifted college graduates might not accept the $3,000 simply to live without responsibility while they were composing the great symphony or the new *Ulysses*. The answer to this one is that the subsidizing of art is not exactly a national disaster; besides, if the young aspirant discovers that he lacks ability, he may decide to marry, have children, shave his beard, bathe, and then get a remunerative job writing advertising copy—in which case he loses the guaranteed income. Indeed, the real protection against widespread abuse is that most people will want two cars, a fur coat for the little wife, and a Florida tan before Washington's birthday. But we shall probably always have some parasites and malingerers among us; penalties and incentives can be devised to keep the number low.

Another problem is that during a transition period, at least, some prices may rise to rather high levels. Apart from the obvious domestic discomfort that this may cause, our balance of payments will be unfavorably affected; foreigners will not buy at our high prices. We have good reason to believe, however, that after the establishment of a new general equilibrium, this problem will disappear. A redistribution of income and a guaranteed annual payment above the poverty level will call for difficult decisions, all right; but it may also lead to better things.

The Official War on Poverty

The alleviation of poverty is being carried out on many fronts and reaches back many years—indeed, even centuries. Groups held together by common interests, from small families to large nations, have frequently harbored sufficient compassion to extend at least a little help to their indigent. The medieval church urged us to put a "penny in the urn of poverty." We have long had almshouses; political machines in our large cities have dumped coal in the streets of urban slums; the Christmas basket is an old story. Many measures which protect those born under a lucky star protect the poor as well, such as the requirement that butchers' scales be honest, that labor unions be given the right to live, or that firemen put out fires everywhere. Our assistance programs, expanded during the 1930's, have prevented starvation, if not poverty. A hundred years of free public education, if it has not yet reached down far enough to fit the very poor for an appreciably better life, has achieved a great deal. For 35 years or so, we have—sometimes unwisely, it is true—sought to keep the economy on an even keel through contracyclical action. Any war on poverty must of course continue all or most of these old programs and probably expand them or develop them more fully. When, however, we talk about the war on poverty in the 1960's, we tend to think of the program suggested by President Johnson and enacted into law. It is the purpose of this section to discuss this program specifically.

President Johnson, in January, 1964, in a message to Congress, proposed that the American people wage an "unconditional war on poverty." The congressional response to this ringing declaration was the passage of the Economic Opportunity Act of 1964. Burton A. Weisbrod has called attention to the mildly bewildering fact that although President Johnson called for a war on poverty, the act that presumably implemented his proposal was named the Economic Opportunity Act. The question may reasonably arise in one's mind as to whether the official aim is to abolish poverty or to increase opportunity. Or are the two ideas really synonymous? That they interact or overlap is fairly clear, but that the goals are identical is open to question. War on poverty seems to be a more comprehensive program than the equalization of opportunity.

In any event, the act provides for many things relating to the problems of the poor and may be briefly summarized as follows:

1. The act provides for a variety of youth programs designed to increase the employability of hundreds of thousands of young people. This includes establishment of a Job Corps, educational centers, programs of vocational training, and aid to young people aspiring to go to college.
2. The next section of the act is rather complex but covers some of the following issues: The federal government will do much to help finance antipoverty programs originating at the community level; this embraces job training for adults, better housing, health programs, help for needy children through supervised foster parents, and rehabilitation of the disabled.
3. Provision is made to help rural indigents and the small farmer; small loans may be made to poor farmers; the migrant farm worker is to receive aid; cooperatives may be financed.
4. Small business is aided by a policy of making liberal loans to small entrepreneurs.
5. The Department of Health, Education, and Welfare may undertake demonstration projects designed to encourage local authorities to fit or retrain needy people for jobs.

6. Various procedural and administrative matters of little interest to us are contained in the last two titles of the act.

It will be noted that the act says nothing about a guaranteed $3,000-a-year income, or an extension of social security benefits, or a minimum wage, or an overall taxation system to relieve the poor. If drastic changes are to be made in these areas—and most antipoverty campaigners think they should be—we must assume that they will be made under some rubric other than that of legislation to equalize economic opportunity. It is doubtful whether the war on poverty can be pursued to the point of victory with this act; but some progress can be made now, and new legislation will perhaps give us new weapons to prosecute a war which, under the very best of conditions, can be won only after many years.

Summary and Conclusions

In this chapter, we have sought to define poverty and measure its extent. For this country and this decade, we can put into the category of poverty all those families of four whose incomes fall under $3,000 annually; using this as a base, the poor may further be defined as those individuals or small or large families whose incomes, adjusted, provide them with a level of living under the $3,000-for-four level. The number of such people runs close to 40 million.

This group includes a hard-core subgroup which transmits its poverty from generation to generation. It contains a disproportionate share of Negroes and other nonwhites. It forms a class which, though embraced within the general American culture, forms a subculture of poverty. This subculture is strange to most of us, who know very few poor people well; as a result, we find it hard to understand them. Poverty—especially through several generations—tends to breed frustration, apathy, and toleration of antisocial behavior, and to smother almost to death any sustained hope of bettering oneself.

Our desire to abolish poverty is founded on the knowledge that we can now—in the great industrial nations, at least, and most surely in the United States—produce enough to feed, clothe, and house everybody adequately. To do this will, however, require sacrifice on the part of the upper income classes, for some redistribution of income will have to be undertaken. But to give the poor a minimum income—say $3,000 for a family of four—is not enough. We shall also have to try to replace the culture of poverty by a culture of hope and aspiration. We shall have to rehabilitate the poor and fit their intelligent members to take a larger part in the life of the community and of the economy. Perhaps, too, they will need better housing and medical care than can be provided for $3,000. Any redistribution of income that goes far enough to matter will mean severer taxation of the rich and a generally more progressive tax system. A program of this sort will not necessarily inhibit the rapid growth of our economy, but may cause some difficult readjustments in both our product and labor markets.

The Economic Opportunity Act of 1964, though providing rather feeble weapons for an all-out war on poverty, is nonetheless a good beginning—but it is only the beginning of a beginning.

QUESTIONS FOR REVIEW AND DISCUSSION

1. "Poverty is never absolute, but is always relative to the culture in which it is found." Explain the preceding statement.
2. Using an income of $3,000 for husband, wife, and two children, make a reasonable budget for such a family. Basic items to include are rent, food, clothing, medical and dental care, utilities, transport, and, if possible, sums for life insurance, savings, and small luxuries such as beer, pipe tobacco, and movies. Compare such a budget with the annual expenses of your own family.
3. Name three groups in our society that contribute a disproportionate number of poor people to the total population.
4. "We have a permanent, self-perpetuating group of people who live in poverty." Do you believe this statement? Give reasons for your reply.
5. What argument can be made to sustain the thesis that increased productivity alone will be of small benefit to the poor in the foreseeable future?
6. What effect would a guaranteed income have on the labor market?
7. "The war on poverty is implemented by an act that increases opportunity for some but does little to help the poor." Is the quoted statement a fair one to make? Explain.
8. "A redistribution of income such that no American family receives less than $3,000 annually is not an adequate attack on poverty." Do you agree with the statement above? Give reasons.

PART IV

Dissenting Economic Theory

Chapter	INTRODUCTION TO
19	DISSENTING
	ECONOMIC THEORY

Economics: Science or Philosophy?

In the preceding chapters, we have looked at economic theory through the lenses of the "governing and academic classes" of the Western world, to use John Maynard Keynes' phrase. In the next few chapters, we shall look at economic theory through the spectacles of those who withhold their assent to some of these doctrines. Because economics is perhaps closer to philosophy than to science, and because many of its theories are unverified, men have built up rival systems of thought to explain our economic world. The data with which economists have to work are so complex and the methods of study so unrefined that several patterns of explanation may be imposed on the same facts.

We all are made more comfortable by certainty. It is reassuring to know that 2 plus 2 always equals 4. Perhaps one of the most satisfactory qualities of physical science is its universality and that of its applications. Though there are French and German automobiles and Soviet telephones and American airplanes, none of these mechanisms would present mysteries to an Arab or Argentinean trained in the physical sciences and their everyday applications. Economics is not sufficiently developed as a science to inspire in us a similar feeling of universal validity.

This is regrettable and, from the pedagogical point of view, presents difficulties. It is always easier to teach material that is undeniably true; to plant seeds of doubt in what has been taught is a thankless task. On the other hand, neither teachers nor students have sought to insulate themselves from the mental stress of uncertainty when the need arose. A course in ethics or in philosophy, for example, forces us to watch a whole parade of contradictory theories as they pass in review—epicureanism, stoicism, existentialism, pragmatism, hedonism, and realism. Literature and painting and music have their classicists, romantics, realists, naturalists, impressionists, and so on. Indeed, it seems that every branch of study, except perhaps mathematics and the natural sciences, demands skepticism and suspended judgment of even its beginning students.

There are, of course, a whole batch of theories and facts in the field of economics that are unchallenged and unchallengeable by all but the philosophical nihilist, who believes that there is no objective basis for truth. Much of what we have discussed in preceding chapters is not open to dispute. We can prove the truth of the law of diminishing returns by experimentation. Though the Soviet Union repudiates the kind of economic theory that colors the thinking of the free democracies, it lowers air transport fares when it wants Russians to make greater use of its Aeroflot planes.[1] This is exactly what any standard theorist would urge. No economist doubts that Joseph was able to sell grain at an exorbitantly high price during the seven years of famine, as the Bible relates. This conforms with supply-and-demand analysis. It is true, of course, that some societies do not respond to the "law" of supply and demand; it is not cross-cultural. But for the moment, we can skip that fact. It does seem to have applied to all of the cultures that most of us know about through our ordinary courses in high school and college history.

To go on, any sensible person can see that a cooling thundershower on a summer's day may be a welcome and refreshing event, but that rain for 40 days and 40 nights is a destructive flood. And this accords with the law of diminishing utility. There is widespread agreement among economists on the degree of accuracy, usefulness, and limitation of such figures as those describing the amount of unemployment and the size of the national debt. This is true also of the GNP, national income, and related figures. Thus, we can safely conclude that there is a solid core of economic theory and fact on which all economists agree.

Disagreement arises over issues of a different and subtler sort: preconceptions, buried philosophical and ethical assumptions, hidden premises concerning the nature of man, and other matters which may seem remote but which are very practical and real in that they determine the nature and scope of economic study—what is included, what is left out, and what is emphasized.

---

[1] *Wall Street Journal*, May 14, 1963, p. 1.

A Specific Case: Marginal Revenue Productivity

Let's take a case to see how some of these issues arise in regard to a specific instance. A basic tenet of standard theory is the marginal productivity theory of distribution, discussed in an earlier chapter. What it says is that each factor of production in a competitive price system receives its marginal revenue product—barring unemployment, imperfect competition, overcapacity, and many other things that characterize a modern economy. Some economists might question whether this is still a basic tenet of standard theory. Leading names have attacked it, but no other distribution theory put forward by standard economists has survived assault as well as this one. No theory could be more bloody yet more unbowed.

To this theory the dissenter has a host of objections, many of which reflect his general objections to standard economic theory. First of all people get their marginal product only under conditions of perfect competition—briefly, in a world that dissenters believe does not exist. The reader will remember from Chapter 3 that many things in science do not exist here below, such as perfect vacuums, the lines and points of geometry, or the perfect sphericity of the earth; but for many purposes, it is useful to postulate them. This, however, does not mean that in the pursuit of truth any figment of the imagination can serve as an abstraction. In a world of mammoth corporations, chronic unemployment, and chronic overcapacity the abstraction or model of a competitive, fully employed world devoid of pressure groups and political power over economic action is simply not worth postulating —at least, so the dissenter would say.

A second objection is that the theory is not a general theory. It concerns itself with incomes established in the marketplace by persons producing goods and services for the market. What about people whose incomes are affected by the market only at a second or third remove—soldiers, teachers, and civil servants at large? What about servants in the home and persons who work in endowed nonprofit institutions and in other places where the calculus of marginal revenue productivity cannot be made? Some incomes are transfer incomes founded on blackmail, thievery, gambling, and a long list of frauds; other transfer payments go to recipients of public assistance or to veterans' pensions. Speculators live in a rather dubious zone in standard theory. Some do seem to perform a useful service which can perhaps find a place in the theory; others, to use Keynes' word for the New York stock markets of the 1920's, operate in a "casino" and often make a negative contribution to production. All of these groups —roughly calculated and estimated—would include about 30 percent of the income-receiving population, an increasing percentage as armies, freeways, madhouses, and other public enterprises proliferate.

Approximately 25 percent of the American income goes to property incomes. Now, if John Doe III has inherited $0.5 million and has invested his money in stocks, bonds, houses, and so forth, he gets his income because he contributes toward production by making his possessions available to labor and entrepreneurship, and the dissenter has no criticism to make at this point of the marginal productivity theory—unless he is a Marxian and opposes private ownership of the means of production and the institution of inheritance. But what the non-Marxian dissenter might wonder about would be the source of the $0.5 million. Suppose it were, as it often is, the result of economic growth. Suppose John Doe's grandfather, a modestly successful farmer, had left a little farm and a few shares of an automobile company to his son, John Doe, Jr. And suppose that in John Doe, Jr.'s lifetime, the original value of the farm and stocks had more than quadrupled, and more than quadrupled again in the lifetime of John Doe III. Now he has $0.5 million and is entitled to the income thereof, not because of any special productivity in his family, not even because of speculative acumen, but simply because, in a rich, growing country like ours, it is rather hard to make an investment that does not grow with the economy. Where do you classify, in the marginal productivity theory, an income which is basically attributable to growth? It must not be thought that this kind of income is an isolated case or applies only to large family fortunes; there must be tens of thousands of American families today whose income is at least a little higher than it would otherwise be because Grandpa once bought a farm for $1,000 in 1890 and his grandchildren were able to sell it for $10,000 or $20,000. And of course, the opposite or, at least, the partial reverse of this is also true. How many Richard Roes today have a lesser income than they might have had if their fathers or grandfathers had not lost all or part of their fortunes in the calamities of the 1930's or 1920 or 1907, or if income had not been eroded by the more or less persistent inflation of the 20th century? The standard economists would of course say that the marginal productivity theory is static and that it does not seek to inquire into the origin of private fortunes; it seeks only to explain the rewards of given factors of production. The dissenter would agree that this attack is limited to the question of scope, but that that is precisely one of the things he is attacking.

Clarence E. Ayres, a distinguished living dissenter, has made the objections which follow.[2] First, he casts doubt on any theory of imputation, that is, imputing specific productivity to a worker or to a machine. If a man cuts firewood, using only his labor and a saw, and sells it for $20 a cord, he can, through bookkeeping, figure that the wear and tear on his saw is 50 cents; therefore, his labor is worth $19.50. This is a mere bookkeeping operation and does not measure specific productivity. It simply measures what it measures, not creative potency.

Going a little farther than Ayres, the question might be asked of many joint enterprises whether one can really impute specific productivity to any process that requires the indissoluble union of different things. To be able to smoke a pipe, you need tobacco, pipe, and fire. Which is most productive of a smoke? Mayonnaise requires egg yolks and oil. Which is the more productive ingredient? In the mammalian world, offspring require both sexes.

Ayres goes on to say that even if we really could attribute specific productivity to either the saw or the woodcutter, where in such a process can we find a way of discovering differences in productivity between a skilled surgeon and a woodcutter? As is well known, surgeons get more income, and perhaps we are prepared, in a commonsense way, to concede that they are more productive. But the specific productivity theory does not help us here.

Ayres's third statement is best quoted *in toto:*

This businessman knows what the items on his ledger are before he knows what his labor and capital have "produced." As critics have pointed

---

[2] Clarence E. Ayres, *The Industrial Economy* (Boston: Houghton Mifflin Co., 1952), pp. 361 ff.

out all along, the whole productivity analysis (like utility analysis) is a matter of "imputation." The rates of remuneration of labor and capital must be known before it is possible to say what their supposed productivity is. Then it is easy enough to say, since all we are saying is that productivity is defined as that which wages and interest measure. We can say this if we want to. But it is only another tautology. We have no independent measurement of the comparative productivity of capital and labor, just as we have no independent measurement of the desirability of the things people buy. Thus the pretty picture of price as the measure of both utility and productivity fades into a set of truths-by-definition which are otherwise meaningless.[3]

The reader may wonder what sort of 12-cylinder, jet-propelled, supercharged theory of distribution is possessed by the dissenters that they can take so lofty a view of the theory put forward by standard theory. The answer is that they have no theory, at least not in the sense in which the word has been used in this book so far and in which standard economic theorists would use the word. This does not mean that they lack interest in distribution—quite the contrary—or that they have not suggested approaches to the problem. One of the most distinguished American dissenters of the first half of the century, Wesley Mitchell, was responsible for the first reliable studies of American income and its distribution, a factual study of the number of Americans receiving income according to certain income classes. Another, Thorstein Veblen, has divided incomes into those received by men engaged in pecuniary employments and those received by men engaged in industrial employments; this dichotomy and its importance will be further developed in Chapter 21. Others, among whom we might cite particularly Clarence E. Ayres, have suggested that our present society still bears the stamp of medieval and even earlier institutions, that capitalism is in part a sort of industrial feudalism. Thus the captain of industry is in some sense the heir and opposite number of the landed nobility, and the workingman of the peasant or serf—and remuneration today is related to concepts of status inherited from a feudal hierarchy. To put it differently, a chief cause for the large inequalities of income (and often wealth) in modern societies is that mankind has always had—at least in the period of recorded history—large inequalities of wealth. In short, our system of distribution is an institution, a way of thinking and behaving. Such explanations are more or less satisfactory to a large group of dis-

[3] *Ibid.*, p. 365.

senters. To standard theorists, they are not enough and, from their viewpoint, do not constitute a *theory*.

For various reasons, an important one being a strong preoccupation with market activity, standard theory has been loath to take part in the development of such explanations of distribution as satisfy dissenters. To standard theory the center of economic analysis has been the marketplace. It is here that consumers cast their dollar votes to guide production, to allocate resources, to reward producers, and to distribute income. Dissenters have, on the whole, sought explanations elsewhere and have minimized the importance of the market. They therefore do not have alternative answers to the same questions as those asked by standard theory. They ask different questions.

Before pushing ahead, we must draw some conclusions from the discussion just above. The reader should note that the objections of dissenters to the theory of marginal revenue productivity was never really met head on. The criticism revolved, rather, on issues of assumptions, postulates, and scope. The dissenter said things like this:

Your theory bases itself on a full-employment, competitive society; there is no such thing.

Your theory assumes—or is limited to—firms employing four factors of production working together to produce profit; but there are many income receivers who do not work in firms. Your theory is therefore of limited scope.

Your theory takes no account of the wealth created for lucky property holders by the nation's growth, or of losses for the unlucky by declines of property incomes arising out of depression or out of the perennial inflationary forces in our society. This means you are satisfied with a static theory. We dissenters are not.

Your theory assumes that specific productivity is something that can be separated out of a complex and then measured. This is a vast philosophical assumption that you need more backing for.

Your theory assumes that you have said something new, given a system of prices already in existence; all you are saying is that wages, interest, and rent measure what in our society is accepted as productivity.

We shall find, as we go on in our study of dissenting theory, that this story is repeated again and again. The objection is not to the logic of standard theory, granted its premises, but to the premises themselves, to the methods and scope of inquiry of standard theory. The dissenter lives in a different world. The above has been a mere foreword to an introduction. We have much more to do if we are to understand the dissenters.

Utopian and Methodological Dissent

Two attitudes appear to have gone into the making of dissenters. One is utopianism, and the other may be named methodological skepticism. Under the utopians, we include socialists, communists, anarchists, and various others who have believed in the perfectibility of man.[4] Under the methodological skeptics, we include those who are and have been dissatisfied with the scope and method of standard economics, who feel that standard economics has often used only a few of the tools of the scientific method. They have lacked interest in making deductions about an abstract, self-equilibrating marketplace in which an impossibly perfect competition prevails. They have felt that before theory can be developed, much more looking and seeing needs to be done.

To the utopians, capitalism—and indeed, all the other economic systems long known to history—exploited the weak and perverted the basic and fundamentally good instincts of man. They have felt that mankind could fulfill its potentialities only under some other kind of social system, usually a system in which private property (except purely personal property, like clothing) would be abolished, and in which full-scale economic planning by the government would be substituted for self-interest as a guiding force.

Man's utopian hopes have been disappointed in recent decades by the recurrence of warfare and by the inability of a socialist state— Russia—to become a perfected cooperative commonwealth, as was once hoped. Indeed, the nation with the most utopian program 50 years ago has turned out to be one of the most oppressive among modern states. We seem to find in Russia one of those frequent but often puzzling cases in which extremes meet, that is, in which the

---

[4] It may seem strange to speak of anarchists and communists as seeking the "perfectibility of man," since we quite properly associate assassination, slave labor, and brainwashing with these words. The ultimate goals of the 19th-century communists and anarchists were, however, very lofty and sought a regeneration of our institutions within which men could—in their view—attain perfection. In the course of the 20th century the communism and anarchism of the 19th century have virtually disappeared. In their place, we have the sometimes brutal Communism of the Soviet Union and China. Its immediate goals seem to have nothing to do with the perfectibility of man, and the means it uses to achieve its goals would have been abhorrent to the gentler utopians of the last century.

extreme of professed utopianism turns out in practice to be a cave of despair. There are perhaps other reasons for the decline of utopianism. The "culture concept" of modern anthropology seems to suggest that our social system—any social system—has the solidity of a glacier. Like a glacier, it can move and change; but movement and change are slow and are invisible from day to day. So, too, our society can change and absorb new ideas, can reform and become a better society—but all slowly, and without earthshaking upheaval. Another reason appears to lie in a better understanding of man. The utopians used to think that human nature is infinitely malleable, that expropriation of the rich and government ownership of the tools of production would somehow destroy in us the temptation to commit the seven deadly sins. This sort of view of human nature is less widely held today, and though few social scientists believe that "you can't change human nature," many of them believe that it is harder to change human nature than men of goodwill thought it was a generation ago.

If 19th-century utopianism is dying, why should we study one of its prophets, Karl Marx—as we shall? There are certain good reasons. First, he is still in good standing in one third of the world and in two of the major powers, the Soviet Union and China. We shall scarcely understand the conflict of ideas between ourselves and the Communists if we do not understand their interpretation of economic life, for this is the key to their other ideas. It is true that Marx might feel lonely in the Kremlin or in Peking; he might even be sent to jail if he were to express his views openly; yet enough Marxism lingers in Communist thinking to be significant. Second, Marx, though not an excellent economist, did see some important things in the field of economic thought. He was the first to make income fluctuations the core of his theory. Today, most economists accept income theory as a major and central issue of economics. They see "boom and bust" in quite a different light, it is true, but they do see the problem. Marx was among the first economists to exhibit genuine insight into the phenomenon of cultural change, something that also has begun to occupy the thoughts of modern economists under the name of "economic growth." Finally, it is an interesting intellectual exercise to see what different patterns of explanation can be imposed on the same facts, for the Marxian pattern is quite different from the pattern imposed by standard theory.

The methodological dissenters are different from the Marxians and other utopians. Though a few may have a utopian streak in them and are perhaps more dissatisfied with our current social and economic system than standard theorists are, their voiced dissent goes mainly to the preconceptions, postulates, axioms, scope, and methods of standard theory. They accept—but only to the degree that any thoughtful man accepts—the world we live in. What they do not accept is the explanations of it given by standard theory.

Dissenters charge that standard theorists are content with unverified "laws" and principles of dubious validity. Their reasoning is sometimes as vain—the charge goes on—as that of medieval scholasticism, which debated long and seriously whether 10,000 angels, being immaterial, could dance on the point of a pin; or whether God, being omnipotent, could make a wheel turn and stand still at the same time. Standard theory is subtly argued, they say, but misses some of the great issues of economic life, such as the prevalence in economic life of coercion, the frequent absence of perfect competition, the nonexistence of that famous state of equilibrium, and the meaninglessness of the "long run"—in the long run, price equals cost; or in the long run, profits go down to zero; or in the long run, fixed costs became variable costs—what do all these things mean in the world of reality? They feel that beyond supply and demand, there are worlds to explore.

A Brief History of Dissent

Our next chore in this introductory chapter is to sketch out, impressionistically, a brief history of dissent. It will make us understand better what we are dealing with if we get acquainted with the utopians and methodological nonconformists of the 19th century. But we shall skip over Marx, since he is to be the subject of the next chapter.

The French were particularly adept at economic dissent in the early part of the 19th century. There were perhaps two good reasons for this. First, capitalism was not so far advanced in France as in England, where standard theory had its chief development. Learned men interested in economic problems lived in an environment in which the capitalists' belief system was less pervasive. It must have seemed possible to them that the economic system might go in any direction; in England, on the contrary, capitalism was already a completely formed system of economic behavior. The second reason was that the French Revolution had brought to the surface many extreme utopian ideas which, despite the return of monarchy and a middle-of-the-road way of life in France, still kept floating about and inspiring successive generations of Frenchmen.

One of the early dissenters was a Genevese, Simonde de Sismondi (1773–1842), whom we shall, by stretching a point, classify as a Frenchman. He criticized the standard theory of the day as being too abstract, which is tantamount to saying that its model left out too many things. One of the things he missed was an adequate study of depressions or of the business cycle. He invented a theory of the business cycle, which, though rather primitive, had two great virtues: It recognized the existence of the problem, and it tried to explain the problem as something more than a temporary failure of economic processes to regain equilibrium. Thus, he further denied the model of standard theory, which assumed that economic disturbances quickly run themselves out and that equilibrium at full employment is restored—a denial that Keynes was able to make his fellow economists believe only in the late 1930's. Sismondi was also impressed by what we would consider to be the imperfections of competition arising out of the increasing difficulties of entering industries. "Today those who trade with a capital of $100,000 are considered of an average size, and the day is not far distant when these will have to face the competition of manufacturers with a capital of $1,000,000." In other words, he saw that the increasingly large scale of industry made entry difficult for those with only small capital—and he spoke of this a century before it began to appear in standard textbooks.

Another dissident Frenchman was Charles Fourier (1768–1830). He dreamed of a world of apartment hotels connected by collective farms within which each individual would perform tasks for which he was best suited. Among the more interesting conclusions of his philosophy of vocational allocation was that children of about 10 should wash dishes and attend to sewage disposal because prepubescents love dirt. These clean-up teams were to be named the "Little Hordes," and they were to march first in all parades. The oceans were to evolve into lemonade as man himself moved to higher levels of civilization. Ferocious animals were to become tame servants of man; Fourier predicted that lions with elegant manners would draw carriages across France in a day. It is easy, a century and a half later, to dismiss Fourier as a crackpot; but really, he exercised considerable influence in his time and left a solid legacy. His followers founded numerous utopian communities in the United States, such as Brook Farm and the Oneida Community. His ideas gave considerable direction to the early American labor movement. His concept of *garantisme* foreshadows the social insurance or social security legislation that is now so widespread. Even the seemingly ridiculous idea of using children to clean up the streets was, about 1897, put into operation by a sanitary commissioner in New York City. Fourier was a forerunner of the "equal rights for women" movement. Some people trace the modern aptitude test to his philosophy of allocating workers to the tasks for which they are fitted and to which they are by their natures attracted.

Claude Henri de Saint-Simon (1760–1825) belongs to the dissenters. He conceived the role of the political state as secondary to that of the economic state. In the economic state, laborers, entrepreneurs, managers, engineers, scientists, and the like were to run the whole industrial system as if all of France were a large factory. What we think of as the true government was, in his world, to occupy the place that guards, night watchmen, detectives, and the like now occupy in a modern factory. Representatives to the parliament were not to be chosen on a geographic basis but from industries. Thus, instead of having a senator from Georgia, this economic state imagined by Saint-Simon would have the senator from agriculture, or the steel or automobile senator. This idea was taken up later by several Marxians, including Nikolai Lenin, and is not completely lost in the Russian government today. Saint-Simon himself was not a socialist or communist and made no sustained attack on the institution of private property. His followers, an active and able group including some of the distinguished Frenchmen of the day (Auguste Comte, Barthélemy Enfantin, and Augustin Thierry), went much farther toward socialism.

France was not the only country to produce unorthodox thought in the science of wealth. German economics until 1918 numbered many dissenters, even without counting Marx, especially among the so-called "historical schools," one earlier and one later. The German

historical school which flourished about 1870 came very close to
keeping its protest within purely methodological limits. Its members
felt that the way to progress in economic study was to pile up mountains of economic facts—most of them necessarily drawn from the
past—and then to disengage basic generalizations from these facts.
They piled up their facts, all right, and their students proliferated
factual theses on almost everything economic, but they did not succeed in making large generalizations. Their example has, however,
heartened many dissenters. And some of their historical work has
given us background to understand capitalism better—has permitted
us to see our society as if projected on a three-dimensional screen.

Two waves of nonconformity arose in the two great English-
speaking countries. In England, dissent found its home around 1900
among members of the Fabian Society: and in the United States, at
about the same time, among the institutionalists. These two groups
were distantly related and had certain sympathies, but were also very
different. The Fabians (named after the Roman Fabius, who opposed
Hannibal with delaying and harrying tactics) sought to bring about
socialism in England by peaceful and evolutionary means. This
socialism, moreover, was to take a form that would respect civil rights
far more than they later were and now are respected in the Soviet
Union. It was based on a program of active reform and soon found in
the British Labour party a numerous following. In all of this, there is
little relationship to American institutionalism, which is neither socialist, activist, nor closely related to a political party; indeed, there
has never been an important and enduring national labor party in the
United States. The Fabians were reforming politicians and pamphle-
teers; the institutionalists were mostly quiet academic men and professional scholars. Apart from political differences, there were certain
philosophical differences between the Fabians and the institutionalists. The Fabians and their Labour party successors had a mildly
Marxian orientation. The American institutionalists did not. We shall,
in Chapter 21, study their contributions more fully.

Summary and Conclusions

Having surveyed—or rather, hastily suggested and barely
sampled—this vast literature of dissent, we are prepared to arrange
our findings in systematic form and to make some useful generaliza-

tions. First of all, we find still acceptable the classification of dissenters into utopians and methodological skeptics. This division should not be looked upon as very rigorous, for many dissenters have been both, but it is an aid to classification.

The utopians may themselves be divided into two classes. First, like Fourier and others whom we have not mentioned, such as Robert Owen, we have the ideal-community, small-scale utopians. This group's influence declined to something like zero as early as 1860 though an occasional blueprint of a small-scale paradise has appeared during the past 50 years. One trouble with these proposed havens of felicity is that they would have to be islands in our culture—and our rock-'n'-roll, superhighway, singing-commercial civilization would engulf anything that tried to stand alone. Another trouble is that the standard of living in such a community—except under almost unbelievably favorable circumstances—would be too low. Microcosmic social and economic units of 10,000 or even 50,000 souls would be inefficient.

The second class of utopians is Marxian. Marx, as we shall see in the next chapter, was an able economist and social scientist. Some of his insights as a scholar are valuable. But even if we were to disregard every hostile action of the Soviet Union and China that has been performed in his name, we would still find him an unsatisfactory theorist.

This leave us with the methodological dissenters. The purest of these were members of the German historical school, now dead. The race of economic historians has, however, not died out. There appear to be several hundred in the United States. This does not mean that all have repudiated standard theory, though many are certainly indifferent to the kinds of problems that hold the interest of the purist in standard theory. And this brings us to the institutionalists, who will be the subject of Chapter 21.

At the close of this chapter we should take note of the fact that the issues as presented above are not always quite so sharp as they are made to appear. Clarity of exposition requires drawing lines more arbitrarily than they are drawn in real life. Between the institutionalists, for example, and the standard theorists, there is no demarcation line that stands out boldly on every issue. The boundary between black and white is a wide gray area, and this area embraces a large field of agreement.

QUESTIONS FOR REVIEW AND DISCUSSION

1. Define, in your own words, each of the following:
   a) Utopian dissent
   b) Methodological dissent
   c) "Culture concept"
   d) *Garantisme*

2. Would you agree that "economics is perhaps closer to philosophy than to science"? A few economists have spoken of the "art" of economies. Is it an art rather than a science? We often speak of a physician as a practitioner of the "healing arts." Does this mean that medicine is unscientific? Would it be proper to speak of a physicist as a practitioner of the "art relating to the behavior of inanimate things"? Explain your replies.

3. Your authors use the word "cross-cultural" in the fourth paragraph of the chapter. How would you define this word? Do you know, from courses in anthropology you may have taken, whether the following are cross-cultural: money, marriage, private property and religion?

4. In biology the concept of evolution is basic. Is biological evolution history or description or theory?

5. Your authors present the argument that specific productivity cannot be measured, since certain creative forces cannot be dissociated. Both oil and egg yolks are needed for mayonnaise; tobacco, pipe, and fire are needed to provide a smoke. Is this argument a valid criticism of the theory of marginal productivity?

6. A six-year-old child, beneficiary of a trust fund invested in stocks and bonds, gets an income of $100,000 annually. In what way may it be said of him that he is a producer?

7. What is the difference between a preconception and an assumption? Would a preconception hinder scientific investigation? What about an assumption? What is a postulate?

8. Some dissenting theorists hold that ancient concepts of status explain, or help to explain, the distribution of income as we know it today. Why would standard theorists reject this as theory? Note that the issue is not whether the statement is right or wrong; this issue is that it is not theory. What is theory, as opposed to a description that explains many cases?

9. Several of the Fabians have received international acclaim for their purely literary achievement. Find out who they were by consulting an encyclopedia. Have you read any plays or novels by any of them? Did you detect any "radical" ideas in their works?

10. William Godwin and the Marquis de Condorcet are two names associated with 18th-century views on human perfectibility. Using encyclopedias and other easily available materials, prepare a 10-minute class report on these men.

Chapter 20

WHAT MARX MEANT

Introduction

Karl Marx was born in 1818 and died in 1883. As an economist, he built up a system as rounded, involved, abstract, subtle, and hard to understand as that of any two or three orthodox economists put together. During his lifetime and after his death, disciples perfected the Marxian system. Among the greatest were his colleague Friedrich Engels and later Nikolai Lenin (who turned theories into reality after gaining control of Russia for the Communist party). It is to these three that we shall principally refer when we speak of the economics of Marx.

Marx was both an economist and a propagandist, or revolutionary. The two roles were fused into a consistent personality. We cannot study the one without studying the other. Yet it is possible to lay stress on the economist and to keep the revolutionary in the background. By doing this in the next dozen pages, we can free our minds from the psychological resistance that his name quite understandably arouses in a nation in perpetual conflict against Communist party aggression. We also need to remember that Marxian theory is not synonymous with the policies of the Soviet Union. Many Marxians are bitterly anti-Soviet—the Trotskyites, for example, who for decades have warned Americans of the Soviet peril. Leon Trotsky's mantle appears to have fallen on Mao Tse-tung; and here again, we have an example of one kind of Marxist who has won the fierce enmity of a second kind.

We shall understand Marx better—indeed, we shall understand any economist better—if we try to figure out what were his hopes and aspirations for the human race. How did he believe man could fulfill his destiny? Orthodox economists, we have already intimated, believed that men realize themselves by trucking and bartering, by disposing economically of scarce goods under current institutions, by constantly comparing amounts of pain with amounts of compensating happiness, by exercising personal liberty and following natural law. To Marx, most of this was nonsense. Without playing the dangerous role of amateur psychoanalyst, we have every right to assume that Marx was consumed by the inner fire of a most uncompromising utopianism. He saw men not as cautious, penny-counting shopkeepers but as potentially little lower than the gods. Since men were obviously much lower than the gods at that moment, how were they to develop upward toward their fullest potentialities?

To Marx the basis of his kind of spiritual development was material and primarily economic. His theory breaks with Christian tradition in that he did not think man could love his neighbor as himself or do unto others as he would be done by unless economic conflict, with its accompanying poverty, were made to vanish from the face of the earth. So long as acquisition of economic goods involved— as he thought—exploitation, war, knavery at large, and the existence of a more or less permanent working class opposed to a more or less permanent wealthy class, so long would all the more exalted human endeavors and sentiments, from friendship and love to art and science, be soiled by economic considerations. Marx proposes, in a manner of speaking, that we simplify and ennoble our lives by taking steps to abolish economic conflict. And you abolish economic conflict by abolishing poverty. And to abolish the have-nots, you have to abolish the haves—but not because sharing their wealth will level things off better. Sharing the wealth, or sharing income, is not an essential idea in Marxism. The haves will be liquidated only if and because they stand in the way of organizing the more productive society envisaged by Marx. A cooperative society that centrally plans its economic activities—the socialist state—will yield a larger product. The real point was to abolish the political power of the haves and their alleged masterclass psychology.

He saw, perhaps more clearly than many of his contemporaries, that the rapid development of science and technology in the dynamic middle years of the 19th century held out the hope of freeing the world from its long curse of hard labor and low productivity—and hence poverty—for the masses. Charles Fourier, though of the older generation, was still fumbling with the idea that lions, not machines, could be induced to supply power for the French transportation system. David Ricardo, Thomas Robert Malthus, and others were so pessimistic about man's economic destiny that they inspired Thomas Carlyle to use the phrase "dismal science" as the synonym for social science.

To Marx, economics was, in a kind of backhanded way, a hopeful science. In the agricultural, low-productivity past, there had been, he said, a reasonable basis for serf and lord, slave and master. But mankind now had iron slaves and the tireless muscles of expanding steam. Abundance for all lay within the realm of probability. But something was going wrong. Steam and science, iron and technology had plunged the working class into even greater misery than before, for the first generation of factory workers was indeed a lost generation. Capitalism seemed to him a more wasteful type of economic organization than the human race deserved to have. The physical basis was here. Yet reasonable expectations had been disappointed. There was no obvious movement in the direction of a better and easier life for mankind; and on the surface, no signs pointed toward utopia.

Marx might, like many of his contemporaries, have sought to usher in a utopian state of affairs by advocating freer education for the workman, or the creation of model factory villages, or a gradual program to be enacted by the parliaments of the newly industrialized countries. He might have enlisted the aid of the churches. But he scorned such methods. He scorned them because in his view the obstacle to immediate realization of a heaven on earth was the inefficient and wasteful capitalist class, the class that in bourgeois democracies is heir to privilege, masterhood traditions, and institutional benefits of an earlier age. Government, press, education, and the church were, he said, owned lock, stock, and barrel by the capitalist class—by the enemy. The enemy was satisfied with the positions he held, the disposition of his forces, and the tribute he was able to levy. There was no hope of budging him or of working out a permanent peace based on the capitalist's willing abandonment of rights and benefits enjoyed.

As for local utopian communities, to Marx they were childish. The system of production in an industrial era, whether under the proposed cooperative or present capitalist state, was necessarily large scale, often nationwide or worldwide. High standards of living could never be achieved by subsistence farming, even if it were hooked up to

Fourier's fancy phalansteries. Large-scale operations were essential to a heavy volume of production, and exchange of goods between specialized regions was indispensable.

Thus, Marx concludes, if you look at things on the surface, there is no basis for hope of a utopia, despite the iron horse and the power of insubstantial steam. "But," he seems to say, "if you will come with me through several fat volumes of *Das Kapital,* I will show you that the house of capitalism is falling down because of its inner weaknesses and that a brave new world is building up."

It is of the essence of Marxism that our capitalist world is plunging toward utopia, even though we are unaware of it, just as the physical earth is turning and plunging through space without our being able to feel its motion. The foundations of capitalism are invisibly crumbling—invisibly, that is, to those who do not, like him, know what telltale evidence to look for. And to pile up metaphors, capitalism carries within itself the seeds of its own destruction. A species of economic termite is gnawing away at the sills. Capitalism is decaying; utopia is rising up. That, in broadest outline, is how Marx's subconscious went after his utopia, since he could not get it through government, church, education, or model factory communities. Our next step is to find the Marxian termites in the sills and the seeds of the alleged decay.

Surplus Value

The basic thing to grasp about capitalism, Marx says, is that under its institutions there is a considerable and inevitable gap between the current wages of labor and the value created by labor. How does Marx support this bold assertion, so fundamental to his other conclusions? Marx's first step is to develop again, partly in Ricardian fashion, the then dominant theory of labor value. This, the reader recalls, is the theory that the value of any product is related directly to the number of hours of labor congealed in it. That is the cornerstone of the edifice. Marx meets naïve objections immediately. Obviously, the things made by labor must have utility to have value. An undesired commodity like a fur-lined bathtub would never sell at its full labor value. In the case of a really useful thing like a boat, only the socially necessary labor hours confer value. By this, he means in part that anybody who builds a freighter in the desert and then transports it overland to the sea cannot hope to be rewarded for the extra work required by so awkward a system of production. Large boats are built at the water's edge—that is "socially necessary."

How this discrepancy between wage and value works out can be shown in an imaginary case. Assume that a man's felt hat has both theoretical economic value and an actual market price that are correctly symbolized by the words "ten dollars." Assume also that it took a total of 10 hours of labor to produce the hat, beginning from the time the rabbit was caught until the time the consumer's initials were stamped in the hatband. These 10 hours are to cover everything, even the small emanations of past labor absorbed by the hat from the machines, chemicals, and kettles used in manufacture. A hatmaking tool or acid or any kind of tangible capital is congealed labor; a little of that stored- up labor rubs off on each hat made. When Marx assumed that it took 10 hours of labor to make a hat, he meant 10 hours of every conceivable kind of labor—current, recent, previously congealed, unskilled, skilled, managerial, and artistic, as well as labor used in transportation to market, storage, retailing, and so on.

Let us agree with Marx that a hat takes 10 hours of labor to make, that it sells for $10, and that therefore the value created by all labor used in manufacture is $1 an hour. "Good," says Marx, in effect, "but now we shall find that the workers employed actually were paid an average of only 60 cents an hour" (or 30 cents, or 80 cents— the exact figure, so long as it is appreciably less, does not matter). Why does the worker get less than $1 an hour? Because he was robbed by the employer? Marx does have some harsh things to say about the employer's being an Old Moneybags and about capitalism's dripping with the blood of workers, but this sort of thing is not the basic explanation. The basic explanation is economic.

The reason the wage is 60 cents an hour instead of $1 is that 60 cents is the true value of an hour's worth of labor power. So? Why, then, the $1-an-hour story with its intimation that the worker was robbed? Oh! That dollar applied to something else. There are really two things involved:

1. Value added by one hour's *labor* = $1
2. Value of one hour's *labor power* = 60 cents

We are talking about two different things—value added by labor and cost of labor power. To understand the two equations, you must think of a human being who belongs to the labor force as you would of a machine: He costs so much to bring into the world; in a normal lifetime, he consumes 60 million calories, as a truck consumes x gallons of gas; he yields 80,000 hours of work, as a truck is able to deliver y ton-miles—and so on to complete the analogy with depreciation, repairs, replacement, and all that. There is a cost of producing men, just as there is a cost of producing horses and cows. Now, all the costs of producing, maintaining, and replacing a worker, divided by the number of hours he can work in a lifetime, figures out in our assumed case at 60 cents an hour, just as we can say that each ton-mile over the total lifetime of a truck figures out to 2 cents. Thus, when the worker gets 60 cents an hour for his *labor power*, he is in one sense getting the proper reward for his time. He is being reimbursed for past and current labor congealed in *him*. To repeat, add up the money value of all the hours of labor required to produce, maintain, and replace a workingman; divide by the number of hours he will work in a lifetime. The figure you get is 60 cents. That is what he is paid for his *labor power*. The employer is under no business obligation to pay more; he has paid the total costs of production of the labor power he has bought. But when the worker actually goes to work, he adds $1 worth of value to whatever he is producing—one whole dollar's worth, not 60 cents' worth. Why?

"Why not?" the Marxians might say by way of reply.

This concept of getting something extra out of one of the factors of production was not foreign to economic speculation in its earlier days. A school of French economists known as the physiocrats (who flourished about 1750) based their principal theories on a similar concept, applied, however, to land rather than labor. Land, they said, yielded an economic superplus—a net product, to use their phrase (*produit net*). Agriculture and mining yielded something special-extra, they said. The physiocrats were wrong about land. But the Marxians believed they were right about the superplus; and it is produced by labor, says Marx. He named the superextra "surplus value," a phrase which has become a most provocative one in the modern world.

Marx also gives a direct and positive reply to this question,

though this does not mean that it is convincing. All through his
economic theory, he makes a distinction between use value and
exchange value. There is no particular relationship between the two,
he says. The exchange value of bread, for example, is about 25 cents a
loaf today; its use value is incalculable, for it is the staff of life. In our
example, we may say that the exchange value of labor is 60 cents an
hour; its use value is $1. The capitalist is able to appropriate this
difference. And there is no reason to believe that use value and
exchange value should coincide. Marx develops this point fully and
interestingly. We are reluctant to burden the reader with an expanded
statement, however, because it is precisely here that Marx is least
convincing. It cannot be said that he has made his point or that he has
been able to convert even sympathetic readers. This is a crucial spot in
Marxist doctrine. If his analysis here were unequivocal, then most of
his other propositions would have to be accepted as true, with all that
this implies. It is one of those things you either believe or don't
believe.

The difference between what a worker consumes and what he
produces, we have said, goes to the capitalist. He is not cheating the
worker or demanding a kickback, as straw bosses sometimes do. Sixty
cents is the proper rate. He is simply paying the worker an amount
equal to what the worker must expend to keep going efficiently. But
why does not the worker see what is going on and demand the surplus
value for himself? Well, the worker is not well organized and anyhow
does not see this clearly because our economic process is rather complex and obfuscating. But the capitalist is in a strategic position to
appropriate the surplus value. Our institutions are such that the
worker is not now in a strong enough situation to take what, according
to Marx, rightfully belongs to him.

To Marx the important economic point here is not so much that
the working class is being exploited, whatever slogan value the
concept may have in propaganda. Marx is, in a sense, hard-boiled
about the "injustice" visited upon the worker, and rather admires
capitalism for the productive miracles it has achieved. Marx's real
interest in surplus value is that it is the jimmy to pry open the door of
utopia—the very thing he was looking for from the start. Surplus
value not only belongs morally to the worker but will also destroy the
capitalist system. Under capitalism the worker is never paid enough

money to buy back all he produces. Thus, wares pile up and find no market. Gluts cause depressions; depressions cause misery; misery causes revolutions.

Crises and Imperialism

The process is a little more intricate than has been suggested just above. Marx is not a pure and simple underconsumptionist. He assumes that technical progress will go on apace and that production will employ fewer and fewer men. This will be hard on labor, but it will also be hard on capitalists. Surplus value, according to Marx, can come only from living labor. Mammoth laborsaving machines cannot produce surplus value, for surplus value is a kind of biological reversal of the law of the conservation of energy; surplus value means that the value of the labor poured into the human organism is always less than the value of the labor that can be drawn from it. This law is Marx's economic fundamental. This basic fact—a fact for Marxians only, of course—is not true of machines, buildings, or land. Thus the capitalist cannot exploit a turret lathe, a factory, or a coal mine. He can only exploit an employee. When he gets rid of an employee (competence assumed), he gets rid of the only agent of production that can be exploited, and thereby lowers his income. Even when he substitutes laborsaving machinery for workers, he loses—at least in the long run. He loses because only human beings can yield surplus value; and in the long run, surplus value is the only substantial and enduring source of the employer's income (or profit).

Marx recognizes the paradox that although surplus value can arise only out of human labor, employers rush to get rid of their profit-returning workers and to substitute for them batteries of expensive laborsaving machinery. He removes the paradox by saying that any *individual* employer who keeps ahead of his fellows by using new laborsaving machinery cheapens his costs while the old price remains current, and may make a large differential gain. But when the others catch up with him—and competition forces them to do so—they all ruefully discover that low costs mean low prices eventually, and that they are now worse off than before. Now they all use less labor to make surplus value for them, and the innovators have lost their former and temporarily favorable position. Thus, what innovating employers really want—on the Marxian theory—is the jump on their competitors, not a reduction of the number on the payroll. The decline is an inevitable outcome but is not the end sought; indeed, it defeats the end sought.

But there is a way of sustaining income after all, Marx tells us, at least for a while. By expanding his existing plant or building new plants, the capitalist can again employ more men; by employing more men—or rather, by employing as many as were employed before the innovations—he can collect as much surplus value as he did in the past. In other words, each dollar invested in new capital now brings in less; but since more dollars are being invested, incomes remain the same. The ratio of income to investment is always going down, but the total amount of income is the same, because the same number of workers is employed in the expanded plant or branch factories. Workers are now spread thin in a large number of expensive factories. The capitalist is thus constantly driven to make new investments. To do so, he must frantically build new plants—here or in Europe, Canada, Africa, Saudi Arabia, or South America—where, incidentally, he comes into conflict with capitalists of other countries on the same mission, a rencontre that (Marxians say) sometimes has serious consequences, such as world wars.

In Marx's view, then, capitalism is at first a dynamic—even in some ways admirable—force that equips the world with machines, railroads, ships, communication networks, and the like. At some point, however, the world's workshops are built. After that, the continued rapid, remorseless building of new and often redundant equipment becomes sheer madness from a community viewpoint. Over a long enough period, it is a losing race.

Fewer and fewer men, relatively, will be employed and paid wages; more and more things will be produced—or at least, will be producible, because of the vast amount of machinery in existence and because of its extraordinarily high productivity. Less and less, *relatively,* can be bought back by the working class. There will be gluts. Capitalists will produce too much to dispose of profitably. Workers will be too poor to buy. It will take months or even years to absorb the surpluses produced. This partly explains—to Marxians—the recurrent depressions with which we have been so familiar. According to Marx, they will get bigger and deeper and worse and longer. To get out of a depression, the price of capital goods will have to be scaled down, or capital goods will have to be destroyed. War is doubly useful to capitalism here, for it destroys factories and surpluses; but peaceful means may also be used, like burning surplus coffee in Brazil or letting crops rot (as Marxians often point out).

The capitalist can expand for a long time, but at some point the waste and futility of overinvesting, overbuilding, overproduction, and underconsumption—with attendant crises and wars—will be plain to all. When that time comes, capitalism will have decayed. Everybody will be sick of it. Society will be turned over to, or be taken over by, the working class under revolutionary leadership. Surplus value will become the property of the workers themselves, not of the owners of capital—indeed, there will no longer be any capitalists. Perhaps violence will be required to achieve the final step; even so, the era of violence is but a moment in a long evolutionary process—like the period of labor in childbirth. Both are the final, decisive, traumatic events in a long process of gestation.

Disappearance of the Middle Class

The main process above will be accompanied by a secondary movement—the disappearance of the middle class or, to use the French phrase, the *petite bourgeoisie*. When Marx wrote, a century ago, the *petite bourgeoisie* was constituted differently from what it now is. Our middle class contains a much larger percentage of teachers, nurses, librarians, salesmen, newspaper reporters, and other well-educated, salaried employees than it did in 1860. To Marx and to his contemporaries, the *petit bourgeois* was a small shopkeeper or small manufacturer primarily. This class, Marx felt, was doomed to extinction. As the process of capitalist development goes on, larger and larger industrial plants are needed, for reasons spoken of above. To go into business for oneself requires more and more money. The end of the process of competition is monopoly, for what is competition but the dropping-out of the less effective competitors? Huge concentrations of capital develop. The difficulties of starting business on nerve and a shoestring, or of hanging on after starting, increase. Many socialists, following Marx, have been less anxious about trusts than standard theorists have been, and have done less about demanding the prosecution of huge firms under our antitrust legislation. On the contrary, they have felt rather pleased at the fulfillment of the Marxian prophecy—at least the part that foresaw the development of mammoth corporations.

During this period of evolution of large firms, the middle class will find opportunities closed; it will be, to use the old socialist rhetoric, ground between the upper millstone of monopoly and the nether millstone of the proletariat, and it will disappear. It will be driven either into the ranks of the working class or into the ranks of what Marxists described as the paid flunkeys of capitalism—junior executives, corporation lawyers, labor management experts, government employees, and so on. Some fine day, before the revolution, society will be divided into only two groups—a few capitalists with their henchmen, and many miserable workers. After the revolution, society will be classless.

The facts of American economic development have half supported Marx and half refuted him. The mammoth firms are here, and today a larger percentage of the population works for wages or salaries than in 1860. The *petite bourgeoisie,* in the sense of small tradesmen and proprietors, has not expanded on a percentage basis; but the middle class has expanded, if we count members of the service industries that existed either not at all or exiguously in Marx's day— physicians, dentists, chiropodists, morticians, public school teachers, pomologists, agronomists, and geologists (it is said that more scientists are living in the United States today than were produced by all of mankind throughout recorded history until 1900). We found in Chapter 2 that many retail stores still thrive, despite Sears Roebuck, Macy's, the A & P, and similar establishments. Thus a strong middle class lingers on, though now of altered components.

Materialist Conception of History

A by-product of Marxism is its effect on almost all fields of knowledge. In support of his doctrines, Marx put to work a type of historical analysis which has sometimes been named the "materialist interpretation of history." One essential point of this method of analysis is that a vast number of social phenomena, usually non-economic ones, are explained in economic terms. With much of this, we can all agree. There is no question, for example, that many wars have had an economic basis. A national holiday, like Thanksgiving, has clear economic roots: Our thanks were initially offered for a good harvest. Wrapped up with the economic interpretation of history one usually finds a measure of geographic interpretation as well. This, too, is quite acceptable up to a point. In the sixth grade, we learn that New York is a great city because it has a good natural harbor, lies at the mouth of a navigable river, and possesses a rich hinterland. Nobody can object to this.

Marx was not, of course, the first to explain social phenomena by material causes. The method is as old as the Greeks of antiquity and was not unknown to his contemporaries. The Marxians have, however, given a twist to this simple and widely acceptable geographic and economic determinism—a twist that puts their brand of economic determinism in a class by itself. In this version the primary economic fact is a conflict between the rich and poor, which they name the "class struggle." History is to be understood, briefly, as an agelong attempt of the rich to exploit the poor and keep them in subjection. Every conceivable means in used to subjugate, according to the Marxians, from brute force to such gentle persuaders as art and religion.

To the Marxian, art and literature are largely forms of propaganda on behalf of the upper classes. The great paintings, dramas, and epics of the world, they would say in proof, are peopled by nobles and kings and men of power, never by common men. Or if the common man does appear, he is, as in William Shakespeare's *Julius Caesar*, represented as a clownish shoemaker or a member of a fickle, unreasoning mob. All of this, according to the Marxians, would be the expression of an attempt to exalt the governing and wealthy classes and to degrade the working classes. As for the art inspired by religion, from the Cathedral of Chartres to John Milton's great poetry, the Marxists would say that since religion is merely a way of diverting the minds of the poor from their harsh lot, religion and all of its products are a form of propaganda that benefits the ruling classes. They do of course recognize the existence of an art of protest, from *Piers Plowman* through Thomas Hood's *Song of the Shirt* to Pablo Picasso's *Guernica*. But, they would say, there can be very little of such art, and it can only be a harbinger of the great and true art which will flourish when the proletariat has thrown off its chains of bondage. A variant of this type of analysis is used to explain some of the abstractions of modern art and some unintelligible forms of poetry and prose. Here, the story is that since capitalism is in its last stages and crumbling away, modern capitalist art, reflecting this crack-up, is indecisive, obscure, and generally as mixed up as is the current economic order in transition.

The modern Communist party appears to believe this most fervently—so much so that they put the idea to work in reverse at home and abroad. In the capitalist countries the party seeks to influence artists and writers under the theory that their counterpunching in the arts will to some degree nullify the propaganda allegedly inherent in capitalist art. At home the party discourages, to the point of Siberian labor camps, all forms of art that do not in some way or other support its belief system.

Even the sciences are viewed in part as bourgeois creations. For a long time, Ernst Haeckel, the German biologist, was much more popular among Marxians than the much sounder geneticist Gregor Mendel. The reason is that Haeckel can be made to say that good education and good environment may permanently affect the genes and may result in the passing-on of greater native endowment by heredity to successive generations. Mendel can be made to say that inferior human endowments will never be remedied much by good environment. The significance of these conflicting genetic theories to Marxism is clear: The Marxists believe that they can quickly arrive at utopia not only by rapid improvement of the environment but also by a rapid improvement of human strains in a good environment. The genetics of Mendel offer no such hopeful shortcut. The Mendelians would concede that you can turn a dead-end kid into a better man by placing him in a favorable environment, but the environment will not improve his genes (the stuff out of which inherited characteristics are made). Thus, there can be no cumulative human improvement through a simple genetic change made by an improving environment.

Though the world of science had apparently buried Haeckel's theories with him when he died in 1919—just at a time when Mendel's conclusions were being reaffirmed by the American Thomas Morgan —the issue arose again in the 1940's. This was the famous Lysenko affair. T. D. Lysenko, the Soviet biologist, sought to bring the theories of Haeckel to life again and received the benediction of Joseph Stalin.

It is true that Lysenko has been discredited in Russia and Haeckel reburied; what is remarkable is that a dead genetic theory should ever have been resurrected at all.

Similarly, the Marxians will have nothing to do with Sigmund Freud. There may of course be sound reasons for dismissing some of the Freudian theories, but the Marxian reason is the rather superficial one that Freud got his ideas from psychoanalyzing many upper-class men and women and that his theories are therefore theories of the capitalist mind. The working-class mind is presumably different.

A joke current in the 1930's sums up the party's persistent class-struggle interpretation of events. The editor of the *Daily Worker,* a Communist party newspaper, picked up from his desk and read a news bulletin stating that a man had been killed by an automobile at 42nd and Broadway. The editor tossed the bulletin to one of his assistants, saying: "Class-angle that for tomorrow's edition." Perhaps this never happened; but the story does indicate, through exaggeration, how the Marxist version of the economic interpretation of history permeates everything from traffic accidents to esthetic theory, genetics, and psychiatry.

Summary and Conclusions

Out of the above discussion, we are able to disengage what might be named the Marxian model, that is, the basic plan of the economic system. The Marxian model is a moving picture rather than a still representation.

Roughly, here is what we see in this cinematic model. Out of the ruins of feudalism a driving, restless class arises to build up a new society, capitalism. It is industrial and urban, as feudalism was agricultural and rural. It seizes—as all economically dominant classes do in the Marxian system—control of the government, of the church, and later of the press and the system of education. It performs miracles of production and encourages and applies science. It fosters democracy of a sort and, in its conflict with the landed aristocracy, concedes to the working class certain rights it never before possessed. But still, capitalism exploits the working class; that is its functional (rather than moral) weakness. For out of this exploitation come the forces that will lead to its decay. In due course of time, this indus-

trious, dynamic class will disappear. It will disappear because it
blindly pursues its own logic to the point of self-destruction. The
verdict of history will always be favorable to capitalism. Its historic
mission was to build up a tremendously productive economic
machine, which, however, it never learned to control. The future
therefore belongs to the working class. QED!

Something like this is the basic model that Marxians have of
contemporary economic society. It resembles a plant that grows, bears
fruit, and dies, rather than physical forces seeking equilibrium, as
standard theory so often suggests. The model is of the whole society
rather than merely the economic part of it. Marx cannot separate the
economic part of society from the rest of society, as standard theory
often seems to do. Everything hangs together in an all-embracing
pattern.

But there are clearly erroneous ideas in this model. The first
thing usually criticized is its theory of value, on which all else is
based. Under capitalism, any theory of value based on costs alone—in
this case, labor costs—is defective and incomplete because it leaves
out of consideration the forces of demand. Marx shares this fault with
his predecessors Adam Smith and David Ricardo. The latter are
obviously antisocialist, and they apparently did not see to what
purposes a labor theory of value might be put.

The second criticism is a little more complex, and we shall only
suggest its nature. Marx was influenced by the great German philosopher Georg W. F. Hegel. Hegel was no socialist, and Marx disagreed
with him in many things; nonetheless, they have much in common,
and many Marxian ideas are rooted in Hegelianism. Among them are
the concepts that being unfolds and that the universe evolves by plan,
that things beget their opposites and then coalesce into a synthesis, and
that the state is a totality above all individuals. Insofar as Marx's
ideas reflect change, destiny, and inevitable goals, they are Hegelian;
and Hegelianism, though full of challenging hypotheses, is also full
of untested ones. One criticism, made particularly by the American
school of institutionalists, is that Marxian Hegelianism is a closed-end
system, a kind of system they do not accept and which, they think, is
not accepted by modern science. Marx is, in short, a metaphysician
rather than a true scientist.

Our final criticism is that Marx's predictions simply have not come true. We have not had serious depressions for a generation. We have in the 20th century had some of the savage warfare that Marx predicted, it is true; but among its many causes, economic imperialism has not been the overriding cause. Capitalism has not been as inflexible as Marx thought it was. It has been able to adapt itself and to remedy—or at least attenuate—some of its shortcomings. It has, for example, shown willingness and ability to reduce the severity of depressions; in the United States, Presidents of both major parties have said that all the resources of government would be used to prevent another decade like that of the 1930's; and in the major capitalist nations of Europe, depression seems to be even more unlikely than in this country.

All in all, then, Marxism holds rather little promise for us today, though it did possess a few interesting insights and did stimulate thought among many able men, not only on economic issues that standard theory ignored, but also on other issues of the social sciences. Marx was a great and stimulating social metaphysician, but much metaphysics has a way of being superseded by facts and by science. It is even doubtful whether the Soviet Union is strongly Marxist. Returning travelers in recent years have, when questioned, almost unanimously testified to the fact that there are comparatively few memorials to Marx; the idols, statues, and portraits have been of Lenin primarily.

QUESTIONS FOR REVIEW AND DISCUSSION

1. Define, in your own words, each of the following:
   a) Utopia
   b) Surplus value
   c) Socially necessary labor time
   d) *Petit bourgeois*
   e) Closed-end system
2. A student was asked on an examination to give an example of economic determinism. He wrote: "A man must work in order to make a living." Is this an acceptable reply?
3. Does a subsistence theory of wages make much sense? Compare the concept of a subsistence wage in the United States in the 1960's with a subsistence wage in 1860. Would you agree that subsistence varies with time and place?

4. The production of good hybrids (plants and animals) is a major cause of
   great progress in U.S. agriculture. Could T. D. Lysenko's theories inhibit
   the production of good hybrids in the Soviet Union? How? Perhaps a
   biology major or an instructor in your department of biology could help
   you in arriving at a reply.

5. Karl Marx said that depressions would get longer and worse as time went
   on. Is this confirmed by the history of the past 30 years? Might it have
   seemed true in 1932? Why, in your opinion, have depressions been less
   serious in the past 30 years?

6. Can one with consistency accept the Marshallian demand-and-supply concept of value and at the same time accept Marxism? Explain your reply.

7. Does "imperialism," according to Marxian doctrine, require actual rule by
   a mother country over a colony? Or military conquest?

8. Some economists have classified Marx as a classical economist because he
   too adhered to the classical theory of labor value. Does this seem justifiable
   to you? Explain your reply.

Chapter 21

DISSENT IN
THE UNITED STATES

Introduction

There has been a moderately steady though perhaps not strong current of dissent in American economic thought. We were a new and underdeveloped nation by British standards; and many of the theories that took root in the right little, tight little island of England, where economics was first developed, often did not fit our sprawling continent. With an intuition the wisdom of which is perhaps more easily demonstrated today than it would have been a century ago, our earliest economic thinkers rejected the classical standard dogma concerning free trade and advocated protection. Today the accepted doctrines concerning growth in underdeveloped nations advocate protectionism for countries struggling through the takeoff period.

Classical economics had for many years before 1875 held to the wages-fund theory of wages. This theory viewed wages in somewhat the same way that a subsistence farmer views his produce. If he must live from harvest to harvest almost exclusively on the rather limited quantity of corn, potatoes, apples, cabbage, and turnips he stores in the fall, then obviously he rations himself carefully to survive in comfort until the next harvest. Any prolonged increase in consumption during February, March, and April will result in scarcity and want during the early summer. So, too, the wages-fund theory assumed a fixed amount of available wages. Such a doctrine might do very well for a nation of subsistence farmers who produced almost nothing from October to July, but it made no sense for a nation like England in 1853. Or rather, it made sense to those who opposed wage increases. An American, Francis Amasa Walker, began attacking this rather silly theory in 1875 and finally buried it for good.

Henry George, reformer rather than economist, attracted a large following. What bothered him was that so many unmerited fortunes had been made in this country by the holding of land for appreciation through the growth of industry, population, and transportation. He proposed a tax on the economic rent of land. Such a tax, he felt, would yield enough to make all other taxes unnecessary—hence the name "single tax" applied to his doctrines. His proposals elicited great interest here and abroad, and in some quarters he generated a vast amount of enthusiasm. In 1886, he ran for mayor of New York City; though the loser, his share of the total vote was impressive. From the right, the chief criticism made of the single tax was that it would abolish private property in the form of land. This would be bad enough; but in addition, it would discriminate unfairly in favor of other holders of private property, such as owners of factories, ships, railroads, and so on, whose private productive property would not be touched by the single taxers' proposals. Although the Fabian socialists in England were sympathetic to Henry George's program, the strict Marxians criticized the single tax as not going far enough. They argued that socialism could not be achieved unless all the industrial equipment of a nation, as well as its land, were put into the hands of the proletariat.

As time went on and other problems came to the fore, such as the growth of trusts, trade unionism, banking reform, and World War I, the single-tax movement lost its attractive power. An organization of disciples of Henry George still exists, but the single-tax movement exerts only a feeble magnetism today.

A large number among the most distinguished economists of the period 1900–1925 had done their graduate work in Germany under the great men of the historical school (Karl Knies, Wilhelm Roscher, and Gustav von Schmoller). They returned with heretical ideas that shocked the conservatives of the classical standard tradition. Some attacked the deductive method of standard economic theory. They suggested reforms which then seemed radical in labor-management relations, urged governmental regulation of transport, and even advocated the income tax! They took an active part in forming the American Economic Association, which is still the chief professional organization of economists in the United States. The rebels, just back from Germany, wanted to insert in their first manifesto that laissez-faire was not enough to organize the economy and that the government must intervene to make human progress possible.

The more conservative among the founders urged the suppression of such extreme viewpoints. As they matured, most of the young rebels—but not all—became more conservative themselves; and with such exceptions as will be noted below, American economic thought has followed the classical or neoclassical tradition, as previously developed in this book. Two or three rebellious names might be mentioned here, though it is scarcely worth describing their work—Simon Nelson Patten, Richard T. Ely, and Scott Nearing. The most enduring form of dissent produced in the United States came a little later; it is known as "institutionalism."

The American Institutionalists

The United States has produced a brand of economic theory known as institutionalism. The name "institutionalism" is not the only one that might have been chosen; but since no one-word description can adequately suggest all the ideas held by institutional economists, this one will do about as well as any other that might have been selected. It was used to describe the work of the first American institutionalist, Thorstein Veblen, and somehow it caught on and stuck.

An institution, as widely used in the present context, does not mean a school, hospital, home for delinquents, or similar establishment. It means a pattern of inherited habits, a "cluster of social usage," to quote Walton Hamilton, who may be classified as an institutionalist. It is characteristic of an institution that it has tremendous hold on us and great governing force. The American family is, for example, an institution, and may be made to include the preceding courtship behavior, engagement ritual, proper conduct in widowhood, and divorce. It has prescriptive force in that no young American man, ready to marry, would first decide whether to found a family based on monogamy, bigamy, or polygamy; no young American needs to make the agonizing decision as to whether he will engage in courtship by adopting the methods of the Navahos or Kshatriyas. When his first child is to be born, he sends his wife to the hospital and later buys cigars for his friends instead of deciding to take to his own bed and groan, as is done in certain other cultures. To an American, free dating, going steady, and monogamy are the "natural" and proper

things to do despite the fact that there are scores—perhaps thousands
—of other natural ways of getting married and founding a family.

Now, economic systems like feudalism or capitalism are institutions. And there are institutions within institutions; within capitalism,
for example, we find the institutions of private property and of money
and credit. One can even argue that the so-called "law of supply and
demand" is an institution. We know of at least one culture that does
not change its prices under conditions of scarcity; and this alone
would be enough to suggest to institutionalists that acceptance of the
law of supply and demand is not a natural basic human response but
is, as it were, an acquired taste—or better, a group habit.

In standard economic theory, particularly at the time institutional ideas in America were first stirring about 70 years ago, it was
assumed that our economic system was the natural order—an obvious
and natural system which to its practitioners seemed to be the inevitable way in which man would organize his economic life. Adam
Smith spoke of the human "propensity to truck, barter and exchange
one thing for another." This, he suggested, might be one of the "original principles in human nature." In short, he felt that there was a sort
of shopkeeper's instinct born in all of us. The early standard theorists
were to some degree aware of the fact that American Indians and
other primitive groups had economic systems quite different from the
capitalism of their day. They tended, however, to interpret such
systems not as being qualitatively different but as being simply more
primitive forms of capitalism. Thus, David Ricardo, an early economist, has a long rigamarole about how, in early stages of society,
hunters and fishermen figure their labor time, number of employees,
and depreciation on their canoes or on bows and arrows and finally
come up with a ratio by which they exchange deer for salmon. It is
most doubtful whether calculations like this went on in the early
stages of society, for early man's economic ways of thinking were
qualitatively different from ours.

The institutionalists were not too much concerned with what went
on in primitive societies, but they were concerned to show that no
economic system is the one and only natural system. In other words,
economic systems are only bundles of institutions and, like institutions, subject to change. For institutions do change. Our courtship

habits today, for example, are quite different from what they were at the frontier or in the days of Priscilla and John Alden. And to go into economic fields, our institutions here have changed a great deal, too. Our social security system and the federal protection of collective bargaining reverse dominant beliefs of the 19th century.

When institutions change, man himself changes with them. There may be such things as "original principles in human nature," but what is popularly thought of as original human nature is often not human nature at all but the powerful force of institutions on man. It is widely assumed, for example, that man is naturally revolted at the thought of worms as a food. Actually, it is our institutions that breed this disgust in us, and it has nothing to do with human nature. Within certain limits, at least, education, environment, and institutions can mold our human nature to do the most surprising things—even to die cheerfully. The self-immolation of the Hindu widow in suttee was done willingly in response to the code institutionally prescribed.

If you postulate that man carries on his economic life primarily driven by the compulsions of his institutions—which, like our prov- erbs, sometimes make contradictory demands upon us—and is only secondarily driven by a truly enlightened pursuit of gain or pleasure, you develop a model of economic life, a cosmos, that differs a great deal from that postulated by standard economic theory. If, further, you consider that our institutions are rather stable—as they are— whereas our physical environment and technology are vastly dynamic, you may conclude that we arrive at a point where we have a dis- turbing imbalance between stable institutions and dynamic tech- nology. An example is the ability of medical science to prolong life, so that we have a larger percentage of older people than we formerly had, coupled with the inability of our institutions to provide a proper place for them in our society, either at the workbench or in the family, in specially designed homes or other proper refuges. The rather despairing cry that we should halt atomic research until man- kind has caught up morally and spiritually with the awesome powers conferred on us by atomic energy is another example of the disturbing situation in which we find ourselves as the result of a lag between the various parts of our culture. Our institutions tell us that international disputes are properly and honorably settled by the threat of force or, if needed, by force itself. Our technology tells us that force is an outmoded way of settling conflicts of interest when the amount of force available can scarcely be calculated and would suffice to return man to a worse than paleolithic world. Here is a dilemma. One of the great institutionalist economists, Thorstein Veblen, describes this type of difficulty in this way:

> While modern men continue to boast and laud the changeless antiquity and stability of the rules [institutions] which govern their industrial relations, it is at the same time their pride and boast that the industrial arts which condition their behavior under these rules are forever changing, progressively and at an ever-accelerating rate. In time, immutable rules of conduct enforced under progressively changing conditions should logically result in a muddle.[1]

Both standard theory and Marxism took root in philosophical fields that American institutionalists find infertile. The soil of Karl Marx is Hegelian; and the philosophy of Georg W. F. Hegel is identified with the absolutism of the old German Empire as well as the dictatorship of Adolf Hitler. The roots of standard theory lie in better earth, but it is a soil that lacks important nutrients. Standard theory has fed on rationalism, hedonistic utilitarianism, a Newtonian conception of science, individual liberty, and Benthamism. The American institutionalists would base economic theory on Darwinism rather than on Newtonian concepts. Newtonian science relates to the static, mechanical, and repetitive. Darwinian science is evolutionary, concerned with growth and development rather than equilibrium. Modern non-Marxian economic dissent has, at least in the United States, based itself on the instrumental theory of John Dewey.

Since this instrumental theory of Dewey's is so important a concept in modern dissenting theory, we ought to try to form some notion as to what it is all about, lest readers get the impression that Dewey—who was a mighty force behind progressive education (so called) and is therefore plausibly but wrongly held responsible for the fact that Johnny can't read or spell—has also corrupted economic thought.

In his primary field—namely, that of philosophy—Dewey urged abandoning the study of problems that had long engrossed the attention of philosophers. Many of them, he said in effect, are pseudo-problems—the real versus the ideal, the phenomenalist versus the

---

[1] Thorstein Veblen, *Absentee Ownership* (New York: Viking Press, Inc., 1923), p. 16.

absolutist. Let us give up, he said, some of our metaphysical and epistemological tasks and try to find out what the problems of man are, not what the traditional problems of philosophy are, and try to understand and rectify specific social ills. As stated here, this may seem to be a mere call to philosophers to abandon philosophy and take up social science for no very clearly stated reason. Perhaps his critics would agree with this statement. In anticipation of such a response from critics, Dewey had previously laid a groundwork which attempts to prove that he is the one who is returning to the primary concerns of philosophy (man's welfare) and that others have strayed; he argues that some of the dualisms (real versus ideal) are simply restatements of the animism, superstition, and ignorance of the past—in short, that man asked the wrong questions thousands of years ago and that we still saddle ourselves with the burden of answering them instead of throwing off the valueless baggage and asking questions that are germane to the day.

As to his psychology—for he wrote at a time when psychology was not so clearly split off from philosophy as it is today—the essential idea is not that man is rational or irrational, good or bad, or has or has not freedom of the will, but that man produces his environment and is in turn affected by it. Our intelligence and curiosity, for example, impel us to produce nuclear bombs; but then the nuclear bombs affect us and help to make us the kind of people we have turned out to be. There is interaction between man and environment. Further, man is not a passive creature, seeking pleasures and rejecting pains, but an active, goal-seeking organism much more interested in problem solving, in attaining desired ends, and often in activity for its own sake rather than in choosing between greater and lesser pleasures.

The reader will presently be able to see, as we continue to describe the concerns of institutionalists, how much they accord with the philosophy of John Dewey. The institutionalists, too, would wish to throw overboard many questions inherited from the past; they too accept a psychology which insists on the relationship between the psyche and the society that nurtures it.

Now, it will be asked, what has all this got to do with running a central bank or stopping our gold outflow in the blessed year 1968 or any of the thousand and one problems with which economists deal?

The answer is that there is no direct relationship, but that a relationship does exist. In trying to define the nature of a similar indirect relationship, William James once quoted G. K. Chesterton approvingly as follows:

> There are some people—and I am one of them—who think that the most practical thing about a man is still his view of the universe. We think that for a landlady considering a lodger it is important to know his income, but still more important to know his philosophy. We think that for a general about to fight an enemy it is important to know the enemy's numbers, but still more important to know the enemy's philosophy. We think the question is not whether the theory of the cosmos affects matters, but whether in the long run anything else affects them.[2]

In similar fashion the institutionalists might say that in economics the general view—or theory or model—that you have of the whole economic system is the most important element of your economic thought. If you believe that the propensity to truck and barter is original human nature; if you think, as the founders of standard theory thought, that the rational search for pleasure and the avoidance of pain are the mainsprings of human action; if you think that capitalist habits of thought are eternal and cross-cultural; if you think that marginal productivity is the "naturally" just way of apportioning the produce—if you believe all these things, then you have one view of the economic cosmos, and this view may affect your belief about how to run a central bank or stop our net gold outflow in the blessed year 1968. If, however, you have quite different ideas—that capitalism is a growing, changing institution that has developed out of former modes of making a living; that man's actions are only partly rational; that human beings were not born to truck and barter; that productivity or undergoing pain are not the only moral bases for consumption; that the things we consume are dictated by our institutions rather than by our rational search for pleasure—then you live in a different economic cosmos, and this may affect your attitude toward central banks and the control of gold.

The first American institutionalist of renown was Thorstein Veblen, born in 1857. He possessed, to a degree perhaps unmatched by few other mortals, the ability to free himself of the institutional prejudices that are so firmly built into most of us. He is often referred

[2] G. K. Chesterton, *Heretics* (London: Bodley Head, 1906), p. 15.

to as "Olympian" or as having Olympian detachment. This appears to be a way of saying that, like the famous visitor from Mars, he felt wonder and perplexity at everything human beings did. Why do we make business loans? Are they really an aid to production, as everybody says they are? Who do styles change all the time? Why do women bind themselves—as they did in his day—with corsets or handicap themselves with high heels—as they still do? Are handmade things really more beautiful than machine-made things, or do we impute great beauty to them because they are more expensive? Ordinary answers did not appease his inquiring mind. He had an insatiable curiosity, a restless "idle curiosity," to use one of his many good phrases. His writing was satiric, partly because he felt that what men did was on the whole rather absurd. His misanthropy is in the grand tradition and reminds one of Jonathan Swift.

His first book, published in 1899, was entitled *The Theory of the Leisure Class*. It may, in part, be considered a theory of consumption. Standard theory has little to say about consumption, except that it is characterized by diminishing utility. For Veblen, this is too little. He surveys primitive, medieval, and modern society to find that consumption is often a form of competition, a keeping-up with or surpassing the Joneses; that goods are often not desired for their inherent function, but to act as evidence that their owner possesses wealth.

Just as headhunters exhibit their shrunken heads, so do the rich like to show off their Cadillacs, and their women to display their clothes and matched accessories. The barbarian culture still lives in us. And much of our consumption is rooted in display. He speaks of this as "conspicuous consumption," a phrase that has become part of the ordinary speech of educated Americans. But the urge to display is not confined to the rich. It filters all the way down to the lowest economic strata. Thus the shopgirl wants her $9.98 basement-store version of a dress designed by Christian Dior; with it, she can snub the girl who bought only a $6.39 dress, originally designed by a nameless *couturier*.

Part of what he is saying, of course, is that our habits of consumption are not always rational and functional, and that they are often wasteful or uneconomic. Much of our produce is destined to feed the needs of vanity. Pondering this, one may well wonder whether the world can ever produce enough for all. That the human race, in another century or two, will be technologically capable of producing enough basic food, clothing, and shelter for all is a reasonable hope. But it is contradictory to hope that the world can ever produce enough to allow us all to consume more conspicuously than our neighbors. This is one of many interesting questions with which we are left by *The Theory of the Leisure Class.*

Perhaps of equal interest is Veblen's concealed repudiation of an assumption of standard theory. Standard theory assumes that consumption is exogenous, that is, rooted in motivations that have nothing to do with economics, such as love of beauty or an innate sense of elegance. If people believe that handmade shirts or shoes or wallets are beautiful and are therefore willing to pay more for them—well, then, that's that, but this is no concern of economic theory. What Veblen is trying to say is that our economic system makes us like some things better than others. Through advertising, through psychological identification with the rich and leisured, through reverence for expensive things that the rich can buy, we allow our tastes to be guided in directions that may be perverse. The Chinese once bound women's feet and found them beautiful—both women and bound feet—because (says Veblen) such women could do nothing useful. This proved that the husband was rich enough to support a completely helpless adult in his family. The corseted Victorian woman proved the same thing. To say that Victorian women both worked and wore corsets is no refutation to Veblen. The hardworking corseted woman simply was able to confer on her husband the best of two worlds; she worked for him at the same time that she inflated his ego by dressing like a woman who did not have to do her share of menial tasks. Thus, Veblen's *Theory of the Leisure Class* tangles with exogenous and endogenous aspects of consumption. Standard theory says that consumers' preferences, choices, and the like are outside the purview of economics; Veblen says that economic considerations play a large role in influencing consumption.

A second important contribution made by Veblen was a series of four essays in which he unflatteringly evaluated standard economic theory. Standard theory, he said, was based on a false pleasure-pain psychology with 18th-century concepts of a natural order, and on false analogies with the physical sciences—equilibrium, statics, dynamics, and all the rest. Economics should be closer to biology and, like it, be an evolutionary science, that is, concerned with the rise, growth, and decline of institutions.

Veblen: Pecuniary and Industrial Pursuits

Veblen took issue with an assumption of standard theory that any legal means of acquiring money also contributed somehow to the making of goods. It was out of this objection that most of his later positive work arose. As has been several times noted previously, one assumption of standard theory is that almost any honest way by which a man can make money is also to some degree connected with the making of a good or service. Hence, it is assumed that acquisition of money is an act that redounds to the benefit of the entire society. Veblen not only disagreed with this but felt that the divorce between moneymaking and goods making could serve as the basis of economic theory.

He put goods makers (and producers of services) into one category. They are the ones whose labors benefit society. They design and construct bridges, heal the sick, grow corn and hogs, cut fabrics for our clothing. They are inspired by the instinct of workmanship and produce our worldly goods. If production were left to this group alone, we would live in a society of relative abundance. But production, he said, is sabotaged by the very people into whose hands the direction of it falls—the entrepreneurs and the moneylenders. They are not really interested in the making of goods. They want to make money, and the process of making money interferes, on the whole, with the abundant and conscientious production of goods. If production can be kept at a low level, relative to potential demand, prices go up, and opportunities to make money multiply. This explains what to him is the ubiquity of monopoly or quasi monopoly. If shoddy and meretricious things can be sold, so much the better, says the money-maker; this helped to explain to him the plight of the exploited consumer. One feels when one reads Veblen that competition in its economic sense does not exist at all. Almost every transaction is one in which some degree of monopoly power—or coercive power—is employed by one of the parties. If the economy is unstable—something that is not socially desirable—opportunities for profit making increase; the shrewd money-maker can make money as a bull during the upswings of business and as a bear on the downswings. Hence, it is to the interest of money-makers to have economic ups and downs—even full-scale "boom and bust"—though to the ordinary goods-making citizen the resulting gyrations of prices are economically injurious. Credit, which is a further manipulation of money by those who understand the arts of acquisition, is a vast superstructure imposed over the process of producing goods. It may enable certain individuals to get rich at the expense of others, but it does not measurably increase production or the welfare of society at large. Thus the harmony of interest between all economic agents, as postulated by standard economic theory, simply does not exist for Veblen.

In the development of his ideas he does not, like Marx, make a frontal attack on the institution of private property, but it is clear that some forms of private property are to him indefensible. We should stop here a moment to observe that private property can be graded according to the degree to which people generally feel its possession to be defensible. Not even communists question the indefeasible right to own one's toothbrush. On the other hand, most people condemn or otherwise question the ammunition maker's right to retain the excess profits he makes during wartime; and the excess-profits tax with which we are familiar is a way of saying that Americans do not believe this property right to be indefeasible.

Veblen does seem to feel that certain forms of property rights are of questionable value to society. He does not directly and unequivocally propose government ownership of industry, but he does speak a lot about the evils of what he calls absentee ownership. "Absentee ownership" is an invidious phrase and a flexible one, and the reader is a little at a loss to know exactly what Veblen means by it. In one place, he defines it as "the ownership of means in excess of what the owner can make use of, personally and without help." It might also be described as "possession of an unearned increase of wealth." Lying behind his hostility toward absentee ownership is his feeling that some forms of property are no longer defensible in a society like ours. Some forms of property ownership will have to be changed if we are to secure the blessings of technology for all.

Now, all this sounds pretty radical, but it must be remembered that Veblen wrote in the early part of this century and that some of the institutions he attacked have changed, and changed in ways that nullify some of his criticisms. We have in the past half century accepted new ideas concerning the indefeasible rights of property. Our progressive income taxes are heavy beyond anything that Veblen knew or perhaps thought possible in a capitalist world. He did not live to see unemployment compensation benefits enacted into law in this country, or old-age benefits; both of these redistribute wealth in ways that Veblen would not have believed possible. Since his earlier writings, banking and stock market activities have been regulated to prevent some of the moneymaking abuses that Veblen saw. If one reads Veblen with the chronology of the past 50 years in mind, one finds that some of his radicalism has become commonplace. Veblen never witnessed as many years of relatively high prosperity as we have seen since 1940. This does not mean that Veblen would retract everything he wrote if he were living today, but it does mean that he saw much more to be dissatisfied about during his lifetime than he would see today. He would probably even agree that standard economic theory itself has taken a slight turn for the better.

Veblen's Theory of Economic Change

The capstone of Veblen's thinking was a theory of change. This we must summarize briefly. Between those who are primarily money-makers and those who are primarily makers of goods, there is, he says, a psychological gulf. There always has been a gulf between the makers and the predators. To Veblen, this does not result in a class struggle in the Marxian sense, though there are resemblances. The influence of advancing technology causes the gap to widen. Under feudalism and most other isms of the past the cleavage between the two groups was held within bounds of a sort. Under capitalism, however, which uses industrial machinery and promotes the development of science, the cleavage becomes deeper and deeper. For the cultivation of science and the tending of the machine nourish the realistic and constructive propensities in mankind while they starve the aggressive propensities and destroy superstition. Thus the machine tenders (factory and transportation workers), engineers, scientists, and all those whose work develops the constructive tendencies will discover a progressive atrophy of their destructive traits. The money-makers, of course, will as before cultivate their aggressive traits. Those with strong constructive tendencies will be willing to change as our rapidly evolving technology and science demand. Those with aggressive and destructive tendencies will resist institutional change.

In this state of affairs, several things can happen. Tension between the people who make money and those who make things will develop to the point at which there is overt struggle. Out of this struggle, if the makers of goods win, we may get an industrial republic modeled on the patterns of utopian thought; or if the makers of money win, we shall get a reversion to a system of status, something like fascism. (Veblen pointed out this possibility years before fascism first appeared in Italy.) Another possibility is that the money-makers —an aggressive breed imbued, as they are, by strong attitudes of national glory—will wage nationalistic wars. Whatever happens, we may be sure that capitalism as we know it will disappear. When it goes, we may have instead a utopian industrial republic, or a long season of warfare or dictatorship, something like what George Orwell describes in his *1984*.

Veblen: A Brief Evaluation

There is, of course, a great deal in Veblen that must not be taken literally. That he was often wrong is undeniable. There is at least a grain of truth in the charges that his view of capitalism was a caricature and that he wrote with "audacious charlatanism"—Eric Roll's phrase. But there is much soundness and challenge in his work, and many varieties of economists have taken his criticisms of standard theory quite seriously. We shall not go into detailed critical analysis here. It is enough to say that he represents a viewpoint and general attitude which are much more difficult to brush away than are some of his specific ideas and fanciful paragraphs.

Veblen's heirs and disciples—if the latter is not too strong a word for them—differed a good deal from Veblen himself. They made normal adjustments to family and daily life, as Veblen could not. Some took—and still hold—important posts in government, business, and universities such as Veblen with his waywardness could not have taken or held. He had no talent for the role of organizational man. His followers have eschewed caricature, satire, literary sadism, and misanthropy. But most of all, they have avoided the large unsupported generalization and have devoted themselves to the search for "opaque" facts, as Veblen had indeed exhorted economists to do, though he was not handicapped by what he preached. The criticism widely made of these fact lovers is that, like the German historical school, their passion for collecting isolated items stands in the way of their developing theories, and that facts without theory are inadequate. This criticism may not be entirely fair, but it is one of the most common criticisms leveled at the institutional school. It is perhaps unfair because standard theory seems to expect aid from institutional theory in the solution of problems and answering of questions that have been posed by standard theory. Except when the questions relate to public policy, institutionalists have little interest in them; they have their own theoretical problems and questions. In the next half of this chapter, we shall look a little more closely at this second generation of Veblenians, particularly at one of them, Wesley Mitchell, who has been among those most widely accused of amassing facts at the expense of theory.

Wesley Mitchell and the Business Cycle

After Veblen the best-known institutionalist was Wesley Mitchell (1874–1948), who spent most of his life studying the business cycle. His long devotion to this task, begun before 1913, was of course fundamentally motivated by what Veblen would have called "idle curiosity," but it must also to some degree have been his way of protesting against the neglect shown by standard theory of this spectacularly visible economic phenomenon. The reader will remember that standard theory got seriously interested in the business cycle only in 1936, but Mitchell had already been working assiduously at the task for nearly a quarter of a century.

To Mitchell the basic reason for the business cycle was a weakness in the organization of our economy. Like Veblen, he repudiated the model of an economy that organized and regulated itself through competition and price. Now, if you deny the self-regulating model of standard theory, you must find some other model to put in its place, or you must be prepared to admit that all economic life is chaos, which it obviously is not. The institutionalists, including Mitchell, have not been explicit about their substitute model, but they have said enough about it to allow us to venture an opinion as to what they might have said had they been more explicit. They would probably have accepted the following propositions as indicative of their attitude toward economic organization.

First, our institutions and basic psychological drives do much to organize not only economic life but also social life generally. Our biology and culture make us beefeaters, clothes wearers, book readers, pet lovers, founders of families, and house dwellers; and these things, up to a point, stimulate suppliers to produce beef, clothing, books, cat food, dog food, wedding rings, bridal veils, diapers, and the like. In other words, a basic economic problem—what to produce—is partly settled by many years of history, not alone by consumers' dollar votes. The human race has been eating wheat for thousands of years, and this fact bulks large as a governor of its continued production. The distribution of wealth, too, has some of its roots in our institutions. We believe in the institution of private property and in the right to transmit a large part of it through inheritance; these are institutional facts. We also believe in the justice of property incomes. Those who inherit a good deal of property are therefore entitled to a larger share of the national income than if they depended for their income on their marginal productivity alone. Assignment to tasks is also partly institutional. Though there is considerable class mobility in the Western capitalist world, and particularly in the United States, it is still true that there is a certain class and vocational stickiness. This results from our institutions. Despite many brilliant exceptions, the sons of the blue-collar class wear blue collars throughout life; and despite some truth in the saying about shirt sleeves to shirt sleeves in three generations, the sons of the professional and prosperous classes become business executives, lawyers, and doctors. In summary, then, institutions are responsible for an enormous amount of economic organizing. The preceding sentences are in sharp contrast to standard theory, which uses supply and demand to explain what is produced and how the product is divided.

Second, we do get much economic organization, the institutionalists concede, in exactly the way standard theory says we do. Price and wage expectations do of course determine whether Smith will manufacture more or fewer water skis or whether Jim will take a production job with General Electric instead of with General

Motors. Just how much pinpoint organization we get in a society where conpetition is so often imperfect is, however, a matter of opinion, and in the opinion of most institutionalists the governing force of price is much smaller than standard theory believes—but price does, after all, help to allocate resources properly and determine what is produced.

Third, government has always played a large role in determining economic affairs. We tend to think that government stayed out of private business until 1933, when Franklin D. Roosevelt became President and started big government. This is quite wrong. Government, through the tariff, forced the rapid rise of American industry after the Civil War. Federal and state and local governments encouraged canal building and subsidized the early railroads with land grants. Neither the tariff wall nor the aid to transport are to be thought of as mere sources of taxation or small public works; they are part of a vast planning program which has left a heavy impression on American life. Today, merely through what they tax or do not tax, governments direct a great deal of economic life even if we leave out of account the specific direction they give to agriculture, home construction, and countless other economic activities marked by direct governmental intervention.

Fourth, these numerous sources of organization are not enough, and there is left a degree of economic chaos. Each firm in such a society is well organized, but there is little integration among the firms. There is no central plan or goal toward which all firms contribute. The partial anarchy of such a system leads to a variety of problems, not the least of which is the business cycle. Our economy gets out of tune as a violin gets out of tune because of the way it is constructed. We do not seek elaborate causes to explain why a musical instrument becomes jangly; the reason is apparent if you stop for a moment to examine how it is made. So, too, our economic system, weakly organized, necessarily gets out of whack.

To return to Mitchell: The basic cause of the business cycle is that our economic system is incompletely organized. This is the fundamental fact. But of course, it is only the beginning. Mitchell goes much farther than this and builds a large superstructure on this basic fact. Part of this superstructure might be described as a study of how men are likely to behave under varying economic circumstances; how their hopes and fears and expectations of gain and loss cause them to engage in behavior that has a definite pattern; how some of this behavior is exaggerated by a cumulation of economic forces. But let us begin at the beginning.

A business cycle, as its name implies and according to Mitchell, is a complete circuit. It has several phases, often described as:

1. Revival (getting out of the depression)
2. Expansion (the boom phase)
3. Recession (heading downward after the peak)
4. Contraction (the depression)

When these four phases have run their course, we start all over again, like sitting several times through a movie. Not *just* like the movies, really, for the next show is never exactly like the last or any preceding one. It may be much longer or shorter, more harrowing or less. We do not always go through a depression as long and deep as that of the 1930's, or through a high, wide, and handsome boom like the one after World War II. Indeed, the best we can say is that business cycles resemble each other only just enough to persuade us that they really do form a species. Like earthquakes, they may be trivial or devastating. They are recurrent rather than periodic.

If these concepts are true, it follows that most readers of this book have lived through several cycles, that we are all living through one now, and that the more venerable among us have lived through as many as a dozen or more. These are proper deductions, granting, of course, that readers have been behaving themselves and have been living in capitalist, money-using, industrialized countries. (There are no business cycles in Cathay or in the wokas berry culture of the Klamath Indians.) Cycles vary in length from one to 12 years and seem to "average" about four years in the United States and a little more in Europe. The word *average* is placed in quotes to remind readers that there are several kinds of averages, that sometimes they have small meaning, and that it would be dangerous to plan to make stock market killings on the basis of four-year pulsations.

Each phase of the business cycle, Mitchell says, generates the next. To see how this happens, we must follow a business cycle through its phases. Start at any point you like—at depression, let us say. Prices at last have fallen so low that consumers with money decide to buy and some businessmen have come to believe that they will never be able to buy cheaper. Interest and wage rates are low and hence favorable to renewed activity. In the home, furnaces or refrigerators have worn out; industrial equipment must at length be replaced, too, unless the factory owner is prepared to go out of business altogether. Firms have been strengthened and reorganized; their owners have come to accept the idea that they are worth less than they formerly thought they were and are ready to operate with less grandiose expectations. A condition like this may be reinforced by propitious events, like a local war far away somewhere that stimulates orders for material without threatening a general debacle.

Once a revival starts, it tends to spread by a cumulative process. A few new men are hired and get wage envelopes. These wages are spent for new things, and the demand for new things requires new hands to make them; the new employment increases spending, and the spending further increases employment. Timid hope gives way to optimism. Profits are good because firms are producing enough to operate efficiently—that is, at low unit costs—and because wage rates tend to rise more slowly than prices. This process, sometimes with temporary setbacks, goes on and on until prosperity is reached.

But Mitchell's "prosperity" is not the same thing as John Maynard Keynes' "full employment." In the prosperous 1920's, Stuart Chase wrote a book entitled *Prosperity: Fact or Myth?* He showed that despite a widespread sense of well-being, many groups such as farmers and the people in the textile industry were having hard sledding. To them and the technologically unemployed, the prosperity of that seemingly golden decade was a myth. Well, it is that kind of fact-myth prosperity that Mitchell is talking about, and to which we are able to return by a self-generating process. This does not mean that full employment cannot be reached; it only means that full employment does not have to be reached when we speak of prosperity.

So now we are more or less prosperous again. Why do we not stay more or less prosperous? How do we lose our grip on this pleasantest phase of the business cycle? Prosperity brings stresses to the business system. Some of the laggard costs are beginning to catch up with the businessman and to threaten his profits: Interest rates go up; taxes may go up; rents go up; wages and even salaries rise. Less experienced or less competent workers have to be em-

ployed; more rejects are produced because greenies' hands are
clumsy; to fill rush orders, overtime at time and a half must be paid.
There is, besides, a tendency for the price of raw materials to go up
higher and faster than the price of consumers' goods. A few industries
begin to feel these pinches severely. Strains are accumulating in many
sectors. Some of the weaker firms may be failing. More cautious
bankers may refuse to renew certain loans. Here and there a spectacular business failure may sound a shrill note of warning to over-
confident businessmen. Sometimes, untoward outside events (like a
series of unprofitable harvests or the destruction of an armaments
market by the outbreak of peace) may add to the more ordinary
stresses and saturate the business community with gloom.

Now the cumulative process is reversed. Caution and gloom may
give way to fear. Everybody is searching for a way to remain solvent
in case the boom turns into bust. This helps to make it go bust.
Orders decline or are canceled, workers are laid off. A process of
liquidation sets in and then gathers momentum. Businessmen frantically throw possessions onto the market—land, houses, securities, and
stocks of goods—to salvage what money they can or to pay loans due.
This causes securities and stocks of goods to fall faster in price. Even
so, buyers hesitate to buy, in anticipation of still lower prices. Now we
are in recession and only a step away from the depression—which is
where we started—and then the whole process is repeated.

The above summary scarcely does justice to Mitchell's analysis
of how this self-generating, cumulative process goes on. It is a mere
suggestion of how he handles this part of the job and gives no hint of
the skill with which he weaves together many strands to form a
pattern.

Mitchell's account of how one phase breeds the next is widely
accepted by economists, but accepted as description rather than explanation. To Mitchell, however, this line between description and explanation is very fine, if it exists at all. To many, his entire performance is disappointing, because he never fastens attention on any one
or two factors (such as investment) as *the* cause. With Mitchell, there
are no specific causes for depression or prosperity or business cycle as
a whole, just as sophisticated men find no single cause for war. The
basic condition under which business cycles occur is that there must
be a loosely organized money-using economy, as we have already

stated earlier in this chapter. But this is not what most people think of as a specific cause. Mitchell suggests that as capitalism evolves and changes, so may business cycles change. Their immediate and precipitating causes, their length, perhaps their severity and frequency, and some of their characteristic phenomena—all these are subject to change as our society changes.

What's to be done about this business cycle? It is obviously an evil, and how can it be corrected? On this point, Mitchell has relatively little to say, though he does make a few suggestions. Yet it was fairly clear to those who read him carefully that little could be done within the framework of American capitalism as he knew it. He was about 60 when the Roosevelt revolution began, and he had perhaps miscalculated the degree of change that our society could absorb. One must guess that in his opinion only a considerable amount of governmental intervention (or economic planning) could prevent depression; and since, before 1933, economic planning seemed to be an impossible hope, he simply refused to waste time figuring out detailed palliatives for the business cycle. This was a task that remained for Keynes and his followers.

But there was a little more to it than that. Mitchell had taken note of the economic planning that had been done by the government during World War I and felt his deepest beliefs vindicated when he saw how vastly desirable the results of planning could be. This stuck in his mind, and he felt that economic planning—as we used to call it in those days—might help to even out the ups and downs of the business cycle. Yet he was rather hesitant to urge planning as a remedy. Perhaps he felt that people were not quite ready for planning except in great emergencies like war. He felt, too, that planning was pretty dangerous stuff to fool with. It was experimentation, but experimentation that necessarily had to be carried out on a large scale and that therefore might have maleficent repercussions on millions of people. Testing things in the social sphere cannot be done by a few daring pilots or by a few heroic men who volunteer to try out a new serum. Caution and some considerable skepticism about how much economists, including himself, really understood about the workings of our economic system made him hesitate to give much advice. Though he knew more about business cycles than anybody else in the world, he had really very little to say about how they might be mitigated. In subdued tones, he made some very sensible suggestions, but they were never couched in terms to stir great public controversy during the 1930's, when the issue was alive.

The differences between Keynes and Mitchell are striking. If the reader will contrast the view given in the past few pages with the Keynesian views given in Chapter 9, he will see wide differences in approach. Mitchell sees the business cycle as the result of man's behavior in a certain institutional setting, a setting in which man organizes his work mainly in business enterprises. Keynes does not center his work on business cycles at all, but rather on the expansion and contraction of the national income. Mitchell sees many small causes contributing toward a result. He sees a self-generating process, one phase inevitably turning into the next. Keynes sees forces straining toward equilibrium.

Since Mitchell is so closely identified with his studies of the business cycle, there is little more that needs to be said about his other contributions here. The reader will notice how narrow his scope was compared with Veblen's, but how much more painstaking and acceptable his work on a chosen topic. Mitchell was among the first of the non-Marxians to believe what many economists have since come to believe, too—that study of the ups and down of business is a central, not peripheral, problem of economic theory; and that a serious study of the cycle would have repercussions throughout economic theory.

John R. Commons and John M. Clark

Another important name among the institutionalists is John R. Commons. Though he is perhaps best known for his historical studies in the American labor movement, our chief interest in mentioning him is to point out the rather radical opposition of his viewpoint to that of Veblen and, to a lesser degree, of Mitchell. Both Mitchell and Veblen, as we have said, possessed an aloofness toward practical programs that, in the case of Mitchell, was a blend of skepticism and modesty for economics, but in Veblen was a profound misanthropy. Commons, on the other hand, seemed to be much more optimistic about the improvement of society. He was an active reformer; he felt that though deep conflicts of economic interest existed among groups, the conflict could usually be attenuated by some sort of reform, ranging from such things as improved education to unemployment compensation. Much of his work was done in Wisconsin, under the governorship of the liberal Robert M. La Follette, where he threw himself into a vast work of reform, from professionalizing the civil service of the state to the drafting of tax laws.

He felt capitalism to be a changing set of institutions which could slowly be shaped to serve man better. He disagreed with Marx about the existence of one great class struggle and with Veblen about the existence of a basic goods-maker and money-maker struggle, but agreed with both that coercion often was part of economic competition. And if there was not one great conflict, there was hostility, or at least tension, among various groups and blocs in the community—debtor against creditor, big business against little business, farmer against industrial worker, and so on. Groups often organize to get their way through political action; thus, government and the courts play a large role in economic life—a concept that is virtually absent from standard theory. This makes a rather interesting suggestion for an economic model—various groups fighting to advance their economic interests with the aid of political action and finally carrying their dispute to government—but one gets the impression that government is less the completely neutral tribunal than the final theater of conflict.

Commons was not an expert on the business cycle; but like most institutionalists, he recognized it as a dominant problem. Before Keynes' *General Theory*, he made certain very Keynesian suggestions about remedying depression. He felt that consumer demand should be sustained by government and that payments should be made to the unemployed, to farmers, to business, and to wage earners.[3]

John Clark, long a professor at Columbia University, is generally classified as an institutionalist. Although contributing to economics until his death, he began making additions to knowledge so long ago and at such an early age that one tends to place him with Mitchell and Commons in time. Like other institutionalists, he was drawn to the study of the business cycle, toward the analysis of which he made important contributions. One was his analysis of how large overhead costs promote instability in the economy. Another was a

3 John R. Commons, *Institutional Economics: Its Place in Political Economy* (New York: Macmillan Co., 1934), pp. 589–90.

study of the relationships between consumers' demand for consumers' goods and the entrepreneurs' demand for the capital goods that made them; the fact that the relationship is not simple and direct was pointed to as a cause of economic fluctuation.

American Dissent in the 1960's

Dissent in the United States is much feebler today than it was a generation ago. One important reason is Keynes. As we have already indicated in Chapter 9, standard economists refused to accept economic depression seriously as the center rather than the periphery of economics. To most dissenters, this seemed an unpardonable oversight. Keynes' *General Theory* appeared in 1936. Since then, income theory, depression, inflation, and the business cycle—macroeconomics, in short—have become the large nuclei around which standard theory groups itself. This has made for a *rapprochement* between standard and dissenting theory.

Another development that has brought them together is the almost incredible growth of good economic statistics. Economists of all persuasions were handicapped, even as late as the 1930's, by a dearth of statistical studies. Occasionally, an excellent and reliable study, often made by a private agency such as the National Bureau of Economic Research or the Brookings Institution, would give us an estimate of the national income, but much was still unknown quantitatively. During the early years of the depression of the 1930's, our statistical knowledge of unemployment was arrived at "by guess and by gosh." The monthly stream of comparable figures that we have today was nonexistent. Creation of a fine statistical service since then has given everybody the same facts and has prevented all economists from straying too far in imagination, since the truth of many propositions can now be checked by briefly consulting the *Statistical Abstract of the United States.* One wonders how many fanciful propositions have been mercifully drowned at birth by the flood of figures now available.

A third area of *rapprochement* lies in the changing attitude of standard theory toward governmental intervention. The hard-nosed, pre-1930 standard theorist had not changed much since the days of Adam Smith, who felt that the role of government should be limited to defense against the foe, the administration of domestic justice, and the building and keeping-up of certain institutions—such as lighthouses, presumably—which could yield no profit to private enterprise. The great depression, World War II, the atomic bomb, and subsequent experiences have demonstrated that the free market—even when it *is* relatively free—can handle only part of the job of regulating a modern economic system. All but a few diehards among contemporary standard theorists now agree that considerable governmental intervention is necessary. Disagreement may arise on kinds of policy, on areas of intervention; but there is no disagreement on the basic issue, namely, that a complex economy must supplement the regulatory forces of the marketplace with governmental regulations. This, too, makes discourse between dissenter and standard theorist possible today—discourse that was less often possible in 1930. The dissenters, of course, have never had much faith in the regulatory power of the market, particularly the imperfect markets of the modern world, and have long felt that, however useful Adam Smith's ideas were in 1750, they had become quaint by 1850 and anachronistic by 1900.

As a result of all this, areas of disagreement have been reduced. At a regional economic conference an institutionalist spoke on the topic of "Institutional Economics Today." At the close of his lecture, during the question and comment period, a standard economist observed: "But we are all institutionalists now." What he meant was that institutional and standard theory have come rather close together, pretty much as described in the three paragraphs above. Elsewhere, under somewhat similar circumstances, economists have noted that institutional theory is virtually dead, because it has served its purpose. Like third political parties in the United States, it stimulated changes; and having accomplished its purpose, it has perished.

Many dissenters would disagree that everybody is an institutionalist now, or that dissent has fulfilled its historic mission. The evolutionary viewpoint has not permeated standard theory; many of its practitioners have stopped looking at the real and troubled world to contemplate the peaceful realms of mathematics—these are among the complaints made by dissenters today.

This last complaint, the one about overindulgence in mathematics, needs a word of explanation. In earlier chapters, we saw how supply and demand curves could be made to symbolize certain

economic entities and to show relationships. This sort of thing can be
carried pretty far, as the page from the *American Economic Review*
reproduced on page 449 will suggest. Now, no educated person will
deny the vast benefits conferred on the human race by the use of
mathematics in science. But many educated persons will also ask
whether mathematical reasoning can take us very far in solving
economic problems. Statistics is of course a different story. The counting of the unemployed, the estimation of GNP, figures on imports,
exports, and demand deposits—all these are important figures, and
though they involve the use of arithmetic, algebra, and the calculus,
they are not what we mean when we speak of mathematical economics.
Mathematical economics is fundamentally the standard economic
theory heretofore discussed in this book but stated in mathematical
rather than verbal symbols. All the economic theories discussed under
standard theory can be put into mathematical terms. For instance, by
employing two equations, we can describe what a monopolist must do
to maximize profits. The first equation would represent the demand
curve for the monopolist's product, and the second equation would
represent the monopolist's costs of production. With the use of the
calculus, these equations would determine the output and price that
would maximize the monopolist's profits. Mathematical economics
claims certain advantages over verbal standard theory. Among the
most important are the fact that mathematical analysis employs precisely defined terms and assumptions, and the fact that mathematics
facilitates more complicated operations than could be handled
through a nonmathematical approach. Another attribute claimed for
mathematical economics is that it more clearly indicates the limitations of economic theory by removing the camouflage of words. However, the use of mathematics does not free standard theory from the
limitations inherent in its methodological approach.

Another area of economics that uses a great deal of mathematics
is called econometrics. An econometrician attempts to represent reality by a set of mathematical equations which are derived through
statistical investigation. The set of equations, or econometric model,
can then be used to explain or predict economic occurrences. Econometrics is limited by the fact that it deals only with quantifiable
variables and therefore neglects many of the sociocultural factors that
influence man's economic activity. Some economists feel that as this

relatively new field of economics matures, it will prove to be an important area of dissent from standard theory. The development of computers in recent years has suggested the possibility of great achievement in this field. Many dissenters feel that most of the problems that can be handled this way are not problems of the real economic world. They are formalized problems, as distantly related to the world as chess is to the modern battlefield. In short, dissenters believe that mathematical economics has for many economists become both a refuge from reality and a game rather distantly related to economic problems—a game that distracts attention from the study of the human condition. Edith Hamilton, the renowned classicist, comparing ancient Egypt and India to the more realistic Greeks of Periclean times, has some interesting remarks to make about mathematics, with which dissenters would agree. Egypt, the reader will remember, fled to an inner universe; its center of interest was the dead. Concerning Egypt and mathematics, Edith Hamilton writes:

It is easy to understand how in these conditions the one department of the intellect that flourished was mathematics. Nothing is less likely to react practically upon life or to intrude into the domain of theology than the world of the idea revealed to the mathematical imagination. Pure mathematics soars into a region far removed from human wretchedness and no priest ever troubled himself about the effects of free inquiry along mathematical lines. There the mind could go where it pleased. "Compared with the Egyptians we are childish mathematicians," observes Plato. India, too, made notable contributions in this field. But sooner or later, if the activity of the mind is restricted anywhere it will cease to function even where it is allowed to be free.[4]

Dissent from standard economic theory in the United States today is formless but pervasive. It is methodological rather than utopian. It is much closer to institutionalism than to Marxism. With a few notable exceptions, modern dissenters are inarticulate—or rather, their voiced dissent is oral rather than written. The leading economic journals of the country do not reveal the existence of a strong minority dissatisfaction with the dominant trends in economic theory today.

One of the more active institutionalists of repute is Clarence E. Ayres of the University of Texas. His influence on students has been considerable, particularly in the Southwest and Middle West. He pursues the Veblen-Dewey train of thought, fleetingly described a few

[4] Edith Hamilton, *The Greek Way* (New York: W. W. Norton & Co., Inc., 1942), p. 16.

SHINOHARA: THE MULTIPLIER

As it is a closed system, $Y = Y_d$. From equation (a), it follows that when $e_p = 0$, $k_r = k_m$, and when $e_p = 1$,

$$\frac{k_r}{k_m} = 1 - \frac{aP}{Y} k_r.$$

Since in general (in rigorous terms, if $S/Y > 0$),

$$\frac{aP}{Y} k_r < 1,$$

k_m will be relatively larger than k_r according as e_p becomes larger. In my previous article (*op. cit.*), a modification of equation (a),

$$\frac{k_r}{k_m} = e_0 + e_p k_r \frac{S}{Y} \tag{b}$$

was called the fundamental equation.

We assume, next, the Duesenberry saving function,

$$\frac{S_r}{Y_r} = \beta \frac{Y_r}{Y_{ro}} - \alpha \qquad \text{(Duesenberry)}$$

where Y_{ro} is the highest real income in the previous peak and S_r is real savings. By multiplying both sides by PY_r, and differentiating this with respect to Y, we get

$$\frac{d(PS_r)}{dY} = \beta \frac{Y_r}{Y_{ro}} (1 + e_0) - \alpha. \tag{c}$$

This value ranges from

$$\left(\beta \frac{Y_r}{Y_{ro}} - \alpha \right) \text{ when } e_0 = 0 \text{ to } \left(2\beta \frac{Y_r}{Y_{ro}} = \alpha \right)$$

when $e_0 = 1$. The ratio between k_r and k_m in the case of the Duesenberry function is,

$$\frac{k_r}{k_m} = \frac{\beta \dfrac{Y_r}{Y_{ro}} (1 + e_0) - \alpha}{2\beta \dfrac{Y_r}{Y_{ro}} - \alpha}. \tag{d}$$

If $e_0 = 1$, then $k_m = k_r$.

Modigliani's saving function was,

$$\frac{S_r}{Y_r} = \alpha^* + \beta^* \left(\frac{Y_r - Y_{ro}}{Y_r} \right). \qquad \text{(Modigliani)}$$

SOURCE: Taken from M. Shinohara, "The Multiplier and the Propensity to Import," *American Economic Review*, Vol. XLVII, No. 5 (December, 1957) p. 623.

pages back. It is difficult to name in order of importance other institutionalists, though certainly the names of Allan G. Gruchy and David Hamilton would belong in any list.

A group much larger than the institutionalists has made itself felt. These, for want of a better name—indeed, of any name—might be called free-floating dissenters. Perhaps the longest known of the well-known names of this group is Gardiner C. Means. Without accepting the authority of Veblen, he has called for the reconstruction of economics in the following fashion:

> The Modern Corporation has undermined the preconceptions of classical economic theory as effectively as the quantum undermined classical physics at the beginning of the twentieth century. An equally drastic reconstruction of economic theory is due and is, perhaps, now in process. It is my purpose here to present a background for this reconstruction. This I propose to do by examining the relation between recent events and economic theory.[5]

Another free-floating dissenter is John Kenneth Galbraith. His model of the economic world is a sort of political model, various power groups keeping one another in check—big corporations, big labor, agriculture, and other groups. The strength of each is weakened by the strength of other blocs.

This group of dissenting economists—which is not a group but rather a miscellany of individuals—has no particular leadership and looks to no economist of the past as the founder of its school, for there is no school. Some of these individuals are specialists in labor problems and feel they get little help from standard theory. Others are students of economic growth and see little of value for them in price theory; and the Keynesian theory, though more helpful than price theory, is still a static theory, only partially useful in a study of underdeveloped, growing economies. Still others, students of the corporation, antitrust, oligopoly, and the like, find that the theories of imperfect competition as developed by standard theory carry them only a step or two toward the solution of their problems. Whether they will be able to respond to unifying forces sufficiently to achieve their aim, namely, the reconstruction of economic theory, remains to be seen. Several hundred have organized themselves into the Associa-

---

[5] Gardiner C. Means, *The Corporate Revolution in America* (New York: Crowell-Collier Publishing Co., 1962), p. 47.

tion for Evolutionary Economics, with a quarterly named the *Journal of Economic Issues.*

Summary and Conclusions

Now, as one looks back upon the work of the institutional economists, one cannot help noting how different their work, their interests, and their concerns are from standard theory. There is little interest in the price-forming process. The words "supply and demand" rarely appear in their books. Neither word appears, for example, in the index of Wesley Mitchell's 1927 book on business cycles; and this fact cannot be blamed on some editorial oversight, for it reflects the general spirit of the whole book. If the institutionalists were lacking in other virtues, they at least can be congratulated for going far without ever saying "supply and demand."

What is most criticized by standard theorists in institutional economics is that it lacks theories. The Veblens, Mitchells, and Commonses have never developed things like the laws of diminishing utility and diminishing returns, or Pareto's law. There is no precise, widely accepted model like the model of pure competition, which becomes the starting point for further elaboration. The institutionalists do have their institutions in common as the basis for a model, but they are not put together to form a neat abstraction on which there is widespread agreement—for Veblen's institutional model is really quite different from Commons', though they are not completely out of touch with one another.

It has often been said in criticism of the institutional approach that since it really has no theories, it has no general solutions and no general policy recommendations. This is not quite true; in the desperate depression years of 1932 and 1933—to take one case—the institutionalists had more intelligent things to say about alleviating the depression than did standard theory. The real trouble seems to be that institutionalists theorize about their own model exclusively, whereas standard theorists find laws to govern only theirs; and since the models vary widely, communication between them is difficult. If Colin is theorizing about the moon and Collette is theorizing about Jupiter, and if both of them think they are theorizing about the same thing, each will think the other's attempts at theorizing rather inferior. And this seems to be the situation in economics. Institutional economics has plenty of theories, but they do not look like theories to standard critics, many of whom do not understand what institutionalists are trying to say.

For whatever reason, institutional theory has not attracted a sufficient number of economists over a long period of time to build up a large community of scholars who revise and check one another's work. Science requires human groups large enough to establish a fruitful cooperation, and the institutionalists appear not to have been able to attract an optimum number of men and women sufficiently imbued with the same viewpoint to develop and refine their theories.

Whatever their faults or merits, institutional theory and other forms of dissent have played the same useful role in economics that third parties have played on the American political scene. Third parties have never thrived here; they could never effectively combat the strength and prestige of our two major parties. Because, however, some of their ideas met real needs, these ideas have been taken over by one of the major parties. So, too, over the decades, standard theory, like either of our major parties, has from time to time taken over—or paid heed to—the objections and arguments of dissenters. It tried to free itself from the shackles of an underlying pleasure-pain psychology; its work on imperfect competition is a tacit admission that the model of perfect competition has its weaknesses; in 1936, under the leadership of Keynes, standard theory at last made a serious study of the business cycle. The National Bureau of Economic Research, headed by Mitchell, began making studies of national income long before the Keynesians used income as a basis for their work. Now, it must not be thought that all this change is uniquely traceable to the prodding of American institutionalists or even to dissenting theory in general. A thousand forces have supervened in the past 50 years to compel change in standard economic theory.

With John Dewey, the philosopher, institutionalism shares a certain general neglect because it has no glittering facade. It promises no final truths, no clear and definite causes for visible effects. It is the enemy of a closed-end system such as Marxism. It is not pessimistic in that it does offer hope for mankind, but it offers no simple solutions to human problems. It demands the eternal facing of opaque facts—

something that disturbs our complacency and deflects us from our quest for easy certainty.

QUESTIONS FOR REVIEW AND DISCUSSION

1. Define, in your own words, each of the following:
   a) Single tax
   b) Institutionalism
   c) Hegelianism
   d) Hedonism
   e) Utilitarianism
   f) Econometrics
   g) Misanthropy
2. What similarities and what differences do you see in the Keynesian multiplier and Wesley Mitchell's "cumulative process"?
3. What made advocacy of the income tax heretical in the 19th century? Consult an encyclopedia and prepare a brief essay on the history of the income tax. Why was the 16th Amendment to the Constitution required?
4. Look up the article on pragmatism in the *Encyclopedia of the Social Sciences*. Prepare a brief essay on John Dewey's ideas and influence.
5. Do you agree with G. K. Chesterton and the implications of the authors of this book that one's general view of the world affects one's view of certain aspects of it? Could not two persons with radically different views of the world agree on the same theories of physics?
6. How would Thorstein Veblen meet this argument: "You seem to say that only expensive things are considered beautiful; but what about sunsets and sunrises, or a painting by Rembrandt, or the music of Mozart?"
7. Veblen states that credit does not increase productivity. Can you agree with this statement? (Actually, Veblen did make a few exceptions, but his position was substantially as stated here.)
8. During Veblen's lifetime, some American Marxians wondered whether or not Veblen was a socialist. The final consensus was that he was not. What arguments might have been adduced pro and con?
9. What are your own responses to the argument that institutionalists neglect theory? What is theory as opposed to description? Are Veblen's predictions concerning economic evolution based on theory or description? What about Mitchell and the business cycle?
10. Assume that costs rise in a period between depression and prosperity. Which of the following, as well as others you might think of, would rise slowly or after a lag: taxes on land, interest, rent, raw materials, wages? What part would two- or three-year contracts play in producing lags?

11. Try to get hold of a copy of the *Statistical Abstract of the United States* for some year in the 1920's. Compare it with the current volume. What topics do not appear at all in the older volume? What do you find on such subjects as GNP, unemployment, or distribution of national income?

12. How would you distinguish between the phrases "statistical economics" and "mathematical economics"?

13. Can one make useful policy recommendations that are not based on theory? Before vitamins were discovered and their function understood, the human race had developed certain sound notions about diet. Are drugs being used today whose action is not understood by theory, but which achieve desired results? Are comparisons of economics and the medical arts valid?

14. In this book and elsewhere, you have read about business cycles, depression, stagnation, recession, crises, "boom and bust," and decline of national income. What are the similarities and differences among the preceding words and phrases?

PART V
Economic Growth

Chapter 22

ECONOMIC GROWTH AND DEVELOPMENT

Introduction

Several of the major economists of the past have given some attention to the problem of economic growth or to what is quite similar, the question of economic change or economic development. The chapters and sections on Karl Marx and Thorstein Veblen have shown how much the dissenters have thought about this, and various of the older standard economists from Adam Smith to Alfred Marshall have also had something to say on the subject—not to mention a wide group of 20th-century economists from Joseph Schumpeter to Wesley Mitchell. But like the work on depression and inflation, the study of economic growth did not take on major stature until quite recently. Indeed, the subject did not come into the economic foreground until after World War II.

Numerous forces have combined to place this problem in the limelight. One is the great impact of Keynesian thought. Under the Keynesian analysis a depression in the advanced capitalist nations may be looked upon as a halt in economic growth, and this view of depression encourages scrutiny of the process of growth itself. Another force has been the "revolution of rising expectations," to use Adlai Stevenson's phrase. For various reasons the underdeveloped nations, such as India and China, are not content to stay backward and are organizing themselves for accelerated growth. This has political repercussions and threatens to disturb the world balance of power; the rich nations, generally sympathetic to the growth of the underdeveloped nations, are nonetheless concerned as to what economic growth may mean in future power alignments, since political power is related to economic growth. Finally, the economic growth of the Soviet Union has been a matter of anxiety to the Free World. Though still far behind us in productivity, she has until recently been growing at a rate twice as fast as the United States. Since Nikita Khrushchev has stated that Russia intends to vanquish capitalism by superior economic achievement, we have something more than academic interest in the question of how economies grow.

What is economic development? How can we measure it? As a first approximation, we can say that the index of economic growth is the long-term rate of growth of real income per capita. There are a few valid objections to this concept, but it will serve as a starter. By saying "real," we exclude a mere monetary increase in income resulting from inflation, since rising prices may accompany a stationary income. We rely on the per capita concept to wash out population increases. Real national income may rise at the same time population increases, but unless real income rises faster than population, our standard of living does not rise. And we say "long-term" to exclude relatively brief depressions or booms.

Now, there are certain objections to the statements made above. For example, assume that income is increased by longer hours of work—by loss of that desirable commodity named "leisure." Is this economic growth? Is a nation really stagnant economically if population and income rise at the same rate? Does economic growth have much meaning if no humane values whatever are attached to the type of increased wealth produced—if, for example, more chromium on vacuum cleaners and more filigree on more boudoir lamps symbolize the nature of the increased wealth? We do not answer these questions but merely ask them to show that the concept of "a per capita increase in real income" is only an approximate definition of economic growth.

The growth rate of the real national product of the United States has in recent decades been about 3 percent annually. It exceeded 4 percent between the Civil War and World War I. The Soviet rate was until recently estimated at 7 percent. To be sure, the Soviets have much more to grow to than we, but this kind of speed is disturbing. The rates of growth of the advanced, rich countries of the Free World during the 1950's were mostly above ours, but reconstruction after World War II may have had something to do with this. Switzerland and Canada, which were not devastated, were a little ahead of us. Sweden and Norway were close to us. England was behind. Japan, with a thumping 9.3 percent, was at the head of the class. Latin-American income, it has been estimated, grew at the rate of 3 percent during the early 1950's, but population growth has been so rapid that per capita income has scarcely registered the improvement.

The approaches to the study of economic growth may be divided into two general categories—historical and ahistorical. The historical studies seek to derive lessons about growth from the experience of nations that are now advanced. The ahistorical seek to explore our present knowledge of economics with a view to seeing what principles from current theory are applicable to the problems of growth. We take up first two interesting historical approaches.

The Contributions of Economic History

W. W. Rostow has captured the attention of economists all over the world with his book named *The Stages of Economic Growth*. His stages are five, as follows:

1. The traditional society
2. Preconditions for takeoff
3. The takeoff
4. The drive to maturity
5. The age of high mass consumption

Traditional societies include those of the ancient world as well as those of the modern world that have not yet begun to apply modern science consistently to their problems of production or health. Economic growth in these societies may be visible over the centuries but not over the decades.

The second stage of growth is the period in which the preconditions for takeoff are developed. One way of describing this would be to say that whatever went on in England from about 1400 to 1780 got the British ready for their takeoff. This included stable parliamentary government, the building of good roads and ports, an economic system in which agriculture declined while trade and manufacturing increased, the development of nationalism, and the purposeful application through science of better and cheaper ways to produce. Rostow seems to feel that humiliation is an important ingredient of this period —an affront to the growing spirit of nationalism—in Germany, the bitter memory of Napoleon; in czarist Russia, Napoleon again, as well as the Crimean and Russo-Japanese wars; and in Japan, Commodore Matthew Perry's menacing ships.

The third stage, the takeoff, may be thought of as a period characterized by events—primarily economic events—such as occurred in England between 1783 and 1802; and in France, Belgium, and the United States roughly between 1835 and 1860. India and China appear to be still in the takeoff period, which may have begun for both in 1952; but since the takeoff period appears to last about two decades, we shall not know until 1972 whether the Chinese and Indians really did take off. During this period the rate of investment must rise to a minimum of 10 percent of the national income. If it is really successful, growth is built into the economy—that is, economic agents, by continuing to do what they have been doing, will cause the economy to grow. Growth is now a normal part of economic endeavor. The economy can be compared to a seedling that has put forth its adult-shaped leaves and caught on; it has germinated, formed roots, and is ready for steady growth.

The next period is the drive to maturity, which lasts for about 40 years after the end of the takeoff period. Investment will continue to exceed 10 percent of the national income and may rise to 20 percent. Industrialization spreads along a broad front. The national income grows faster than population. France, the United States, and Germany all reached this stage by 1915. Such nations have mastered the technology required to produce, within reason, almost anything that can be produced anywhere else in the world.

The last stage is that of high mass consumption. This is the era of consumers' durable goods, such as sewing machines and typewriters in the home, and of the wide diffusion of electric gadgets of all kinds—irons, shavers, blenders, mixers, and, at long last, the battery-powered toothbrush. This period began for the United States, the first nation to enter this blissful era, just after the depression of 1920–21; for Canada, the second mass-consumption nation, a year or two later.

So much for the five stages of growth. Rostow, the author, goes on to connect some of his insights into the nature of growth with warfare, colonialism, and foreign policy—areas in which it would be digressive to follow him. For our purposes, it is perhaps enough to make note of the fact that he has created a useful taxonomy, or system of classification. The names of his stages are used by economists everywhere in the Free World, at least; he has in a sense standardized the periods of economic growth in somewhat the way that, in human growth, we use such standard terms as "preschool," "infancy," "adolescence," and "senescence."

Other economic historians have sought to explain other aspects of

growth. The German historical school explained the rise of capitalism by finding causes in religious beliefs. To put it much too briefly,
they looked to the rise of Calvinism, the migrations of European
Jews, and the decline of Roman Catholicism, as shapers of a new
belief system that made the rise of capitalism possible and, with it,
economic growth.

A living American, Clarence E. Ayres, has made a most valuable
contribution, though less widely known than Rostow's stages of
growth. We begin a summary of his theory by noting that until about
400 years ago, differences in levels of living throughout the world
were relatively small, if we except the exiguous groups that still lived
under barbarism or savagery, such as the Indians of North America.
Men were using wheels and waterpower to lighten their tasks; they
had long ago domesticated animals and understood the cultivation of
the soil. Pottery, cloth, fire, boats, sails, and other basic discoveries
and inventions were old stories. But in about 1500, first England and
then the nations of Western Europe began to pull away from humanity
elsewhere and by 1800 or so had attained to such a high level of
technological development that their produce surpassed that of the
rest of the world. This technological development, by cultural diffusion, was shared with Australia, New Zealand, Canada, and the
United States, and a little later with Japan.

It is not too hard to explain why the transplanted children of
Western Europe shared her capacity for economic growth, and only a
little more difficult to explain why Japan joined the ranks of the
advanced nations. What is really hard to explain is why Western
Europe forged so far ahead of Asia; or—for it amounts to the same
thing—why Asia, as far advanced as anybody in 1550, stayed behind
after that.

To explain this, Ayres[1] asserts that Western Europe was the
frontier region of Mediterranean civilization. A frontier is a region of
many cultural contacts, of free and easy manners; the ceremony and
institutions of life back home are easily thrown off. Religion may not
lose its force; but theology, ritual, and strict doctrine change and may
lose some of their authority. Marriage remains, but the traditions
surrounding courtship may break down. The ceremonial needed to

[1] Clarence E. Ayres, *The Theory of Economic Progress* (New York: Schocken
Books, Inc., 1962).

celebrate a marriage with a wasteful seven-day festival may disappear. As institutional resistance breaks down, technology can come
into its own. For technology does not necessarily gain acceptance
simply because it exists. The Chinese invented gunpowder but used it
only for firecrackers; in the West, its potentialities were more widely
exploited—often for human woe rather than for man's weal, it is true,
but if it is immoral to kill people with bullets and cannonballs, the
fault is in man, not in gunpowder. Two thousand years ago, Hero
invented a jet-propelled steam engine, but his culture found no use for
it. The Arabs, despite their well-developed technology, refused for a
long time to embrace printing because of an institutional proscription
about graven images.

Technology, as conceived by Ayres, is not a simple thing. It
includes mathematical symbols and printing; it includes all the instruments we use to further knowledge, such as thermometers and
microscopes. It includes "human skills and know-how and the complement of tools and equipment in which such skills and know-how are
embodied."[2] It includes science and the scientific method.

Now, this frontier region of Western Europe was exposed to the
technology of previous ages—of Greece, Rome, Egypt, the Middle
East, and Byzantium. Its institutions were weak. According to Ayres,
"technological revolution spreads in inverse proportion to institutional resistance."[3] Because resistance was weak, the capacity of
Western Europe to absorb, assimilate, recombine, and develop technology was great. Thus, it came about that the people of Western
Europe were "endowed with a full complement of tools and materials
derived from a parent culture and then almost completely severed
from the institutional power system of its parent."[4]

Leaving institutions aside for a moment, it should also be recognized that any technology grows through contact with another technology. For example, well-rigged, sturdy, deep-draft ships were developed by combining the clinker-built boats of the Vikings with the
large, well-rigged, shallow-draft, often oar-propelled ships of the
Mediterranean. Such hybrid ships had to be built before the great
voyages of discovery could be made. Institutional resistance might

[2] *Ibid.*, p. xxi.
[3] *Ibid.*, p. xix.
[4] *Ibid.*, p. 137.

have prevented the fusing of the northern and southern shipbuilding virtues; but it did not, and now Western Europe was in contact with the East Indies and West Indies.

Ayres uses this historical analysis to justify his emphasis on the role of literacy and education in establishing the preconditions of economic growth. There can be no Rostovian "takeoff" without literacy. This is where the big initial push must be made. He downgrades efforts to supply copious flows of capital to underdeveloped areas unless massive educational efforts have been made. In partial support of this, he cites cases in which advanced capital goods have been introduced into underdeveloped nations—pipelines, oil-drilling rigs, plantations, mines, and factories into Latin America, the Middle East, and India. Wherever this has been done without education, we find islands of modern capital goods surrounded by oceans of illiterate agricultural or nomadic people, not much different today from what they were a hundred or even a thousand years ago, except perhaps that they are even poorer. In short, here are people with the most modern technology in front of their very noses; but their institutions and resistance to change, not yet undermined by education, prevent them from copying what they see.

Joan Robinson, the imperfect competition lady of Chapter 6, reviewing sympathetically Ayres's analysis, notes casually—even perhaps half humorously—that if Ayres's theory is right, Black Africa will outstrip us all economically, for she finds that in the world today the frontierlike situation closest to that of Europe centuries ago is to be found in Black Africa.[5]

It is hard to know what lessons the historical studies described above are able to teach us. Human beings tend to find in history what they are looking for; the "lesson" is known in advance and then history is dredged to find evidence in support. Some things do seem clear, however. Much of the world, if no longer in the traditional society, still has far to go before the preconditions for takeoff are fulfilled. There must be political stability and good government. It must be good government in the sense that despite a little graft here and there and some partiality to favored groups, the welfare of the whole nation now and in the future receives adequate consideration.

---

[5] Joan Robinson, *Economic Philosophy* (Chicago: Aldine Publishing Co., 1963), p. 113.

This is not yet true of Latin America, with which we, as North Americans, are deeply concerned. How long will it take? Where are the frontiers in which institutions have but a tenuous hold, to follow Ayres? Or how many more humiliations, to follow Rostow? One cannot help feeling, as one looks over the record spread by history, that half the world is in for a long and difficult period before the underdeveloped nations arrive at the takeoff stage. Inefficient and corrupt governments by the dozen will have to be overthrown, institutions sacred to large masses of humanity will have to relax their grip, and new belief systems will have to be adopted by reluctant populations.

It is interesting to speculate on what the next stage of human and economic development may be. Earlier, we noted Rostow's suggestion that in the United States, now that high mass consumption has been achieved, our affluence will go into accelerated human reproduction, Malthusian fashion. But elsewhere, other predictions are being made and other possible pathways being pointed out. Such American economists as John Kenneth Galbraith, Seymour Harris, and a group of neoinstitutional economists feel that we are now ready to improve the quality of American life, that is, to divert our wealth-creating power away from redundant automobiles, radios, and TV's, away from electric salad-tossing machines and automatic back scratchers, to cleaner air and water, better-landscaped junkyards, better schools, hospitals, prisons, police systems, and insane asylums.

A British publicist, speaking of his country, suggests that self-generating growth—or at least, rate of growth—declines; that industrial equipment even in an advanced nation may wear out faster than it is being replaced; and that a second "takeoff" must be planned and achieved before his country can move forward to meet the increasing expectations of an affluent society.[6] Ben B. Seligman, in his book *Most Notorious Victory*, is chary of firm prophecies, but he does call attention to the danger of man's being overwhelmed by the machine. His fears are based on a down-to-earth knowledge of the computer and automation rather than on a poetic hostility to science and its works.

Aldous Huxley and George Orwell were not economists, and their forecasts were based on artistic intuition and inspiration rather

[6] Andrew Schonfield, "Britain Needs a Second Industrial Revolution," *New York Times Magazine*, August 21, 1966, pp. 32 ff.

than on a sound statistical extrapolation of current and measurable trends; yet their dread predictions concerning the post-high-mass-consumption economy cannot be discounted.[7] And as has been said in an earlier chapter, man's capacity to make technological changes is so much greater than his capacity to make appropriate institutional changes that he may go down in defeat. This, at least, is one of the prospects held out by Veblen.

Nonhistorical Studies of Growth

If, now, we turn to the nonhistorical studies of economic growth, we find a dark and bewildering jungle of theories, growth models, mathematics, statistics, empirical wisdom, and policy recommendations. Elementary textbooks are devoting as much as one fifth of their pages to growth, and economists in droves are publishing books and articles on the subject. The following discussion can scarcely do more than suggest the kinds of problems economists are trying to solve. It will help us to work if, before we start talking directly about growth, we clear away a certain amount of underbrush by putting down a few brief clarifying statements, which follow immediately.

We may assume that any economy which has taken off in the Rostovian sense has built-in growth and will continue to grow—as will a normal six-year-old child, quite unconscious of what he is doing, but for different reasons. In the case of an economy, the institutions and the aspirations and abilities of its members are all stable enough to impel them to carry on in the future as they have carried on in the past.

Thus, to take ourselves as an example, we shall probably grow at an annual rate of about 3 percent in the future as in the past, without doing very much about it, or at least not consciously doing much more about it than fiddle around with taxes and the discount rate. It is true that some economists believe capitalism must eventually slow down, and they are possibly right. To go into this problem would take us rather far afield.

All the stir about American economic growth revolves around an increase of 1 or 2 percent. We are now growing at about 3 percent. No responsible person has suggested that we seek to grow at a rate higher

[7] Huxley's *Brave New World* and Orwell's *1984*.

than 5 percent, and a rate of 4 percent is nearer the consensus. But to achieve this extra 1 or 2 percent, we shall probably need governmental intervention.

Leaving aside the possible surprises of the future, no economy will sustain growth at a rate faster than about 10 percent. Indeed, the most rapid rate of growth on earth today is about 9 percent—the Japanese rate. The reasons growth rates cannot soar to 20 or 50 or 100 percent are easily perceived by common sense: Population grows slowly, and all production requires human labor; new resources are not made quickly available—it takes time to develop new mines, to build new buildings, and to clear new land; livestock, orchards, and woodland require definite periods of gestation; new technology is developed slowly—not every year sees a new basic discovery that has revolutionary applications to increased production.

When we talk about growth beyond current rates in capitalist countries, we have two kinds of problems to deal with. First, there is the pure act of industrial growth, which is more or less the same everywhere. Everywhere, growth requires more and improved capital goods, a better educated population, an increasingly skillful working force, continued access to raw materials either through discovery of new sources or good substitutes for old materials, and so on. The second problem is how to stimulate growth and plan for an increased rate within our institutions without disturbing too much our present sense of how much government should intervene.

A Communist dictatorship is to a large degree unhampered by the second problem. It can intervene at many more points in the economy than can the democratic governments of the advanced capitalist states, particularly the United States, which has stronger traditions of nonintervention than most nations of the world. Thus the Soviet Union can focus attention with greater exclusivity on what, in the paragraph above, was named "the pure act of industrial growth." There are, however, even in a Communist dictatorship, limits as to what it can do. Perhaps the Soviet Union could grow faster if the underlying population were willing to eat cottonseed and soybean cakes, as cattle do; but even a dictatorship cannot, except in such emergencies as war, force so much austerity on its citizens. The Soviet Union, too, is handicapped by its own belief system—largely the quasi-religious dogmas of Marxism.

The underdeveloped nations, though varying a good deal among

themselves, are on the whole probably more willing to accept governmental intervention as an aid toward achieving an increased rate of
growth than we are. But they too are distracted from the act of pure
growth by their institutions, belief systems, traditions, and the like.
Thus, Latin America could probably grow faster if the population
increased at a slower rate. Its belief system precludes an aggressive
attack on this problem. The strong feeling in India about not destroying any kind of animal life inhibits its growth; the Indians neglect an
important resource and put up with the depredations of roaming
monkeys and cattle.

Growth can be defined as increased and improved production.
There are, according to standard theory, four factors of production.
The way to increase production is, then, to get more in the future than
in the past out of the four factors. Although this statement is an over-
simplification, it is a useful guide. Growth everywhere requires an
improvement in the industrial quality of the working force and more
capital. In backward nations that will probably take the capitalist
route, the development of entrepreneurship is a desideratum; and in
communist nations, better managers and planners. Land cannot really
be improved, though we can drain it or irrigate it or fertilize it or
protect it from floods. Here, students have given much attention to
land tenure, which, among other things, means dividing it up into
parcels that are neither too large nor too small.

While recognizing that economic growth can result from changes
in the quantity or quality of any of the four factors of production,
standard economic theorists have based most of their models of
economic growth on increases in the size of the capital stock. In most
of their models, it is assumed that a definite relationship exists
between the quantity of capital a nation has—its capital stock—and
its capability to produce. If a nation's capital stock is increased, so is
its productive capacity. This relationship between capital and national
product is put in terms of a "capital coefficient." If the capital stock of
a nation is valued at $400 billion and its full-employment level of
national output is $100 billion, the capital coefficient is 1:4—one unit
of output for each four units of capital. If the capital stock of our
hypothetical nation should increase from $400 billion to $800 billion,
the full-employment level of national income would rise to $200
billion, assuming a constant capital coefficient.

By incorporating both the capital coefficient and the Keynesian savings concept in a single equation, standard economists have developed the following simple equation of economic growth. If:

g = The yearly percentage growth in national income
v = The capital coefficient
s = The percentage of the national income saved each year

then:

$$g = s/v$$

It can be seen from this equation that, holding v constant, the rate of growth in national income (g) will be determined by the rate of savings—which, of course, represents capital accumulation. If s and v are both known and constant, the nation's growth rate can be predicted. The capital coefficient, by itself or within the context of the growth equation, can be of value in making investment decisions. If the capital coefficient is 1:5 for an investment in a steel mill, 1:4 for an investment in a textile plant, and 1:3 for an investment in a university, then certainly investment in higher education should be a prime consideration.

As a portrayal of the underlying structure of economic development, the above equation leaves much to be desired. Nowhere does it take into consideration such essential factors of economic development as technological change, human attitudes, political structure, or class rivalry. In addition, the measurement of s and v is still beyond the dexterity of the most competent econometricians. Even the concept of g is of limited value, for it deals not with per capita income but with changes in total income. If g proved to be 2 percent per annum but population growth was 2.2 percent, economic growth would not increase human welfare.

With the above points in mind we should be able to move quickly forward in our discussion of growth.

Growth under Capitalism: The United States

We have in several previous chapters shown how one obstacle to growth—namely, depressions—can be remedied by monetary and fiscal action and other contracyclical measures. In an advanced nation like ours, it is sometimes easy to confuse two rather different concepts, namely, growth and stability. Thus, we sometimes say that our unemployed cannot be absorbed unless we increase our rate of growth. This may be true, but it does mix up the idea of depression unemployment with growth. Perhaps a couple of diagrams will clarify the issue. Suppose a society like ours becomes stationary and between 1961 and 1970 keeps its per capita income at a level of $2,500. Experience suggests that the business cycle will cause constant deviation from this amount. Under these assumptions the nation's economic activity can be plotted as shown in Figure 22–1. Here, we have fluctuation but no growth. Figure 22–2, in contrast, shows a growing society. Per capita income rises over the decade from $2,500 to $3,700—approximately

FIGURE 22–1

A STATIONARY SOCIETY AND THE BUSINESS CYCLE

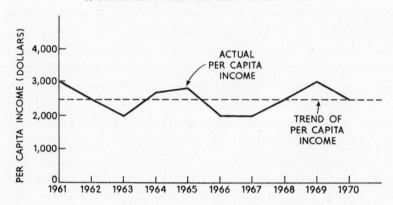

FIGURE 22–2

A GROWING SOCIETY AND THE BUSINESS CYCLE

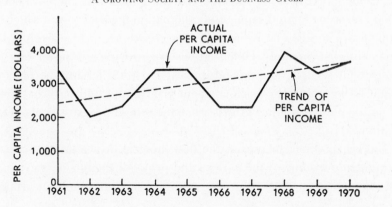

4 percent growth cumulatively. But Figure 22–2 also shows that the rise is unsteady because of the business cycle.

Now, if, as in Figure 22–1, we are in the postulated depression of 1966–67 and simply wish to get back to normal, we can do several things: First, we can let events take their course and hope to get back to prosperity; there are apparently forces in the economy which will bring us back to prosperity of a sort after depression, but they may be very slow and unreliable; this is pretty much how we handled depressions before 1932 and what we have apparently repudiated as a solution.

Second, instead of waiting for nature to take its course, we can use the countercyclical policies that have been discussed in various places in this book; these include lowering the interest rate, reducing taxation, and continuing to pay unemployment benefits as long as depression lasts even if rights to them have expired.

If, now, we are trying to do more than mitigate the business cycle and want to follow the path of the broken line in Figure 22–2, if we want to go from a per capita income of $2,500 to one of $3,700 in 1970, what do we do? Here the answers are not quite so easy, mostly because growth theory is not so well developed as business cycle theory. We might of course say, as we did in our first reply to the business cycle question: "Leave it to time and circumstances; growth is built into our economy; we've grown in the past, and we'll do it again." Well, it is just conceivable that this is the only answer needed and that if we sat back and relaxed and minded our own business, we would keep on growing at a satisfactory pace.

The economist, however, is not satisfied with this answer. First of all, economic growth may just not take place after all. There is enough good reasoning behind some of the stagnation theories—into which we cannot go—to keep us from accepting growth as an inseparable part of a capitalist economy. Other nations are growing at a faster rate. To protect our security and our position of world leadership, perhaps we ought to become self-conscious about growth and find out what kinds of public policies induce growth when the rate of progress tends to fall behind.

Perhaps then, to repeat, the first thing to do would be to try to straighten out some of the valleys and peaks of the business cycle, as shown in Figure 22–2. We may assume, when as much uncertainty pervades the economy as the roller-coaster chart suggests, that the general atmosphere for growth is not favorable. What else might we do? One of the most important ingredients of a growing economy is the improvement of the industrial quality of its citizens and hence of its labor force. This means better health, physical and mental; improved education; and rehabilitation of persons with skills made valueless by automation. It means reducing school dropouts and searching for high intelligence among low-income groups and then training its possessors. It is the very rare young person among the gifted poor who gets to college. We must improve our schools for Negroes and other disadvantaged groups.

A second important ingredient of growth is technology. It must be constantly improved through our own research or imitation of others, or both, and it must be embraced and incorporated into the productive process. Although the United States is not noted for its excellence in basic research, we do have considerable skill in the adaptation of research to increased production and considerable flexibility in the introduction of new processes. There are, however, several institutional drags. The building construction unions, often in alliance with local contractors and politicians, have saddled us with trade practices and building codes that leave the stamp of the handicraft era on most of our buildings. Unions in general resist new machines and new methods. They are not to be blamed for this, however, since the cost of change is in the short run greatest of all to the working class. Our belief system does not allow us to make a serious and frontal attack on reducing the human costs of switching from old to new industrial processes. So long as technological unemployment is treated casually and hit-or-miss attempts at solving it are allowed to hold sway, so long will intense resistance to the introduction of more productive processes prevail. And this is only one example. Medicine and education appear to be hampered by institutional drag.

The third element of growth is increased capital per member of the working force. Capital is composed largely of tools, from tack hammers to diesel locomotives to jet airplanes. But the point is not to give the worker a lot more of the same. A cabinetmaker could not produce more if he were given two or three identical sets of hand tools, and a locomotive engineer could not produce more ton-miles if he were given six diesels. What the cabinetmaker needs is power tools; and the engineer, a more powerful locomotive that will pull 30 more freight cars. This has been called a "deepening of capital" by numerous economists.

The reader may wonder—and economists worry about this—how we can keep on deepening capital when the propensity to invest is low. We invest (in the Keynesian sense of buying new inventory or equipment) when prosperity looms ahead; but on the level of high stagnation, investment is not widely attractive. Part of the remedy may be found in the fact that although investment may not—in 1968, let us say—seem attractive to John Doe or Richard Roe, if a great wave of investment were to sweep the country, investment would be interesting to entrepreneurs as a class and therefore to John Doe and Richard Roe. Investment means buying machines and inventory; people who make machines and inventory get wages; people who get wages spend their money on inventories and the product of machines. The trick is to get everybody investing together.

The government can encourage general investment in various ways. Low interest rates are encouraging, but probably not enough so. Tax exemptions for new investment may be more encouraging. Economists are rather ingenious at working out various lures; whether they will be opposed by a few parliamentarians who seem to belong to another world and century remains to be seen; whether the lures will really work when enacted into law also remains to be seen. After all, even the best economic ideas, like the best-designed machines or buildings, reveal faults after the blueprints have been converted into three-dimensional substance.

Another anxiety of economists is that growth and full employment will cause creeping inflation. If the rate of growth is not excessive (as it might have to be in wartime), there is no good, strictly economic reason why inflation should set in. Inflation has been defined as too much money chasing too few goods. Growth does not demand an imbalance between goods creation and money creation (by banks). For every loan, there should be a compensating volume of goods. What could happen, of course, is that strategically placed sellers would increase their prices. Full employment in the United States and a 5 percent growth rate would create a fantastic prosperity. Sellers outside competitive markets—and this means quite a lot of sellers—might be able to raise their prices and still keep on disposing of satisfactory quantities of goods, particularly if their products were characterized by inelastic demand. The consumer, intoxicated by steady wages and employment, would probably not complain; but the government, if it wished to protect him in his euphoria, might take various measures to keep prices down. We have already discussed these in Chapter 16 on the preservation of competition. They included the encouragement of foreign competition, vigorous antitrust action, and the like. Perhaps it should be repeated here that another group requiring protection from inflation even more than the consumer is the fixed-income group, including retired people on pensions.

Some economists have argued that we do not save enough to allow us to invest as much as we should if economic growth is to equal or exceed recent rates of growth. If this is the situation, what are we to do? Our propensities to save and to spend are very personal matters; and in our kind of society in peacetime, not much can be done to make us save more. In wartime, we have bought government bonds under the spur of patriotism; we refrained from overconsumption because of shortages and legislation that forbade the buying of certain items, such as autos, and through limitations, such as ration cards. The Soviet Union may use these and allied methods in peacetime to compel saving, but we cannot. We could place limitations on install-ment buying—increasing the initial deposit and shortening the period —but this would meet with much resistance and might not accomplish very much. Although current doctrine holds that if incomes rise, savings increase, this hypothesis might not be true if we were to have a long period of full employment and uninterrupted growth. We do not know how much is saved for a rainy day—for fear of future un-employment, to be more exact. If this fear were removed, savings might decline relative to income. On the other hand, much of our new investment arises out of institutional saving, such as the undistributed profits of corporations. It might be more feasible to encourage them to save even more than they now do than to try to influence the ordinary citizen's choice between spending and saving. This problem of under-saving may have to be met some day, and with policies that have not yet been devised.

Growth in the U.S.S.R.

In the Soviet Union the problem of stimulating growth, though by no means easy, is to some degree simplified by disregard for human rights and the rights of property. In a dictatorship committed to planning, problems of growth are solved on a quite different plane. If saving seems to be required, people are made to save by such simple expediants as taxing them more or paying them less, or not producing certain goods for consumers in the first instance, or rationing. There are restraints on the bureaucrats, to be sure: Consumption goods must be produced in sufficient volume to secure cooperation and goodwill from the underlying population, in the extreme case, to prevent revolution; in the short run the Soviets are restrained by the inferior industrial quality of their population and their capital; natural resources must be adequate; population must not grow too fast; and in general, they are held back by the fact that production everywhere demands hard labor, mental and physical—work and sweat, blood and tears.

All of the above is not to say that a socialist economy under dictatorship is a more efficient economy than a nonsocialist, democratic economy. It can, however, pursue a limited number of objectives with great vigor: In Russia, there have been vast and successful drives to increase capital, to stamp out illiteracy and otherwise improve the industrial quality of the population, and to build up vast military and paramilitary (satellites) power. But as in almost any other sort of human activity, these vigorously pursued goals are pursued at the expense of other achievements. A Soviet state cannot dodge opportunity costs—everything produced is at the cost of what was not produced. Despite some successes currently, agriculture is still an unsuccessful Soviet industry. Under Joseph Stalin the peasant was kept a stepchild of the revolution; he was organized into unsuitable productive units; he was denied adequate mechanical aids and fertilizer. Now, farm production is incrasing. Housing is even less developed than agriculture. The very low production of automobiles makes the bad and few roads tolerable but deprives the Soviet citizen of mobility and the joys—such as they are—of turnpike slaughter. A vast quantity of consumers' goods is of low quality. The system of retail distribution is poor. Thus a socialist economy is limited in what it can do, and some things it does very badly.

Socialist economies are also hampered by their belief systems and, like all other societies, by the institutional weight of the past. Marxism, for example, repudiates Malthusian theory partly on the ground that Thomas Robert Malthus' bourgeois economics was a mere apology for capitalist exploitation, and partly on the ground that under socialism the efficiency of production and the justice of distribution would provide food enough for all. This disavowal of a population problem—particularly in the early days of the Russian revolution—has caused some backing and filling in population policy in both China and Russia. In the latter nation, too, it has caused some backtracking on such social issues as the place of woman and of the family. It is not easy to assess the damaging influence—if any—of T. D. Lysenko, the Russian agronomist and geneticist, on Russian agriculture; his theories, opposed to those of most of the world's geneticists, conformed to Marxian ideology. Certainly, much more of Lysenko, who was the head administrator of Russian agriculture, could not have been beneficial in the long run. It is interesting—but perhaps profitless—to an economist who knows little about psychology or learning theory to speculate on whether, in the improvement of Russia's industrial quality, the Pavlovian doctrines have been helpful or harmful. Ivan P. Pavlov's experiments and insights accord with Marxian positivism and materialism, but their rigorous and dogmatic applications in education and psychiatry may do more harm than good.

The detailed and invasive planning of the Soviet Union has probably hindered growth. It is possible to meddle too much with an economy, to give excessive supervision, to spy to the point of hurting producers' morale. This is the result of a belief system that refuses to tolerate any outcropping of the spirit of business enterprise.

We can summarize by saying that the communist nations do have a lesser problem in maintaining a target rate of growth than have nonplanning, private enterprise nations. But they have their problems, too. We must nonetheless recognize them as worthy competitors on the economic plane.

The Underdeveloped Nations

Growth has become a great branch of economics, as we have said; and if growth can be divided into compartments, the area of greatest concern and attention is growth in underdeveloped countries. If an economist dines with half a dozen colleagues, he must be prepared to listen to what they have recently been doing to promote the growth of Darjeeling, Ifni, Malagassy, Swaziland, Zanzibar, and other places he has either never heard of or remembers only as names strewn among the martial accents of Rudyard Kipling's poetry of empire.

If we agree that an underdeveloped nation is one in which the per capita annual income in 1957 fell under $300, then 72 percent of the world's population lives in underdeveloped nations. Included in the wealthier 28 percent would be such doubtfully rich areas as the Soviet Union and Puerto Rico. If we lower our sights and define an underdeveloped nation as one in which the per capita income was $100 or less, then we include only a little more than half the world. To be sure, per capita income figures expressed in dollars tell us less about the underdeveloped nations than they do about the advanced nations; but they tell us enough to make us know that half of the world's human beings live in a state of poverty almost inconceivable to the American college student.

What may be even more shocking is that the gap between the underdeveloped nations and the more highly developed nations is widening. Sixty percent of the world's population received 13.2 percent of the world's income in 1950, but only 11.1 percent in 1964. The richest 40 percent increased their share from 86.8 to 88.9 percent in the same period. The United States, however, constitutes a surprising exception: Our share of global income in the same period has fallen from 40.8 to 34.7 percent.[8]

The economic doctrine which sheds the greatest light on the problems of underdeveloped nations is the Malthusian doctrine. James Bonar, an English economist of the 19th century, once made a joke about Malthus which suggests that we might rename the famous

[8] James H. Weaver and Leroy P. Jones, "International Distribution of Income: 1950–1964" (unpublished paper). The authors made their study at American University, Washington, D.C.

essay on population *An Inquiry into the Nature and Causes of the Poverty of Underdeveloped Nations*—a parody of Adam Smith's famous title. There is little doubt that almost all students of economic growth in underdeveloped nations are perturbed about the population question. Although we have long talked about the teeming throngs that live along the great rivers of Asia, it is not until recently that the danger has been aggravated almost to the point of hopelessness. The great trouble is that it is easier, cheaper, and less threatening to a widespread belief system to prevent death than to prevent birth. A few simple and cheap measures, such as malaria control through DDT spray, have prolonged life in the underdeveloped regions. Life may be prolonged through public health without the knowledge or consent of those benefited. No equally cheap and easy methods to prevent birth have been found. Moreover, the multitude applauds an increase in the life-span but decries the limitation of families. Thus the world's underdeveloped nations, when they do increase their food supply, immediately share it with a larger population. Efforts to increase the food supply seem as fruitless as the labor of Sisyphus, not because the birth rate has zoomed upward, but because more people live longer.

This Malthusian view helps us to understand what is going on, but it does not tell us what to do about it; indeed, Malthusianism has always been looked on as a pessimistic doctrine, holding out little hope for the future of mankind. The only solution visible on the horizon is the possibility of discovering cheap, effective, and harmless contraceptives; but even if the technical means are found, the question of institutional acceptance remains to be solved.

This situation contrasts most unfavorably with our own history of growth. As the nations of Europe were approaching the takeoff stage, public health had made no great progress. The same decades that brought growth of knowledge on the prolongation of life taught men to increase material production. The underdeveloped nations have to contend with a problem of lopsided development; years can be added to men's lives by a few short months of easy work, such as an intensive campaign of vaccination against smallpox; but the way to increased production of food is long and hard.

A second great problem of the underdeveloped nations is to improve the industrial quality of their populations. This, of course, means schooling; and schooling means the denial of other things. In the long run, few investments pay off more handsomely than education, but its effects cannot be seen in a few months. Much has been done in Mexico and the Soviet Union on a volunteer basis by dedicated teachers, after hours, in classrooms under a tree in summer and in a peasant's hovel in winter. But perhaps this sort of thing succeeds best in an atmosphere of revolutionary *mystique* and lasts for only a few years of emotional exaltation.

Those who are specializing in this sort of thing have asked whether primary education for all should be the first goal, then high school for all who have the intelligence, and finally college; or whether the same resources should be expended on all three levels together, excluding at first some children—perhaps half of them—from elementary education in order that a fraction of the population may be highly trained through college without having to go abroad. Perhaps the second plan is the better one, though in many of the underdeveloped nations the rising expectations of the mass are not unconnected with the ideals of democracy and of public education for all; and the economic advantages of training an elite at home may be counterbalanced by unfavorable political repercussions. Also, when stated in the above terms, education is made to appear to be a mere classroom affair. Some of the teaching should be done by agricultural agents, by posters (don't use a common drinking cup, spitting spreads disease), by apprenticeship, and by requiring foreign companies to hire indigenes as junior executives.

But improvement of industrial quality is not just a matter of literacy or what you learn in school. Most Americans absorb a great amount of industrial knowledge simply from living in the environment; almost any American youth can operate a lawn mower, an elevator, an automobile, or an outboard motorboat by simply living a normal life in our highly industrialized environment. He can care for them, too; he knows they must have oil, a method of cooling, and dozens of other things needed to keep them in operation. Contrast this with the spectators of a movie in the heart of some of the underdeveloped countries who even today stampede when the pictured locomotive rushes down on them. Will a youth from such a community ever learn to fly a jet plane? Perhaps, but at what cost?

The problem of education is always complicated by the problem of institutional beliefs, social myths, superstition, taboos, and the like.

We all know about the sacred cow in India. Although freethinking upper-class Hindus love a rare filet mignon, the Indian prohibition against killing animals is a very real drag on Indian development. But there are many such problems—the place of women, for example. Males, in their infinite wisdom, have never really been averse to having women work so long as they stuck to laundering, cooking, cleaning, or pulling a plow. But men might object to having women enter factories, work alongside men, take off their veils, or wear streamlined clothes that would not easily get caught up in whirring machines. The breaking-down of resistance to such changes is not a matter of education in the ordinary sense; but if it is not broken down, some of the underdeveloped nations may have difficulty finding an adequate labor supply or using available resources.

After population of proper quantity and good industrial quality, the next most important need of an underdeveloped land is capital. Capital requires saving—not necessarily or primarily or exclusively individual thrift, in the way that money was saved by the middle classes of Western Europe during the 18th and 19th centuries; but it does mean that somehow, somewhere, decisions will be made to postpone consumption now so that tractors, motors, generators, and the like may ultimately enhance production.

Here we face a tough problem. The underdeveloped nations are so poor that undernourishment is the general lot of the population. Yet, if they are to progress, they must save out of their undernourishment to build up capital. One economist, back from a mission to an underdeveloped country, estimated that the deprivation required to build a certain large dam would cost 100,000 deaths among the poorest inhabitants. This may be an overstatement, but it points toward a sad truth. Because of the unequal distribution of income, there are a few rich—very rich—people even in underdeveloped nations and still more who live above the malnutritional level. Studies by the United Nations indicate that many underdeveloped nations are able to save 7 percent or more from domestic sources. This much alone would not be enough to attain the 10 percent that W. W. Rostow considers to be necessary for takeoff. With foreign borrowing, however, the 10 percent is easily achieved by a large number of nations, though India, the Philippines, and several Latin-American countries in which we are particularly interested do not attain this figure.

The successful merchants, the speculators, and the rich of most underdeveloped nations of today are temperamentally different from the thrifty Puritans and bourgeois of Western Europe 300 years ago. The very rich are big spenders on the Riviera, in Paris and Rome and London; when they invest, they are likely to invest in sound American or European stocks, not in native paper mills or agricultural process-ing plants; and when they do "invest" in their own countries, they are likely to buy land or palatial homes. In short, their excess funds are not used to buy capital for use at home. Part of their trouble is a mistrust of their own government; part of it is a fear of communism, which, to some degree, is a threat in many underdeveloped nations. As a matter of fact, the urge to get on with economic growth is widely associated with a strong spirit of nationalism, anticolonialism, unrest, and a kind of revolutionary fervor, whether communist or not. It is easy to blame the poverty of the poor on the wealth of the rich, and in a situation which is far from quiescent the property of the rich may be in danger. It must, however, be said that the rich of the underdevel-oped nations even in quieter times were not great investors at home. The phenomenon is sometimes explained as an absence of entre-preneurship—if that is an explanation. It is probably better explained by an aristocratic tradition that can be easily traced back at least as far as Aristotle, and on through Cicero and the Middle Ages—a tradi-tion which holds trade and the industrial pursuits to be debasing and unworthy of a gentleman.

Even so, there is a little money to get hold of for investment. There seem to be three ways of getting these savings away from the potential savers and placing them in the hands of investors or entre-preneurs for the purchase of ordinary capital, or in the hands of government for the creation of roads, bridges, dams, and similar kinds of capital, often called "social overhead capital." They are (1) foster-ing private saving, (2) taxation, and (3) inflation. To entice private saving, a sound system of banks should be created—sound enough to coax hoarded gold and silver from their hiding places. For social overhead capital, the government may have recourse to taxation or inflation, or both.

Taxation policy, as recommended by economists in the advanced nations, is largely countercyclical and when possible incorporates automatic stabilizers. In backward nations the control of the cycle has less significance. The underdeveloped countries may feel the depressions of advanced nations, as when decline of American income causes us to cut purchases of Brazilian coffee. But over our purchases they have no control; and even if they did, the large population engaged in subsistence agriculture is almost as independent of business tides as a squirrel that lives off the land in summer and buries nuts for winter. The aim of fiscal policy in a subsistence country is to cut down consumption; various forms of sales, excise, and import taxes may be used for this. These may be made less regressive than such taxes might otherwise be by placing much lower taxes on necessities (bread or rice) and higher taxes on imported luxuries such as autos, wines, liquors, and home appliances—the latter not luxuries in the United States, but certainly luxuries in Gambia, Ghana, Guadeloupe, and Guinea. A tariff on foreign goods would raise money and protect infant industries.

Inflation can be used as a method of forced saving. The government can simply print money and use it; more likely, it will print bonds and sell them to a bank, which can create means of payment, as has been explained in an earlier chapter. All of this will make prices go up; people will buy less. As long as the inflation is moderate and the money supply well controlled, all will be well. It is really no different from taxation. It is, however, dangerous because it is too easy politically, and the temptation to abuse the method is great. Unless the government is reliable, honest, and in full control, inflation may get out of hand and be harmful—indeed, self-defeating.

Capital may also be acquired by borrowing from advanced nations, for whom the sacrifice of saving is less than it is for underdeveloped nations. We are of course talking about hardheaded investing by Americans, English, French, or Dutch in the industries of India, Ethiopia, Libya, and Bolivia—object, the making of profit. One roadblock, looking at the matter from the viewpoint of a supplier of loanable funds, is that the very thing that makes these nations still underdeveloped countries in the second half of the 20th century makes investment in them unattractive. We citizens of the United States, because of our vast wealth, are the ones on whom the greatest share of foreign investment would fall, as it fell on the English a century ago.

As a nation with a long isolationist tradition, still physically isolated from so much of the remainder of the world,[9] possessing only a brief experience in international finance and some of that most discouraging, we are probably less interested in making foreign loans than were the advanced nations of the 19th century. And anyhow, taking all the advanced nations together, it is doubtful whether they have great excesses of savings to lend. European reconstruction absorbed a lot, and now savings go to investment needed to sustain and supply full employment. It is conceivable that this situation is temporary and that in the 1970's potential suppliers will be scouring the underdeveloped nations for investment opportunities.

Looking at the matter now from the viewpoint of potential demanders, the underdeveloped nations are bidding rather weakly for private loans. They'd like to have loans, all right, but in the vague way that most people would like to own a 30-room house, complete with private marina and two dozen servants. Loans must be made on their own terms, which are—exceptions conceded—rather risky. Few credible guarantees against the dangers of nationalization, expropriation, confiscation, inflation, or discriminatory taxation are given—and probably cannot be given. American, British, Dutch, and French investors want their rewards (interest, dividends, or repayment of the principal) to be in their own currency or in a form that can readily be converted into a major currency; here again, the underdeveloped nations cannot or will not give adequate guarantees. Many underdeveloped countries want to keep railways, telegraph, telephone networks, electrical distribution, and broadcasting in their own hands, thus closing many avenues to investors. Others, reacting to a previous colonialism, want to keep foreigners out of mining, petroleum, and plantations. There are, of course, exceptions. Americans and Europeans have invested heavily in the oil wells of the Middle East. A few areas, Jamaica and Puerto Rico, for example, have welcomed foreign investment by tax exemption during an initial period.

[9] It is true that you can take a jet at Kennedy Airport and reach almost any part of the world in less than a day and that people therefore speak of all nations as being every other nation's next-door neighbor. But we are still isolated physically by comparison with Europeans. From Amsterdam, you can reach any one of five foreign countries in one day's drive; and from one of them, France, you can swim to England, a sixth. Europeans have long had to deal daily with foreigners. Most of our border lines go through thinly populated areas, and relatively few Americans have constant contact with the natives of Canada or Mexico, much less Albanians or Egyptians.

The governments of several advanced nations are ready to make certain loans and occasionally outright grants. The Soviet Union, too, is lending to underdeveloped nations. Two international banks also lend. One, the International Bank for Reconstruction and Development, makes only hard loans, that is, loans on the same strict terms that would dominate ordinary loans between businessmen. The other, the International Development Association, is a soft-loan agency, that is, the terms of the loan and the rate of interest are easier than in ordinary business practice.

We must not leave this section on the international financing of loans without calling attention to the fact that foreign loans are of less significance than deduction might suggest. A good deal of development has gone on in the underdeveloped world without much foreign investment. Japan's growth after 1868 is more clearly traceable to its educational policies and institutional changes than to loans. Much is made of the role of foreign investment in the development of the United States, but a recent study by Wendell Gordon[10] suggests that its importance has been overemphasized.

Where to Start?

Assuming, now, that underdeveloped nations can get a little capital, where and how will it be first applied to get best results? There seems to be more agreement among economists on how than on where. It should normally be applied in such a manner as to result in a labor-intensive industry. Thus, if the decision is to increase the amount of capital in agriculture, it is better to start by providing more fertilizer and pesticides than mammoth tractors or picking and harvesting machines. This follows the rule that when labor is in relatively large supply, as it usually is in underdeveloped nations, you combine the factors of production in such a way as to use more of what is abundant.

The question of where you start is harder to answer, and each expert in this field seems to have his own theory. Some would argue that agriculture is the place to begin. They would sustain their case by citing that in England the agricultural revolution preceded the industrial revolution and that Japan a century ago placed agriculture very

---

[10] See Ayres's discussion of this matter, *op. cit.*, p. xxii.

high in its list of priorities. By increasing farm productivity per head, labor is released for industry—not to mention the fact that the nation is better fed and healthier, and hence capable physically of greater production. Land taxes can also be increased if agricultural prosperity increases.

Others would stress the need to create external economies in various ways. In economic theory the phrase "external economy" refers to a reduction of cost arising from actions taken outside the firm benefited. Suppose your business requires a lot of long-distance telephoning. If the telephone company reduces the price on long-distance calls, your costs will fall through no effort that you have made; this is an external economy. External economies are often the fruit of "social overhead capital"—that is, the building of roads (or better roads), canals, public utilities, and the like; these are most likely to be supplied by government and can therefore be easily planned for. But industries normally within the scope of private enterprise can also create external economies. For example, the establishment of a weekly newspaper in a small town might cut down everybody's printing bills directly; and as a training ground, the shop would tend to increase the general supply of skilled printers. Because social overhead capital is a veritable fountainhead of external economies, many economists would place emphasis on this as a place to begin.

The disadvantage of social overhead capital is that it is expensive and that expensive individual projects are all-or-nothing affairs. You cannot build half a dike to hold back the sea or a miniature dam to impound the water of a mighty river. To be sure, one can be satisfied with a narrow gravel road rather than a divided six-lane highway, or a modest bridge rather than a double-decker, 12-lane affair. Another alleged disadvantage would be that nobody would use the overhead capital, initially at least. Why build a canal in India between Madrepore and Apelcore if nobody in Madrepore has anything to ship and nobody in Apelcore has any money to buy anything if something were shipped? Let the canal wait until a supply is created at one end of the canal and purchasing power comes into being at the other end.

Some economists advocate balanced growth. At first, stimulate the development of a little of everything—agriculture, light manufacturing, heavy industry, and social overhead capital. All branches or sectors of an economy should grow synchronously, they say. Others would favor unbalanced development and would cite our own successful imbalances as proof of their thesis: We had a canal-building era, a railroad era, and an automobile era. Each newly growing industry tended to pull a host of other industries along with it—automobiles helped to develop steel, petroleum, rubber, glass, and so on. Each, by rapid, unbalanced development, created a desirable disequilibrium.

Summary and Conclusions

One could go on indefinitely discussing the subject of growth and any stopping place would be as arbitrary as any other. The subject, though old in one sense, is in its modern context so young that the field of theory is unorganized—in fact, disorganized and discursive. A few generalizations do disengage themselves, however. The secret of development is to improve land, labor, and capital to the end that greater output will result. Entrepreneurship, too, must improve; and if the society does not recognize this function, then leadership will have to improve, whether the officer in charge be named commissar or Great White Father of the Red October Dawn Cooperative. In the underdeveloped nations, all the human material of the society must be improved, or at least brought into line with the demands of modern technology. Housewives must learn to use better home and kitchen equipment, to prepare and serve health-giving meals, to stop feeding betel nuts and quicklime to their children. Consumers must be flexible about new commodities—perhaps not the first by whom the new are tried, but not the last to lay the horse and buggy aside. In short, the problem is to pull everybody out of a pre-Newtonian world into the post-Newtonian world. For this, education of every kind is necessary, from schools and posters to on-the-job training. But education must be defined, or redefined, in pragmatic or instrumental terms. The prerevolutionary Chinese were cultivated beyond Western standards, but they studied Confucianism, calligraphy, literature, and conjectural history. Very little of this was related to the natural environment which must be manipulated if production is to be increased. And none of it developed the inquiring mind, which is an enemy of the prescriptive forces of unsuitable institutions. Whether the training of the inquiring mind in backward areas will produce revolutions and civil war before it induces growth is still an open question, perhaps one of the greatest questions facing the world. Finally, population must come under human control.

For those who have made the step from pre-Newtonianism to post-Newtonianism, whether capitalist or communist, the problem of growth is easier. Barring the cataclysmic effects of nuclear warfare and other perverse events, growth seems to be built into the economies, or rather the cultures, of the advanced and semiadvanced nations. But we, too, have the problems of improving our factors of production and of combating institutional resistance. Ours is not the problem of stepping over into the post-Newtonian world, but perhaps we must learn how to manage ourselves in the post-Darwinian and post-Einsteinian worlds. It is a little humiliating to think that we cannot yet handle unemployment, automation, or the increased productivity of the farmer. Such things, too, will perhaps be mastered—and partly through a wider diffusion of economic knowledge.

QUESTIONS FOR REVIEW AND DISCUSSION

1. Define, in your own words, each of the following terms:
   a) Real per capital income
   b) Built-in growth
   c) Basic research
   d) Underdeveloped nation
   e) Foreign investment
   f) External economies
   g) Social overhead capital
2. Discuss the historical and ahistorical approaches to the study of economic growth.
3. Modern free economies, such as that of the United States, contain within themselves certain obstacles to economic growth. What are these obstacles? What policies can be employed to overcome them without changing the basic nature of a free economy?
4. Many economists feel that major institutional change must take place before underdeveloped countries will experience economic growth. What institutions now of importance in underdeveloped countries hinder economic growth? What new attitudes must underdeveloped countries cultivate for successful economic growth?

5. Some underdeveloped nations have resorted to using government-instigated inflation as a method of forcing economic growth. How can planned inflation stimulate economic growth? What dangers may a nation encounter under such a program? What effect will planned inflation have on a nation's balance of payments?

6. What political and economic factors help assure the Soviet Union a high rate of economic growth? What economic and political factors hinder the Soviet Union's economic growth?

7. "The economic growth problems of underdeveloped nations can best be understood by examining the society and culture of these nations, because economic growth is social change." Discuss.

8. America's foreign aid program has sustained increasing domestic political attack in the last few years. What are the purposes of our foreign aid program? What information would be necessary to evaluate the program? Using the resources available in your college library, collect as much of this information as possible. Then, through discussion with fellow students, evaluate America's foreign aid program.

Index

INDEX

This book has been set in 12 and 10 point Bodoni Book, leaded 2 points. Part numbers and titles are 18 Spartum Medium. The size of the type page is 27 by 46½ picas.